Introduction to Psychology

Introduction to Psychology

for teachers, nurses and other social workers

D. E. JAMES
Director of Adult Education
University of Surrey

revised edition

CONSTABLE LONDON

First published in 1968
by Constable & Company Limited
10 Orange Street London WC2

Second revised edition 1970

Copyright © D. E. James 1968, 1970

ISBN 0 09 451011 3

Reproduced and Printed in Great Britain by
Redwood Press Limited, Trowbridge & London

to my wife

Contents

9

10

List of Illustrations

11

I should like to thank Messrs Duckworth and Co Ltd
for their kind permission to include 'Some types of
electroencephalograph records' from W. Grey Walter's
The Living Brain.
I am indebted to Miss B. N. Faukes, S.R.N., R.N.T.,
D.N. (Lond.), B.S. (Columbia Univ.), Chief Education
Officer of the General Nursing Council for England
and Wales, on whose suggestion this book was written.
I am also very grateful to Miss C. M. Fleming, M.A.,
ED.B., PH.D., F.B.PS.S., formerly Reader in Education at
the University of London Institute of Education, Mrs.
C. A. Hyman, B.SC. (Econ.), M.A., A.B.PS.S., Lecturer in
Psychology at the University of Surrey, and Paul
Halmos, PH.D., Professor of Sociology at the
University College of South Wales.

D. E. JAMES

University of Surrey
April 1968

FOREWORD

Perhaps the main tasks of an introductory course in psychology are to help students to see perspective within the subject, to understand principles and extract them from superficial detail and to differentiate between fact and opinion. This is as true for students following the course as a major subject in their professional training as it is for the interested layman studying psychology for its own sake. Despite its fundamental importance to their work, however, many students concerned with human problems are not allowed adequate time for the study of psychology. Consequently a text-book comprehensive yet elementary in both content and style is essential for such persons to increase the benefit gained from their studies.

Deciding upon what might be considered an appropriate introductory level for such a book can be a major problem when catering for groups of students not only working towards a variety of end-points, but also having varied backgrounds, abilities, language facility, etc. A suitable text-book to fit these requirements must not only explain basic concepts simply for the weaker candidate but also provide an introduction to more advanced reading for the stronger student. The approach followed here is such that this text is really 'a first introduction'; consequently few detailed references are included, but a bibliography is appended in which the interested reader may follow topics which he selects and also find many valuable references for further reading.

There are many possible approaches to psychology and no two introductory books are identical in the line they follow. When presenting the subject to potential teachers, nurses or other social workers, two major aspects are of prime importance:

  a. the reader must be introduced to a brief, elementary but comprehensive survey of general psychological principles which have not been distorted by premature application to any particular complex set of circumstances;

15

Introduction to Psychology

   b. this must be followed by a course which will enable the student to interpret the application of these principles in the very complex human situations which he will find in his professional work in e.g. classrooms, hospital wards, or in life in general.

It is common practice to attempt to combine these two approaches into a single introductory course and the results on the whole speak for themselves. The lack of knowledge, appreciation and interest in psychology among many trained personnel concerned with the amelioration of human problems is lamentable. If similar paucity in their knowledge and attitudes was found in other aspects of their work they would be seen in a very poor light. Yet surely in dealing with any human problem, a knowledge of psychology is of the utmost importance.

Almost without exception the reason behind this negative attitude towards the social sciences in general and psychology in particular boils down to ignorance about the true nature and scope of these subjects. They become complex, unwieldy, and often incomprehensible when taught by a specialist in a narrow field in a very brief course geared to the needs of a specific profession. Many of the difficulties of understanding which do arise could be avoided by prefacing the applied course by one of a less specialized and more basic nature. It is for such an initial general course that this book is designed. In most aspects of applied psychology the literature is excellent but designed for readers with some psychological knowledge and perspective within the subject. This book has been written for students with only everyday lay experiences to draw on.

Three major criteria have governed its content:

   a. brief but comprehensive coverage of the main areas of psychology which are important to the beginner;

   b. logical development both between chapters and within chapters, with emphasis on examples chosen from everyday experiences, in an attempt to dispel the common criticism of nebulousness and irrelevance to the man-in-the-street;

   c. simplicity and brevity to aid orientation and perspective within the subject.

Psychology is treated as a subject in its own right with a vital part to play in our modern world. At the same time its relevance and interrelationships with the biological and physical sciences on one hand and the social sciences on the other are of great importance in making the subject meaningful and giving it perspective.

The book can be considered to fall into three interrelated sections:

A. BIOLOGICAL FOUNDATIONS – the concept of psychology as the study of our reactions to our surroundings; interaction and co-ordination between ourselves and the environment; introduction to receptors, the nervous system and effectors.

B. THE PSYCHOLOGY OF THE INDIVIDUAL – a survey of the major processes going on within the human mind; interpreting and misinterpreting ourselves and our surroundings; motives, the forces which direct behaviour; the importance of past experiences in dealing with present problems, i.e. an introduction to learning and thinking.

C. THE PSYCHOLOGY OF GROUPS OF INDIVIDUALS – the uniqueness of each individual; the problems of individual differences and techniques for assessing these differences; the effects of persons on one another when sharing a common environment; problems of coming to terms with ourselves and our surroundings, i.e. an introduction to mental health and mental illness.

The ground which could be covered under these headings is very wide indeed. Where selection has been necessary topics have been chosen which are likely to be of most importance to teachers, nurses and other social workers. For example, with the needs and interests of nurses in mind the discussions of the nervous system and mental defence mechanisms have been expanded. For teachers some detail on examinations and intelligence tests has been included. For social workers of all kinds, the general problems of communication, leadership, mental health and mental illness are among the topics given special emphasis, while references to pressing social and educational problems arise in most chapters. Nevertheless the overall approach avoids strong application to the problems of any particular profession. Some suitable texts which perform this function are listed in the bibliography.

Any text, however elementary, is bound to reflect the interests of the author. Some readers will feel that undue stress has been placed here on biological aspects of psychology. Psychology today is more closely tied to other life sciences than has been the case in the past, and it is my own view that the study of behaviour is most valuable when considered as an aspect of human biology. In a book covering such a wide field controversial points can hardly be avoided. The responsibility for their treatment here lies solely with the author.

Chapter One

Psychology – The Study of Behaviour

INTRODUCTION

This volume is an attempt to explain and put into perspective
some of the more common psychological concepts which will
be encountered by nurses, teachers and others concerned with
people and their problems. Although our subject is, to a very
large extent, personal and human, our approach to it must be
scientific and objective if it is to be valuable.*[1]

It is a good scientific principle to begin by defining and
limiting the field which is to be examined. *Psychology* is not
easy to define in a way acceptable to everyone. Basically,
however, it may be considered to be the study of behaviour
and this is the meaning given to it here. Now we must consider
what we mean by *behaviour*. This general term is given to the
outward activity of a person or animal in response to the
situation in which it finds itself. To appreciate what is involved
in psychology, therefore, we must examine the nature of
behaviour and the processes underlying it.

SIMPLE FORMS OF BEHAVIOUR

Although our main object is to study the behaviour of human
beings, the task will be less overwhelming and more easily
seen in perspective if we first consider comparatively simple
behaviour[2] such as is found in jellyfish or sea-anemones.

Behaviour in its simplest form is the direct reaction of an

* For references, see the end of each chapter.

animal to changes in its surroundings (*environment*). Specialized cells on or near the body surface are sensitive to alterations in the intensity of heat, light, sound, chemicals, pressure, etc., coming into contact with them. These sense cells are called *receptors*. Animals can react to this information from receptors by one of two main methods:

a. They can move in relation to the stimulus (either towards it if pleasant, e.g. food or a mate, or away from it if unpleasant, e.g. a poisonous chemical or an enemy). These reactions involve the use of *muscles*.

b. They can secrete substances on to the stimulating object (either to take advantage of it, e.g. digestive juices on to food, or to counteract it, e.g. neutralizing secretions on to unpleasant chemicals or repellent secretions on to enemies). These reactions involve the use of *glands*.

Muscles and glands, because they are used by organisms to respond to stimuli, are called *effectors*.

When a receptor is activated by a stimulus from the environment, it releases energy. This is carried as electrical impulses along *nerves* (specially insulated conducting pathways) away from the skin and into the animal's body. In this simplest case these nerves lead directly to muscles or glands. When nerve impulses reach these effectors they activate them. Hence stimulation of one part of the body produces a response in another. By the development of suitable nerve pathways an effector capable of a satisfactory response can be associated with any particular receptor.

BEHAVIOUR IN MORE COMPLEX ANIMALS

As animals evolved and became larger and more complex such direct nervous links would have considerable limitations which would be very restrictive in the competitive and complicated environment with which these organisms had to cope. If this type of nerve connection was retained there could be one of two possible developments:

a. only one effector could be linked to any one receptor thereby greatly limiting the responses that the animal could make;

b. each receptor could be linked with many effectors (giving a variety of possible responses to any one stimulus) but the whole nervous system would be so large and cumbersome as to be most inefficient.

In these more highly evolved organisms, such direct nervous connections are reserved for certain basic reactions particularly:

a. safety reactions, e.g. withdrawal from hot or other painful stimuli, blinking, coughing, maintaining balance, etc.;
b. essential processes which we do not voluntarily control, e.g. heart beat, digestion, etc.

Such direct connections we call *reflexes*. We shall be returning to them in the following chapter.

In these more highly organized animals (including, of course, Man himself) the nervous system has so developed that the limitations suggested above do not occur. A central co-ordinating system (called the *central nervous system* – C.N.S.) has evolved which consists of the brain and spinal cord. This C.N.S. acts in a similar way to a telephone exchange (Fig. 1 1, p. 22):

a. Receptors send their nerve connections to the C.N.S. These nerves supply to the C.N.S. information about the environment (they are called *sensory nerves*).
b. Effectors are activated via nerves coming from the C.N.S. (These are called *motor nerves* because they result in movement or secretion.)
c. Within the C.N.S. decisions are made as to the best course of action to take in response to the information coming from the environment via the receptors and sensory nerves. It instructs suitable effectors accordingly by sending impulses down the appropriate motor nerves.

The great benefit which such a co-ordinating system confers on an animal is obvious. It enables the creature to develop complex and varied behaviour patterns so that it can deal effectively with the situations it encounters.

THE C.N.S. AND PSYCHOLOGY

The processes going on within C.N.S. are extremely complex and very little understood. It is common practice to refer to the sum total of these activities as the *mind* (the adjective derived from it being '*mental*').[3] As teachers and nurses we are constantly dealing with people. Their behaviour (and, of course, our own) is the direct result of mental activities and we must consider in more detail what psychologists have so far

21

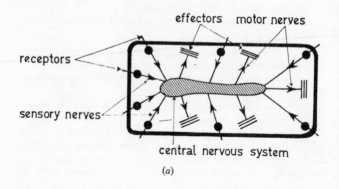

(a)

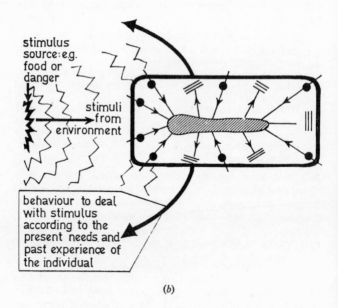

(b)

Fig. 1 1 Diagram of an animal with a simple central nervous system
  a. Structure of nervous system
  b. Functioning of nervous system

22

discovered about the processes that cause and direct behaviour.

The plan upon which this book is based is designed to introduce the major mental processes in as simple a manner as possible. We shall begin with a brief consideration of some of the more important facts about the *structure and functioning of the nervous system*, for this, after all, is the physical basis of psychology.

The mind of a person deals with information picked up by receptors and passed to the C.N.S. The way in which we picture (or *perceive*) ourselves and our surroundings is fundamental to how we respond. Our next task must be, therefore, to understand how we interpret this information coming from our sense organs, and some of the mistakes we are likely to make in our interpretation. As a result of the messages we pick up we decide how we are going to respond. We must then consider the mental energy forces behind our responses (our *motives*).

Observations of the behaviour of an individual during his lifetime show clearly that his responses change. Some of these changes are the result of growing up and growing old (i.e. *maturation*) while others are produced by experiences from the environment (i.e. *learning*).

Such a piecemeal approach to the individual as these early chapters present is obviously artificial but does help the beginner to see basic psychological processes more clearly. The situation is partly remedied by the next two chapters which attempt to integrate these themes, first, from the viewpoint of co-ordinated mental processes (*thinking*), and then as interrelated *developmental* processes. We next turn our attention to the uniqueness of the individual asking what makes us unique and how differences between individuals may be assessed in terms of certain characteristics (*examinations* and *intelligence tests*). Chapter 11 looks at the major difficulties of assessing and comparing whole unique individuals (i.e. *personality evaluation*). The book ends with a brief introduction to some of the problems of how individuals live together, communicate and co-operate (i.e. *group psychology*) and suggests some of the underlying concepts in *mental health* and *mental illness*.

SUMMARY

1. Life in the modern world is complex, varied and in many ways unnatural. The scientific study of how Man copes with problems of adjustment to his environment is difficult. It involves extracting general principles from the mass of available detail and distinguishing between facts and opinion if worthwhile results are to be obtained. This is the task which the psychologist sets himself.

2. We can define *psychology* as the study of behaviour. We can define *behaviour* as the activity of an organism in response to the situation in which it finds itself.

3. Simple forms of behaviour consist of direct reactions by muscles and glands (*effectors*) in response to information picked up from the environment by sense cells (*receptors*).

4. In more complex animals such an arrangement is very limiting and is retained only in *reflexes* which are reserved mainly for safety reactions and essential involuntary processes.

5. In complex animals (including Man) a *C.N.S.* has developed. To this run *sensory* nerves from the receptors and from it *motor* nerves to the effectors. The great value of such a system is that decisions can be taken and responses varied according to the information received by the receptors.

6. The activity of the C.N.S. we have called the *mind*. It is very complex and imperfectly understood. However, some of the most important processes involved in this activity can be investigated and the findings applied in the solution of human problems.

REFERENCES

1. Iliffe, A. H. 'The Scientific Status of Psychology' in *Readings in General Psychology*, edited by Halmos and Iliffe (Routledge & Kegan Paul, London 1959) pp. 1–8.

2. Dethier, V. G. and Stellar, E. *Animal Behavior: Its Evolutionary and Neurological Basis* (Prentice Hall, New Jersey 1961).

3. For a discussion of a variety of views on brain-mind relationships see Laslett, P. (editor) *The Physical Basis of Mind* (Blackwell, Oxford 1950).

Chapter Two

The Physical Units of Behaviour

INTRODUCTION

In this chapter we shall look more closely at the physical mechanisms involved in behaviour.* In the first chapter we described three stages in the performance of a suitable response by an animal to a change in its environment:

  a. information regarding the change had to be picked up by receptor cells;
  b. this information was then carried by nerves from the receptors to effectors;
  c. these effectors, when stimulated by the message reaching them via nerves, responded and through their activity the animal was able to deal with the change in the environment which had been encountered.

It is the nature of these receptors, nerve cells and effectors that we are mainly concerned with here.

All living cells are sensitive to changes in their surroundings. In a very simple animal like *Amoeba* there are no specialized receptors, the whole surface of the cell being sensitive to all types of change which may occur in the water in which it lives. Moreover, the effectors of the cell are close enough to the receptors to be easily stimulated directly by chemicals which are produced by the latter when they are activated. In a larger, more complex body, e.g. that of a human being, receptors and effectors are much further apart. Also different

*The beginner should first read the concluding paragraph on page 41 if he finds that the physical basis of behaviour is of little interest to him.

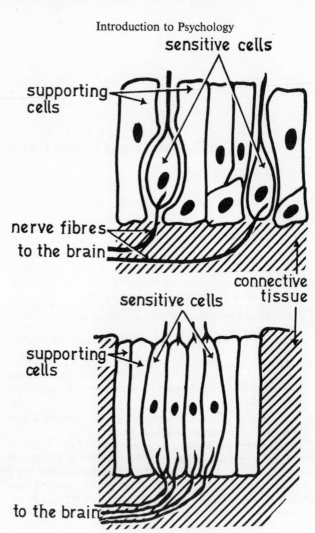

Fig. II 1 Some types of receptor cells
above Receptors in the nose
below Receptors in a taste-bud
above opposite Receptors sensitive to light
below opposite Receptor sensitive to pressure

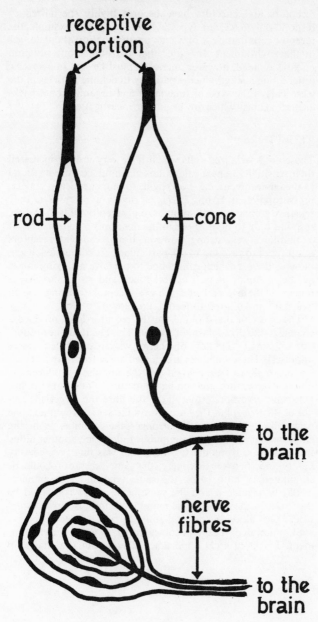

receptors and effectors have become highly specialized to respond only to certain types of stimulation. For example, the receptor cells in the eye may pick up information about danger in the environment. In order that the unpleasant situation may be avoided, however, messages must be sent in a specific order along a lengthy nerve pathway to definite muscles in the legs. This is the type of functional and organizational background against which we begin our investigation.

RECEPTORS [1]

These are specialized cells which have very greatly increased their sensitivity to particular kinds of stimuli commonly found in the environment, e.g. heat, light, sound, chemicals, gravity, pressure (Fig. II 1, pp. 26–7). Normally a receptor is only sensitive to one type of stimulus, e.g. receptor cells in the eye respond only to light, those in the nose only to chemicals. (If a stimulus is very strong, however, it may cause all receptors of all types to respond in the particular part stimulated, e.g. a blow to the ear which causes one to perceive a singing noise, i.e. hear sound, as well as feel touch and pain; similarly a punch in the eye activates the eye receptors causing one to 'see stars' in addition to feeling the blow.)

The effect of the stimulus on the receptor is to produce a change in the protoplasm of the cell. This results in the production of small 'bundles' of energy which are called 'nerve impulses'. These impulses are carried away from the receptor via nerve fibres (see below). All the impulses produced by different receptors are similar in nature. They vary in size between nerve fibres (the bigger the fibre the larger the impulses it carries) but they are always the same size on any one nerve fibre. However, the stronger the stimulus from the environment the faster the impulses follow one another along the nerve (i.e. if middle C on a piano was first pressed very lightly and then very strongly, the same receptors would be stimulated in both cases, the same type and size impulses would be produced and the same nerve pathways would be used, but in the second case many more impulses per second would pass along the nerve than in the first instance).

Stimulation of receptors comes from *changes* in the environment. This is of great importance. To an animal a change in

The Physical Units of Behaviour

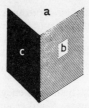

Fig. II 2   A retinal pattern of stimulation

The pattern shown here results from more light being reflected per unit area from 'a' than from 'b', and more from 'b' than from 'c'. The effect of focusing light on the sensitive cells of the retina is to cause them to generate nerve impulses. The greater the intensity of light falling on a receptor cell, the higher the rate of impulse production. This pattern then will be represented in the retina by a similar pattern reflected in rate of impulse-production. This 'impulse-pattern' can be transmitted to the brain and the individual can perceive much more than simply the presence or absence of light in the environment.

its surroundings (e.g. a new sound, a fresh smell, an object coming in contact with its body, a movement picked up by its eyes) can mean danger or food or some other information of importance. A non-changing environment is likely to be of much less importance. If the animal can survive at the moment, and the status quo is maintained, then it will probably continue to survive. Consequently receptors are designed to respond to changes in the environment but not to static conditions. For example when one puts one's clothes on in the morning, one feels them for a few seconds, but one is not normally aware of them for the rest of the day; when one enters an atmosphere with a strong smell or a regular noise (e.g. a ticking clock), one notices it at first but soon 'becomes used to it'. All our receptors are sensitive to changes in the environment. When there is no change, information about the situation ceases to be picked up and nerve impulse generation gradually fades. When no further impulses are produced the receptor is said to be *adapted* to its present condition.

These impulses coming from receptors are the only sources of information for the C.N.S. regarding the environment. If too much new information is received at once the brain cannot deal with it (e.g. on starting school or entering hospital); consequently the person's behaviour is confused and he feels insecure and anxious. Conversely, if too little information reaches the C.N.S. (as, for example, on a long space journey or during a prolonged stay underground when conditions are relatively stable and the receptors soon adapt and cease to transmit impulses) then the C.N.S. has inadequate information upon which to base its interpretations of the outside world. We shall return to this topic when discussing 'perception'.

In order to increase their efficiency, receptor cells often occur together in groups. Such groups are called *sensory tissues*. The value of such tissues is obvious. Each isolated receptor cell can only transmit limited information to the C.N.S. Take, for example, a light-receptor cell in the retina of the eye. If light falls on to it impulses pass to the brain. The brightness (intensity) of the light is represented by the rate of impulses passing to the C.N.S. This is the limit of the information which the single receptor cell is capable of transmitting. However, if a large group of light-receptors are situated together a pattern of light from the environment will produce a pattern of excitation among the receptors. This pattern can be passed to the brain and more detailed information of the environment is available to the C.N.S. (Fig. II 2).*

A sensory tissue needs other types of tissue to protect it, support it, feed it, remove its waste products, etc. Such a group of tissues centred round a sensory tissue constitutes a *sense organ*, e.g. the eye, the ear, a taste-bud, etc.

Sense organs are often classified according to the source from which they obtain their information.[2]

A. EXTEROCEPTORS collect information from outside the animal's body either:

    a. at some distance, e.g. eyes, ears, nose;
    b. in contact with the body, e.g. tongue, skin.

B. INTEROCEPTORS collect information from surfaces within the body, e.g. situated in gut or blood-vessel walls.

C. PROPRIOCEPTORS collect information from within tissues themselves (especially muscles, where they record tensions from which the brain can determine the relative positions of various parts of the body).

Each of these receptors makes contact with a nerve fibre that will convey its information away towards effector organs.

*Other more complex patterns occur which are based on distribution of impulses in time rather than space, but these are beyond the scope of this discussion here.

NERVE CELLS [3]

These are much specialized cells designed to carry electrical impulses between various parts of the body (Fig. II 3, p. 32). Each consists essentially of a *nerve cell body* which is not greatly different from other non-specialized cells. It contains a nucleus and most of the cytoplasm of the cell. It is here that the basic life processes (e.g. nutrition, respiration, excretion) of the cell are carried out.

From this nerve cell body grow out projections called *nerve fibres*. In the simplest case two such fibres are produced:

- *a.* a *dendron* which carries impulses (either from a receptor or from another nerve fibre) towards the nerve cell body;
- *b.* an *axon* which carries this information (brought in by the dendron) away from the cell body and passes it on to another nerve fibre (dendron) of another neuron or to an effector.

These fibres are prolongations of the surface of the nerve cell body. If a fibre is cut, the part separated from its cell body dies because it has lost its energy supply. The portion still connected to the cell body, however, may grow outwards (along the path of the severed section which degenerates) and complete the original nerve connection.

The fibres are conducting strands coated on the outside by an insulating layer of fatty material which prevents their electrical impulses from leaking away into surrounding tissues during their passage through the body. Often many nerve fibres follow a very similar pathway, e.g. all the fibres from the left eye to the brain travel together; similarly all the fibres from the C.N.S. to the calf muscle of the right leg will run side by side. These delicate fibres, during their long journey through the body, pass near structures which are capable of movement and exerting pressure on them, e.g. contracting muscles, pulsating arteries. To give them added protection bundles of these fibres, wrapped in packing tissue, are bound together in sheaths. Such a bundle of nerve fibres is called a *nerve*.

From our description in the first chapter of the nervous system of a complex animal it is obvious that there are three quite different functions for the nervous system to perform. Each function is carried out by its own specialized type of neuron:

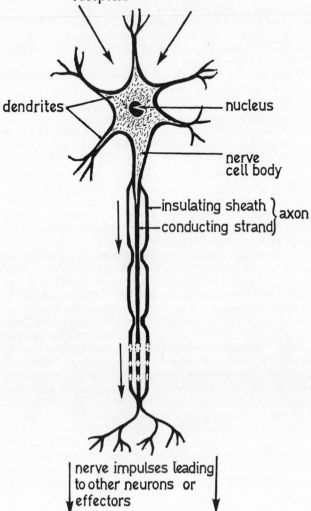

Fig. II 3 A generalized nerve cell

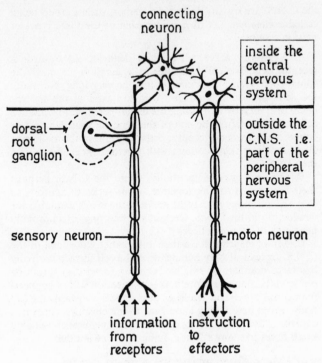

Fig. II 4 Specializations in nerve cell structure

a. Sensory neurons carry information from receptors to the
   C.N.S.;
b. Connecting neurons transport this information through the
   C.N.S.;
c. Motor neurons bear directions from the C.N.S. to effectors.

In order to carry out these tasks efficiently, variations on
the basic structure of a nerve cell have developed (Fig. II 4,
above). A complication in this structural specialization is that
nerve cell bodies normally lie in or near the C.N.S. The reason
for this is probably that food and oxygen are more easily
obtained and protection is greater for these delicate structures
when they are not widely scattered. Those cell bodies outside

the C.N.S. are usually collected together, such a group being called a *ganglion*. Let us consider each of the three types of neuron separately.

A. A sensory nerve cell sends a dendron out towards a receptor cell. The cell body lies in a ganglion just near the spinal cord. Hence the dendron may be very long. Normally the dendron connects directly with the axon of the sensory nerve cell, thereby by-passing the actual ganglion in which its cell-body lies. Often the end of the dendron branches and so connects with several receptor cells. The end of the axon may also branch, making contact with several connecting cells in the C.N.S.

B. Connecting cells lie wholly within the C.N.S. Perhaps their function is to link together whole series of neurons so that an enormous variety of nerve pathways is available for conduction in the C.N.S. Certainly connecting cells normally bear very many nerve fibres.

C. Motor neurons have their cell bodies embedded in the C.N.S. Instead of only one dendron the cell surface normally has large numbers of smaller branches (*dendrites*) sprouting out in tufts. Each dendrite makes connection with a connecting neuron fibre. The dendrites pass impulses towards the cell body. From here a long axon runs to the effectors which it is capable of activating. At its end the axon may branch, sending small fibres to many effectors lying near one another.

RELATIONSHIPS BETWEEN NERVE CELLS

Although much of this chapter is devoted to describing the structure and arrangement of nerve pathways, we must bear in mind that such pathways exist solely for the conduction of information to and from the C.N.S. or between various parts of it. This information is of course in the form of nerve impulses which we have already mentioned.

The exact nature of these impulses need not concern us here, except to say that they are electrical in nature and probably are the results of chemical changes in the nerve fibre itself. The passage of the impulse along a fibre is comparatively straightforward. We must consider here what happens when an impulse reaches the end of an axon.

Neurons lying next to one another in a nerve pathway do

34

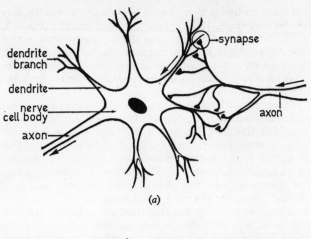

(a)

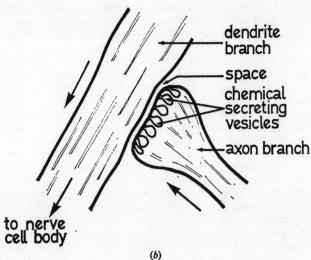

(b)

Fig. II 5 A synapse
a. Connections between two adjacent neurons
b. High-power detail of one synapse.

35

not make protoplasmic contact. There are always small spaces left between them. These spaces are called *synapses* (Fig. II 5, p. 35). Nerve impulses must jump across these synapses, rather like electrical sparks jump between two wires in a circuit. Synapses are very important to us in our study of nerve pathways because they are the places in which control of impulses can occur.

There are two other concepts which relate to synapses that must be mentioned here, namely facilitation and inhibition.[4]

A. FACILITATION. We find that if one impulse is passed along a nerve fibre, it reaches the end of the axon but can go no further. If we take another nerve fibre and pass two impulses along it, only one jumps over the synapse and passes on along the next nerve cell. The other impulse has been used as a 'bridge' across the synapse (in fact, the first impulse arriving at a synapse probably causes a chemical to be secreted into the space, and through this chemical the next impulse can pass). This bridging of a synapse is called *facilitation*. We shall return to it again in later chapters when discussing learning. Let us note at the moment that if one or a few nerve impulses were generated, e.g. by a very small stimulus on a receptor, or by a slight accident, the number of impulses might be too small to reach far into the C.N.S. and the person might not be made aware of the trifling and unimportant stimulation.

After the passage of an impulse and the secretion of the first chemical, a second destructive chemical (enzyme) is normally produced which removes the facilitating bridge (i.e. the first chemical). The pathway is now returned to its original condition. However, if a pathway is used over and over again it is likely to be very important to the person. In such cases, by mechanisms which are not properly understood, it becomes easier for impulses to pass over synapses. (This may be due to the destructive chemical not being produced, or to the nerve fibre ends growing closer together, or to some other unknown change.) Impulses follow such permanently facilitated pathways much more readily than they do normal ones. Perhaps this is the physiological basis of habit-formation.

B. INHIBITION. In complex nervous systems it is sometimes necessary to prevent a usual reaction from occurring in response to a particular stimulus, e.g. to stifle a cough near a

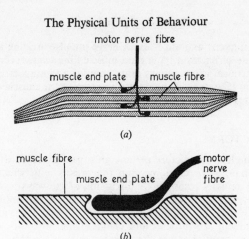

Fig. ii 6 Muscle end plate
a. Diagram of a motor nerve ending on muscle fibres
b. Detail of section through a muscle end plate region

sleeping baby, to stand still as a savage dog approaches or to stop yourself performing an irritating habit. There appear to be two main ways in which inhibition of such movements can be brought about.

i. Some neurons exist in certain parts of the C.N.S. which, when activated, secrete a chemical into the synapse at the end of their axons. This prevents the next neuron from being stimulated by other nerve cells converging on it. For example, a train of impulses from the C.N.S. running down a motor nerve to the muscles which raise the left arm, will at the same time, block the pathway for impulses travelling to the muscles which would pull the left arm downwards.

ii. Antagonistic sets of muscles may be brought into action to counteract the particular unwanted movement, for example, muscles which move you backwards come into play just at the moment when the doctor sticks a hypodermic needle into you and you start a reflex forward movement. If these two sets of muscles should act one just after the other, the effect will be that you jump.

The activities described for synapses (junctions between nerve fibres) are basically similar to those occurring at junctions between axons and effectors. A nerve impulse arriving at the *end-plate* of an axon lying on a muscle fibre causes secretion of a chemical which allows other impulses to jump across the junction (Fig. II 6). These impulses entering the muscle cause the fibres to contract.

EFFECTORS[5]

To complete our picture of how an organism copes with its surroundings we must mention the organs with which the animal actually responds. A discussion of the ways in which these organs act, however, is beyond the scope of this book. Let us state that the major tissues involved in reacting with the environment are muscles and glands. Other effectors which might be mentioned are the pigment cells in the skin which protect us from the sun; ciliated cells in the respiratory tract which clean the inhaled air, amoeboid cells in the blood which destroy foreign bodies, etc. With the exception of the muscles used for movement all these effectors react quite automatically to the changes with which they are designed to cope.

The muscles used for movement however are under the control of the C.N.S. Impulses from receptor organs enter the C.N.S. and a mental picture is formed of what is going on in the environment. In the light of this mental picture the C.N.S. 'decides' how best to respond to the situation in which the body finds itself. Impulses then are directed off down suitable motor nerve fibres to the effectors which can most suitably respond. For example, a receptor informs the C.N.S. of the presence of food in the environment. Muscles are activated which will cause the body to move towards the food source. (Automatically, at the same time the salivary glands will start to secrete to cope with this aspect of the environment for which they are designed.) This physical reaction of the body in response to a stimulus is called *behaviour*.

REFLEX ARCS[6]

Basically a reflex arc is a nervous link running directly from a receptor to an effector through a series of nerve cells and synapses. However, the information to which it is necessary to make an immediate response by certain effectors is also likely to be important to the whole animal. Hence most reflex arcs pass through the C.N.S. (Fig. II 7 below).

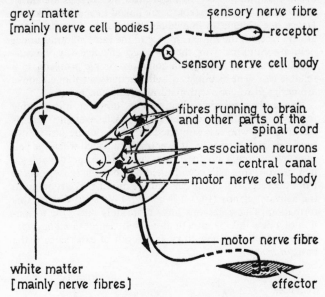

Fig. II 7 Diagram of a simple reflex arc

In the simplest case, the sensory neuron from the receptor makes contact with a connecting neuron in the spinal cord. This connecting neuron performs two functions:

a. it passes the message from the sensory neuron on to the correct motor neuron so that a response can be made immediately;

b. it sends information to the brain about the stimulus which the receptor has received. This information enables the brain to decide how the effectors should respond. The intensity of reaction can be adjusted according to the emotional state of the animal (see later) and if necessary, in some cases, the response of the effectors can be prevented (probably through some form of inhibition), e.g. a parent can stifle a cough near a sleeping baby or one can hold on to a valuable hot teacup until it can be safely put down.

Introduction to Psychology

Human beings have many inborn reflexes, e.g. coughing, blinking, swallowing, and many others of which we are not aware, e.g. gut movements, heart beat, pupil contraction in bright light, and so on. In these cases the nervous system so develops that certain receptors are linked to specific effectors. Hence one obtains an immediate response to a stimulus and always receives the same response to the same stimulus under natural conditions. This, then, is a very effective way of ensuring that the body copes with common, simple problems in a reliable way. The examples of reflex activity mentioned above are designed to cope with natural circumstances.

Besides these inborn natural reflexes, however, it is possible to develop artificial reflexes. The classic example here is Pavlov's dog who was subjected to a bell ringing just before food was presented to it. It eventually salivated when the bell rang even though no food was given. Here, presumably, a new nervous link had been forged between the sensory nerve from the receptors of the ear and the motor nerve running to the salivary glands (Fig. II 8 below). (We shall discuss this formation of new nervous links more fully later; the formation of a new link by growth alone is an aspect of *maturation*, while formation of new links as a result of experience is the basis of *learning*.)

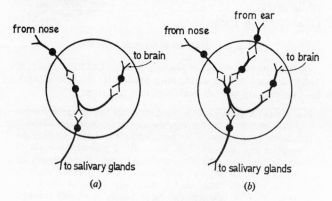

Fig. II 8   Diagram of reflexes
a. An unconditioned reflex
b. A conditioned reflex

NEURONS AND MORE COMPLEX MENTAL PROCESSES

Modern psychologists are becoming increasingly aware of the fact that they have a great deal to learn from physiology and neurology. An excellent attempt at integrating concepts from these sciences into our present findings in psychology will be found in the writings of D. O. Hebb, Professor of Psychology at McGill University. His *Textbook of Psychology*[7] is a comprehensive overview of his own interpretations. The interested reader should not confine himself to Hebb's approach alone but explore among the other texts indicated in the bibliography.[8]

It is not possible to follow this line of investigation further in this book. However, as our techniques for investigation of the nervous system improve, it may well be that the human brain will give up its secrets in the way in which other major organs like the kidney and heart have done.

CONCLUSION

We began this chapter by dealing with the anatomy and physiology of nerve cells and then extended our discussion into the realms of 'higher mental processes', e.g. co-ordination, learning, integration. It is not our aim in this book to try to explain all psychological phenomena in such basic physical terms. Whether or not such an interpretation will ever be possible is a matter of great dispute among psychologists.[9] Nevertheless, it is important for us to realize that such concepts as these are rapidly developing and they very closely tie psychology to other branches of biology and indeed to all other sciences.[10] It is upon such grounds as these that scientific methods of investigation have been designed for and can be profitably used in psychology. It is important for everyone concerned with modern psychology to be aware of some of these basic physiological ideas even though they may not appear to be directly applicable to the psychological problems of dealing with people. They help to give the subject a definite objective basis which is essential to a true scientific approach. The fact that we shall mention them less as the book progresses in no way diminishes their underlying importance.

SUMMARY

1. It is convenient to discuss initially the physical mechanisms underlying behaviour, i.e. receptors, neurons and effectors and the connections between these structures.
2. Various types of nerve pathways have been described by biologists and psychologists. These have raised a good deal of discussion as to the possible functions served by such neural arrangements in the nervous system.
3. Synapses and their facilitation and inhibition are probably of central importance in our understanding of the role of the nervous system in the control of behaviour.
4. The nature, functions and limitations of reflex arcs give a useful introduction to the way in which the nervous system functions as a unit at a simple segmental level.
5. Our knowledge of complex psychological processes is not completely divorced from what we know of the anatomy and physiology of nerve cells. It is not intended to follow this type of approach throughout the text. It is important, however, that the student should be aware of its existence.

REFERENCES

1. See Young, J. Z. *The Life of Mammals* (Oxford University Press, London 1957) especially pp. 462–74.
2. Any general physiology text-book will give an introduction to the form and function of human sense organs. For more advanced treatment the following may be recommended:

    a. Best, H. C. and Taylor, N. B. *The Living Body* (Chapman & Hall, London, 4th ed. 1958; 1st ed., 1938) pp. 574–648.
    b. Young, J. Z. *The Life of Mammals* (O.U.P., London 1957) pp. 475–526.

3. See Walsh, E. G. *Physiology of the Nervous System* (Longmans, London 1957) pp. 1–16.

4. For more general information on facilitation and inhibition see Morgan, C. T. *Physiological Psychology* (McGraw-Hill, N.Y. 1965).
5. Walsh, E. G. *Physiology of the Nervous System* (Longmans, London 1957) pp. 16–33.
6. Any introductory human biology text will expand on the function and nature of reflex arcs. For more detailed treatment on the spinal cord see:

The Physical Units of Behaviour

    a. Walsh, E. G. *Physiology and the Nervous System*, pp. 78–109.
    b. Young, J. Z. *The Life of Mammals*, pp. 323–72.

7. Hebb, D. O. *Text-book of Psychology* (Saunders, London, 2nd edition 1966; 1st edition 1958).
8. Useful introductions to physiological interpretations are:

    a. Wooldridge, D. E. *The Machinery of the Brain* (McGraw-Hill, N.Y. 1963) which is an attempt to translate the results obtained by workers in biology and psychology into terms intelligible to the physical scientist.
    b. Walsh, E. G. *Physiology of the Nervous System* (Longmans, London 1957) emphasizes the neurophysiology of the C.N.S.
    c. Buddenbrock, W. von *The Senses* (University of Michigan Press, Ann Arbor 1958) examines the more biological concepts of sensitivity.
    Several other valuable texts are included in the references of Chapter 3.

9. Sidman, M. *Tactics of Scientific Research* (Basic Books, N.Y. 1960) discusses the use of scientific method in psychology.
10. Harlow, H. F. and Woolsey, C. N. *Biological and Biochemical Bases of Behavior* (University of Wisconsin Press, Madison 1958) gives an interesting but difficult account of some of the major areas of physiological advancement in psychology. For a more elementary treatment see Zangwill, O. L. *An Introduction to Modern Psychology* (Methuen, London 1950).

Chapter Three

Co-ordinating Ourselves with Our Surroundings

INTRODUCTION

We have emphasized the importance to organisms of being able to respond to changes in their environments if they are to survive. It is obviously essential that their behaviour should be synchronized with and suitable for dealing with the particular circumstances in which they find themselves. This involves taking into consideration not only external stimuli from their surroundings but also internal needs and conditions of their own bodies. An understanding of these processes of co-ordination is of the utmost importance to all persons concerned with the study of behavioural problems, yet their analysis and interpretation presents some of the greatest technical problems that Man can imagine.

Our organs of co-ordination are the brain and spinal cord, collectively termed the central nervous system (or C.N.S.). Biological and psychological research is only now beginning to discover the possible mechanisms through which these organs function.[1] However, within these organs the processes about which this book is written are constantly taking place. It is essential therefore that we outline simply and within the limits of our knowledge the place and function of this co-ordinating system within our bodies.

In order to facilitate perspective, let us go back through time and trace the evolution of our C.N.S.[2] The very simplest forms of living creature evolved along two diverging lines. One line (the plants) developed the capacity for building up their own food substances from simple materials such as carbon dioxide (from the air) and water and mineral salts (from the soil). The other branch (the animals) could not perform this function and had to eat ready-made food in the form of plants or other animals. Obviously plants can obtain their food requirements by remaining stationary in a suitable spot and pushing roots into the soil and branches into the air. Animals, on the other hand, need to be able to move around in the environment to discover plants or chase other animals to eat them.

Moving around and catching food involves not only being aware of what is happening in the environment, but also of being able to respond to the information received in an organized, efficient manner. This presents many problems, particularly when animals become large and the various parts of their bodies become differentiated and highly specialized.

The co-ordination mechanism obviously must come between the sensory nerves bringing information from the receptors and the motor nerves carrying instructions to effectors. We can think of a simple C.N.S. as a complication of links between sensory and motor nerves. These links form integrating pathways running the length of the animal's body. Information is collected from receptors all over the body and passed up sensory nerves into this C.N.S. To these stimuli, responses are made which are satisfactory for the needs of the whole organism, rather than just for that area of the body which was stimulated.

We said that one of the main functions of the C.N.S. was probably to co-ordinate the activity of an organism so that it could catch food more efficiently. (Obviously other uses of movement have been made, such as avoidance of danger from other moving animals, pursuing a wandering mate, etc.) If you are hunting an animal for food it is obviously an advantage if your mouth enters new environments first. The appearance of a great lumbering body before the mouth would be likely to frighten away your prey before you had time to attack it. Very early on in evolution therefore, we find differentiation within the body of a 'mouth' end (anterior end) which is normally at the front end of the animal and so enters new environments first, and a 'tail' end (posterior end) which normally follows.

This anterior end is the exploring region of the animal. It is here that a large number of sense organs will be required (especially distance exteroceptors, e.g. eyes, ears, nose) to pick up information of what lies ahead. With the consequent increase in input to the C.N.S. at this anterior end, a proliferation of co-ordinating and integrating neurons is necessary, resulting in a swollen area at the front end of the C.N.S. In higher animals including Man this swelling is called 'the brain' whilst the rest of the central co-ordinating system is 'the spinal cord'.

There is a general tendency in evolution for species to become more efficient at coping with the environment. In order that maximum value be obtained from the large anterior sense organs it is desirable that they (and the mouth) should be easily turned to explore any part of the environment which appears interesting. To move the whole of a massive body every time you wish to turn your eyes towards a new point of focus is obviously quite inefficient. In higher animals we find a pivoting mechanism (the neck) between the anterior brain-sense organs-mouth complex (or head)[3] and the rest of the body (the trunk).

Each of the major structures in the head is protected by a bony case, essential for parts of the animal which are constantly entering new and often hostile environments. The mouth has its jaws, the brain its cranium, and the sense organs are encased in bony capsules. Over this basic framework lie a few muscles and the skin of the head. The bony cases, however, give the head its characteristic shape (Fig. III 1, p. 47). We shall discuss the development of the brain below. Here let us simply state that through evolution of higher animals there has been a general gradual increase in the size of the cranium in proportion to the size of the jaws. (Exceptions to this may occur where animals have a well developed brain but eat food which demands large jaws for mastication, e.g. the dog family.)

Although for the rest of this book we shall be concerned mainly with the head (and more particularly with the brain) we might at this point notice that general increase in efficiency of form and function has also occurred in other parts of the animal. The major motor organs (i.e. the muscles of locomotion and their skeletal bases) have moved out of the trunk

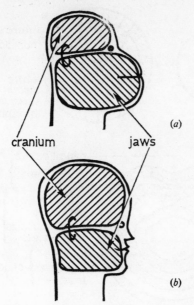

cranium   jaws

Fig. III 1   Examples of vertebrate heads
     a. Ape
     b. Man

into special projections called limbs. Whether these be fins or paddles, wings or legs, on the principle of levers they are much more efficient than they could ever be if embedded in the trunk. Morèover they can contract with the violence essential for rapid sudden movement without damaging soft internal organs. These latter have remained in the trunk. In the case of mammals (including Man) the trunk is divided again into a rigid walled anterior chest (or thorax) which contains the heart and lungs lying in chambers within which they can change size and shape with little impediment and a larger posterior abdomen in which other vital organs lie.

In the rest of this chapter we shall be discussing various aspects of the brain. We described this as a swelling at the front end of the C.N.S. The reason that it appears to be 'on top' of the human body is, of course, due to the fact that man

47

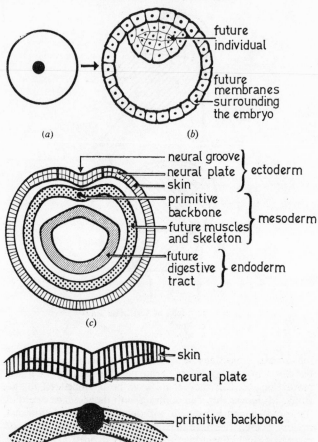

Fig. III 2 Embryological development of human nervous system
  a. Zygote
  b. Hollow ball of cells
  c. Later stage of human development (cross-section through the individual)
  d. More detail of neural plate

48

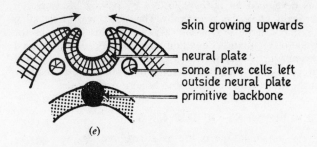

skin growing upwards

neural plate
some nerve cells left
outside neural plate
primitive backbone

(e)

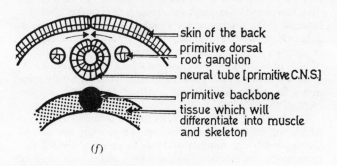

skin of the back
primitive dorsal
root ganglion
neural tube [primitive C.N.S.]
primitive backbone
tissue which will
differentiate into muscle
and skeleton

(f)

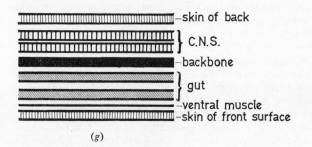

–skin of back
} C.N.S.
–backbone
} gut
–ventral muscle
–skin of front surface

(g)

e. Slightly later stage
f. Later stage still
g. Longitudinal section through body at stage f

has developed an upright posture by pulling his trunk up vertically above his hind limbs. The advantages of elevating his major sense organs and also freeing his fore-limbs for tasks other than locomotion are obvious. The increased nervous supply that is needed to co-ordinate these newly sited structures also adds to the amount of nervous tissue necessary in the brain, hence causing it to become even larger.

DEVELOPMENT OF THE C.N.S.

Every individual starts life as a fertilized egg (or *zygote*) formed by fusion of a sex-cell from each of his parents. We shall return to this concept at various points in this book, for example when discussing the relative importance of inheritance and environment in learning, or individual differences, or theories of personality development. For a full treatment of the embryological processes involved the reader should consult a general biological text.[4] Here we shall briefly mention a few points basic to our understanding of the development of the C.N.S.

The zygote divides many times to give a ball of cells from which the individual will develop. These cells are not all identical with one another and can be roughly divided into three categories according to the tissues and organs to which they give rise. There is an outer layer (called *ectoderm*) which forms the skin and nervous tissue, a middle layer (called *mesoderm*) which forms skeletal, muscular and blood tissues and an inner layer (called *endoderm*) which forms the linings of the digestive and respiratory tracts.

We shall concentrate on the ectoderm (Fig. III 2, pp. 48–9). Down the centre of the top of the embryo a strip of cells of the ectoderm becomes enlarged. This long thin plate is the beginning of the nervous system and is called the neural plate. The ectoderm at the sides of the neural plate grows up and over the top of it, pulling the edges of the plate up with it. The ectoderm from the two sides joins in the midline, as do the two sides of the neural plate. Now we have a hollow neural tube of nervous tissue lying just beneath the skin of the embryo's back. This is the primitive central nervous system from which the spinal cord and brain will differentiate.

Some nerve cells (those on the edge of the neural plate) are

Co-ordinating Ourselves with Our Surroundings

left outside the neural tube, lying free just below the skin.
They form the dorsal root ganglia of the spinal nerves (Fig.
III 3, p. 52). These ganglia lie in pairs, one on each side of the
neural tube, all down the body. Each nerve cell in each ganglion
puts out two processes, a long one running to a part of the
body outside the nervous system and a shorter one running
into the neural tube. These nerve cells are sensory in function,
i.e., they carry information to the C.N.S. from various parts
of the body.

Other (motor) nerve cells inside the C.N.S. send out
several outgrowths, one long one running to a muscle or gland,
and shorter ones making contact with fibres from a sensory
nerve cell. This contact is not usually direct but is achieved by
way of association neurons (as described in our discussion of
reflex arcs in the previous chapter).

A section across the spinal cord of a mammal will show this
arrangement which we have described, i.e. sensory nerve
fibres running up a dorsal root into the top of the cord, and
motor nerve fibres running out through a ventral root. Nerve
cell bodies are composed mainly of protoplasm and in a mass
appear grey (grey matter). Nerve fibres are covered with a
fatty insulating material and appear white (white matter).
In our section (Fig. III 4, p. 53) we find sensory grey matter in
the swellings (ganglia) on the dorsal roots and motor and
association grey matter in the centre of the cord around the
central canal of the original neural tube. Around the outside of
the motor grey matter lies white matter, consisting of fibres
which link motor, association and sensory neurons together in
any one part of the C.N.S. and also fibres which run up
and down the cord linking different parts of the C.N.S.
together.

The dorsal and ventral roots described above unite just
outside the spinal cord to form spinal nerves which run out
into the body of the animal. A short distance along each spinal
nerve is an off-shoot leading to another ganglion. From these
ganglia a fine network of nerves spread out to all parts of the
body. This is the autonomic nervous system[5] which controls
automatic functions of the body, such as movements of the
digestive tract, changes in diameter of blood vessels, activity
of glands, etc. Obviously the efficient working of this system
is of vital importance to the organism. However as it is

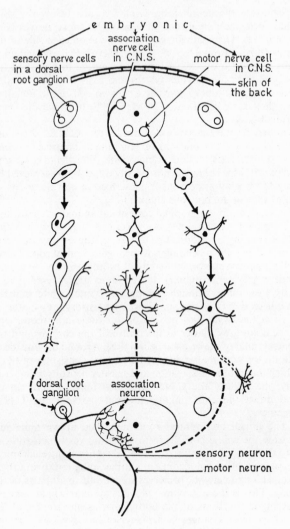

Fig. III 3 Development of a spinal nerve

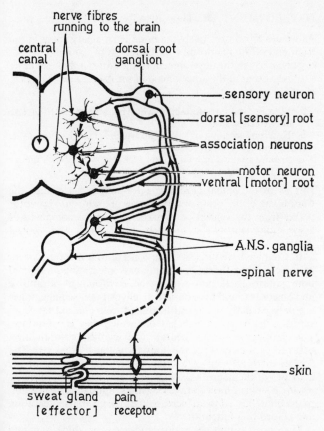

Fig. III 4   Transverse section through the adult spinal cord showing an 'involuntary' pathway

If the stimulus, i.e. heat, is very intense, it is likely that a pathway from the association neurons to voluntary motor neurons would be activated to involve muscular contractions and withdrawal of the skin from the stimulus. (See Fig. II 8)

beyond our conscious control we tend to take it for granted. We shall return to it later in our discussion of emotions.

DEVELOPMENT OF THE BRAIN

As we described previously the brain is an enlargement at the front end of the neural tube in the region of the major sense-organs. Early in the development of the embryo three separate swellings occur at the anterior end of the neural tube (Fig. III 5, pp. 56–7):

    a. the front swelling or fore-brain which is associated with the nose and perceives smell;
    b. the second swelling or mid-brain which is associated with the eye and is the visual centre;
    c. the third swelling or hind-brain which is associated with the ear and is the centre for both hearing and balance.

Just as in the spinal cord this information passes into the dorsal part of the brain and responses are sent out via motor nerves from the ventral part. Association areas composed of association neurons lie between these dorsal and ventral centres.

In Chapter 1 we discussed the concept of a nervous system as a mechanism for co-ordinating and integrating an animal both within itself and within the environment. Primitive nerve-nets as found for example in jellyfish and sea-anemones are only partially successful in this process and are far from versatile in the types of behaviour which they can produce. The development of a neural tube enabled co-ordination between various parts of the body to be much improved. The further establishment of a brain to dominate and direct the activities of the neural tube increased efficiency even more by having a single centre to take decisions. Subsequent evolution of the brain has led to an increase in efficiency of its integrating and controlling functions.

The most primitive brains consisted of three separate swellings each concerned with a different sense. As evolution progressed two concurrent trends occurred. The sensory, motor and association areas of the brain became larger and more complex and varied. At the same time there was a gradual migration of control of these centres forwards to the fore-brain leaving behind in the mid-brain and hind-brain direction of those automatic functions of which we are not normally aware, e.g. heartbeat, respiration, posture and balance. The result has been a gradual increase in size of the forebrain and the subordination to it of the rest of the nervous system. The more closely collected the various brain centres are, the greater can be their integration and the more flexible and advanced is the behaviour which they direct.

Let us examine this evolutionary process more closely. Even in such lowly vertebrates as the sharks we find some re-distribution of brain centres. The fore-brain is still the smell-centre, the mid-brain perceives visual stimuli but also receives the sensation of hearing which has migrated forwards from the hind-brain. This latter is concerned only with balance, respiration and other automatic processes. Moving on up the evolutionary ladder to the amphibians (e.g. the frog) we find a most important development. While the distribution of senses is the same in the frog as in the fish, in the upper part of the fore-brain lies a strip of tissue which acts as a sensory reception centre for nerve fibres from the mid-brain. This strip (or 'new-brain' as it is often called) really repeats the work of the mid-brain but its significance is that it lies in the fore-brain. Notice, however, that in fish and frogs much of the mental life of the animal is run by the mid-brain.

The 'new-brain' from now on is the area in which most evolutionary progress is made. In the reptiles it becomes a much more substantial neural mass. From the reptiles two major lines of animals evolved, the birds and the mammals. In birds the 'new-brain' is very much reduced in size, plays no important part in the creature's mental activity, and birds, like fish and frogs, perceive most of their sensations in the mid-brain. In mammals, however, the 'new-brain' has increased enormously and this lies behind their very characteristic behaviour. In general, fish, frogs, reptiles and birds are un-affected by stimuli unless they directly affect them (we say, are biologically relevant). For example, food, danger or, in the breeding season, a mate, will elicit responses directed towards them, but the enormous variety of other stimuli present in the environment not immediately affecting them are meaningless to them. Mammals are quite different from all other animals in that they can learn from these incidental

Fig. III 5   Evolution of the vertebrate brain
a. Primitive central nervous system
b. Primitive central nervous system with brain developing
c. Simplification of situation in C.N.S. of shark
d. Transverse section through line A–B of diagram c
e. Section of same region in frog
f. Similar section in reptile
g. Similar section in bird
h. Similar section in primitive mammal
i. Similar section in a more advanced mammal

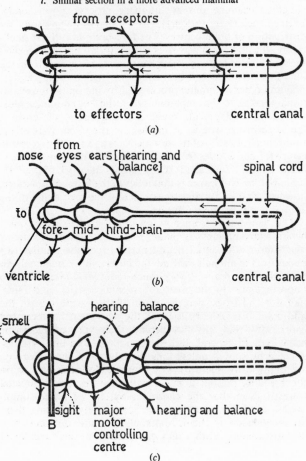

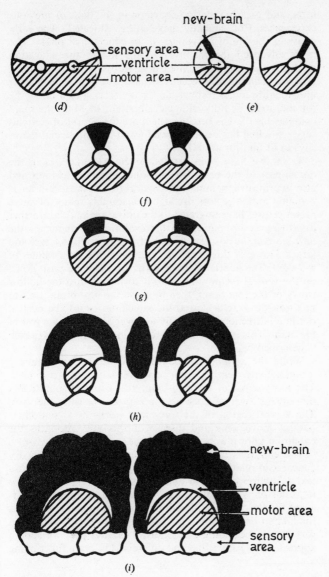

facts, and greatly modify behaviour in the light of previous experiences. Consequently they can be 'educated'. The early phase in the life of a mammal is an educational phase. The more advanced the mammal is, the longer the education necessary to cope with life successfully. This educational phase or 'childhood' precedes sexual maturity, for before the individual becomes responsible for the rearing of a family he (or she) must be fully competent himself. In Man, the more complex his life has become, the more the period of compulsory schooling has been extended (even beyond sexual maturity) to fit him for adult life.

So far we have been discussing sensory processes in the dorsal part of the brain. In birds and lower vertebrates and also in primitive mammals the ventral part of the fore-brain is a major motor region. In higher mammals many of these motor centres have migrated to the dorsal region, thus further improving co-ordination. In the evolution of mammals the new-brain in the dorsal area of the fore-brain grows larger and larger. However this expansion occurs within the confines of the skull. The effects of this growth are firstly to push down on the ventral region and cause it to buckle into the hollow cavity of the fore-brain, then to cause the new-brain itself to be thrown into folds and at the same time for it to be pushed out in all directions, eventually to cover almost all the rest of the brain. This is the condition found in human beings (which is described below).

While the mammalian new-brain controls the voluntary motor activity, ventral motor regions still have a part to play. The motor area of the mid-brain still controls some reflex movements such as cocking the ears or focusing the eyes. The ventral region of the fore-brain works as a 'smoother-out' of movements and disease of this area produces the condition known as St Vitus's Dance.

The emphasis which we have put on these evolutionary concepts in relation to the brain may seem out of place in a text devoted primarily to human psychology. The reason for its inclusion is two-fold. First, in order to attempt to understand the structure and functioning of anything as complex as the human brain it is essential to trace its development from very simple beginnings. Secondly, it is vital that we should appreciate the similarities and differences in brain functioning between groups of animals when interpreting experiments and applying findings of investigations on animals to human situations and problems.

It is an indisputable fact that a major reason for the success of mammals in becoming the dominant animals in the world today stems from the development of the 'new-brain' area of their nervous systems.[6] All living organisms are moulded by the environment, and all, to some extent, leave their mark upon it. Mammals (especially the more advanced forms) however, have been able to mould the environment considerably to suit themselves.

If you mark off the sensory and motor areas of the new-brains of reptiles and primitive mammals you will find that there is very little left. However as you go up the evolutionary scale the regions which are not primary sensory or primary motor centres but which are association areas lying between and around these centres, increase quite rapidly. In monkeys and apes these association areas are quite substantial and in Man they are very large indeed. Increasing complexity of mental activity appears to be directly related to increase in size of these association areas. We still know very little indeed about these areas. Evidence suggests that information coming up sensory nerves into the brain is fed into the primary sensory areas, e.g. the visual, auditory or tactile areas. Nerve fibres from these sensory areas run out into the association areas and carry information to them. Presumably these association areas can hold information as memories or images in such a way that items received at different times can be stored and connected and utilized in the directing of future behaviour. We shall return to a fuller discussion of such processes in the chapters on 'Learning' and 'Thinking.'

THE HUMAN BRAIN[7]

So far in this chapter we have discussed brains in rather general terms. While it is important to realize that all vertebrate brains are based on the same plan and apparent variations are simply due to development of different parts to different extents in different types of animal, it will be useful to conclude our study with a rather more specific examination of the human brain (Fig. III 6, pp. 60–1). When anatomists first described the contents of the human cranium they named the various structures they discovered in a haphazard way, often attempting to describe their appearance or position. We still retain many of these terms today and the main ones which the reader may encounter elsewhere must be introduced.

We described the original neural tube of the embryo as running the length of the animal's body. It therefore runs into the skull. We can think of the front end of the very early embryonic neural tube as being a hollow tube. We can think

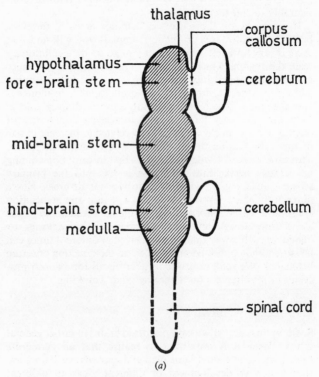

(a)

Fig. III 6 The human brain
a. Diagram indicating relationships of parts
b. (opposite) Diagram of gross appearance

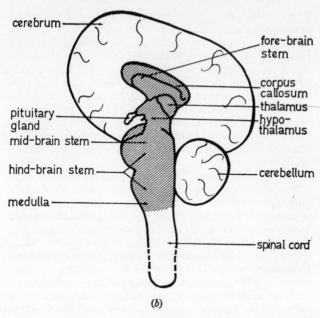

(b)

of the front end of the adult organism's neural tube (i.e. brain) as being a hollow tube (or *brain stem*) bearing three swellings, one in the hind-brain (the *cerebellum*) and two in the fore-brain (the *cerebral hemispheres*). Throughout the brain the brain stem is basically concerned with control of reflexes and the channelling and passing on of information in much the same way as the spinal cord.

In the hind-brain the brain-stem region is called the *medulla oblongata*. It controls such reflexes as relate to the heart, the gut, e.g. swallowing, and the respiratory system, e.g. coughing and sneezing. Developing out of its roof is a swelling about the size of a tangerine called the cerebellum (which means 'little brain'). This controls posture and balance and is very important in co-ordinating complicated activities such as locomotion. It is very well developed in Man who, because of his upright posture has great problems of balance. The complexity of this part of the brain is considerable, e.g. it can control about fifty muscles which must be synchronized and integrated to move each leg when walking. Moreover it can modify its patterns of control to allow a person to walk, jump, hop, dance, etc. or remain still in a variety of postures. As we can perform these locomotive activities while thinking or talking about something else it is clear that the cerebellum controls a very large number of complex *reflex* actions related to movement. If it is damaged, a person's balance is upset and he takes on a drunken gait as he tends to over-compensate. One of the effects of alcohol is to anaesthetize the cerebellum resulting in the characteristic rolling gait and loss of balance of drunkards.

The human mid-brain has remained only as brain stem. While in the lowest vertebrates it controlled vision, and in later types vision and hearing, in Man the major parts of these centres have migrated forward into the fore-brain. The mid-brain now only controls visual and auditory reflexes.

The fore-brain of Man contains the most anterior part of the brain stem. The dorsal part of the brain stem (or *thalamus*) is basically sensory and functions as a directing or sorting centre for information going into the two large swellings on its roof (the cerebral hemispheres). Before discussing these further let us briefly describe the ventral portion of the fore-brain brain stem, which is the *hypothalamus*. This basically motor region is responsible for the control of such reflexes as water balance, temperature regulation, and appetite. It is also intimately concerned with the expression of emotions through involuntary physical reactions, e.g. sweating, trembling and blood-pressure. The experiencing of emotions however occurs in the cerebral hemispheres. We shall return to a discussion of this subject in Chapter 6.

The cerebral hemispheres originate as two small swellings on the roof of the fore-brain but they increase in size very rapidly during embryonic development. The cell bodies of the neurons of the cerebral hemispheres migrate towards their surface giving an outer layer of grey matter called the *cerebral cortex*,[8] which is the organizing area of the hemispheres. The nerve fibres from these cell bodies run inwards from the cortex making their various connections and forming a central mass of white matter, which carries information to and from the cortex. In the human cortex there are some 10,000,000,000 cells and, in order to accommodate them all on the surface this latter is thrown into a large number of folds.

While the whole of the human nervous system consists of two symmetrical halves, nowhere is this more marked than in the cerebral hemispheres. For purposes of co-ordination the two halves of the nervous system are connected by fibres running crossways between them at all levels. In the case of the cerebral hemispheres the connecting bridge is very large and well-developed and is called the *corpus callosum*.

In the light of the previous chapter the reader may well be saying that discussion of the gross anatomy of the brain is not very valuable. Surely it is the pathways and connections between neurons that are important. In the final analysis this may well be true but our present state of knowledge, while allowing us to discuss the architecture and lay-out of 'the telephone exchange', cannot yet throw much light on the 'wiring system' and its mode of operation. Evidence suggests that primitively the brain consisted of a great criss-cross mass of fibres all inter-connecting with one another. Such an inter-lacing mass of association fibres does run widely through the brain. However there is a tendency for neurons apparently concerned with common functions to gather together in specific centres (or *nuclei*) and groups of fibres following common paths to be collected into bundles (or *tracts*).

We can go further in our investigations of the functions of various parts of the cortex by experimenting in various ways, e.g. cutting out certain regions of the hemispheres of animals, or stimulating specific areas electrically. Work on human beings is, of course, very difficult, but observations of behaviour of people suffering brain damage in accidents or comparing behaviour abnormalities in life with lesions in the brain discovered in post-mortems have proved useful, as also have techniques of electrical stimulation of parts of the exposed brain during operations. However the information so obtained is not as illuminating and straight-forward as was originally supposed (see below).

It is convenient to divide each hemisphere into four lobes, the frontal, parietal, temporal and occipital, the relative positions of which are most easily understood from the diagram (Fig. III 7, p. 64.) The two hemispheres appear to be mirror images of each other in gross structure, and as we have

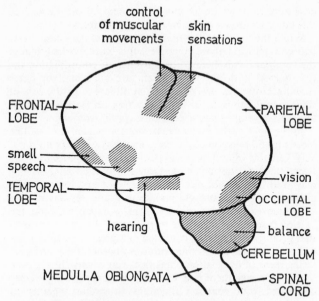

Fig. III 7   Map of the cerebral hemispheres of Man

said they are connected by bridging fibres. It is interesting to note that in general we find a crossing over of nerve fibres as they pass through the corpus callosum. Consequently sensations from the skin or ear on the left hand side of the body are passed to the right cerebral hemisphere and vice-versa. Again the left cerebral hemisphere controls movements of muscles on the right side of the body. There are complications to this situation, e.g. the eyes send fibres to both hemispheres, while the speech centre is normally found only on the left hand side. Normally, one hemisphere dominates the other, the left one in right-handed people and vice versa, and recent evidence suggests that it may be in the dominant hemisphere that the majority of psychological processes, e.g. thinking, learning, etc., goes on. If this is so, perhaps this is a further step in the process which we previously discussed of concentrating major controlling centres very close together to facilitate efficient integration.

FURTHER ON THE HUMAN CEREBRAL CORTEX

There has been a tradition in psychology to think of the brain as being composed of a number of different parts each with its own specific function (or faculty), e.g. the memory, the intelligence, the conscience, the reason, etc. Because these functions were considered to be essentially human and because the human cerebral hemispheres were so much larger than those of other organisms, these faculties were believed to reside in the cerebral cortex, as comparatively isolated, specialized tissue masses. Investigations indicate, however, that this view is quite erroneous. The brain must be considered as a whole, rather than in terms of disconnected units. Direct evidence for this can be experimentally produced. For example while the processes of reasoning, thinking, etc., can be shown by evidence from evolution and development or by removal of fore-brain tissue to reside in the cerebral hemispheres, destruction of parts of the brain stem will also impair these processes. Again we have said that the spinal cord and brain stem are responsible for control of reflexes, e.g. withdrawal from pain, coughing or sneezing. If connections between the brain stem and the cerebral hemispheres are severed these mechanical responses will still occur when suitable stimulation occurs. However in the intact C.N.S. the cerebral hemispheres take a part in such reflexes, e.g. in feeling pain, or controlling coughing and sneezing when they are socially unacceptable. This and other evidence suggests that under normal circumstances we should consider that the nervous system functions as a whole.

The general plan upon which this complete system works seems, in principle, to be as follows (Fig. III 8, p. 66). The spinal cord and brain stem consist of inborn direct links between sensory and motor nerve fibres, the activation of which produces reflex responses. The cerebral hemispheres are composed basically of extra connections which are inserted between sensory input and motor activation to modify subsequent responses. These new pathways are affected by learning and by their utilization behaviour is more likely to be suitable for the whole body and adapted to environmental conditions. We have already discussed reflexes in the preceding chapter. Now we must consider further the activation of these

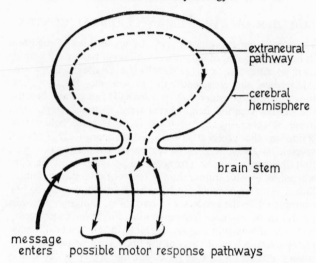

extraneural
pathway

cerebral
hemisphere

brain stem

message
enters   possible motor response pathways

Fig. III 8   Possible relationship between brain stem and cerebral hemispheres

more complex links running through the cerebral hemispheres.

Studies of information entering the brain from receptors
indicate that there are two distinct forms of activation:

A. THE SPECIFIC SENSORY SYSTEM where information runs
up direct pathways to areas of the cortex specialized for their
reception, e.g. cortical centres for sight, hearing, touch. These
areas are well developed and minutely organized so that
patterns of information coming from receptors can be efficiently and accurately interpreted. For example, there appear
to be point-to-point connections between the retina or the
cochlea, or the skin-receptors of touch, and specific groups of
cells in the cortex. This type of specific excitation is very
rapid, and so we see or hear or feel immediately after the
receptors concerned have been stimulated.

B. THE NON-SPECIFIC SENSORY SYSTEM through which some
of the information passing up sensory nerves is directed off
down branches to many parts of the brain. The function of
this system is to arouse the cortex to a suitable level of activity
so that it can respond effectively. When we are asleep, the

non-specific system is working at a very low level, while when we are attentive and noticing everything going on around us, it is very active. We can define consciousness (the state of being aware) in terms of level of activity of this non-specific system. When it is damaged or anaesthetized we become unconscious, i.e. we are not aware of our surroundings. When we are unconscious our specific sensory system does not function either. This non-specific system is apparently essential for responses to specific stimuli to occur. Information is supplied to this non-specific system from a variety of sense organs. This is all intermingled and gradually accumulates or dies away. Consequently we gradually get sleepy or more attentive. It is important to note that this non-specific system depends not only on input from sense organs but also on information fed back to it from the cortex. For example, we do not necessarily drop off to sleep in a quiet dark room. If we are excited or worried about a problem we can lie awake all night thinking about it. Our C.N.S. is kept aroused by feedback from the active cerebral cortex. In order to go to sleep we must stop thinking as far as possible, i.e. 'make our minds go blank'.

Information leaving the cerebral hemispheres to direct behaviour also can take one of two pathways:

A. THE SPECIFIC MOTOR SYSTEM where messages are sent directly and quickly to motor centres in the brain stem and spinal cord to guide specific responses to specific stimuli.

B. THE NON-SPECIFIC MOTOR SYSTEM which determines the general overall responsiveness of these motor centres. For example, if a person is very sleepy his responsiveness will be low and should he fall out of bed, he will only slowly 'come to', i.e. he must wait for gradual accumulation of non-specific sensory arousal which in turn will eventually produce a more active non-specific motor condition. If on the other hand, he is in a very attentive state, e.g. nervous or worried, his motor responsiveness will be high and he will jump at the slightest sensory stimulation, e.g. a slight noise, a gentle touch. Again a small child who is upset or angry will cry about anything that happens to him no matter how innocuous it may be. Obviously the autonomic nervous system mentioned above can be considered as part of this non-specific arousal system.

Our knowledge of the non-specific sensory and motor

systems is very meagre indeed. More work has been carried out on the specific systems but the information collected raises more questions than it answers. Certain areas of the cortex are primarily concerned with specific functions, e.g. the visual area, or auditory area, or speech area. However, it is important to note that while these specific areas perform a vital *part* of the mental process with which they are concerned, they are not by any means responsible for the whole of the process. Vision is impaired or destroyed by damage to the visual area. However it is also adversely affected by interference with optic sensory pathways from the eye, with visual association areas in the brain, etc. Other mental processes such as memory, learning and thinking cannot be localized at all.[9] Lashley showed in experiments on the cortex of rats that impairment in ability to learn is proportional to the amount of cortex destroyed and is virtually independent of area of damage. This and other evidence suggests that it is not the place in the cortex which is important in learning but some other feature, e.g. the pattern of activity which the stimulus produces in the cortex. The nature of such patterns if they exist has yet to be elucidated.

Another problem of localization of functions in the cortex arises from the fact that all nerve impulses are identical, irrespective of the receptor from which they originated. Impulses in the optic nerve are identical with those in the auditory nerve or sciatic nerve or nerves running to the diaphragm. Consider as an example the reception of stimuli by the human body. Light or sound or heat or chemical particles (smell) will fall on all parts of the body surface. Different sense organs are sensitive to different stimuli, e.g. eyes to light, nose to chemicals. However they all convert the stimuli to which they are sensitive into the electrical energy of nerve impulses. The brain receiving these nerve impulses cannot, from their nature, determine whether they represent visual or chemical or touch stimulation. However, as eyes are only sensitive to light, impulses in the optic nerves must represent visual stimulation. Again impulses in the auditory nerves must have been produced by sound stimulation. The specific sensory pathways from the eye run to the visual area of the brain. Impulses arriving here are interpreted by the brain as being the result of visual stimuli. If you cut an organism's optic nerve and electrically stimulate the cut end of it 'light' will be 'seen' in its visual area. Theoretically if you could graft the stump of an optic nerve (still attached to the visual area of the brain) to the cut end of an auditory nerve still attached to the cochlea, sounds stimulating the cochlea would be seen as light in the brain. Again the sudden jarring of the visual area of the brain by a blow on the back of the head will cause it to be stimulated and you perceive light (i.e. you see stars).

While we interpret sensory input according to the part of the brain into which it is fed, there is a good deal of evidence to suggest that accurate location and interpretation of stimuli must be learned by experience in at least some brain centres. [10] For example, a chimpanzee whose limbs were encased in plaster of Paris for the first two years of its life had great difficulty in locating pin pricks on its limbs when unable to see what was happening. Again human beings cannot easily locate internal abdominal pains or objects stuck somewhere in their gullets. This would suggest that we have to somehow learn to relate stimuli entering the cerebral cortex with specific locations in the body. We shall return to this point in our discussion of learning in Chapter 7.

Earlier in this chapter we mentioned association areas as parts of the cerebral cortex which are not primary sensory or motor centres. Those association areas lying between such primary centres probably act as connecting pathways or even storage tissues for past experiences. There is a very large association area in each cerebral hemisphere forming the anterior part of each frontal lobe and called the prefrontal area. The mode of functioning of these areas is very obscure but they seem to convert the impulses entering them into 'feelings' (a concept we shall discuss further in Chapter 6). Some mentally ill persons feel extremely anxious and will not respond to normal methods of treatment. In some cases, cutting the fibres between the thalamus and the prefrontal areas (i.e. removing much of the areas' sensory input) greatly relieves the patient's anxiety. This operation (now largely obsolescent) called prefrontal leucotomy, [11] does not in any way affect the individual's intellect but it frequently tends to make him less neurotic. Observations on persons who have had this operation lead us to the view that the probable function of these particular association areas is to somehow make a person more socially acceptable. Leucotomized patients tend to lack a sense of responsibility, cannot take initiative and are inconsiderate. It is interesting to note that when an electric current is passed through the brains of certain types of mental patient, there follows an improvement in their condition which is similar to, but less permanent than the effects of prefrontal leucotomy. This type of treatment, called electrical convulsant therapy (E.C.T.), will be referred to again in Chapter 14. Here let us simply note that its probable effect is to somehow inhibit the nerve pathways between the thalamus and the prefrontal areas.

In such a brief discussion as this it is impossible to touch on all the interesting and important aspects of the cerebral cortex. The reader is referred to specialist texts in the bibliography if he wishes to cover the subject more fully. Let us, as our final task here, mention some of the evidence which electrical studies of the brain have produced. When neurons are active there is movement of electrically charged chemical particles (called *ions*) across the nerve cell membrane. When one cell becomes active it appears to excite other cells adjacent to it, presumably through the movement of these ions. Consequently the activation of a nerve cell will cause a wave of excitation around it in the cerebral cortex. Evidence suggests that when two nerve cells are activated at the same time they change physiologically in such a way that the next time one of the cells is excited there is a strong possibility that the second cell will be also. This could perhaps be the basis of learning.

The cells of the cerebral cortex are always electrically active in life (even in unconsciousness).[12] If all the cells are 'firing' randomly the level of activity in the cortex as a whole will appear to be more or less constant. However should large numbers of cells fire together, then recover together and fire again together, there will be pulses of activity followed by periods of comparative inactivity in the cortex. The electrical changes of the brain can be recorded on a chart called an electroencephalogram (E.E.G.) (Fig. III 9, p 71). The results obtained are fairly constant for most human beings of the same age group.

The adult at rest in a quiet room with his eyes closed shows

70

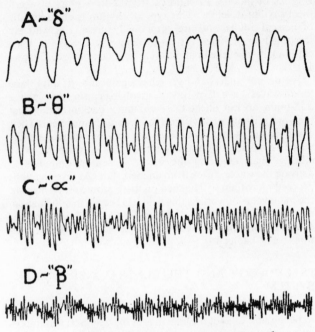

Fig. III 9   Some examples of electroencephalograph records

a. Delta—0·5 to 3·5 cycles per second
b. Theta—4 to 7 cycles per second
c. Alpha—8 to 13 cycles per second
d. Higher frequency (Beta)—14 to 30 c/s

a fairly regular rhythm of firing of about 10 beats/second
(called the alpha-rhythm). On his waking and becoming active
this rhythm breaks up in a way which depends both upon the
person and the type of activity in which he becomes involved.
This is due presumably to some groups of cells firing more
quickly, and others more slowly, giving a combined E.E.G.
of several rhythms which is very difficult to interpret. In sleep
the E.E.G. shows delta waves (1–5 beats/second), suggesting
reduced but closely synchronized activity of large numbers of
neurons. Such delta-rhythms are also characteristic of the

E.E.G.s of infants. In children from 2 to 5 years of age a theta-rhythm develops. This type of rhythm is characteristic of normal adults who are emotionally upset, e.g. who are frustrated or irritated. It also frequently occurs in some emotionally disturbed patients (e.g. psychopaths, see Chapter 14).

We do not understand yet what significance (if any) these 'brain-waves' have. Experiments involving cutting through the mid-brain do not affect these rhythms, demonstrating that they are self-initiated within the cerebral hemispheres.Their existence shows that the brain is in a constant state of activity which is modified by sensory input. This is obviously more efficient than requiring the incoming sensory impulses to activate the whole cortex from an inert state. As investigations proceed more light will be shed on these problems. At present, the main value of work in this field has been in the elucidation, diagnosis and treatment of certain mental conditions such as epilepsy, brain tumours and psychopathic personality conditions (see Chapter 14).

PSYCHOLOGY AND THE CENTRAL NERVOUS SYSTEM

In Chapter 1 we suggested that the mind might be considered to be the sum total of the activities of the C.N.S. It was important at that early stage to take some such single concept as a working basis for introducing the subject of psychology. However, we are now at a point in the book where we have, to some extent, defined our field of study, and it is important that we now consider the pros and cons of this concept before proceeding further.

Approaches to the nature of 'mind' are numerous and varied. Taking two extremes, theology, parapsychology and various philosophical doctrines maintain that the physiological workings of the nervous system are in themselves quite inadequate explanations of human psychology. On the other hand, extreme behaviourists would say that physiological and mental processes are synonymous with one another.

There can be no doubt that there is a very close physical-psychological association. This has been realized by Man for centuries. Originally the seat of mental activity was thought to be the heart and so we find our vocabulary sprinkled with phrases like 'to know in your heart', 'to learn by heart', 'heart-broken', 'sweethearts', etc. Today evidence proves beyond doubt that behaviour is controlled by the nervous system. Studies of inheritance, brain damage, senility, effects of drugs and electrical treatment, and many other instances bearing out this conclusion will be found in this book. The *existence* of a body-mind relationship, however, does not in itself shed any light upon the *nature* of such a relationship.

The root of the problem of understanding the concept of 'the mind' is ascribed by many writers to the limitations of our vocabulary. The term 'the mind' tends to conjure up a picture of a complete entity like 'the tongue' or 'the kidney', and this can lead to the expectation that an organ called 'a mind' exists somewhere in the body of each of us, probably situated in the brain. The fact that no such structure can be distinguished is no criticism of the concept that the mind is a 'non-material entity' whose existence cannot be proved or disproved by physical means. Theories of mind based on this type of approach suggest that the brain acts as an intermediary between the mind and the body and so any damage or modification of the brain will affect the way in which the mind can influence the body.

It would seem to be more feasible to think of a person's mind as being a term applied to processes going on in the nervous system, just as 'breathing' refers to activities in the lungs and 'digestion' to the functioning of the alimentary canal. While such a concept is convenient and acceptable to many psychologists it does not shed much light on the nature of the mind, because the processes going on in the nervous system are still so little understood. Are all mental activities synonymous with physiological processes, are they based on physiology, or are they by-products of such processes? Can the solving of world problems, the planning of a child's future, or the appreciation of literature all be explained in terms of chemistry and physics? Are mental activities properties of neurons which we cannot observe with our present instruments? These and a host of other questions may be asked but not yet in any way answered.

It is important to realize, however, that even if one day we can relate the *occurrence* of mental processes to physiological activities of neurons, this will not necessarily mean that we shall be any closer to understanding the *nature* of these processes. The situation is analogous to saying that we feel pain when a stone flying through the air strikes us on the head. The occurrence of pain is related to the moving stone making contact with our skin, but this does not give us insight into the nature of pain. Similarly the colours we see are caused by light waves, but we cannot describe greenness or redness in terms of light waves.

We must conclude, therefore, that while the structure and functioning of our nervous systems are the probable physical bases of mental events, our present knowledge is so scanty that to use this approach to our study of human problems would be extremely limiting. Consequently the rest of this text turns away from physiological accounts and takes up more psychological interpretations. This is not meant in any way to detract from the importance of work at the neuro-physiological level, which is going on apace in modern psychological laboratories. However it is probably better to concentrate on such an approach subsequent to the completion of a general psychology course rather than to use it as an introduction to the subject.

SUMMARY

1. Co-ordination with the environment is the basis of behaviour and so is the subject matter of psychology. As the C.N.S. is the co-ordinating system, an introduction to its mode of activity is an essential part of a psychology course. Our knowledge in this field, however, is at present very meagre.
2. Because of the great complexity of the human C.N.S. it is useful to approach it from an evolutionary point of view. Simple organisms fall into two main groups:

   a. plants which manufacture their own food from nutrients in the soil and atmosphere;
   b. animals which feed on plants or other animals.

   In order to obtain their food animals must move. This involves responding to the environment in an efficient organized manner, a situation which has been achieved by the development of a nervous system.

Co-ordinating Ourselves with Our Surroundings

3. A simple C.N.S. can be considered as a complication of the association pathways between sensory and motor neurons. Co-ordination and efficiency are more important at the front end of the animal than elsewhere and so we find anterior swellings in the C.N.S. which we call the brain.

4. The neural tube is the embryological structure from which the spinal cord and spinal nerves develop.

5. The autonomic nervous system which controls automatic bodily functions is briefly introduced.

6. The primitive brain consists of three separate swellings each associated with a major sense organ: the fore-brain with the nose; the mid-brain with the eyes; the hind-brain with the ears. For efficient integration however it is necessary to bring the major centres of sensory and motor control as close together as possible. In evolution, while these centres have increased in size, they have also migrated forwards into the fore-brain, leaving behind only reflex actions in the mid- and hind-brains.

7. Early in vertebrate evolution (at the amphibian level) a sensory reception centre for fibres from the mid-brain arises in the fore-brain. This centre is called the new-brain. It is of the greatest importance in mammals, expanding to form the bulk of their cerebral hemispheres. Control of behaviour by this new-brain has been greatly responsible for the success of mammals as a group.

8. The great expansion of the new-brain takes place within the confines of the skull, thus causing it to spread backwards over other parts of the brain and also being responsible for its folded surface.

9. The value of a knowledge of the development and evolution of the vertebrate C.N.S. is two-fold:

   a. it helps us to understand the great complexity of the human brain;
   b. it enables us to evaluate the application of the results of experiments on animals to human problems.

10. A major evolutionary advance in the human brain is the considerable development of association areas between and around the primary sensory and motor centres. These areas may well be involved in the 'holding' and 'organizing' of information within the brain.

11. It is convenient to consider the human brain as an extension of the neural tube into the head region. This tube once within the skull is called the 'brain stem'. On this stem arise three main swellings, the cerebrum in the hind-brain and the two cerebral hemispheres in the fore-brain. The brain stem still functions

much as does the spinal cord, i.e. for controlling reflexes. The cerebellum is concerned with balance and posture. The cerebral hemispheres are the site of the higher mental processes, such as learning, thinking and reasoning and they control voluntary thought and action.

12. In considering the mode of functioning of the brain, it is essential to think of it as an integrated whole. The brain stem and spinal cord basically consist of inborn, fairly direct pathways between sensory and motor nerves, which are responsible for the control of reflex action. The cerebral hemispheres consist, in part at least, of extra connections, modifiable by experience which can be included in the pathways linking sensory input and motor responses. They have the effect of adapting behaviour in the light of previous experience to cope with the environment as efficiently as possible.

13. Information entering the brain apparently follows two systems of pathways:

   a. a specific system which gives an accurate representation in the cortex of the stimulus being transmitted;
   b. a non-specific system which arouses the cortex to a suitable level of activity to respond effectively to the stimuli it is receiving.

14. Responses leaving the brain also follow two systems of pathways:

   a. a specific system sending messages direct to motor centres in the brain stem and spinal cord to guide specific responses;
   b. a non-specific system which determines the general level of responsiveness of these motor centres.

15. A variety of problems relating to localization of function in the cerebral cortex are introduced to indicate the difficulties involved in interpreting the mode of activity of this area of the C.N.S.

16. The prefrontal areas of the frontal lobes are association areas whose functions are obscure. In some mental patients suffering from extreme anxiety, cutting through the fibres running between these areas and the thalamus relieves the anxiety and makes the individual less neurotic. This operation is called prefrontal leucotomy. Electrical convulsant therapy has similar but less permanent effects.

17. Electrical studies of the brain suggest that when nerve cells are activated they change physiologically. This may be of great importance in such mental activities as perception or learning.

76

Co-ordinating Ourselves with Our Surroundings

When large numbers of cells in the cerebral cortex 'fire' together, recover together and 'fire' again together, electrical 'brain waves' can be recorded (as an E.E.G.). We do not yet understand, however, the significance of E.E.G. patterns.

18. While the structure and functioning of our nervous systems are the probable physical bases of mental events the exact relationship between them still is not understood.

REFERENCES

1. For discussion of possible interpretations of behaviour in terms of activity of the brain see:

    a. Eccles, J. C. *The Neurophysiological Basis of Mind* (O.U.P., London 1953).
    b. Hebb, D. O. *The Organization of Behavior* (Wiley, N.Y. 1949).

2. An elementary treatment of the evolution of the C.N.S. is given in Morgan, C. T. *Physiological Psychology* (McGraw-Hill, N.Y. 1965) pp. 36–60). A more advanced treatment is given in Romer, A. S. *The Vertebrate Body* (Saunders, London 1955) pp. 530–90.

3. For a simple discussion of the human head and brain see Harrison, R. J. *Man, The Peculiar Animal* (Pelican, Harmondsworth 1958). For more detail on mammalian heads and brains see Young, J. Z. *The Life of Mammals* (O.U.P., London 1957).

4. A good general account of embryological development can be found in Waddington, C. H. *Principles of Embryology* (Allen & Unwin, London 1956). For a more specialized account of the development of the nervous system see Hamburger, V. 'Development of the Nervous System', *Ann. N.Y. Acad. Sci.* 55 (1952).

5. Any introductory text-book of physiology will give a general account of this topic. For more detailed examination see Mitchell, G. A. G. *Anatomy of the Autonomic Nervous System* (Livingstone, Edinburgh 1953).

6. See Romer, A. S. *The Vertebrate Body* (Saunders, London 1955) pp. 580–7. This source also includes several more detailed references for the interested reader.

7. See Pfeiffer, J. *The Human Brain* (Gollancz, London 1955).

8. For a detailed treatment see either:

    a. Penfield, W. and Rasmussen, T. *The Cerebral Cortex of Man* (Macmillan, London 1950).
    b. Sholl, D. A. *The Organization of the Cerebral Cortex* (Methuen, London 1950).

9. Adrian, E. D. 'Localization in the Cerebral Cortex' in *Readings in General Psychology*, Halmos and Iliffe (eds.) (Routledge & Kegan Paul, London 1959) pp. 9–14.
10. For a further discussion of this and related experimental work see Hebb, D. O. *Text-book of Psychology* (Saunders, Philadelphia and London, 2nd edition 1966; 1st edition 1958) especially pp. 139–64.
11. For a general survey see Sargent, W. and Slater, E. *An Introduction To Physical Methods of Treatment in Psychiatry* (Livingstone, Edinburgh 1948). For a more advanced treatment see Petrie, A. *Personality and the Frontal Lobes* (Routledge & Kegan Paul, London 1952).
12. For an excellent simple discussion of E.E.G.s see Grey Walter, W. *The Living Brain* (Pelican, London 1961).

Chapter Four

Interpreting Ourselves and Our Surroundings

INTRODUCTION

In previous chapters we have been examining the human nervous system from the point of view of the structure and functioning of its anatomical parts. While such an approach is of fundamental importance in psychology,[1] it is (at our present level of knowledge) an inadequate basis for a full introductory course and we must now discuss some aspects of psychology from a less physical point of view.

In this chapter we shall consider what happens to information from the sense organs after it has passed into the central nervous system, i.e. we must discuss how the brain forms within itself a 'mental picture' of the outside world. It is convenient and useful to distinguish between two closely related but rather different aspects of the processes involved,[*] namely:

    a. Sensation which consists of the picking up of information by sense organs and the passing of this information into the brain;
    b. Perception which consists of the activities in the brain as a direct result of the messages coming from the sense organs.

Sensation was the subject of Chapter 2. Here we are concerned with a deeper examination of perception.

*Many psychologists consider this separation to be artificial. It is retained here for convenience of introduction to these processes. The discussion of concept formation is taken up in Chapter 8.

THE NATURE OF PERCEPTION

Perception is the term given to the mental activities involved in becoming aware of and interpreting the happenings in ourselves and our surroundings in order that we may respond to them in a manner most likely to satisfy our existing needs. The processes involved in perception are conveniently subdivided into:

1. *ORGANIZATION* of the multitudes of scattered nerve impulses entering the brain into a meaningful picture of what they represent. Such a picture we call a *percept*. For example a patient 'coming round' in bed after an anaesthetic will have vast numbers of impulses suddenly being dispatched from his sense organs to his brain, informing him of a variety of aspects of his surroundings and his bodily and mental condition:

receptors in the eye	— sight of screens, nurses, etc.
receptors in the ear	— sound of voices, footsteps, etc.
receptors in the nose	— smell of disinfectant, polish, etc.
receptors in the tongue	— taste of anaesthetic, blood, etc.
receptors in the skin	— pressure of bed clothes, temperature, etc.
receptors in muscles	— information regarding his posture
receptors in the gut	— information that he feels sick.

All this information and a great deal more must be so organized as to give the patient a meaningful interpretation (percept) of his situation. At first he may well be confused as his percept will still be disorganized. As time passes he 'sorts out' the information and forms a more coherent percept. We all have similar experiences on waking suddenly from a deep sleep and needing time to become orientated. If we wake slowly we gradually 'come to' and so do not experience such disorientation. Misinterpretation and incorrect percept information, however, is very common in human behaviour. We shall leave discussion of this vast subject to the next chapter.

2. *UTILIZATION* of the percept formed out of the incoming information to so organize (or 'set') the mind that when the person responds to the environment he may do so in the most satisfactory way possible. This re-setting of the mind is very much affected by other factors already present, such as past experiences stored there or motives active in the mind.

For example, two patients having had the same operation at the same time and recovering consciousness in similar situations might behave quite differently. One may have an unco-operative attitude towards the nursing staff, may demand to be the centre of attention and may constantly be worried by memories of a previous similar operation which was unsuccessful. The other may be helpful, co-operative and considerate, may wish to be left alone, feels thankful the operation is over and hopes that he will recover as quickly as his doctor assured him he would. These two patients had virtually the same sensation but the organization of their percepts and their subsequent utilization were quite different due to attitudes, memories, motives, etc., present in their minds at the time. We shall return to this subject again when discussing more fully how percepts differ between individuals.

We have established, then, two different aspects of perception: (*a*) the organization of sensations into percepts; (*b*) the utilization of percepts in the control of responses to the environment which caused the original sensations. The rest of this chapter examines specifically:

- *a*. which of the available information from the environment we select for use in our 'mental reconstruction' of it;
- *b*. the basic principles of perception that appear to be common to everyone;
- *c*. the ways in which each individual adds his own unique ingredients to the mental pictures he forms.

THE CONTENT OF PERCEPTS

Our surroundings constantly bombard our sense organs with stimuli. It is from these stimuli that our minds build up our percepts. This information is received constantly in such great quantities that the brain could not cope with it all. We therefore find that some information is selected for percept-formation while much is rejected. It is this process of selection that we are concerned with here.

Selection occurs at two levels in our nervous system:

- *a*. At the sense organ stage where information is picked up from that part of the outside world towards which the sense organs are directed, e.g. on which the eyes are focused or which the skin is touching.

81

b. In the brain where the information picked up by the sense organs is examined for relative importance in terms of the needs of the person, his past experiences, etc. This selection of material in the brain is called *attention*.[2] We pay attention to that which is important to us.

There is, of course, close co-operation between these two parts of the selection process. The brain can only select from the sensations which the sense organs send it. Conversely if the brain finds little of importance in the sensations it is receiving, it directs the sense organs to continue examining the environment; if vital information is passed to the brain, the sense organs are directed on to its source and attention is paid to it. For example, in a cinema before the lights go down and the picture starts your eyes wander round, you listen to snatches of other people's conversation, you fidget, you keep noting the time, etc. Your sense organs move over the environment but attend to nothing in particular. When, however, the film begins your eyes and ears focus on it. You pay attention to the screen and ignore the rest of the environment. You fail to notice the time passing, the exit of the person next to you, how uncomfortable or how hungry you have become. If, however, during this time someone had screamed or flashed a light in your eyes you would at once have paid attention to this new stimulus. It may have been important to you, so your brain selects that part of the environment for your sense organs to attend to until it is satisfied that there is no danger and your attention can safely be returned to the screen.

This example gives us some indication as to which aspects of our environment are likely to attract our attention. In simple animals concentration of attention seems to be confined to those parts of their surroundings which are important for them to stay alive, e.g. sources of food or danger. In human beings, also, this satisfaction of bodily needs can play a large part in selection of important stimuli, e.g. if we are hungry, cold, tired or in pain we search our environment in an attempt to satisfy the particular need we are experiencing. This tendency is easily observed in persons who, although satisfied in most of their bodily needs, require satisfaction of their sexual appetite. Consequently they pay considerable attention to attractive members of the opposite sex (whether at work, in the street, on television or anywhere else) and will find their attention easily distracted from other areas of their surroundings towards that part which could satisfy this basic need.

Besides this involuntary attention to parts of the environment which satisfy bodily needs, human beings also have the ability to choose certain parts of the environment which interest them (see Chapter 6) and voluntarily focus their attention upon them, e.g. an exciting novel, a pretty dress, an object of historical interest. Such voluntary attention, if repeated often enough, can become automatic, e.g. a mother automatically listens for the cry of her baby; a teacher recognizes at once when her class is not following her; in both these instances attention is constantly being paid to that part of the environment likely to produce information of importance.

Let us consider, by means of an example, how these various types of attention can cause different percepts to be established in a group of individuals all receiving a basically similar sensation. Let us take as our example a woman in labour being rushed to hospital in her next-door neighbour's car. The woman's husband (a garage mechanic) and her teenage son accompany her. As the car enters the hospital gates each person in the car will have a similar sensation. Their percepts, however, will differ according to the parts of the environment to which they attend:

a. Car driver	attending to signposts	Voluntary
	watching for danger ⎫	Involuntary
	manipulating controls ⎭	and Habitual
b. Husband	watching for danger	Involuntary
	listening to tone of engine	Habitual
	concerned about his wife	Involuntary
c. Wife	attending to labour pains	Involuntary
	noticing appearance of hospital	Voluntary
	concerned about family at home	Involuntary
d. Son	concerned about mother	Involuntary
	concerned about conditions at home	Involuntary
	noticing passing nurses	Habitual

All these individuals had a similar sensation but each interpreted it differently according to the features of it on which the attention was focused. The contents of their percepts were different.

Although we have divided 'attention' into the three categories of 'involuntary', 'voluntary' and 'habitual', we find that in each of these forms certain types of information more readily attract attention than do others. These types of stimulation are those which are most likely to be important to the organism. It is convenient to place some of the major 'attention-attracting' characteristics in the following three classes:

A. Information which is *unusual*, i.e. which is different from that previously experienced and which, in biological terms, needs further investigation to decide how useful or harmful it is likely to be; e.g. a pushchair placed in a field with cattle will attract them; a person with a new style of dress or a peculiar walk attracts attention; similarly the use of coloured chalks for important words on a blackboard or the underlining of certain words in a text-book will have attention directed towards them. Our attention is always attracted by new and unusual stimuli, while it tends to be withdrawn from that with which we are familiar.

B. Information which *changes*, e.g. in loudness, brightness, appearance, or which moves. Those parts of our surroundings which are changing are likely to be more important or need attending to more quickly than the rest of the environment. Hence a cat stalking a bird gives as little indication of movement as possible in order not to attract the attention of its prey; a teacher raises her voice to attract a child's attention; a flashing neon-sign causes us to attend to it, etc.

C. Information which *stimulates the sense organs to a great extent*, e.g. a loud noise, a large object, a bright colour, a strong smell, a heavy blow will all attract attention. Biologically speaking, the stronger the stimulus the greater the effect there is likely to be on the person as a result of coming into contact with it. Similarly, information which is repeated is likely to be important and therefore attracts attention, e.g. a flashing light, a repeated cry (e.g. help, help, help). Of course, if any one of these stimuli is repeated too often we become 'used to it', i.e. *adapted* to it (e.g. the ticking of a clock), and our attention is directed elsewhere. We then require a change of intensity to re-attract our attention.

We have previously discussed the ability of the brain to hold information within itself long after the sense organs which picked up that information have ceased to be stimulated by it. Such stored information can be aroused (i.e. we can remember it) when another associated piece of information enters the brain. For example, the sight of a text-book will remind us of homework not completed or the sound of a dog howling at night will bring back the memory of a ghost story. Similarly we can activate several related pieces of information at the same time and out of a recombination of memories we can create quite new relationships (*ideas*). For example I can activate a memory of the problem of what to give my child for its birthday. At the same time I can activate memories of the possessions it has and its needs and interests not yet completely satisfied. Within my mind I can decide on a suitable present without information coming directly from my sense organs. These mental processes may be as important to me as the surroundings in which I find myself. Indeed, if I have a difficult problem to tackle I should move into an environment where little of importance would be picked up by my sense organs, e.g. the peace of a library or a quiet room. I could therefore attend to my internal mental processes at the expense of my surroundings. The same basic rules apply to attention turned inwardly as did to that relating to the environment. We shall return to this point in our discussion of thinking and problem-solving in a later chapter.

In conclusion, let us put the process of attention into perspective in our study of perception. Attention is the selection technique by which important information from our surroundings is fed in great detail into the brain. Other parts of the outside world which stimulate our sense organs are perceived as a general background which is not clearly defined. Should part of this background, however, take on any of the attention-attracting characteristics that we have mentioned above, our attention will be immediately focused on to it. The process of attention decides, therefore, which material should be clearly defined in our percepts and which should be of less importance.

THE NATURE OF PERCEPTS

In the previous section we have been discussing which information from the outside world will be the basis or raw material of our percepts. These percepts, however, have meaning for us. They are not simply collections of randomly scattered impulses arriving at the brain from sense organs. They represent the situation in which we find ourselves. It is the way in which such a percept can be organized and have meaning that we are concerned with here.[3]

Evidence from experiments and observation of development of normal behaviour in children and animals show that the ability to organize sensations into meaningful percepts is probably inborn. However, this capacity is greatly developed and made much more efficient with practice in perceiving new situations: consider the well-known experiments in which a new-born goat kid was placed on a sheet of thick glass.[4] The kid appeared to be standing on a ledge to the side of which was a deep drop. In fact the whole ledge and drop were covered by the glass. However, the kid carefully avoided stepping on to the glass above the drop. A similar situation was found with young children just starting to crawl. In these instances care was taken to ensure that as little relevant practice as possible was involved in each case. The ability to attribute meaning (here danger) to the situation must have been inborn.

The improvement of this inborn ability with practice is shown very clearly by clinical records of persons who have had part of the normal content of their percepts withheld during the period in which they were practising percept-formation.[5] For example, persons born with cataracts (clouded lenses) learnt to organize their percepts and understand their surroundings without incorporating any visual sensations into their mental pictures. When such persons receive their sight they can only distinguish very rudimentary visual patterns, shapes, relationships, etc. They must practise interpreting what they see in terms of what they know from their other sense organs. Visually they are going through a process which most of us follow in infancy. In the normal infant the practice of organization of sensations from all the sense organs goes on at the same time. Details gradually become distinguished and the percepts formed represent more exactly the environment of the child.

It will follow from this that there are certain inborn features of percept organization that are likely to be common to us all. However, our individual past experiences and the situations in which we have practised percept-formation will be different for each of us. It is these similarities and differences which we must now examine.

1. *COMMON PERCEPTUAL FEATURES* With the multiplicity of ever-changing sensations entering our minds (e.g. as we turn our heads, listen to a conversation, put on our clothes, eat a meal) it is essential that the information received should be reduced as far as possible to a stable, meaningful, overall picture. Psychologists are divided as to how this might be attained[6] and two major theories must be mentioned:

A. ATOMISM which suggests that each separate item of information from a receptor is fitted to other items giving a conglomeration of isolated units from the sense organs which together make a meaningful whole, i.e. similar to the building up of a jig-saw puzzle.

B. GESTALT THEORY[7] which holds that an overall meaningful whole is extracted directly from the sensations entering the mind. Such organized configurations (or *Gestalten*) would consist of more than simply the sum of their parts, e.g. a tune is more than the total of its notes played separately; a poem has properties not shared by the isolated sounds or letters of which it is composed.

It is beyond the scope of this book to examine this controversy to any extent. However, it might be noted that there is a good deal of support for the idea that although as adults we may perceive our surroundings as meaningful wholes, we probably have to learn to do this through past experiences of perceiving the parts separately.

Let us now consider some of the principles of organization and interpretation which appear to be basically similar in everyone.[8]

A. THE PERCEPTION OF SPACE. The outside world exists in three dimensions. Somehow our sense organs must be able to convey information to our minds which will enable the percepts formed to include these spatial relationships. The sense organs which are mainly concerned with space perception are the eyes, ears and the sense of touch in the skin. This last sense can be used for exploration of objects with which we come into physical contact. We can explore with sensitive parts of our skin, especially the fingertips (and in babies the tongue and lips), the shape, texture and relative positions of parts of an object. The sensory system involved in space perception with the eyes and ears is less directly appreciated and a brief word of explanation of these must be given.

The sensitive area (retina) of each eye is a two dimensional surface. Either eye alone cannot perceive depth. Stand a book on end on the table in front of you, its broad cover facing you. Close one eye and try to bring a finger up level with the book from the side. It is not easy to estimate the distance of the book from your body. Now use both eyes and the task is easily performed.

What are the factors which are involved in depth perception when two eyes are used together?

i. For near objects (up to about 20 to 25 feet from the observer) the tension in the muscles which move the eyes in their sockets is of great importance. The nearer the object the more the eyes turn inwards to focus on it; hence the greater the contraction of the eye muscles on the inside (nose side) of the eyeballs and the greater the tension set up in them.

ii. As the eyes are some distance apart, a slightly different picture of the surroundings is obtained in each eye. For example, place your two little fingers horizontally with their tips touching about two to three inches in front of your eyes. Look into the distance through these two fingers, first with one eye then with the other. Notice where the point of contact occurs in both cases and you will see that two quite different interpretations are obtained. Now look into the distance with both eyes and you will see a picture composed of the two original interpretations, i.e. two points of contact, one on either side of the visual field. In this case the fingers were not being focused on and therefore were unimportant parts of the visual field as far as the brain was concerned. If the eyes are focused on the fingers a clear three dimensional picture is perceived. The brain has the (as yet inexplicable) ability to fuse together two slightly different two dimensional visual pictures of the environment to which it is attending and from them produce a single three dimensional percept. This cue for depth perception is of great importance for all but very great distances (where accurate distance estimation is not possible).

iii. In order to focus clearly on an object the shape of the lens of the eye is changed by a special internal circular muscle (the *ciliary muscle*). From the tension set up in this muscle the brain can determine the degree of curvature of the lens and hence estimate the distance from the eye to the object being focused on. This is a most ineffective method for estimating depth and can only be used for very short distances, i.e. up to six feet from the observer.

iv. Nearer objects overlap and partially conceal those that are more distant. This gives the observer relative positions but not much indication of actual distances from him.

v. Detail becomes much less clear as distance from the observer increases.

vi. Brightness diminishes and colours appear more blue from a great distance (e.g. hills on the skyline).

vii. When we move, near objects appear to move relatively rapidly, while more distant ones move quite slowly. For example, walking down a country lane on a moonlight night the trees we pass seem to move rapidly, a hill in the distance only slowly, while the moon appears stationary.

These are the major visual factors that are important in our perception of depth.[9]

Let us briefly consider how the ear can perceive space. The stimulus from the environment here is sound.

i. Sound waves travel at a much slower speed than the light waves involved in visual space perception. Therefore sound coming from a source which is nearer one ear than the other (i.e. is to one side of the listener) will be picked up by the nearer ear appreciably before the further one. From this slight discrepancy in time of stimulation of the two ears the brain can (with practice) determine the direction from which the sound is coming. If the sound is coming from directly in front or behind the listener and his eyes cannot come to his aid in location of the source, it is a simple matter to turn the head so that one ear is nearer to the source and the other further away. Now the direction of the sound can be easily determined.

ii. There is another means by which the direction of a sound can be decided. It depends on the fact that high notes have short wavelengths and low notes have long wavelengths. Short waves are more easily blocked by the head than long waves and so the ear nearer the source of a mixture of notes hears a higher pitched sound than the ear further away.

iii. The greater the distance between the sound source and the listener the weaker the noise he hears. If the perceiver knows the approximate strength of the sound being made he can judge, with practice, the distance between himself and the source.

Before leaving this topic of space perception by hearing, we must just mention the phenomenon of *echoes*. The principle involved is that a person (or animal) makes a noise which travels out as sound waves through the air until it reaches an object in its path. The sound waves bounce off the obstacle (i.e. are reflected) and are picked up again by the person's ears. Depending upon the distance of the object from the person, the time taken for the sound to return to him will vary. If the distance is slight much of the sound will be reflected back (e.g. speak into a book held just in front of your face and notice how much louder your voice sounds). Using high pitched sounds enables you to determine the direction of the object (as discussed under *ii*. above). For this reason bats, which use echo-location to guide them in flight, emit a very high pitched squeak. Similarly, a blind man who uses a cane to tap on the ground as he walks is making a high-pitched noise that he can use to estimate the distance and direction of obstacles in his path from the echoes which he receives.

The whole process of space perception is very complex and imperfectly understood. Any short introductory account is bound to be selective as to the information it contains and so is likely to convey an incomplete or inadequate picture. Nevertheless, it is of paramount importance to us in our interpretation of relationships and perspective of our environment.

B. FIGURE AND GROUND SEPARATION. We have described earlier in this chapter how impossible it is for the brain to cope with all the information that the sense organs pick up at any one time. The process whereby the most important information is selected has been described already. The important part of the perceptual field on which we concentrate our attention normally stands out more or less clearly against the rest of the field of which we are aware but on which we are not concentrating. This clearly perceived feature is called the '*figure*' which stands out against the more vague '*ground*'. As our sense organs move over our perceptual field the area to which we attend will change. Any feature of the ground on which we

90

concentrate can become a figure if it stands out from its surroundings. For example, look at a house on the other side of the street and your eyes will focus on a door, a window or a drainpipe. Whichever of these you select becomes a 'figure', while the rest of the building and its surroundings form the ground. This selection of a particular part of the field on which we concentrate and which we see as standing out from the rest is apparently inborn. Persons born with cataracts and having them removed later in life see at once the area on which they concentrate standing out from the rest of the perceptual field. There are, however, certain conditions that must be fulfilled by an object if it is to stand out from the background. It must be different from its surroundings in brightness or colour or perhaps distance from the observer in order that it can be distinguished. *Camouflage* is based on the principle of making the object to be concealed as similar to its surroundings in colour, brightness, etc., as possible.

The whole process of figure-ground separation is the basis of our perception of objects and regions of space. Moreover, because only the figure of a field is clearly perceived the content of percepts is much reduced and simplified.

C. GROUPING OF ITEMS PERCEIVED. In our previous discussion we have frequently referred to 'wholes' and 'entities'. When we look objectively at the meanings of these terms we find that they are only relative concepts. The whole world is built up on a hierarchical basis where units can be looked upon either as entities in their own right or as parts of larger combinations of units, or indeed as collections of smaller units. For example, a book may be considered to be a whole unit or a collection of many pages, or a small part of a library. We shall return to this problem again when discussing thinking and communication in later chapters. Here we are mainly concerned with deciding which aspects of our perceptual field our sense organs group together as wholes (i.e. figures) standing out from the vaguer ground (Fig. IV 1, p. 94).

i. Similarity – stimuli which are like each other but different in some property (e.g. size, shape, colour, loudness, rhythm) from the rest of the field are seen as constituting a whole. For example, the 'strings' in an orchestra or the pansies scattered in a flowerbed are seen to constitute a group.

ii. Proximity – stimuli which occur together in space or time constitute a group. For example, a collection of notes are perceived as a tune or several different wild flowers held together as a bunch.

iii. Common movement. If several objects appear to move together they are seen as constituting a whole. For example, look through a dirty window and your visual field will be marred by smears on the glass. Now move relative to the window and the smears all appear to move at once and at a speed different from that of the objects outside the window. You immediately see the dirt on the window as constituting one group and the objects outside as another.

iv. Continuity and symmetry. Objects which lie in a straight line, a curve or occur in a regular pattern are all seen together. For example, looking at this moment through a lattice window, I see the pattern or the lead strips as an entity. Similarly, the patterns on wallpaper or the rhythm of drums in the background of a gramophone record appear as entities.

v. Completeness. We perceive a continuous object as a whole much more readily than we do a discontinuous one. In actual practice, this is shown most clearly by our tendency to complete any discontinuous percepts which we might have. For example, three dots spaced out from one another are seen as a triangle. The closer the dots are together, the more easily the triangle is seen. This tendency to complete our percepts is probably a technique for overcoming gaps in our sensations caused by limitations of our sense organs (e.g. the blind spot or faulty light receptors in the retina).

We have previously stated that it is essential for easy, efficient perception for us to be able to interpret our surroundings in terms of figures (wholes) and ground. These techniques for grouping are the bases upon which we decide which of the information being picked up should be placed together in one figure and which should be kept out of that figure.

D. CONSTANCIES. We have already stated several times in this chapter the fact that our sensations are continuously changing. Yet in order to be able to interpret and cope with the situations in which we find ourselves we must be able to create some form of order and simplicity out of these multitudes of stimuli picked up by our sense organs. One of the major ways in which such order is obtained is by developing the ability of always perceiving the same object in the same way regardless of its shape, colour, size, brightness, etc., picked up by the eyes at any one time. For example, a pencil will create quite different retinal shapes when seen from different angles; its size will appear to change as we move towards or away from it; its brightness and colour will vary according to the light falling on it. Yet we always see that pencil as the same unchanging object. The biological value of such a perceptual technique is obvious. How the psychological processes involved can bring about this apparent disregard of physical laws has not yet been satisfactorily explained.

This section has been concerned with some of the main principles which appear to be active in the perceptual processes of each of us. Now we must consider some aspects of perceptual interpretations which are individual and personal and in which we are quite different from anyone else.[10]

2. *INDIVIDUAL PERCEPTUAL FEATURES* Earlier in this chapter we established the point that while the ability to organize our sensations into meaningful percepts is probably inborn, it undoubtedly improves with practice. It will follow, therefore, that although each of us will use the common basic organizing processes described above, our actual perception will also be affected by the varying conditions in which we, as individuals, practise our perceiving. Consequently, a percept will depend not only on the content of the sensation being received at this moment but also on:

a. the past situations which we have perceived (i.e. learning);
b. our present needs, values, desires and interests (i.e. motivation);
c. the type of person we are (i.e. personality).

As these factors are fairly constant for any one person it follows that his perception will have some degree of stability. As these factors are different in each of us it follows that the percepts formed by two or more people in the same situation are likely to be quite different. Each of these factors complicates perception to some extent, although the actual degree to which they are involved is not easy to determine. In this section we shall consider each of these three factors in turn.

A. PAST SITUATIONS PERCEIVED BY THE INDIVIDUAL. We have said that our ability to understand and interpret our percepts improves with practice. This means that to a large extent we have to learn to perceive the world in the way we do. In fact,

Introduction to Psychology

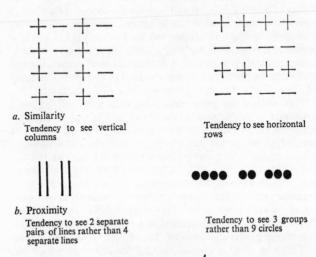

a. Similarity
   Tendency to see vertical columns

Tendency to see horizontal rows

b. Proximity
   Tendency to see 2 separate pairs of lines rather than 4 separate lines

Tendency to see 3 groups rather than 9 circles

c. Continuity
   The dotted curved line is seen as an entity running through the straight lines

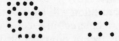

d. Completeness
   The dots are not seen separately but are integrated into a familiar shape

Fig. IV 1   Factors affecting grouping in perception

how we interpret ourselves or our surroundings at any time depends not only on what is present in our sensations at that moment but also on any relevant experiences we have had prior to that moment. Let us consider a classical example to illustrate this point.[11] The image formed on the light-sensitive layer (retina) of the eye is inverted (turned upside down), having passed through the lens (Fig. IV 2, p. 96). However, our brains interpret these inverted retinal images as if they were the right way up. If an adult (who is used to perceiving the world the other way up from that which his eyes suggest) is fitted with a pair of inverting (i.e. turning upside down) spectacles he will now perceive the world the wrong way up. At first he is completely unable to cope with the new situation but with constant practice for two or three weeks he will be able to orientate himself perfectly well and will be able to perform the most complex of tasks (even driving in traffic in the rush hour) as completely as he could before the experiment began. On removing the spectacles, however, he now perceives the word upside down again and has to relearn to orientate himself normally.

Considering a more common everyday example of this principle, we find that, having learned to organize our percepts in a particular way, we have difficulty in accepting and dealing with new sensations which do not fit into our preconceived patterns. For example, an older person who tries to interpret modern music, art, dancing or discipline in schools in terms of his own past experiences and training will have great difficulty in understanding and appreciating the new situation. He will almost certainly reject the new unacceptable sensation as being less satisfactory than his own previous experiences stored in his mind. (This tendency to reject new material increases with age.) Consequently, an adolescent and his grandfather both listening to the same modern popular song are likely to interpret it quite differently in view of their past experiences.

Taking a more biological view of the rejection of new, unfamiliar sensations, it is probable that an animal might have some difficulty in coping with situations that give rise to such sensations. An extreme instance here might be the case where information coming from various sense organs is conflicting, e.g. if you twist round and round and suddenly stop, your

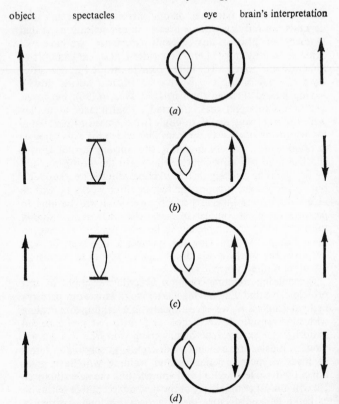

object   spectacles   eye   brain's interpretation

Fig. IV 2 The effect of inverting spectacles

a. Normal sight before spectacles worn
   Brain interprets retinal image by inverting it. Therefore perceives world right way up.

b. When inverting spectacles are first introduced
   Brain still inverts retinal image. Therefore perceives world upside down.

c. When subject has 'got used' to spectacles' effects
   Brain ceases to invert retinal image. Therefore
   perceives world right way up.

d. When spectacles are first removed
   Brain still does not invert retinal image. Therefore perceives world upside down.

eyes tell you that you have stopped but your ears inform you that you are still going round (due to the continued swirling of the fluid in the inner ear). The mind cannot cope with such conflicting information. Perhaps the feeling of dizziness which results is an indication to you to move out of this unsatisfactory situation. If so, this is a physical technique for avoiding unacceptable sensations.

We have been considering how past experiences affect present percepts and have discussed the rejection of unacceptable new sensations. Let us now examine what happens to sensations which are acceptable but are subject to a variety of interpretations. Take, for example, the interpretations of a statement of a government's policy by its own supporters and by members of the opposition. The statement will be viewed quite differently according to the preconceived ideas of the individuals concerned. These preconceived ideas are the results of past experiences. Similarly, a physicist will perceive a complex mathematical formula quite differently from most schoolboys or bus conductors. A consultant's percepts of a patient will be quite different from those of a nurse who knows the patient as an individual or members of the family of which the patient is part. These are examples of different percepts being formed from similar sensations, the variations being due to differing past experiences of the perceivers. We must now consider in more general terms how our past experiences affect our present percepts.

Percepts are constructed in the mind in the presence of the sensation from which they are formed, i.e. while the sense organs are receiving the information which will be the content of the percept. After the sense organs stop receiving a particular sensation, the percept in the brain remains in its organized form. Such an 'after-percept' is called an *image*. For example, I look at my hand on the table in front of me. The mental picture formed is a percept. I close my eyes, or look away from the table, but I still have a clear mental picture of my hand. This retained picture is an image of my hand. Similarly, I have mental images of people I know, places I have visited, etc., which exist in my mind regardless of the fact that I am no longer receiving the sensations that caused them.

Early on in this chapter we distinguished between two aspects of perception:

a. Organization into a meaningful percept of the nerve impulses entering the brain from the sense organs;
b. Utilization of the percept formed to 'reset' the mind so that the behaviour which it directed could cope with the situation being perceived.

In many of the instances which we have been discussing so far this 'reset' mind has been used immediately to respond to the environment. For example, a car comes along the road in which you are standing. Your eyes and ears pick up information about it which is passed to your brain as a sensation. Here the brain organizes this information into a meaningful percept. This percept resets your mind so that any behaviour you perform will deal as well as possible with the situation, e.g. cause you to step back if you are just on the kerb, run forward if you are in the middle of the road, stand fast and hold up your hand if you are a policeman on point duty, etc.

Often, however, we pick up information to which we do not wish to respond at once. For example, I may be waiting at a bus stop for a No. 33. While I am standing there I perceive a No. 45 bus stopping a little further up the road, a taxi rank on the corner, a large new supermarket which has just opened on the opposite side of the road, a great deal of traffic passing by, etc. Each of these items of information will be perceived (i.e. will form percepts which will reset my mind) and will be remembered as images. My mind has been reset or modified by my experiences. We say that I *know* this information. My subsequent mental activity will be affected by this information which I know.

Any one of such items of information, however, may be used in many situations. For example, the image of the large new supermarket which I perceived while waiting for the bus could be used in several different instances, such as:

a. if I ever want to change my grocer;
b. if I want to describe the position of No. 33 bus stop;
c. if I am discussing new developments in the town in which I live.

This general resetting of the mind in relation to specific previous percepts which subsequently can be used in many different situations is called *knowledge* of the specific original percept. (In the example above I show knowledge of the supermarket when responding to the three instances suggested.) Consequently, you can see that if a new percept is relevant to anything we have previously perceived our minds will be already modified to some extent and we will expect the new percept to fit in with our previous experiences. This is why different people perceiving the same situation form quite different percepts. For example, a field of corn is perceived differently by a farmer, an artist and a picnicker, due to their previous experiences, training and interest.

So we can see that what we perceive and how we perceive it is greatly affected by our past experiences.[12] If a new sensation does not fit into our expectations of it we may misinterpret or distort this new item of information to make it more acceptable, or we may reject it altogether. (Such aspects of faulty perception are the basis of Chapter 5.)

B. OUR PRESENT NEEDS, VALUES, DESIRES AND INTERESTS. In Chapter 6 we shall be discussing mental driving forces which direct our behaviour. These forces we call *motives*. They become active because of some need which a person is experiencing. The behaviour they produce leads to the satisfaction of this need. For example, hunger is a need which a person will experience after a period of going without food. Such a person will be motivated to obtain food to satisfy this deficiency. His behaviour towards satisfying his need is activated and directed by a motive. We will leave a fuller discussion of these energy forces until later. Let us here simply note that motives can activate a person to satisfy needs ranging from the most biological, for example hunger, pain avoidance or sexual desire, to the most psychological, for example security, social acceptance or the need to be interested.

Obviously, the presence of such motives active in a person's mind will affect the way in which he perceives a given situation. Take an obvious example of an individual perceiving the scent of fried steak and onions. If he is hungry he will find this smell attractive, if satiated he will be repelled by it. If he is very tired, this or any other stimulus may irritate him, while if he is upset or afraid, he might be too busy to notice it.

Different people perceive the same situation differently according to their particular needs, values and interests. For example, an orchestral concert may be pleasurable to some people, a crashing bore to others. Again, a group of students being required to speak at a debating society meeting may

99

perceive the situation as challenging or embarrassing, humiliating or pleasurable according to their existing needs and interests. Notice how in these last two examples it is impossible to separate 'motive force' from past experiences of the individual. We shall return to this point in Chapter 6.

In general, we try to interpret our surroundings in such a way that we may respond to them in a manner most likely to satisfy our existing needs and as our needs change so will our percept of any given situation.

C. THE TYPE OF PERSON ONE IS.[13] In Chapter 11 we shall be discussing the uniqueness of each individual. One's overall individuality is called one's *personality* and it includes all those qualities of a person which differentiate him from everyone else. It consists not only of those aspects of his make-up which we have already mentioned in this chapter, but many others besides. All his physical, psychological and social qualities; his interests, attitudes, and skills; how honest, reliable, pompous or selfish he is; all these factors are part of his personality.

The way in which a person interprets the environment will be affected by his personality. For example, a weak, inadequate person will perceive the world as a more difficult, terrifying place to live in than most people do; a person of very high principles will see more evil and condemn more freely than will the average individual; an anti-social person interprets the presence of others in a less favourable light than is normal. Similarly some people are emotionally more stable than others, some more tolerant, others more self-centred, etc. The manner in which a person responds to his surroundings is part of his personality. This is, of course, dependent upon how he interprets his surroundings in the first place. These two aspects of behaviour are very closely interrelated. We shall return to them in a later chapter.

PERCEPTION OF OURSELVES AND OTHER PEOPLE[14]

In the perception of the tremendous variety of situations which any one person meets in the course of his lifetime, the only feature common to all these perceiving situations is the individual himself. For example, whether I am ill in hospital or away on holiday, in school or at home, in a traffic jam in London's rush hour or mowing a lawn, in each of these situations I am the constant factor. We have pointed out that an individual changes as he gains new experiences and as his biological and psychological needs alter. Nevertheless, he is sufficiently stable for his behaviour to be to some extent predictable. We have said that we would expect some people, wherever they are, to be selfish, thoughtless, or pompous, others to be reasonable, kind, hasty or conscientious. Of fundamental importance in the interpretation of how a person behaves is the understanding of how he perceives the world around him. How he perceives his surroundings in relation to himself will be very much affected by how he sees himself. Self-perception is a complex, little understood subject which is basic to a full appreciation of the behaviour of ourselves and others.

As infants we perceive ourselves as being all-important and the focal point on which our parents and the rest of the environment should concentrate attention, i.e. we obviously interpret the world in terms of ourselves. This tendency is also basic to our interpretations in later life although with experience we modify our views and do not express our self-centredness so uninhibitedly as do young children. As we grow older social acceptability plays an increasing role in modifying our behaviour. We worry about what other people will think to such an extent that this becomes one of the major controlling forces for adult behaviour. In very obvious forms this concern for social approval is illustrated by such expressions as 'what will people think', 'I would not be seen dead in . . .', 'keeping up with the Joneses', 'when in Rome do as the Romans do', etc. However, the desire for social approval also works in more subtle ways. How successful we are is determined not only by the extent to which we can cope with situations ourselves but also by comparison with the performance of others in similar situations. When we learn by imitation and from suggestion we are following patterns approved by others. Moreover, we have to learn to accept criticism in all kinds of ways. By these processes we build up an ideal of what we should be in terms of socially acceptable standards. Frequently the percepts which we form of what we actually are fall short of this ideal. Techniques for overcoming such discrepancies are dealt with in the next chapter.

One final point will be made here on this vast subject. We have discussed how past experiences, attitudes, motives, etc., of a person affect the way in which he perceives his surroundings. Every situation which you perceive includes some aspect of yourself. These past experiences are stored in your mind and become part of the standard against which you compare the future percepts which you form. This is part of what leads to stability in your own perception. However, you also use this standard for interpreting the behaviour of other people. These other individuals will have different past experiences, interests, values, personalities, etc., from you and you will get a wrong impression of the reasons behind their behaviour when you compare it with your own standard. For example, abruptness on the part of a patient may be considered rude and unpleasant by a sensitive nurse who is perceiving the patient's reactions in terms of 'what would I mean if I behaved in that way?' In fact, the patient may well have an abrupt way of speaking or perhaps be using abruptness to cover up fear about being in hospital. He would certainly not wish to alienate the nurse.

Consequently we can say that we tend not to see ourselves as others see us. One of the major tasks of all of us who work with people is to put ourselves as far as possible in the place of the other person and try to understand his problems from his point of view. Self-perception when projected on to the environment leads to misperception. This and many other aspects of misinterpretation of ourselves and our surroundings form the basis of the next chapter.

SUMMARY

1. In the study of *perception* we consider what happens to information picked up by the sense organs when it eventually enters the brain.
2. Perception consists of two main processes:

    a. *Organization* of the multitudes of scattered nerve impulses reaching the brain into meaningful pictures (called *percepts*);
    b. *Utilization* of the percepts formed to so reset the mind

that when the person responds he does so in the most satisfactory and appropriate way.

3. At any one time there is always more information available in the environment than the brain can cope with. Therefore the brain selects the most valuable items for mental reconstruction of the surroundings. This selection is called *attention*. The chapter then includes a discussion of which aspects of the environment are most likely to be selected, i.e. attended to.

4. Evidence suggests that the ability to organize and utilize the information picked up by our sense organs is inborn, although it is greatly improved with practice. It follows from this that although we probably all have similar inborn basic tendencies in percept organization, depending upon the conditions under which we practise perceiving, we all will each develop individual features of the process.

5. Important principles of perception which are believed to be common to everyone are:

   a. The perception of space;
   b. Figure-ground differentiation;
   c. Ability to group items perceived as separate entities depending upon their similarity, proximity, common movement, continuity and symmetry, etc.;
   d. The ability to perceive objects as more or less constant irrespective of the way in which they stimulate the eyes.

6. Individual variations in perception may be usefully grouped under three headings:

   a. the past situations the person has perceived
   b. the present needs, desires and interests of the person
   c. the personality of the individual.

7. The way in which we interpret our surroundings and other people is very much influenced by our perception of ourselves in relation to them.

REFERENCES

1. For further discussion of this approach see Hebb, D.O. *A Text-book of Psychology* (Saunders, London, 2nd edition 1966) and Adrian, E. D. *The Physical Background of Perception* (O.U.P., London 1947).
2. For a full discussion of 'attention' see Vernon, M. D. *A Further Study of Visual Perception* (Cambridge University Press, London 1954) pp. 200–56.

3. Solley, C. M. and Murphy, G. *Development of the Perceptual World* (Basic Books, N.Y. 1960) consider this problem with special reference to the importance of learning in perception.
4. Gibson, E. J. and Walk, R. D. 'The Visual Cliff', *Scientific American* 202 No. 4, 1960, pp. 64–71, describe the experiments on goat kids.
5. Von Senden, M. *Space and Sight* (Methuen, London 1960) gives a review of the work performed on persons blind from birth who subsequently receive sight.
6. Allport, F. H. *Theories of Perception and the Concept of Structure* (Wiley, N.Y. 1955) gives a critical review of the more important theories of perception.
7. Ellis, W. D. *A Source Book of Gestalt Psychology* (Harcourt Brace, N.Y. 1938) includes a collection of important writings in the field of Gestalt psychology which are relevant both here and in later chapters of this book.
8. For a useful introduction to some of the more important problems here see Geldard, F. A. *The Human Senses* (Wiley, N.Y. 1953). For a full treatment with experimental demonstrations see Gibson, J. J. *The Perception of the Visual World* (Houghton Mifflin, Boston, Mass. 1950).
9. For further discussion see Carr, H. A. *An Introduction to Space Perception* (Longmans Green & Co., London 1935).
10. Each of the topics in this section is discussed in more detail in Vernon, M. D. *A Further Study of Visual Perception.*
11. Ewert, P. H. *A Study of the Effect of Inverted Retinal Stimulation Upon Spatially Co-ordinated Behaviour* (Genet. Psychol. Monogr., Provincetown, Mass. 1930, 7: 177–368.
12. For a full discussion of the effects of learning on perception see Solley, C. M. and Murphy, G. *Development of the Perceptual World* (Basic Books, N.Y. 1960). Also of great interest here is Fiske, D. W. and Maddi, S. R. *Functions of Early Experience* (Dorsey Press, Homewood, Ill. 1961).
13. See Blake, R. R. and Ramsey, G. V. *Perception: An Approach to Personality* (Ronald Press, N.Y. 1951).
14. For a useful survey of findings in this field see Tagiuri, R. and Petrullo, L. *Person Perception and Interpersonal Behavior* (Stanford University Press, Stanford 1958).

Chapter Five

Misinterpreting Ourselves and Our Surroundings

INTRODUCTION

In previous chapters we discussed how we build up mental pictures (percepts) of ourselves and our surroundings. We described how information gathered by our sense organs was transmitted by nerves to the brain. Here the information received was moulded by past experiences, attitudes and motives into meaningful interpretations which could be used subsequently for directing our behaviour. Some of the terms of reference used in these interpretations could easily be checked against the environment to ensure their correctness. For example, with the combined use of our eyes, ears, and sense of touch we could verify that objects round about us exist in three dimensions, or that although distant objects appeared to show less detail than similar nearer ones this was simply due to the inability of our eyes to discern detail at a distance. Other terms of reference, however, were built up inside ourselves and could not easily be checked, e.g. an attitude towards another person or one's opinion of oneself. In these instances every new percept formed to try to examine the correctness of our original attitude or opinion is affected by previous percepts and so any misinterpretations are perpetuated.

We can see then that any percepts that we form as a result of sensations from the outside world or from within ourselves may be, at least partly, incorrect. The only indications of what our surroundings are like come from our sense organs (either directly as when we see, hear or feel a sensation, or indirectly through memories of past experiences). How, then, can we know that we are misinterpreting? In many cases we cannot know. There are some simple instances where our mistakes become apparent as when we form a percept which does not agree with information later received from the environment, e.g. coming out of an examination convinced that you have failed but subsequently learning that you have passed easily; or a small child picking pretty flowers in the garden as a present for Mummy, but getting into trouble when the damage he has done is discovered. Generally speaking, misinterpretations which are recognized can be rectified, the fact that our original response was wrong being remembered and used to mould future responses to similar situations.

In many cases, however, our misinterpretations may not be apparent to us and we go through life not realizing that they exist. For example, early in life we may form an antagonistic attitude towards persons of another religion, race or political party. Such an attitude may be based on an isolated unfortunate encounter or, more likely, may have been imitated from our parents or friends. We go through life misinterpreting all our experiences of such people in this unfavourable light. Because we are so used to our bias we may fail to recognize its existence.

WHY WE MISINTERPRET

Obviously misunderstanding of the outside world tends to counteract the whole purpose of perception for the organism. To be unable to recognize danger or a mate or food would put an animal at a great disadvantage in its environment. In human beings where the environment is extremely complex, misinterpretations are more easily made than for most other organisms. In situations such as teaching and nursing, misunderstanding on the part of the pupils and patients as well as teachers and nurses is very common yet extremely undesirable. In this section we shall be concerned with some of the main ways in which misinterpretation can arise. It is convenient to classify these processes of misinterpretation into the following categories but there is much overlap between the classes as the examples show.[1]

A. Information reaching the sense organs from the environment may be ambiguous or inadequate.[2] We are all familiar with diagrams that can be interpreted in more than one way (Fig. v 1, below). Such examples are extreme and are rarely met with in everyday life. A more common example is the situation where one does not see a step, e.g. in a dark passage or on uneven paving stones. Here the scanty information reaching our eyes has been interpreted as representing a flat surface when in fact it is uneven. In a young child much information may appear ambiguous on first encounter. However, by exploration with various sense organs (eyes, ears, skin, tongue, etc.) the child learns the correct interpretation to attach to his sensations. When an adult enters a new situation where he has no previous frame of reference that can be applied, orientation can be difficult and misinterpretations may result. For example, a person entering hospital for the first time may well be bewildered and anxious; similarly a child starting school may be ill at ease and insecure. In both these instances, explanations and assistance from nurses or teachers can be invaluable in helping the newcomer to interpret his surroundings correctly.

B. The observer may be concentrating on parts of the environment which are not particularly important, while not

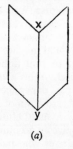

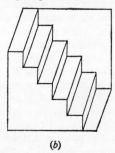

(*a*)   (*b*)

Fig. v 1   Some examples of ambiguous figures

a. Focus your attention on the line x–y and it will sometimes appear to recede from you, sometimes project towards you.

b. The 'Schröder Staircase'.

attending to those which are of more value to his interpretation. An obvious example here is the conjurer who
attracts our attention to some unimportant but exaggerated
action he is performing with one hand, while preparing the
next trick quietly and unobtrusively with the other. This type
of misinterpretation is probably fundamental to much
misunderstanding in young children at school. They pay
attention to detail but neglect underlying principles. Consequently later application of these principles to new problems
is quite beyond them. This is a specific example of the saying
'you cannot see the wood for the trees'. Extreme concern
about detail or example will often lead to incorrect perspec-
tives in subsequent thinking. The man-in-the-street or the new
student nurse may concentrate too much on superficial
details of a patient's illness and may well neglect more
fundamental aspects. There are many well-meaning people
who are more concerned with revengeful acts against the
juvenile delinquent than with discovering the underlying
reasons for his behaviour.

C. Correct interpretation of our sensations depends upon
our degree of understanding of the situation we are perceiving.
We may lack the type of past experience necessary for us to
appreciate fully what we see or hear. A biology student looking
down a microscope to try to observe an *Amoeba* is quite likely
to focus on an air bubble if his previous experience of *Amoebae*
and air bubbles is limited. Similarly a person with no psychological knowledge, listening to two psychologists discussing a
difficult child may well reject their ideas as nonsense because
his previous experiences do not permit him to understand
their approach to the problem. A patient in hospital may well
misconstrue discussions, charts, etc., relevant to him if he
tries to understand a complex situation in the light of his own
scanty knowledge. It may be that the type of past experience
which a person has is unsuitable for correct interpretation of a
new situation. For example, a pedestrian sees a small child
run over by a car. Later in court he is asked to give an account
of the accident. If that pedestrian was a car driver who had
narrowly missed being involved in a similar situation his
percept of this accident might be biased towards the motorist;
if he was the parent of a child who had been run over he
would probably be prejudiced against the motorist. In either

of these instances the pedestrian's interpretation of the present accident would have been partially incorrect. We tend to see new situations in the light of our past experiences. This fact must be borne in mind by all teachers and nurses when imparting information and instructions to their charges. (This topic is more fully discussed in Chapter 4.)

D. We may have been expecting a sensation which was slightly different from the one which our sense organs actually received. We interpret what we perceive along the lines which our past experiences indicate is most likely to be correct. The blue notice board with white letters which say:

POLITE NOTICE
NO PARKING

is often misinterpreted as a Police Notice.

E. When discussing the 'structure of percepts' in Chapter 4 we described the tendency to make our percepts as complete, symmetrical and rhythmic as possible. This may be due to the need to (*i*) compensate for deficiencies in our sensations (due to inadequacy of our sense organs or insufficient information reaching them) and so make the percept formed more meaningful or (*ii*) place information in categories for ease of understanding and storage. While such processes have obvious advantages when correctly used, they can easily become sources of misunderstanding. If a percept is completed incorrectly this is obviously direct misinterpretation. But equally, putting a new experience into a category where it does not exactly fit can cause you to read far more into that experience than is justified and consequently misunderstanding occurs. For example, to say that a child is just like his father because of one or two specific similarities can cause you to interpret many other of the child's features in the light of your knowledge of his father. Similarly, to know that a patient is suffering from a particular disease may well cause a nurse to think that she knows far more about the patient than is justified. This basic tendency to categorize, while biologically useful, can lead to extreme misunderstandings. Sweeping statements in the press about 'children today', 'the younger generation', 'the good old days', etc., are examples of this tendency taken to extremes where they become inaccurate.

F. It may well be that the sensation from which a percept is to be formed gives us an unacceptable impression of ourselves or our surroundings. It might show us up in an unfavourable light, or indicate that we are incapable of coping with our environment. In such instances we may actively reject those parts of the sensation which are unsatisfactory, while at the same time exaggerate or invent more satisfactory parts. For example, a person at a party who already has imbibed too much alcohol may well be convinced that he only 'drinks to be sociable'. In this way he is able to accept the sensations of his behaviour that his sense organs are receiving.

The whole process of perceiving, thinking, recalling, etc., involves the compromise or modification of the actual situation to match it with what the individual wishes to perceive or avoid perceiving, to remember or avoid remembering. This has been summed up by Woodworth[3] in the most useful phrase 'trial and check', which serves to emphasize the way in which we interpret ourselves in relation to our surroundings and our surroundings in relation to ourselves. An 'expectancy' is set up within the individual and tried and checked, accepted or rejected, until the expectancy and incoming information match each other sufficiently well to give a stable, workable perception organization.

In this chapter we are mainly concerned with how and why people misinterpret themselves and their surroundings. Obviously we cannot observe directly the percepts which another individual forms. We can only examine such percepts through the behaviour which results from them. If we can examine the situation which a person perceives and subsequently note his behaviour we shall be able to decide for ourselves whether or not he has misinterpreted his surroundings. Notice that we can only 'decide for ourselves' in such observations. Whether or not we consider that a particular response to a given situation involves misinterpretation will very much depend upon how we (the observers) interpret both the original situation and the response of the individual concerned. Moreover, in many instances we shall not be able to discover which of the factors listed above was responsible for the misunderstanding we believe has occurred in the person that we are observing. In most cases, probably more than one factor will be involved.

There is one other consideration that must be borne in

mind. We may perceive the environment as it really is but consciously decide to respond to it in a way which would suggest to others that we have had quite a different sensation, i.e. we behave in a way which is intended to mislead others, e.g. on being found with a broken vase in his hand a child may tell his mother that the cat knocked the precious ornament off the window ledge. The child's percept in fact contains information that he (the child) broke the vase. Before translating this percept (i.e. what really happened) into behaviour (i.e. telling mother) other forces in his mind have become involved. Here the child did not misinterpret his environment. He purposely made a misleading response to endeavour to cope with the environment more satisfactorily. Misinterpretation involves the formation of an incorrect percept. Behaviour which is not representative of the percept formed is not the result of misinterpretation.

HOW WE MISINTERPRET

From our discussion in the previous section of this chapter it is clear that misinterpretation may occur at two different levels of perception:

a. At the sensation level where ambiguous, inadequate or incorrect information may be picked up from the environment.
b. At the percept-forming level due, e.g. to inadequate understanding, incorrect expectations, placing in faulty categories or simply the unacceptability of the sensation being perceived.

Misinterpretations due to factors at the sensation level can only be overcome by altering the stimulus to make it more meaningful or by practice on the part of the perceiver in coping satisfactorily with such scanty or incorrect information. In the rest of this chapter we shall be mainly concerned with problems of misinterpreting at the percept-forming level. In order to understand better the problems of unconscious misinterpretation by adults let us examine very briefly some aspects of how a small child learns to understand his environment. There is a basic desire in all of us to have our bodily needs satisfied immediately. For example, a baby demands food when hungry and is not prepared to wait; if afraid he wants to be comforted at once. One of the major lessons that a child must learn is that he must come to control his desire for need-satisfaction. For example, he must not poke his fingers into any new object that interests him; he must not fight against a parent who thwarts his immediate whims. The learning of this lesson is basic to the training of all young animals. Most of these latter learn by natural consequences which responses are satisfactory and which are not. For example, a kitten stalking a bird learns that an uncontrolled movement or noise will adversely affect its hunting; a young puppy learns to be submissive to older members of the pack by the unpleasant results of being too forward. In the complex and difficult environment in which children are brought up punishment by natural consequences may be too drastic or too slow to be efficient. Instead the child's parents take upon themselves the responsibility of attaching unpleasant consequences to unsatisfactory behaviour and vice versa. The child is not allowed to eat soil and discover that it may cause illness, not allowed to run into the street to encounter dangers which exist there. Rather, the parent with sharp words, withholding of treats, physical punishment, etc., helps the child to control his behaviour and so learn to cope with his environment. It is in this way that much of the child's interpretation of himself and his surroundings develops.

Let us consider the situation we have just described from the child's point of view. At first (when he is very young) parental interference seems quite arbitrary, the child not knowing what response will be evoked by his actions. With experience the child soon learns to expect disapproval for some of his acts and reward for others. He establishes a 'social code' which is learned from past experiences. Children from different cultures, social classes or even from different families in the same neighbourhood will develop different social codes depending upon the way in which their parents bring them up. A social code is the guide against which a child will judge his behaviour (and also, of course, the behaviour of others). Providing parental interference (discipline) is consistent it does not greatly matter whether control is comparatively strict or lax. The absence of parental control, or control which is inconsistent, has a very harmful effect on the social code which the child is trying to form.

During this period of development of a social code the

child experiences a conflict between (1) what his basic nature desires and (2) what his social code permits. In the adult this conflict still exists but in a more sophisticated form. Here these two aspects may better be expressed as (1) what the person actually is and (2) what he wishes he was. For example, a schoolteacher may in fact be an unreasonable, uncompromising bully. He wishes he was a strong, reliable, popular leader. If the sensations resulting from his behaviour constantly present him with percepts which are unsatisfactory or unacceptable to him there are various ways in which he can change the situation.

A. He can change his sensations, i.e. he can 'change his ways' (his behaviour towards his children); he can change his profession or move to a new post where his bullying approach would be more acceptable, e.g. in a reformatory school where toughness may be considered a desirable attribute.

B. He can change his attitude towards the sensations he is receiving so that conflicts no longer arise, i.e. he can 'change his ideas' as we say in everyday language. We have said that past experiences are important factors in deciding what form our percepts take. With frequent perception of a certain type of sensation we come to incorporate this new sensation into our minds. Later percepts regarding this type of sensation become acceptable to us. We get used to that type of sensation. A young, sensitive woman marrying a harsh, cruel man will tend to become hardened herself and will gradually find her husband's behaviour more easily acceptable. A patient who has developed a disability which he knows he will never overcome becomes resigned to it as his experiences relating to his problem gradually accumulate. In both these examples all new percepts formed are moulded more and more by experiences relating to the unpleasant situation in which the persons find themselves.

C. A major difficulty arises when an individual receives conflicting sensations but is unable to compromise to alleviate the mental conflict he is experiencing. This must frequently happen when two or more desires are aroused which both demand satisfaction but are directly opposed to each other. For example, you may be very tired and want to go to bed but at the same time there is a late night television programme which you want to see. You may have persistent abdominal

113

pains and know you should visit the doctor, but your fear of what he might tell you makes you wish to avoid the situation. In such instances you must consciously decide to satisfy one desire and ignore the other. Frequently, however, conflicting situations of which we are not aware arise in our minds. For example, we may receive sensations regarding our own behaviour that give rise to percepts which make us appear inadequate or inferior yet we cannot change our situation or our ideas to counteract our shortcomings. In order to overcome such discrepancies between our actual selves and our ideal selves we have a series of unconscious mental techniques whose purpose is to reconcile what we actually are with what we wish we were. These processes are called *mental defence mechanisms*.[4] Recognition of them is very important for our understanding of the behaviour of other people (and, of course, also of some of our own reactions). They are particularly common in the behaviour of people who are in difficult and distressing situations, e.g. patients in hospital or children unable to cope with their environment. We must therefore examine some of these mechanisms more closely. We shall return to a more generalized discussion of this subject when considering 'mental health' in a later chapter.[5] Let us simply state that the more closely one's actual self and one's ideal self converge the better adjusted an individual one is and the fewer defence mechanisms occur in one's behaviour.

MENTAL DEFENCE MECHANISMS [6]

These defence mechanisms act as a form of mental anaesthetic to 'lessen the pain' caused by conflicts between what our sensations tell us we are and what we think we ought to be. Remember, however, that they are purely unconscious and we are not aware of their existence while we are using them. The actual details of the mental mechanisms used will depend very much on the problematic situation which we are experiencing. For example, a student may have performed very badly in some important examinations and her parents are disappointed in her. The conflict between what she is and what she wishes she was is quite clear to her. She may respond to the situation in a variety of ways. She may simply ignore the whole unpleasant experience and leave the matter to be forgotten. She may (quite unintentionally) misplace the blame (the teacher does not understand me; I did not have the right text-book). She may withdraw into herself and sulk or avoid her parents. She may even take to drink or contemplate suicide if she finds the situation too unbearable. In each of these suggested instances the driving force behind her behaviour may not be a conscious desire to mislead or avoid but is unconscious. If she is aware of lying or misleading then she is not using mental defence mechanisms (as we have defined them) but is performing behaviour which is out of keeping with the percept she has formed.

How you actually respond to a conflicting situation depends upon you as an individual (your past experiences, present motives, attitudes, etc.), on the nature and seriousness of the conflict with which you are coping and on the environmental situation in which you find yourself. Any classification of defence mechanisms which might be constructed is bound to be somewhat artificial. However, it makes our very brief study of these mechanisms more logical and useful if we adopt the normal procedure of distinguishing between some of the more common and interesting types.

1. *MECHANISMS INVOLVING SUBSTITUTION* Suppose that the behaviour you are displaying in a particular situation fails to come up to the standard demanded by your ideal but you are unable to improve your performance in this task which you find difficult. If you redirect your energy from that situation where you are inadequate and rechannel it into an activity where you have previously had some success you will probably perform very well in this second task. This process is called *compensation* and is a very common feature in the behaviour of persons with a pronounced weakness or inadequacy. For example, a dull boy may constantly come bottom of his class in academic subjects. If he directs all his available time and energy resources towards games, art, music or any other ability which he might have, he will probably be very successful. Primitive races with little opportunity for activities other than physical outlets become very successful in these pursuits because of the time and energy spent on them. (This may well be a major factor behind the athletic and sporting successes of American Negroes who have lacked opportunity for developing activities in other fields.) Another

common instance of compensation is the plain girl who has difficulty in finding a boy friend. She will often turn her attention to working hard at school and so become very successful academically or professionally. Thus mental compensation is comparable with physical compensation, e.g. where an insurance company pays money for goods that cannot be replaced or a blind man develops his hearing facility and the sensitivity of his fingertips to compensate for his lack of vision.

Closely allied to such compensating mechanisms are forms of behaviour called *sublimation*. In such cases we do not direct our energies into a pre-existing channel quite different from the original. Instead we turn our energies towards a new goal similar to the original but more acceptable and attainable. For example, the young woman with a maternal desire may have no opportunity for expressing it in its natural form. If she turns to teaching or nursing she can sublimate her maternal drive into a worthwhile satisfactory outlet. This same mental mechanism may well be one of the bases of creative art, where unexpressed energies naturally designed for creation of new members of the species can instead be utilized for creating art, music, literature, etc. It is suggested that many great artists and scientists produce much of their important work when young and fired with procreative energy. A final point on sexual sublimation may be made from investigations on primitive tribes in various parts of the world. It is found that in tribes where sexual precocity is permitted the level of culture is low. Where rules relating to sexual activity are strict the cultural level is correspondingly higher. If the relationship here is as direct as the evidence suggests then the cultural level of mankind today is very much a result of his sexual restraint and the rechannelling of the creative energy made available. We have discussed sexual sublimation at length because of its frequency and importance. However, other forms of sublimation are extremely common, e.g. the redirection of aggressive energy into competitive sports or other activities; crude, untutored curiosity may be turned to investigation of important problems, etc.

Not all redirections of energy are satisfactory or acceptable. Sometimes, through force of circumstances, persons turn their natural desires towards other available but unsatisfactory goals. For example, a woman living alone may turn her maternal instincts towards a dog or budgerigar sometimes to an unhealthy degree (see Chapter 13); boys in a single-sexed boarding school may direct their sexual desires towards their fellow pupils. Such unacceptable redirections of energy (particularly those relating to sexual energy) are called *perversions*.

The final instance in this category of substitution goals that we shall mention is the situation where there is no suitable goal available in the environment towards which you can redirect your energy. In such cases it is possible to create your own goal in your mind. You can reach this non-existent goal in your imagination. Such a process is called *day-dreaming*. For example, a person with an inferiority complex may imagine that he holds his own and is aggressive towards his com-petitors; a down-and-out beggar may day-dream about riches and power; a teenager may imagine that he is independent and successful or that he has 'changed the world' round to his way of thinking. Such processes are widespread among persons who feel insecure, inferior or unable to cope with their environments but can see no way out of their dilemma.

In each of the examples discussed above a second more easily attained goal has been introduced into the situation. In other words, we have changed our environment so that we can cope with it more successfully and the divergence between our actual self and our ideal self has been lessened.

2. *MECHANISMS FOR IMPROVING OUR CHANCES OF COPING WITH OUR ENVIRONMENT* There is a tendency in each of us to copy other persons who cope with life's problems in a more successful way than we do ourselves. This goes far beyond conscious imitation. It occurs without us being aware of it. It is one of the major ways in which children learn from adults. This process of putting ourselves in the place of others and behaving (and thinking) as they do is called *identification*. If used in the way described above, it is a most valuable mechanism. However, there is no safeguard to ensure that the persons with whom we identify ourselves are desirable models to follow. While a child may adopt the attitudes of its teacher and cope with its problems more adequately than before, a nurse may identify herself with a patient, experience her fears and suffering and so be incapable

of doing her job objectively. (It is along these same lines of undesirable identification that films and horror comics concerning gang warfare, monsters and death are condemned by many people as unsuitable literature for children.)

Another commonly used mechanism to deal with conflicts, loss of face, feelings of inferiority, etc., is to resort to behaviour which previously solved a problem we experienced. This returning to earlier forms of response we call *regression*. For example, a child of ten or eleven years, when sleeping in a strange house where he feels insecure, may start wetting the bed; an adult may, under stress, break down and cry. In both these cases childish behaviour that once brought assistance from mother is, quite unintentionally, being used to help in the present crisis. Regressive behaviour can often be seen in persons in difficult situations. When confronted with a problem people often make silly remarks, adopt childish attitudes, become unnecessarily dependent on others, etc.

In these two mechanisms just described we have substitution of approach to the problem rather than redirection of energies towards a new goal. These techniques of identification and regression aim at reducing the divergence between 'what we wish we were' and 'what we actually are' by trying to ensure that this latter coping with the environment is as satisfactory as possible.

3. *MECHANISMS FOR CONVERTING MENTAL ANXIETIES INTO PHYSICAL TERMS* Frequently mental conflicts are difficult for the individual to cope with and often it is impossible to get sympathy and help from others in the solving of such problems. There are several mechanisms which function to make mental anxieties obvious on the physical plane so that the individual, with or without external assistance, may deal more effectively with the unsatisfactory situation.

Probably the most simple instance here is the use of a physical action to counteract the mental activity which is causing distress. For example, under stress, some people smoke heavily, others fiddle with their clothes (notice the fidgeting, tie-adjusting, uncontrollable behaviour in a dentist's waiting-room, or in a fathers' waiting-room at a maternity hospital). Such activities are called *compulsions*. The exact reasons behind such acts are difficult to assess. They may be an alternative outlet for the energy involved in the conflict; they may be methods of taking the person's attention off the problem. Whatever causes them, their value is undoubted as a method of reducing tension.

Another closely related, widespread mechanism is the development of *psychosomatic illnesses*.[7] The close connection between mental tension and physical reaction is obvious in us all, e.g. feeling sick at the thought of a very unpleasant experience, trembling with fright, 'butterflies in the stomach'. It is not surprising, therefore, that prolonged extreme mental conflicts may manifest themselves as physical illnesses. The best-know examples probably are ulcers in the stomach or duodenum as a result of constant worry, or asthma in persons lacking self-confidence. There are, however, many such physical illnesses which have their roots in psychological anxieties. One particularly interesting form is called *conversion hysteria*. Here an individual develops a physical incapacity to enable him to withdraw without loss of face from a situation where he will be unsuccessful. For example, a girl may actually develop a severe headache to prevent her from going out with a boy whom she dislikes. A mother who unconsciously wishes to keep her grown-up son at home may become ill and so be physically dependent upon him. A person who wishes to retire may develop an impediment which makes him unfit for his work. Such examples are often called 'unconscious malingering' but this term is misleading. The persons involved really have got a problem. However, it is basically mental rather than physical and it is in the mind that the cure must be effected. Perhaps faith-healing and cures through suggestion under hypnosis come into this category.

A well-known manifestation of this type of mental defence mechanism is *accident proneness*.[8] Statistics show that the vast majority of industrial accidents are caused by a very small number of workers. This suggests that the cause of these accidents lies not with machinery or manufacturing processes, but with the people involved. Further examination of these individuals shows that they fall into two main categories: (1) those that are hostile towards society or the management but cannot obtain satisfaction by direct aggression; (2) those that are hostile towards and wish to punish themselves. In both instances a solution is found through an indirect approach to the problem. Taking this second (self-punishing) approach to its extreme, we have *suicide*,[9] where anxiety and conflict in the mind cause a person to take the most drastic way out of the situation. Suicide is a very wide topic beyond our discussion here. On one hand attempted suicide may be designed to attract attention. On the other it may be the reaction to conflicts and anxiety which are so intense that the desire to go on living is subordinated to the desire of relief from mental distress. It may well be that when such extreme tensions arise in a person it is no longer possible to keep them out of consciousness and the person becomes aware of them.

4. *MECHANISMS FOR IGNORING THE EXISTENCE OF CONFLICTS* Due to the limits of our minds, we can only be aware of a very small part of our experiences at any one time. We normally are conscious of information from the environment which is at present reaching our sense organs. However, past experiences and other processes going on in our minds are not always in our consciousness. We can become aware of many of them if we so desire by remembering them. But equally we can reject or forget experiences of which we do not wish to be reminded. If a conflict is very unpleasant and the conscious knowledge of it causes us great anxiety we can actively forget it. This process is called *repression*. For example, a trained nurse with an incurable disease would have a tremendous conflict in her mind between what she knows about her condition (i.e. that she is going to die) and what she wishes was the case (i.e. that she would go on living). In such an instance she might well repress her knowledge of her actual situation and carry on planning for her homecoming and rehabilitation, being cheerful and optimistic about her circumstances, having actively repressed her anxiety. Such repressions can often be found in relation to a feeling of guilt. For example, a selfish or cowardly act is readily repressed; a situation where we could not cope with a problem is actively forgotten. Teenagers who are called upon to behave as adults when they have very little experience upon which to draw may often make fools of themselves. The whole period of adolescence is beset with such unpleasant situations. There is a very strong tendency in adults, therefore, to repress memories of this stage in their development. Consequently, adults have

much more difficulty in understanding and helping their teenage children than might be expected from their own past experiences.

As might be expected, such powerful memories stored in the mind of an individual usually colour his behaviour in one way or another. In many cases the outlet for the energy involved in such a conflict is found in dreams. However, in most people a repression also colours their waking behaviour. It is common practice to classify these influences on behaviour according to whether their effect is the same as that of the repressed material would be, or whether it is the reverse. For example, suppose a spinster is repressing a sexual desire which is incompatible with the life she is leading. This repression may influence her behaviour to make her antagonistic towards anything which has sexual involvement, such as co-education, bikinis or heterosexual friendships. She may become a prude to a quite unreasonable extent. Such an influence is called *reaction-formation* where the behaviour now displayed (i.e. prudery) is the reverse of that which is repressed (i.e. sexual desire). Alternatively, the spinster may repress her own sexual activities but manifest an interest in sexual matters in an indirect way, e.g. by wallowing in scandal, reading pornographic literature, having naked statues in her home or telling smutty stories. Such behaviour is termed *indirect expression* of a repression. Similarly repressed feelings of inadequacy, of aggression, etc., may appear in a modified form or as the reverse of the original desire which is repressed. In all forms of repression an individual unconsciously wants to forget. The results of repression, however, are normally harmful due to tensions created in the unconscious as well as adverse influences in conscious behaviour.

Another technique for ignoring the existence of a conflict is the process of *rationalization*. Whereas with repression unsatisfactory mental aspects of 'what we actually are' were discarded, in rationalization the information that we are receiving about ourselves is so interpreted that it approximates to what we think we should be. For example, the schoolgirl mentioned earlier in this chapter who, having done badly in her examinations, excuses herself by saying that she did not have the requisite books for her course; the person who puts off a visit to the dentist because he has no time to spare; to say 'all is fair in love and war' when you wish to play a dirty trick on the boy friend of a girl you think is attractive. Rationalization is the production of logical reason for an act, even though it is quite the wrong reason. It is the basis of making excuses and is a common mechanism (even a habit) in many people.

5. *MECHANISMS FOR SEPARATING THE TWO ANTAGONISTIC ASPECTS OF A CONFLICT* The classic example of conflicting forms of behaviour that can be easily separated is the person who has one set of moral values for Sundays and another, less rigorous set, for weekdays. He is able to divide his mind into 'separate compartments' and simply utilize the appropriate compartment demanded by the situation in which he finds himself. Although this type of defence mechanism is probably more widespread than we realize (i.e. our standards change according to the people we are with, the situation we are coping with, etc.) it is often difficult to isolate instances in ourselves. We tend to rationalize and explain away any apparent incongruity that is pointed out. It is in mentally sick patients that such *dissociations*[10] (as the use of these separate mental compartments is called) become clearly apparent. For example, 'the prophet' bringing tidings of heaven soon to be established on earth will, during lax moments, steal a cigarette from a sleeping neighbour; 'the mighty fearless warrior' does as the student nurse tells him. In extreme cases it is possible for a person to develop two or more completely separate personalities on this principle of dissociation. Such cases of *multiple personality* are rare. A more common instance is the dissociated condition known as *fugue* where a person suffering from extreme tension may temporarily repress all knowledge of his life, work and family. Such persons who have lost their memories may be found wandering miles from home with no recollection of how they got there or what has happened to them.

Another technique for separating the two conflicting aspects of our behaviour is to transfer the blame for unsatisfactory responses on to another person or object. In this way we identify ourselves with 'what we ought to be', but we misplace the inadequate 'what we are' on to some part of the environment. For example, a poor workman blames his tools; a lazy child fails his examination because his teacher was

122

inadequate. This direction of our own shortcomings away from ourselves is called *projection*. It is often indicative of a lack of courage to take the blame for our own inadequacies. These examples we have noted are rather special types of projection. In its wider sense, projection really means seeing the world around us in terms of our own past experiences, present attitudes, etc. Consequently, seeing the world through rose-coloured spectacles is a more positive approach to projection than blaming another for our own shortcomings. We shall return to this wider concept of projection when discussing personality in a later chapter.

6. *MECHANISMS FOR AVOIDING CONFLICT BY RETREATING FROM IT* In this category come those forms of behaviour which are withdrawals from difficult situations rather than being positive attempts to cope with them as in previous mechanisms discussed. A very common example, particularly in persons with a general feeling of inadequacy, is *shyness*. In such cases the person withdraws 'into his shell', will not participate in social situations and generally tries to prevent his inadequacies from being noticed by others.

The reverse type of behaviour may represent retreat by some other persons. For example, an individual may take part in as many activities as possible in order to prevent himself from having time to think about his real problem. Such *hyperactivity* is found particularly in energetic people who would find passive retreat unacceptable.

Finally we might mention that some persons, particularly those that are emotionally immature, may tend to take drugs or alcohol as a means of dulling the tensions of mental conflict. They retreat behind a more physiological screen than do persons using other psychological defence mechanisms. However, they fit very well into this category of avoidance of conflict through retreat.

We have discussed mental defence mechanisms at some length because of their considerable importance to us in the interpretation of our own behaviour and that of others. Most people believe that they know why they respond in the way they do, and think they can judge the behaviour of others equally efficiently and objectively. However, a closer examination of the behaviour and judgements of anybody will reveal all kinds of possible alternative explanations. Such mechanisms as we have described here are present in some degree in most people. They are in most cases valuable, anxiety-relieving techniques which do little harm. However, should they reach proportions where the individual loses contact with reality then some form of remedial treatment is desirable. A very advanced state of this condition would be classed as *psychotic* (see Chapter 14). Such cases are fortunately rare. However, many of us suffer at times (or even constantly) from over-active defence mechanisms which interfere with our efficiency, understanding, co-operation, enjoyment of life, etc., to an extent which is undesirable. To overcome such a situation it is essential to understand the conflict which exists and the mechanism being employed to resolve it. In most cases the best results are obtained by 'opening your heart' to a friend who listens sympathetically but lets you sort your problem out in your own mind. In really severe cases a psychotherapist should be consulted. He is a trained professional worker who is able to listen to and help persons in such situations.

MISINTERPRETING OTHER PEOPLE[11]

In later chapters we shall discuss some advantages and problems for individuals living together in groups. We shall emphasize the point that for such groups to be maximally efficient the individuals composing them must understand each other as well as possible. Earlier in this chapter we described how easy and common it is for us to misinterpret our physical surroundings and also to fail to understand ourselves and the reasons behind our own behaviour. We must now briefly consider how we misinterpret other people who are much more complex than objects and of whom we have much less knowledge than we have of ourselves.

We can have no absolute standards for interpreting the behaviour of other people and the probable forces causing them to respond as they do. Consequently we use ourselves for purposes of reference. We think of ourselves as being normal, consistent and logical and the beliefs and attitudes which we hold as being those of maximum importance. Our earlier discussion of mental defence mechanisms will suggest how unsatisfactory this is likely to be. Turning to the persons we are attempting to assess, we presuppose that while they are complex and each is unique, nevertheless we are able to understand them and evaluate their attitudes and responses fairly and adequately (although when asked how we achieve this, the answers given are unconvincing). We shall return to these problems in our discussions of 'Personality' in Chapter 11.

Let us consider some common examples of the ways in which we may misinterpret other people. When information is received about another person frequently it is ambiguous. To infer the internal conditions of a person (e.g. his motives, attitudes, interests) from observation of his external behaviour and appearance is very difficult, especially in cultures like our own where we are trained from infancy not to show our feelings but to put on a socially acceptable front. As we suggested in the last chapter, even when a conscious attempt to conceal our feelings is not made, the same affective state can produce quite different forms of response in different people. For example, anxiety may cause some people to work hard, others to be unable to concentrate, some to become aggressive, others shy and retiring. Again different motives operating in different people can produce similar forms of behaviour. For example, members of a football crowd queue putting money in a flag-day tin may do so because they approve of the cause behind the charity, or because they want to impress their fellows or because they want to conform with their neighbours who are subscribing, or because they have a financial interest in the cause and hope to encourage others to support it. It is very easy to form the wrong impression of another person from interpreting his behaviour as if it were a response you were making yourself.

Because of the great variety of information available to our sense organs at any one time it is easy to pay attention to certain characteristics of an individual while ignoring others. The parents of a new baby will be familiar with this fact when some people think that their infant is like his mother while others can 'see his father in him'. Both parties may well be right to some extent but they are not taking into account all available information. Similarly with adults we may select some perhaps quite superficial aspect of an individual's personality and from this construct a whole erroneous picture

125

of him. We have referred to this tendency to complete our percepts earlier in our discussions on perception. When we see a long-haired young man on a railway station and assume that he is work-shy we are adding information which we may have gleaned from any of a variety of sources. Some *may be* fairly reliable, e.g. our own observations or reports from disinterested observers on this individual's conduct. Much may be quite irrelevant, e.g. our previous experience of people who look like him or our interpreting his behaviour as if it were our own.

How often your impression of a person can change when you 'get to know him better'. Lack of relevant prior experience of an individual can often lead to misinterpretations. Teachers and nurses, businessmen and social workers all know only too well the great value of personal contact and full understanding of their charges. We tend to expect other people to have the same values and attitudes that we have ourselves, to respond as we would and if they do not, we consider that they are misguided or have made a mistake. People with no children may expect youngsters to behave like small adults. Again persons from other cultures may be regarded as inferior or ignorant because they possess different customs, habits and attitudes from ourselves. This whole process of expecting something different from what actually happens, the concepts of attitude and set will crop up repeatedly in later chapters. In one sense it represents a tendency to over-simplify, to try to make people fit into categories. This may involve trying to make one person consistent over a long period during which he changes, e.g. not allowing a child to grow up or not letting a subordinate utilize knowledge and skill which he has acquired during a long apprenticeship served under you. On the other hand it may consist of generalizing about many quite different individuals, e.g. all Scots are mean, all Welshmen can sing.

We form percepts of other people based on information from a variety of sources. Yet we are not aware of summing up these separate factors. We see each individual as a whole. Consequently we have great difficulty in distinguishing between fact and subjective addition. Generally the picture is complicated by the fact that we each try to interpret ourselves as favourably as possible (no matter how well trained we may be to believe that we do not). We 'put on a front' which is designed to show others who are assessing us what we want them to think about us. All factors considered the interpretation of other people is a very complex process which is probably performed much less efficiently than most of us realize.

SUMMARY

1. Although some of the terms of reference which we use for interpreting ourselves and our surroundings can be objectively checked, many of them cannot be so confirmed, e.g. opinions, attitudes, etc. The percepts which we form using such unconfirmed terms of reference may well be incorrect. The indications are that this occurs to a much greater extent than most people realize. Consequently, misinterpretations and wrong percepts are utilized and perpetuated in our perceptual processes.

2. Such misinterpretations work against the whole purpose of perception, which is to enable us to know what is going on around us.

3. Some of the major factors in misinterpretation are:

   a. inadequate or ambiguous information gathered by the sense organs;
   b. attention being directed towards the wrong part of the perceptual field;
   c. previous relevant experiences being of the wrong type for present sensations to be correctly and objectively interpreted;
   d. the perceiver expecting a different sensation from the one which he actually obtains;
   e. the incorrect completion of a percept based on an incomplete sensation – this may lead to the inclusion of this percept in an incorrect category;
   f. the percept may be unacceptable to the individual as it conflicts with other predetermined views, e.g. his impressions of himself.

4. Misinterpretations of perception show themselves through the behaviour of the individual. However, it is important to distinguish between:

   a. formation of incorrect percepts, i.e. misinterpretation;
   b. formation of correct percepts but performance of behaviour out of keeping with the percepts formed.

Both these activities will manifest themselves in behaviour incompatible with the environmental situation. It is with the first category that we are concerned here.

5. Misinterpretations may occur at two levels:

   a. at the sensation level, i.e. wrong or inadequate information being collected by the sense organs;
   b. at the percept level, i.e. incoming information being built into incorrect percepts.

6. Many of our terms of reference are built up during childhood. We learn what is satisfactory and what is not according to the success we have in coping with our environment and also by the responses to our behaviour by our parents and others with whom we come into contact. We develop two separate aspects of the self:

   a. the actual self – which is what we perceive ourselves as being;
   b. the ideal self – which is what we know we should be or wish we could be.

7. Frequently information regarding our actual self conflicts with the wishes of the ideal self. To overcome this discrepancy various techniques may be employed:

   a. the incoming sensation can be modified (i.e. you change your ways);
   b. the attitudes and acceptable percept structure can be modified (i.e. you change your ideas);
   c. where compromise or conscious choice is impossible unconscious mental defence mechanisms are employed.

8. A mental defence mechanism is an unconscious technique for reconciling a conflict, e.g. between the situation as it actually is and as we wish it was. Such mechanisms are particularly important and widely used when our actual and ideal selves strongly diverge. Consequently, a study of such mechanisms is of great value to nurses and teachers who deal with persons in stressful situations.

9. What form the mental defence mechanism actually takes will depend on the individual involved, the conflict being resolved and the environmental situation in which he finds himself. However, it is convenient to distinguish between the following categories:

   a. mechanisms involving substitution;
   b. mechanisms for improving our chances of coping with our environment;

    c. mechanisms for converting mental anxieties into physical terms;

    d. mechanisms for ignoring the existence of conflicts;

    e. mechanisms for separating the two antagonistic aspects of a conflict;

    f. mechanisms for avoiding conflict by retreat.

10. Mental defence mechanisms are used by everyone to some extent. In most cases they are valuable anxiety-relieving techniques. However, in advanced cases a person may lose contact with reality. Such a person is classed as *psychotic*.

11. In most of us during times of trouble and stress our mental mechanisms become over-active and impede our efficiency and enjoyment of life. At such times it is important to understand the stress which exists and mental mechanisms being used to alleviate it. A heart-searching talk to a sympathetic friend (or, in severe cases, to a psychotherapist) is the best method for relieving the situation.

REFERENCES

1. For a general introduction to some of these problems see the essays by Vernon, M. D. 'Attention and Visual Perception', and Drever, J. 'Perceptual Organization and Action' in Cohen, J. (editor) *Readings in Psychology* (Allen & Unwin, London 1964).

2. For further discussion of optical illusions see Tolansky, S. *Optical Illusions* (Pergamon Press, Oxford 1964).

3. Woodworth, R. S. *American Journal of Psychology* 60 (1947) pp. 119–24.

4. For a general discussion and criticism of the concept of mental defence see Fleming, C. M. *Teaching: A Psychological Analysis* (Methuen, London 1958) especially Chapter IV.

5. Hadfield, J. A. *Psychology and Mental Health* (Allen & Unwin, London 1952) is a useful introduction to mental health and mental illness.

6. Maslow, A. H. and Mittelmann, B. *Principles of Abnormal Psychology* (Harper, N.Y. 1951) and O'Kelly, L. I. *An Introduction to Psychopathology* (Prentice Hall, New Jersey 1949) both give an extended treatment of mental defence mechanisms.

7. Alexander, F. *Psychosomatic Medicine* (Norton, N.Y. 1950) examines this subject more fully.

8. Csillag, I. and Hedri, E. 'Personal Factors of Accident Proneness', *Industrial Medicine* 18 (1949) pp. 29–30.

9. Raines, G. N. and Thompson, S. U. 'Suicide: Some Basic

Considerations', *Digest of Neurology and Psychiatry* 18 (1950) pp. 97–107.

10. See Prince, M. *The Dissociation of Personality* (Longmans Green, London, 2nd ed. 1930) or Thigpen, C. H. and Cleckley, H. M. *The Three Faces of Eve* (McGraw-Hill, N.Y. 1957).
11. For a valuable summary of present ideas relating to perceptions and misperceptions of people see Vernon, P. E. *Personality Assessment* (Methuen, London 1964) especially pp. 25–46.

Chapter Six

The Forces Which Produce Behaviour

INTRODUCTION

In the previous two chapters we have been considering the collection and interpretation by the individual of information relating to himself and his surroundings. In this chapter we begin a consideration of how he utilizes this information which he has obtained. We are then concerning ourselves with the basis of human activity whether this takes the form of building, repairing and maintaining the physical body of the individual or of exploring, dealing with and modifying his physical and social environment. This subject, so vast as to be almost commensurate with psychology itself, can only be introduced at this point. We shall return to it again and again in subsequent chapters.

The study of dynamic aspects of science is a comparatively new departure.[1] For example botanists in the last century spent their time writing massive systematic descriptions of leaves and flowers, while today emphasis is placed more on physiological and evolutionary processes. Again in physical medicine biochemical and physiological studies accompany the descriptive anatomy parts of a medical student's course today, and even this anatomy is more closely related to function than previously. So also in psychology we find that the earlier studies centring around sensation, perception, learning, etc., have in this century been considered more and more from a dynamic point of view. The study of a dynamic process is bound to be difficult especially when it is manifested in the behaviour of different persons in a variety of situations. A host of concepts and terms has arisen to attempt to describe different aspects of the forces producing and directing behaviour in different contexts. For example, the biologist refers to appetites, instincts, goals and homoeostasis, while the clergyman talks of aspirations, passions, wishes, wants and the will; the school teacher employs in his thinking rewards, punishments and the stimulation of interest while industry refers to incentives, aims and targets. The psychologist, while rejecting many of these terms because of their imprecision, accepts others which together with such concepts as needs, drives and emotions are basic to the description and interpretation of experimental findings in the study of dynamic aspects of behaviour. The general term given by psychologists to the production and direction of behaviour to satisfy an individual's needs or to enable him to achieve a particular goal is *motivation*.[2]

MOTIVATION AND BEHAVIOUR

In the first chapter we defined behaviour as the activity of a person or animal in response to the situation in which it finds itself. This 'situation' is the product both of external stimuli perceived via the sense organs and internal experiences generated within the individual himself, e.g. interests, feelings. We have already described some simple types of behaviour when discussing reflex actions, e.g. the stimulus of a pin pricking the skin causing a person to jump away from the painful part of the environment. The central problem which faces us in this chapter is that the majority of situations to which a person must respond are far too complex for reflexes alone to be adequate. No stereotyped reaction will always allow a person to obtain food or avoid danger, find a mate or bring up a family, decorate a house or solve a scientific problem. The most efficient technique for performing these activities will obviously vary between situations.

In order to cope adequately with the multiplicity of problems which a person is likely to encounter, flexible patterns of response are essential, which can come into action when required, can be modified by experience and can be adapted to the specific circumstances in which the individual finds

The Forces Which Produce Behaviour

himself. Systematic studies in this field of psychology are many and varied. Nevertheless they are all primarily concerned with answering two fundamental questions:

    a. What makes an individual active rather than inactive?
    b. Once active, what determines the form of his activity?

For example, why are the children in the road outside my window expending their energy in a variety of ways instead of sitting quietly doing nothing? Why do they chase each other wildly, fighting over a sweet at one moment, yet cooperate and help each other over a garden fence to retrieve a lost ball in the next.

In general, behaviour is produced which promotes the survival of an individual or which makes his existence more acceptable* to him. Psychologists ask what are the factors (or *needs*) which must be satisfied for an individual to enjoy such an existence. Surely if these can be isolated we shall be much nearer determining what makes him respond in the first place and also be nearer predicting the nature of the responses which he is likely to make. Psychological literature contains many attempts at isolation and classification of these basic needs. The problem arises that you can only determine the existence and nature of a need by observing the behaviour which the person produces to satisfy that need.

Frequently there is no directly discernible link between a need and the way in which a person responds. A rat in the wild state will eat when hungry or copulate when sexually aroused. A man in his own home may go to a tap for a drink because he is thirsty or may stop mowing the lawn and sit down because his muscles are fatigued. But such simple obvious instances are comparatively rare. Take an employee at an office party given by his boss. Can we say that when he eats he is hungry and when he refrains from eating he is

*The 'acceptableness' of a piece of behaviour is assessed by some psychologists in terms of how efficiently it enables the person performing it to attain pleasure or avoid discomfort. The connection between behaviour produced and the pleasure obtained may be direct as when you eat to satisfy hunger or move into the shade when the sun is blazing down. It may be much less direct, however, in such cases as owning up at school to a misdemeanour, or giving to the poor, or sacrificing your life for your country. Past experiences have taught us what is expected of us by society and doing that which is acceptable to others is a very strong motivating force in most of us.

satiated? We see him with a plate of scones in his hand. Is he eating them because he is hungry, because he does not want to offend his hostess who made them, because he does not want to be different from the rest of the group who are all eating, because although he is not really hungry he has a great liking for home-made scones, because he wants to hand the plate to an attractive new office member with whom he wishes to make contact, because he feels that the boss is giving this party on the profits gained by the firm from his labours and so feels he is entitled to eat as much as he can? Similarly a new junior member of the firm at his first office party may refuse a scone offered to him because he is not hungry, because it is the last on the plate and he has already had two, because he is so nervous that he cannot eat, because he is hoping to rush away as soon as possible, etc. A single reaction may be the expression of any one of a variety of motives or may be based on a combination of several motives acting together.

Similarly a single motive may produce many different responses in different individuals. Look at the reactions of the various persons at the party discussed above. Many will be nervous in the home of their superior and this lack of security will underlie much of their behaviour. Some of the more accomplished social performers will appear quite at their ease while others will be jittery and unable to keep calm. Some will be shy and not say a word while others will talk too much, perhaps making fools of themselves or telling boring stories, some will be unable to eat, others will drink too much.

To attempt to isolate the motives underlying any particular piece of human behaviour is very difficult indeed:

a. because motives often act together producing behaviour based on, for example biological requirements, the need for social acceptance, the individual's own particular interests;
b. because even when only one motive is active or dominant, the behaviour produced to satisfy it can be very varied;
c. the same behaviour pattern can be produced to attempt to satisfy many different motives.

In any situation in which it is necessary to determine the underlying motivating factors behind a person's responses the observer must always take into account the type of person he is dealing with, the past experiences of that person, and the nature of the present circumstances facing that person.

Obviously these factors must be considered by the teacher coping with problem pupils, the nurse faced with difficult patients and all of us in dealing with unco-operative colleagues or with personal difficulties where we seem to be the odd man out.

PROBLEMS OF TERMINOLOGY

The student reading a variety of elementary text-books on motivation may well be confused by the terms which are used and the concepts described. It is vital that he should attempt to understand why different approaches to the topic arise and why it is possible to have several complementary ways of describing the same topic. Different workers in different fields may all encounter a common basic psychological phenomenon such as 'motivation' and will each describe it and interpret it in terms appropriate to his own sphere of work. For example, the physiological psychologist in his studies on states of arousal in rats will develop physiological interpretations, the educational psychologist may prefer theories based on learning, while the social or industrial psychologist may be more concerned with 'field theories' or culture patterns. Each, therefore, will describe motivation in different terms and from these descriptions a variety of interpretations and theories will arise. No one is necessarily right and others wrong. They may all be describing different facets and manifestations of the same process. We shall find similar situations arising in later chapters on 'learning' and 'personality'.

It follows from what we have just said that it is likely that no single theory, certainly as stated at the moment, is likely to be wholly satisfactory in explaining all the findings accumulated in the field of motivation. Among the most important attempts made so far may be mentioned:

A. INSTINCT THEORIES [3] which describe motives as inborn universal tendencies which are present in each of us. The concepts involved here have had a history of chequered popularity. Although in modified forms they are gradually attaining more acceptance than they had twenty years ago, they probably present an over-simplified view of motivation

135

and much which was once thought to be inborn is now known to be learned early in the individual's life.[4]

B. PHYSIOLOGICAL THEORIES which base motivation on physiological deficiencies, behaviour being produced to remedy the imbalance. While these concepts are perhaps appropriate to the basic biological needs it is much more difficult to apply them directly to psychological or social needs.

C. FIELD THEORIES[5] present a very comprehensive approach to the problem of putting emphasis on the interaction of all forces internal and external to the individual as being instrumental in the production of his behaviour. We shall mention other theories of motivation in our discussion of 'learning' and 'theories of personality' later in this book. It is impossible to extend our discussion on this point further here. The interested reader should consult the bibliography for further reading.[6]

Despite the wide variation to be found in the use of terms in discussions of motivation, it is essential that in order that we can proceed we must select and define some relevant concepts. The definitions given here, however, should not be attributed to these terms occurring in other works before establishing the views of the other authors concerned. We shall use the word *'need'* to mean any deficiency suffered by a person whether this is physiological, e.g. the need for food, warmth, or psychological, e.g. the need for security, social acceptance. When a person is suffering from what is obviously a physiological need his aroused condition in which he will perform activities designed to remedy this physiological lack we shall call a *'drive'*, e.g. a hunger drive to obtain food, a sex drive to find a mate. In many instances however, present environmental effects together with learning from previous experiences so disguise the true origins of a state of arousal in human beings that the concept of a specific drive is inappropriate. Such a state of readiness we shall call a *'motive'*, e.g. ambition, interests. Whether or not a motive is a drive modified by experience is a matter of dispute. Some psychologists refer to motives as acquired or secondary drives. For convenience sake we shall distinguish between them as suggested above.

We might perhaps note at this point that just as there are a multiplicity of theories of motivation, so for similar reasons we find many different classifications of motives. Any classification then can be considered to be a matter of convenience to the person proposing it.

INDIVIDUAL NEEDS

Let us first consider some general concepts relating to the physiological needs and their related drives which arouse an individual so that he may perform suitable activities to remedy these needs. We are all constantly using up food and oxygen from which we obtain energy for growth, repair and movement. We therefore need constant supplies of these substances and constant removal of waste by-products. However, in the higher animals including Man, conscious life is not continuously concerned with basic biological functions.[7] Within the bodies of such creatures are storage facilities, e.g. the gut and fatty tissues for food, the bladder for waste, which enable exchange with the environment to take place periodically. The constant exchange between living cells and stores within the body occurs automatically without the individual being aware of it. (Oxygen cannot easily be stored, but breathing is sufficiently simple and invariable for it to be carried out at the reflex level under normal circumstances.)

When our food-store runs out or our bladder becomes over-full, messages are sent to the C.N.S. to inform it of the existing need. The C.N.S. will then become aroused and act (or be ready to act) in a manner which will produce behaviour to satisfy the need. At present our knowledge of how we become active is very meagre indeed. (We suggested some physiological evidence in Chapter 3.) There is much speculation as to whether the aroused state (or drive) produced in the C.N.S. is always the same state of general excitation whatever the need initiating it may be, or whether there are many drives each specifically related to one or a group of needs, e.g. hunger drives, pain-avoidance drives. The form of the behaviour produced will depend both on the nature of the existing need and the circumstances in which the creature finds itself. For example, a hungry cat will become active in his search for food, but what form his behaviour takes will depend upon the environment. In the garden he might hide in the hedge to stalk a bird or scratch on the door to be let into the kitchen. In the kitchen he might jump on to the shelf where the remains of a joint has been left, or he may rub round the legs of his mistress who feeds him.

The relationship between motivation of behaviour and our own physiological imbalance is obvious to each of us. Because of our rigorous social training, however, adults tend not to make obvious their biological needs in their social behaviour. Small children, on the other hand, demonstrate the effects of deficiencies and tensions very clearly. They can work or play or be sociable when their biological needs are satisfied, but should they become very hungry, over-tired, or need to urinate they have great difficulty in thinking about anything else. Although these physiological drives only become obvious in extreme cases they nevertheless have some effect on our responses and attitudes even when our needs are more moderate. For example, just after a large luncheon a person 'couldn't eat another crumb'. Some time later, although not really hungry, he might take a cup of tea and a biscuit if pressed to do so. As the evening progresses he begins to look forward to his supper, finds his homework being interrupted more and more easily by smells and noises from the kitchen. If he went to bed with no supper he might well feel very hungry next morning and find it impossible to think or do anything which did not bring him nearer to his breakfast.

This example illustrates some other interesting points about motivation. When we have a specific need we tend to pay attention to stimuli relevant to the satisfaction of that need and often ignore other irrelevant stimuli. In modern society most of our physiological needs are satisfied but one which may well not be satiated yet be very strong particularly in young people is the sex-need. Individuals in such a condition often cannot help looking at, talking about or more positively pursuing members of the opposite sex. We first introduced this concept of 'how we see other people being related to our own needs and interests' in our discussions of perception. We shall return to it again when examining how we assess each other, e.g. in personality interviews.

Not only does the C.N.S. select certain parts of the environment for us to concentrate on according to our existing needs. It also enables us to take advantage of improving our storage situation should a suitable opportunity arise. For example, we frequently eat a meal when not really hungry, or use a public convenience when we meet it on a shopping spree. The C.N.S. then is not entirely dependent on a need to produce behaviour. Conversely a need might arise but behaviour may not be produced to satisfy it, e.g. when a tired child will not go to bed, or a patient gradually starves himself to death. The precise relationship between need, drive and satisfying behaviour is not clear. Another manifestation of the problem comes from the ability of the body to cease performing a certain type of behaviour when a store is replenished but before the physiological need is satisfied, e.g. we stop drinking when water is in our stomach but before the fluid imbalance in the body tissues which made us thirsty has been corrected.

As we collect more and more experiences of the best way to satisfy our needs we develop more and more complex patterns of response. This whole process of learning will be the subject of the next chapter. Let us note here that its effects on motivation are far more complex than learning to take a deep breath before diving, or to pot a child before it goes to bed. A man may perform activities which will improve his status and salary at work. He may be motivated simply by a desire to shine above his fellows or to make more money than they do. On the other hand he may have learned that such behaviour will bring him security and respect, the wherewithal to set up home (with the attendant blessings of companionship, love, shelter, regular meals, etc.), will enable him to follow his own interest or be accepted into a group which he wants to join, etc.

We must very briefly consider some of the more important physiological needs of the individual, although as will become apparent as out discussion proceeds, in our modern man-made society most of them are so regularly and fully satisfied that they may cease to play the large part in the motivation of *our* behaviour which they do in that of lower animals.

Obviously basic to our discussion are the essential substances of metabolism, viz., *food* and *oxygen*. We all need regular supplies of many different food substances (including water) in order that we may produce energy for chemical and physical activities, and build up our bodies or make good those parts which become worn. There is evidence to suggest that we possess some ability to know which particular food constituents we are lacking, for children and animals presented with a variety of types of food select fairly widely. Again cattle which are fed on a diet lacking in minerals will eagerly go to a salt-lick. Excess of any one sort of food soon causes a person to lose his appetite for it even though he may be very fond of it (as students making meringues in cake factories, or picking strawberries as holiday tasks will tell). Many problems relating to this group of needs for foods and the related hunger drives have been worked out in the laboratory as they are particularly convenient for experimental work. An interesting field of investigation beyond the scope of discussion here, relates to the study of artificial hungers (or addictions). Some chemical substances, e.g. nicotine, alcohol, morphine,[8] when taken into the body in some way modify the physiology of the bodily tissues so that they no longer function properly in the absence of the drug in question. Now the individual has a need for the drug and his behaviour is motivated towards obtaining it.

The need for oxygen is supplied through the process of respiration. We described earlier how drives and motivated behaviour were essential for the survival of an organism which has to satisfy its needs by variable patterns of behaviour according to the situation in which it finds itself. Under normal circumstances the processes involved in respiration are sufficiently invariable as to make their control by automatic reflex mechanisms quite adequate. Should unusual circumstances arise however, e.g. a blockage occur in the air passages, pressure be placed on the chest to prevent its expansion, then the C.N.S. is informed and the whole body responds to remedy the situation. Although the physiological nature of these biological needs is really beyond our scope, it is interesting to note here that the body is sensitive to accumulation of the waste products of respiration (i.e. carbon dioxide) rather than to oxygen lack. Under normal circumstances increased carbon dioxide concentration is directly related to decreased oxygen supply and remedial action (e.g. coughing, gasping) relieves both undesirable conditions. However in instances where oxygen is lacking but where carbon dioxide is not accumulating (e.g. in high-flying aircraft or in coal-gas poisoning) the C.N.S. is not informed of any outstanding need, no remedial action is taken and the individual's oxygen deficiency is not made good.

Many of the other waste products of metabolism (i.e. the chemical activities of the body) are passed in solution (*urine*) to the bladder. The indigestible parts of food travel through the gut and collect in the bowel as *faeces*. Both urine and faeces must be voided from the body but this is not a continuous process, the waste materials being stored until a substantial quantity has been collected. There are several possible biological advantages in this periodic evacuation, e.g. the risk of infection is reduced when openings on the body surface are kept closed except for short periods of excretion; again the risk of attack by predators and enemies is reduced if the animal can hold these natural processes until it is in a safe spot. Many animals use urine for territory marking (as dog-owners taking their charges for walks past trees and lamp-posts will know). Other creatures, e.g. hippopotami, leave piles of faeces on the edges of their territories. There are obvious biological advantages in control of these processes. The individual is not aware of the accumulation of urine or faeces until sufficient quantity has collected to stretch the wall of the bladder or the rectum. Information then passes to the C.N.S. to inform it of the existing bodily condition, i.e. of the need to relieve the tension. In human society one has to learn to control these processes in socially acceptable ways. All kinds of taboos and expressions of disapproval are associated with them. We shall return to some of the general problems related to the regulation of urination and defaecation when discussing learning and theories of personality formation.

The complex chemical processes going on in a living body must all synchronize and work together if the individual is to be healthy. All chemical reactions are effected by *temperature* and for a given species of animal a specific temperature is essential for optimum activity (e.g. in man about 98·4°F, in the rabbit about 100·8°F). Reflex control of temperature regulation is possible over a wide range around the optimum temperature, but, as in respiration, should the need (here the deviation from normal) become too great the C.N.S. will be informed and the whole body will be involved in taking appropriate action. Anyone subjected to working in an environment which becomes overheated in summer or very

cold in winter will know how difficult it is to perform behaviour which has any other purpose than remedying the
temperature deviation.

One of the basic needs much used in earlier times for the
direction of behaviour of children by parents and teachers is
that of *pain-avoidance*. In biological contexts it is obviously
valuable to move away from a painful stimulus to stretch a
cramped and uncomfortable limb or to avoid moving or
bumping a dislocated joint or tender sore. Experimental work
on this need is extensive and has established some interesting
conclusions. One of the more important is that animals
brought up not experiencing pain of any sort, seem to be
insensitive to pain when eventually they are subjected to it.
This would suggest that learning is involved in the perception
of pain. Perhaps this throws some light on the fact that while
some people find pain pleasant (i.e. are masochists) no one
enjoys hunger or thirst or cold.

Two needs which are probably closely related are those of
rest and *activity*. When the mind and body have been active
they use up energy and release waste products. The resulting
condition (*fatigue*) demands a period of rest so that supplies
can be replenished and by-products cleared, e.g. 'I cannot
dance another step', 'I must sit down before we start on the
return journey'*. On the other hand if the environment is not
stimulating and the person, although 'full of energy' has
'nothing to do', e.g. during an uninteresting lecture or sermon,
the resulting condition is known as '*boredom*'. For a full and
happy existence a state intermediate between these two
extremes is desirable. Animals in the wild do not get bored as
the satisfaction of their biological needs keeps them occupied
and under normal conditions this can be achieved without
exhaustion. However, put a lion in a cage or leave a dog in a
house alone, supply its biological needs but give it nothing to
do and you will find it pacing the floor, listening and watching
for any interesting stimuli or in some other way making itself
active.

This need for mental and physical activity is all too apparent
in our human society. School children on holiday, businessmen

*Recent investigations show that the nervous mechanisms controlling a
repeated muscular activity become fatigued (and so stop the activity)
considerably before the muscles themselves become fatigued.

in retirement or patients in hospital are all common examples of people 'fed-up' with having nothing to do. In more extreme forms these psychological problems occur in prisoners in solitary confinement or astronauts embarking on long journeys into space. Our own experience indicates that both mental and physical activity is important to us. Children cannot sit still for long but when they become active they do not simply use their muscles in meaningless repetitive movements. They play games which involve imagination and the utilization of past experiences. Adults who must perform a tedious physical task such as weeding the garden or mowing the lawn often find that their minds are active, thinking about all kinds of problems. Workers on humdrum factory tasks can improve their efficiency considerably if background music is available to stimulate their brains. Again if a person is physically tired at the end of a day's work he may still get much satisfaction from mental exercise either of a strenuous nature, e.g. playing chess or bridge, or of a more moderate kind, e.g. watching television or chatting.

This concept of a need to be active is fundamental to much of our motivated behaviour. It appears however that we need a *variety* of types of activity both physical and mental. In fact we say 'a change is as good as a rest'. Every teacher knows that she obtains the best results from a lesson in which the children have a variety of experiences, e.g. listening, reading, writing and doing. Excess of one type of experience is undesirable. After a day in the office a short stroll does you good; when the children are in bed at night mother needs to 'put her feet up'. Again excessive danger is avoided but we like 'a bit of excitement' in a film or book. We cannot stand horror in our own lives but find that the lurid details of murders and disasters in newspaper reports have a morbid fascination for us. We take care not to disgust ourselves and our fellows through indecent exposure or physical assault yet we enjoy smutty jokes and songs or suggestive comments. We approve of low cut dresses and bikinis on other young women but dislike them on our wives and daughters. A modicum of a variety of types of activity seems to be essential for us all.[9] We shall return to this concept in the chapters on mental health and mental illness.

Probably closely related to this need for activity is the

curiosity motive. We all have a tendency to explore and become better acquainted with the environment. A strange object or environment will cause a person to ask questions, manipulate and experiment. This surely is the motive force behind exploration both in physical terms (e.g. in science, geography) and in mental terms (e.g. in philosophy, theology). However whatever the origins of such behaviour may be their final manifestation in terms of interests and attitudes is so modified by past experience, social pressures, etc., that we will find it easier to discuss them in the section on 'social needs'.

In concluding this section, which may at first sight seem peripheral to the work of teachers, nurses and other social workers, we must remember that it is only because of our man-made need-satisfying environment that these drives do not manifest themselves more obviously. You have only to consider the patient in pain, the children in a hot class-room, the drug addict or the homeless family cold and hungry, to see how fundamentally these needs can effect behaviour if they are not satisfied. Nevertheless because of Man's ability to control and satisfy these physiological drives, he has been able to liberate his nervous system from concern with biological functions to follow those social and intellectual pursuits which distinguish him from the rest of the animal kingdom.

SOCIAL NEEDS

It is convenient to distinguish between those needs which are essential to the survival of the individual and those related to propagation of the species because the behaviour patterns producing satisfaction of the needs in these two categories are often the reverse of one another. For the individual to survive, selfish desires must have priority, e.g. he must take, fight, criticize or even kill his competitors. For the race to survive the individual must compromise his own desires with those of his fellows, e.g. he must give, approach, co-operate, praise and help them. A common example of the difficulty of modifying behaviour patterns in this way comes from the individual who marries late in life after having had 'no one else to think of' for many years. When he is called upon to fit into a family he may have great difficulty in 'changing his ways' and so remain a selfish individual whose needs must be satisfied at the expense of the good of the whole group.

Even in our discussions of comparatively simple biological needs it was possible to see the influence of the group to which an individual belongs showing itself in the actual behaviour which he performs. For example, in satisfying hunger drives the Chinese learn that octopi and bird's-nest soup are good, while the French acquire the habit of eating frog's legs and snails. These valuable sources of nourishment are rejected by British people because they have not learned to accept them as food materials.

The customs of the group to which we belong influence behaviour produced to satisfy social needs to a very great extent.[10] Many of these needs can only be satisfied in association with other members of the group, e.g. sexual and parental activities, love acceptance, respect. Depending upon the attitudes and values of different groups so the types of behaviour learned by their members as being socially acceptable will vary. For example, while in Britain and U.S.A. much emphasis is put on the needs and rights of the individual (even if this is to the detriment of the nation as a whole), in communist countries the reverse is the case and individuals are sacrificed for the good of the State. Such differences in attitude make communication between the two parties very difficult as the present 'cold war' situation bears out.

As another example let us consider acceptable forms of behaviour in British society both in Victorian times and today. Social attitudes and pressures in the last century were, for a variety of reasons, antagonistic to positive social need satisfaction. Life was hard for most individuals and little love was shown for other members of society. As a reaction against this way of life, various enlightened social reforms were brought in and today we have moved almost to the opposite extreme. The harsh expression of social motives by Victorian society has been replaced by more humane attitudes. Hanging which was common even in public, has now been abolished. Other punishments for debtors and criminals are much less severe than before. Much more enlightened attitudes to the deformed, incapacitated and mentally ill have arisen. Slum clearance, the replacement of work-houses by a scheme of national assistance, the development of universal education and franchise and a host of other social reforms are all indicative of a change in social attitude. These same trends are reflected in sexual attitudes; ankle-length dresses have become shorter eventually leading to the appearance of the mini-skirt; bathing costumes have decreased in area resulting in bikinis. Mixed schools, the disappearance of chaperons, and the suggestive nature of many modern dances are all reflections of changes in attitude towards sexual expression. Equally many examples of a decrease in harshness of parental attitudes could be cited. At the beginning of this chapter we said that the great advantage which motivated (as opposed to stereo-typed) behaviour gives an organism is that flexible forms of behaviour can be produced to satisfy its needs in the way best suited to the situation in which it finds itself. All people have the same basic needs but the behaviour they produce to satisfy them depends upon the attitudes, values and pressures of the environment in which they live.

Two of the most obviously biological of the social needs are those related to *sexual* and *parental* activity. However well we conceal the fact, we all have a fundamental desire to find a mate. Many of our social customs, attitudes, regulations and taboos have evolved to control and direct this very powerful activating force. Pressures against sexual expression and the concepts of it being evil, dirty, sinful and so on have already been mentioned as possible sources of frustration and conflict in our discussion of mental defence mechanisms.

Biologically speaking, the species is more important than the individual. Disease, starvation, epidemic diseases leading to survival of only the fittest are normal methods of progress in nature. Amongst lower animals, therefore, activities relating to reproduction are of the greatest importance. In human society, however, there are many vital roles to be fulfilled which, although important for the continued success and progress of the species are not directly linked with reproduction. Consequently non-reproducing human beings while not fulfilling their supreme biological function can be extremely valuable members of society, especially when they channel their resources into activities which benefit society as a whole.

Just as individual selfish desires have many devious in-fluences on our behaviour so also have our sexual desires.

146

The Forces Which Produce Behaviour

Apart from obvious directly sexually motivated activities and interests we express our sexual needs in the literature, art, romantic novels and films, which we enjoy, in the clothes we wear and the pursuits we follow. Smoking a pipe or drinking beer are considered masculine occupations, while using an ornate cigarette holder or drinking gin and orange are more feminine. The advertising industry again, makes great play of sexual motivation in its campaigns. There are many other examples which may be quoted as being based on sexual motivation but, as we have said before, it is very difficult to ascertain which underlying need (or needs) is responsible for the production of a particular piece of complex behaviour. We shall not expand the concept of sexually based social responses any further at this point. Let us simply bear in mind that when bitches, queen-cats, ewes or does are 'on heat' their behaviour and certainly that of their male counterparts aroused by their receptive condition, is to a very large extent governed by sexual interest. In human beings where both sexes are more or less continuously sexually receptive sexual interest may well be involved in much of their behaviour. That such influences are usually shown in a controlled and sophisticated manner may well be the result of the social regulations to which we are subjected. It does not detract from their underlying importance.

In everyday language we speak of some women or female animals as being 'born mothers' while others are 'not very good with children'. We are referring, of course, to the type of behaviour they produce when coping with their offspring, but this is a reflection of the strength of parental motivation which the individual possesses. In rats we can assess this in such terms as the intensity of pain which a mother will endure (e.g. by running over an electrified grid) to reach her young in distress. In women we use more complex, less objective measures of behavioural changes during pregnancy and at child-birth, e.g. 'how much she has settled down', 'how much less self-centred she has become'. She will now perform activities which previously she would not have considered, e.g. getting up at 2 a.m. and 6 a.m. to feed her infant whereas previously she may have refused to rise before 9 a.m. whatever happened. Although we often say that it is a case of having to do these things, there is a good deal of evidence to

147

suggest that the woman has a motivating force to help her to forget herself and direct her behaviour to the benefit of her offspring. In lower animals these behavioural changes are mainly controlled by hormones secreted into the mother's blood at the time of her infant's birth. In human beings, behavioural changes in both female and male parents appear to be, in part at least, controlled by the C.N.S. and consequently can be modified by learning.

The essential nature of parental care is obvious in animals such as Man in which the bulk of future behaviour is patterned by experiences from the environment. A duck or frog learns little by experience. They are born with their basic stereotyped patterns of response firmly laid down in their nervous systems. Human infants on the other hand are born with minds which are to a large extent unpatterned but receptive to experiences which they can build into future activity. During this period of accumulation of experience the individual needs care and protection which is provided by its parents. Obviously the more complex the life the individual will lead the longer this protective phase must be. Length of 'childhood' varies not only between Man and other species, but also in Man himself. As his life has become more complex, so the length of education adequate for coping with it has been lengthened as the gradual rise in school-leaving age reflects.

Parents make great sacrifices for their children, giving to them at their own expense and feeling great joy at being able to do so. The possible repercussions of this in social behaviour have been widely debated. Sublimated parental motivation may be responsible in part at least, for our desire to help the weak, the ill, the small and the under-dog. We show pity for the helpless rather than being thankful for the ineffectual competition which they can put up. We help them rather than taking advantage of them. We are affronted at cruelty to 'poor defenceless animals and children'. yet in selfish terms such attitudes make no sense. We applaud people who give up their time to raising money for charity, or who undertake voluntary work for the blind or crippled. If these activities can be considered as manifestations of parental motivation, then surely the driving force which makes people want to become teachers, nurses or other social workers is likely to be the same. It is also possible that our love for small perfect objects of art, intricate patterns, fine lace and pottery may all stem from our positive attitude towards that which has some of the qualities of an infant.

There are obviously very close biological ties between sexual and parental motivation. A young sexually mature adolescent is excited by almost any member of the opposite sex. This form of passion is a manifestation mainly of sexual desire. We learn by experience to become selective among suitable partners (although individuals lacking suitable experience may remain indiscriminate in their sexual interest). The 'love' of a socially and emotionally mature adult involves much more than the expression of sexual lust. It is tempered not only by learning, but also by the need to have someone to care for and to be cared for by another. This could be a form of expression of parental motivation. The 'companionship' of middle age and onwards is perhaps more predominantly the parental aspect with declining sexual interest. 'True love' if it is to last a lifetime, while being able to satisfy sexual and parental desires must also provide opportunities for satisfying other social needs, e.g. security, affection, acceptance and respect as well as mutual interest in at least some experiences (e.g. a family, a house, a job, or social activities). How often a married couple with no children spend much energy on maintaining and improving their home. While we say that with no children they are 'able to do this', the motivating force which 'makes them do this' may be based on the need for a common binding interest.

Human behaviour in relation to sexual and parental interests is very difficult to identify. These powerful forces enter many of our daily activities. As in other animals, in order that we shall become aroused by motives which propagate the species, we must be in a suitable bodily state and have a suitable object for our attention. Human beings, however, are not only almost always in such a suitable state, but because of their complex minds can remember or imagine suitable objects which can arouse these motives and which will therefore colour their perception and behaviour.

Let us leave this topic with a specific reference to behaviour related to reproduction.[11] In courtship (i.e. pre-reproductive activity) we find patterns of behaviour which perform a variety of functions, e.g. the establishment of interest in reproduction

149

in each of the partners, the staking of a claim to the partner, the synchronization of excitement so that both partners are ready to copulate at the same time. The behavioural exchange between male and female partners is very similar to that between mother and child. In obvious cases, e.g. sparrows or seagulls, we can observe the female begging for food from the male and being fed by him in precisely the way in which a mother bird feeds her nestlings. Many male mammals and birds groom and clean their potential mates. In Man, holding hands, presenting gifts, performing services which are reminiscent of the way in which a mother assists her child, e.g. carrying heavy bags, opening doors, and kissing, cuddling and general petting all can be related both to sexual and parental activities.

We must now turn to other social needs which have less obvious biological counterparts. It is extremely difficult to classify them in a form which has general acceptance among psychologists. It will be convenient to consider them under four very broad groupings:[12]

a. The need for security which may perhaps be the counterpart of the need to show protective parental care;
b. The need for acceptance by a group;
c. The need for recognition and respect within the group;
d. The need to be interested and to perform new and exciting activities (to which we have already referred in our discussion of individual needs).

Of course these groupings overlap one another and also cannot be separated from individual needs. This is in part because they are all directing behaviour towards the same ultimate goals, i.e. survival of the individual and propagation of the species. Other major problems in isolating underlying needs have been discussed above. They boil down to the fact that while many apparently inborn motives can be isolated in the behaviour of animals (e.g. aggression, gregariousness, dominance, submission, acquisition), Man is so moulded by his environment that underlying needs become obscured even to the individual himself.

We have just discussed the need found in young animals and children for care and protection while they are learning to cope with life's problems. They must, of course, be protected not only against physical danger but also against psychological and social upset. It is obviously important that these young-sters feel a need to be cared for, and want to be helped by their parents and teachers, otherwise they will rebel against their interfering. The motivating force behind the need for security and affection has been well demonstrated by experiments on baby monkeys, who, although brought up without their real mothers, always ran to a cloth dummy mother to be 'protec-ted' in the presence of danger. The extreme importance of gratification of this need has been widely studied in relation to the development of human personality and problems of motherless children.[13]

As we grow up and become more experienced, each of us needs to lead our own life,[14] take decisions and carry respon-sibility and so our dependence upon our parents must decrease. If such an acquisition of personal responsibility comes too soon, e.g. if a child suddenly leaves an over-protective home, it can be extremely difficult to him to re-adjust to his new situation. It is the duty of all parents and teachers to help their charges to turn their need for security away from their elders and direct it towards obtaining a regular steady form of work, making suitable friends. We all need security throughout life and a person with this need unsatisfied is far from happy and his behaviour reflects his basic deficiency.

Obvious forms of security-seeking behaviour are found in taking out insurance, saving money, buying a house on a mortgage. Perhaps turning to religion may also be included here. In more subtle ways, the security need has much wider effects. We discussed in the last chapter how we build up a body of values and standards against which we judge ourselves and others. If we fall far short of our own standards we may well feel insecure and in an attempt to cover this up the whole pattern of our behaviour may change. For example, we may become aggressive, or show off, we may be over-active or defeatist. There are many forms of behaviour designed to camouflage an unsatisfied need for security. Equally however, any one of these types of behaviour may demonstrate the existence of a variety of different needs. For example, ag-gression can be the manifestation of parental care (when a cow attacks a stranger approaching her calf) or hunger (when dogs fight over a bone), of insecurity (when a child thumps its new baby brother) or sexual desire (when two stags fight over a hind).

The concept of social security is very closely bound up with *acceptance* of the individual by his fellows as a suitable group member.[15] Most of us need to be accepted by our family, friends, work-mates or society in general. The teddy-boy, failing to obtain this, seeks acceptance by members of his gang. We make friends, join clubs, or perform other activities which bring together individuals of similar interest, training or background. The strength of professional bodies and trade unions and concepts of loyalty and friendship are all manifestations of behaviour based on this need. While worrying about 'what people will think', 'being one of the lads', 'following the latest fashion' or wearing school or hospital uniform are obvious, often conscious examples of such behaviour, it also shows itself in more subtle ways in the clothes we wear (e.g. men wearing ties and jackets at business), the papers we read, the way we speak. We shall return to a fuller discussion of this need in the chapter on 'group behaviour'. Let us leave it here by emphasizing the strong motivating force which is aroused by this need for acceptance. Parents and teachers use it in directing behaviour of children, e.g. 'Mummy and Daddy are eating their pudding. Johnny eat his too', or the use of class participation and personal involvement as important activators of motivation. On the negative side, the rejected child, 'go to bed', 'I don't love you when you do that' are punishments which thwart the need for acceptance. On a wider front such social problems as racial and religious discrimination, class distinction and the like can be attributed, in part at least, to a rejection of others different in some way from ourselves.

For most of us it is not sufficient simply to be accepted into a group. We also need to be recognized as a useful member of the group and be respected for the job we are doing. This is the motivating force behind much competition, ambition and striving to 'better yourself'. This pride in our social position may come directly from our status in the group, e.g. royalty and landed gentry do not need 'to put on a show' as they are respected without it. The social climber, however, has to 'create an impression' that he is important and well to do. He may talk in a very artificial voice, or run a large expensive car, boast about his two television sets or spend much time and money keeping the front of his house beautiful. Perhaps we are all guilty of such 'impression-creating' behaviour if we put on our best clothes when going courting or for an interview, or show off our technical knowledge in front of laymen in our subject or interest. Snobbery and one-up-manship can be considered to be forms both of pushing yourself upwards and of running down your competitors so that you shine above them.

Not only do we need to be aware of our own success but we want positive approval from others. Praise and encouragement are great motivators whether you are learning to read in a primary school, or to walk after an injury. In our modern materialistic society social approval is often shown in the form of financial reward. While increasing your own well-being and security, a pay rise also indicates society's recognition of your worth. In a rather less obvious way the importance of recognition of the individual has led to many changes in names of occupations and categories of person. For example, rat-catchers are called rodent operatives, sanitary inspectors are now public health inspectors, mentally deficient children are called educationally subnormal and old age pensioners are senior citizens. Such modifications in terminology help to remove many undesirable attitudes and ideas attached to these names by earlier usage and so increase the prestige of the persons to whom they are applied.

In our discussion of individual needs we noted that there is a basic need in all animals to examine the environment so that it may be dealt with efficiently. Certainly in human beings this exploration of physical and non-material situations which they encounter is very important. It takes them into realms which they would never discover if they were only concerned with those circumstances which naturally impinge upon them. We 'do things because they interest us' and not because they have any obvious survival value. It is very difficult to generalize about 'what interest us'. Each of us has his own personal interests which develop with experience. We are usually interested in topics which are relevant to ourselves, and which we understand and appreciate. A subject can be drudgery to a child in a secondary school until he reaches the sixth form, finds its relevance to his future career, begins to understand

and see perspective within it and so becomes interested in it. Interests represent individual tendencies to undertake and continue certain forms of activity.

If our work satisfies our interest we shall continue to pursue it in our leisure time, e.g. the mechanic who tinkers with old cars in his back garden, the biology teacher who spends his evenings and holidays on natural history expeditions. Hobbies may be considered as outlets for interests which work does not satisfy, either because you cannot follow an occupation in which you are interested or because you have several interests, only one of which can be satisfied at work. You may work in an office but enjoy competitive physical exercise. As a young man you play football on Saturdays and as you get older you enjoy watching others play it. Pools firms may cash in on your existing motivation by adding financial interest to it.

The vital importance of being interested in the task at hand if you are to be successful at it, cannot be overstressed. You can go to a dance or a party and be very active but can be too tired to mow the lawn. You can read an interesting novel far into the night, but half an hour with a text-book is enough. Obviously being really interested in a course of study or a future career is basic to ultimate success in that activity.

We have been discussing some of the major needs which will cause us to be active. In actual behaviour the situation can be much more complex than we have suggested here.[16] Not only are many motives often operative at once, but frequently they may conflict with one another. For example, we may have difficulty in choosing between doing a job which really interests us and one which will bring in more money, security and respect. Again his desire for social acceptance may make a man strike with his fellows, even though this thwarts his need for self-respect. We have mentioned some of the consequences of such conflicts in the last chapter. They will crop up again frequently in this volume.

FEELINGS AND EMOTIONS[17]

So far in this chapter we have been emphasizing what the individual is attempting to obtain through behaviour, i.e. satisfying a deficiency, attaining a goal, etc. But there is more to motivation than action. Each motive has a 'feeling' attached to it. For example, you are motivated to escape from danger and you perform behaviour to achieve this. You also feel afraid. You experience the loss of a very close relative and you feel grief-stricken. Motives are forces which produce and direct behaviour. The internal state of the individual associated with being aroused is described as a *feeling* if relatively mild (e.g. feel awkward holding a new baby, or feel satisfied after a good meal) or an *emotion* if more intense (e.g. terrified as a snake crawls over your foot, enraged at your neighbour creosoting his fence and killing your prize plants). Obviously the distinction between a feeling and an emotion is arbitrary and psychologists group them together as *affective experiences*.

We usually keep the words 'feeling' and 'emotion' for comparatively brief affective states in a person. More prolonged states we call *moods*, while more or less permanent states characteristic of the individual we call his *temperament*. For example, I feel sad when I hear some bad news. If I remain sad for some time I shall be in a depressed mood. If I am always sad then this is a reflection of my temperament. Again I might feel afraid of a thunderstorm. After a severe shock I might 'be on edge', i.e. in a nervous mood for some time. If I am a 'nervous person' then temperamentally I am always nervous whatever happens. We have several descriptive terms in everyday language which apply here. A person who has high affective reaction to stimuli is called *emotional*. A person whose mood changes rapidly is called *moody*. We talk of being of even and uneven temperament according to whether a person's normal state is relaxed and predictable or excited and fluctuating.

These affective experiences colour our lives to a very great extent. When we say that we are happy or sad, annoyed or amused, surprised, disgusted, eager or embarrassed we are describing how we *feel*. The actual physical responses which we discussed earlier in this chapter could, in most cases, be performed by a machine. Goals can be reached or deficiencies made good. But human behaviour has the additional quality of feeling. We are aware of whether a course of action is pleasant or unpleasant both to ourselves and others. We describe individuals as 'having no feeling' when they continue with a form of behaviour which takes no account of the effects which it is having on themselves or others. (We shall return to

155

this point in later discussions of communication for *sympathy* involves the sharing of a common feeling.) All human behaviour is probably accompanied by some form of feeling or emotion.

But these affective experiences can be much more than a colouring accompaniment to a need-directed piece of behaviour. We may perform an act for the feeling which it arouses, i.e. because we like doing it. We find the smell of certain types of flower pleasant, prefer certain colour combinations in our house decoration and enjoy some types of music and art while rejecting others. It is difficult to separate clearly the satisfaction you derive from these experiences from, for example, the mild fear enjoyed at a horror film or a good cry brought on by a romantic novel which may well be forms of behaviour which satisfy our need for activity.

On the other hand an emotion can cause us to perform certain types of behaviour. I might run because I am afraid, hit a child because I am angry or walk out of a film show because I am disgusted with the material being shown.

Obviously then the connection between affective experience and motivation is very close. Emotion can accompany the motivated behaviour, can be the goal to which the behaviour is directed, or can be the motivating force causing the behaviour to be produced.

Motivation is the production and regulation of organized effective behaviour to deal with the situation in which a person finds himself. We have already described how this involves both the external environment and the internal state of the individual. Emotion has been defined as the internal state of arousal of the individual. Within limits, the more aroused the individual is the more effective his response will be. For example, a student often obtains a better result in an examination in which he is a bit anxious than in one where he 'is not worried'. Again you can tell someone off far more convincingly if you are annoyed with him.[18]

However, if we become too emotional (i.e. too aroused), we begin to lose control over our responses and they therefore become less efficient. For example, we may be too angry or upset to realize what we are saying, a soldier may be too frightened to shoot at the oncoming enemy, on a mountain ledge the inexperienced climber may not be able to move on

upwards or back down; the boxer who loses his temper, the
actor suffering from stage fright and a host of other examples
of inefficient behaviour due to interference between motivation and emotion can be seen in everyday life. One of the
reasons behind doctors or police not taking part in cases in
which their relatives or close friends are involved may well be
this decrease in efficiency through emotional interference.[19]

Our knowledge of the physiology of the nervous system,
while still very inadequate, does throw some light on the
physical basis of emotional response. In Chapter 3 we mentioned the autonomic nervous system (A.N.S.) as an offshoot
from the spinal nerves near the spinal cord. This A.N.S. is
concerned only with regulating the purely automatic functions
of the body, e.g. activity of glands, constriction of blood-
vessels. Closer investigation shows that it consists of two
sub-systems, the sympathetic and para-sympathetic nervous
systems, each of which sends nerves to most organs of the body
which are not under voluntary control. The function of the
sympathetic system is to get the body ready for action in fight,
flight or fright situations. The heart-beat quickens, the blood
supply to muscles increases while that to the gut decreases,
salivary gland secretion is modified and the mouth feels dry,
the iris of the eye dilates, hair begins to rise (or where hair-
erecting muscles contract under soft skin, 'goose pimples'
appear). In general the person becomes aroused. The effects
of the para-sympathetic system are to conserve and build up
the body, e.g. heart-beat slows, digestion proceeds and the
person is generally quiescent. The state of arousal in an
individual at any one time depends upon the relative activity
of these two sub-systems.

The A.N.S. as a whole is not well controlled by the cerebral
cortex as are the nerves responsible for voluntary movement.

For example, in a stressful situation such as a visit to the
dentist you can control your voluntary muscles so that you do
not fight or run away, but you cannot prevent your heart
racing, your palms sweating, your mouth going dry, 'butterflies in your stomach' and dilation of your irises. These
'emotional responses' are directed through the A.N.S. The
hypothalamus which we described as the ventral part of the
brain stem in the fore-brain, seems to play an important role

in the organization of emotional expression. On the other hand we are usually aware of our feelings and emotions and we can often learn to control them, e.g. we can conquer a fear, or come to like a certain type of food. This indicates that the cerebral cortex is in some way involved in the experiencing of emotions. The exact roles and relationships between the A.N.S., the hypothalamus and the cerebral cortex are still imperfectly understood.[20]

Many attempts have been made to relate specific bodily reactions with specific emotional experiences, but this has proved very difficult. The same bodily response can be made to a variety of emotions, for example, you may cry with rage, fear or anger. Again any one emotion may produce a variety of different responses, for example fear may cause you to run, freeze or attack, to scream, whimper or to be struck dumb.

Some of the problems involved in attempting to analyse the complex emotional activity of adults have been tackled by systematic observation of emotional development in children. A pioneer in this field, K. M. B. Bridges, elucidated the following pattern of development.[21] A new born infant, when not quiescent, shows only a *general* state of excitement. By the time the child is two months old, however, one can recognize two different categories of response. There is that related to *distress*, i.e. wanting the present situation to change, e.g. if it is being jerked up and down or is subjected to loud noises. The second category is related to *pleasure*, i.e. wanting the present situation to continue, e.g. if it is being fed or rocked in its mother's arms. Further differentiation occurs until at 18-24 months the child can show several distinguishable emotional responses appropriate to existing circumstances. Distress reactions have by now been separated into anger, fear, jealousy and disgust while pleasure responses have differentiated into elation, affection for adults and affection for other children.

It is very difficult to explain how this differentiation comes about. All emotions are states of arousal caused by the situation in which the person finds himself. The specific form which an emotional response takes must depend upon thoughts relevant to that particular situation. For example, *anger* is arousal plus thoughts of attacking, *fear* is arousal plus thoughts of escape, *disgust* is arousal plus thoughts of avoidance. Obviously our thoughts will determine the way in which we direct our activity, e.g. a woman angry with her child may strike it, with her husband may cry, with the local council may write to the Press. Whether or not the same state of arousal develops in different emotions is not clear.

The regular pattern of emotional development in each of us suggests that maturation is fundamental to this process. In many instances however whether or not an emotional reaction should be shown, and the particular form it should take, appears to be learned. For example a small infant does not have to learn to smile or cry under appropriate circumstances. As he grows older however, through praise and discouragement from others he learns when it is socially acceptable to smile or laugh, to cry or scream. In some cultures he learns that he should try to repress all his emotions as much as possible, in others he may develop them either in a natural or in a stylized manner. 'The enforced smile', 'the stiff upper lip' and many other forms of emotional control are found in British convention and in our normal environment which largely avoids extremely stressful situations they work quite adequately. However, should suitable circumstances arise, e.g. in instances of racial or religious riots, cruelty to children, blood sports or capital punishment, people become uncontrollably emotionally aroused, 'hot under the collar', etc., indicating that this affective part of our nature is still present in us all even though custom prevents our showing it under normal circumstances.[22]

UNCONSCIOUS MOTIVATION[23]

It follows from much of what we have said in this chapter that we do not know the real motives behind many of our acts of the reasons why we like or dislike performing them. We tend to put common-sense explanations on them, which help us to save our self-respect and which are acceptable to our friends, but there may well be selfish, sexual or undesirable social influences involved of which we are not aware. The fact that we do not fully understand and control our own behaviour goes against the general view of the man-in-the-street that common sense explains all things. It is widely believed that we can behave logically and rationally if we want to and because we do not choose so to do we are stupid, lazy, weak-willed, etc.

Yet each of us has had experience of performing behaviour which is pointless (e.g. cannot break a stupid habit) or inefficient (e.g. never do myself justice in an examination) or down-right harmful (e.g. always make a fool of myself in front of the boss; cannot concentrate even though it is vital to do so). What 'makes us' behave in these inappropriate ways, i.e. what is the motivation behind these acts?

In the previous chapter we introduced this topic when discussing mental defence mechanisms. Much of our motivation is unconscious. By this we mean here that we are not aware of the full reasons for our performing a certain act. A parent slapped his child which had answered him back. The parent says he did this for the child's sake to teach him to behave in a way which would make him acceptable to others. While this may be true is it the whole reason behind the act? May not the parent be asserting his authority, or getting revenge or even releasing tension caused through pressures at work? If these forces were involved but the parent was not aware of them, they would be unconscious motives. If they were involved and the parent, knowing of their existence, invented stories and excuses to conceal them, then they would be conscious motives.

There is diversity of opinion among psychologists as to the exact nature of unconscious processes. Is there a set of mental processes similar to those of the conscious but of which we are not aware? Are all experiences inconsistent with our own self-image 'pushed' into the unconscious? Do we repress all anxiety causing experiences into the unconscious? We cannot at this point extend our discussion of this topic. Let us simply note that most acts achieve more than one result. For example, an evening 'out with lads' is also an evening away from the wife. A drink with a friend is a social act but also an excuse for imbibing alcohol. The lawn-mower lent to your friend is helpful to him but also puts him in your debt. It is very difficult to analyse your own motives or those of anyone else. Let us simply reiterate the point that frequently (perhaps usually) we do not know the full reason behind the behaviour we perform.

In this chapter we have been considering some aspects of

the driving forces which cause us to respond to the situation in which we find ourselves and also to a large extent determine the form of our responses. As we said at the beginning of the chapter we can only introduce the topic at this point. Motivation is fundamental to all aspects of psychology and we shall return to it again and again throughout this book.

SUMMARY

1. Human beings are active to a greater or lesser extent throughout their lives. The general term given by psychologists to the production and direction of behaviour to satisfy an individual's needs or to enable him to achieve a particular goal is *motivation*.

2. Psychological studies of motivation attempt to answer two main questions:

   a. what makes an individual active rather than inactive?
   b. once active what determines the form of his activity?

3. In general, behaviour is performed which promotes survival of the individual or propagation of the species. Psychologists are concerned with isolating the factors (or *needs*) which must be satisfied for such ends to be achieved. This raises many problems mainly due to the lack of direct correlation between underlying need and specific form of behaviour produced to satisfy.

4. Different workers approaching a common topic (e.g. motivation) from a variety of points of view will develop different interpretations, theories and terminology. These need not be mutually exclusive and no one theory is likely to give a wholly satisfactory explanation.

5. The following commonly used technical terms may be defined thus:

   a. need is any deficiency whether physiological (e.g. food or warmth) or psychological (e.g. security or social acceptance);
   b. drive is a state of arousal to remedy a physiological need, e.g. hunger drive, sex drive;
   c. motive is a state of arousal whose origins are too obscure to be related to a specific drive, e.g. ambition, interest.

6. It is convenient to classify needs into those relating to survival of the individual and those relating to propagation of the species. Behaviour patterns which satisfy these two groups of needs are often the reverse of one another, selfish acts advancing the individual and social acts the species.

7. The basic individual needs, for example food, oxygen, warmth, rest and activity, pain avoidance, curiosity, etc. are fundamental to the organism's existence. However our bodies automatically satisfy these needs for most of the time and our C.N.S. is liberated from constant attention to biological function. Only when our needs become very great do we become aware of them.

8. When we experience a particular need we attend to stimuli relevant to satisfying that need. The specific relationship between need, drive or motive and satisfying behaviour, however, is not clear.

9. Individual need satisfaction can be greatly modified by learning. This is true to an even larger extent of our social needs, many of which can only be satisfied in association with other people. Motivated behaviour is flexible and can be adapted to the situation in which we find ourselves. As attitudes of society vary, so does the type of behaviour which is considered acceptable.

10. Sexual and parental needs are very important basic biological, social motivating forces. Their influences and implications in everyday human life are probably much wider than is generally realized.

11. It is very difficult to classify other social needs in a manner which is generally acceptable. Here they have been put into categories of:

    a. security; *b.* acceptance; *c.* recognition and respect; *d.* interest.

    However these classes overlap not only among themselves, but also with individual needs. It must be remembered that any classification tends to be artificial, the ultimate objects of motivation being individual survival and species propagation.

12. Associated with each motive is an effective experience (a feeling or emotion). You are motivated to escape, you feel afraid. Affective aspects describe the internal state of the individual when aroused. All human behaviour is probably accompanied by some form of feeling or emotion.

13. Affective experiences can be much more than a colouring accompaniment to need-directed behaviour. We may perform an act because of the feeling it arouses, e.g. I do it because I like it. We may perform an act because of the emotion we are experiencing, e.g. I shouted because I was angry.

14. Within limits the more aroused an individual becomes, the more effective his responses will be. However, should these limits be exceeded, efficiency will decrease.

15. Emotions have a strong physiological basis and much work with

human and infra-human species has been carried out in this sphere. Investigations of the emotional development of infants indicate that both genetic and environmental factors are involved. Although the constancy of the pattern of emotional development suggests that maturation is basic to the process, learning is also involved in determining whether emotions should be shown or not and in deciding upon the form of expression of the emotion concerned.

16. This analysis of the motives underlying any particular piece of behaviour is extremely difficult. Any one motive can produce a variety of forms of response, while any one form of response can be produced by a variety of motives. Moreover, rarely in Man do motives act in isolation and combinations of motives can be very difficult to analyse. The subjective interpretation of the person motivated is often of little value as he is likely to be unaware of many of his motives.

REFERENCES

1. See Mace, C. A. and Vernon, P. E. *Current Trends in British Psychology* (Methuen, London 1953).
2. For a general discussion of the problems introduced in this chapter see Bindra, D. *Motivation: A Systematic Reinterpretation* (Ronald Press, N.Y. 1959).
3. Of the many instinct theories of motivation perhaps the most famous is that of McDougall, W. *An Introduction to Social Psychology* (Methuen, London 1950).
4. For example see Tolman, E. C. 'Motivation, Learning and Adjustment', *Proc. of the American Philosophical Society* (1941).
5. Lewin, K. *Principles of Topological Psychology* (McGraw-Hill, N.Y. 1936).
6. See especially Knight 'Children's Needs and Interests – Contemporary Psychological Theories of Motivation', *Studies in Education* No. 7 (Evans, London).
7. For a full discussion of this point see Cannon, W. B. *The Wisdom of The Body* (Norton, N.Y. 1939).
8. Experimental work on morphine addiction is described by Spragg, S. D. S. *Comp. Psychol. Monogr.* 15, No. 7 (1940).
9. For discussion of work on problem solving for its own sake in monkeys see Harlow, H. F. *Psychological Review* 60 (1953), pp. 23–32.
10. See Davis, A. 'Child Training and Social Class' in R. G. Barker (ed.). *Child Behavior and Development* (McGraw-Hill, N.Y. 1943) pp. 607–19.
11. For a full and interesting discussion of courtship and related

activities see Milne, L. J. and Milne, M. J. *The Mating Instinct* (Robert Hale, London 1955).

12. Adapted from the work of Maslow, A. H. *Motivation and Personality* (Harper, N.Y. 1954).
13. The interested reader should consult Bowlby, J. *Child Care and the Growth of Love*, ed. M. Fry (Pelican, Harmondsworth1953).
14. For a discussion of the problems of increasing independence in personality development see Fromm, E. *Escape from Freedom* (Rinehart, N.Y. 1941).
15. For further discussion see Homans, G. C. *The Human Group* (Routledge & Kegan Paul, London 1951).
16. Cameron, N. *The Psychology of Behavior Disorders* (Houghton Mifflin, Boston, Mass. 1947), discusses the concept of needs in relation to frustration and conflict.
17. Reymert, M. L. (ed.) *Feelings and Emotions* (McGraw-Hill, N.Y. 1950) gives a full discussion of many problems and concepts in this field.
18. For a further discussion of the effects of emotion on efficiency of response see Hebb, D. O. *A Text-book of Psychology* (Saunders, London 2nd ed. 1966) Chapter II.
19. Young, P. T. *Motivation and Emotion* (Wiley, N.Y. 1961) discusses the relationship between motivation and emotion.
20. Cannon, W. B. *Bodily Changes in Pain, Hunger, Fear and Rage* (Appleton-Century-Crofts, N.Y. 2nd ed. 1929) discusses physiological aspects of emotion.
21. Bridges, K. M. B. 'Emotional Development in Early Infancy', *Child Development* Vol. 3, pp. 324–34 (1932).
22. For a discussion of the expression of emotions in the mature individual see Saul, L. J. *Emotional Maturity* (Lippincott, Philadelphia 1947).
23. Lindgren, H. C. *Psychology of Personal and Social Adjustment* (American Book Company, N.Y. 1953) especially pp. 39–59.

Chapter Seven

The Processes through which Behaviour Changes

INTRODUCTION

In the previous chapter we discussed responses of organisms to their environments in terms of the end-points towards which their behaviour was directed, i.e. need satisfaction or goal attainment. Throughout our discussion we stressed the importance of flexibility and adaptation to changing circumstances if such responses were to be efficient. Here we examine in more detail the processes through which the behaviour of an individual changes during his lifetime.

We are all familiar with changes in human behaviour both in the short-term (e.g. as a result of a particular lesson or encounter) and in the long-term (e.g. growing up or growing old). We can recognize these changes as modifications in appearance (e.g. size, muscular strength, growth or loss of hair) and in responses (e.g. attitudes, stability, interests). It is much more difficult, however, to isolate the factors which bring about these changes. It is convenient in theory but difficult in practice to separate these changes into two categories based on the factors responsible for them:

A. Those changes which are brought about through growth of the individual which are relatively independent of the environment (providing it satisfies his basic needs) and which follow a fairly constant pattern for all members of the same species. The effects of these factors constitute the process of *maturation*.* Examples of their influence are found in changes in bodily proportions during childhood and adolescence, modifications of attitudes to other people, especially to members of the opposite sex, changes in level of physical vitality with increasing years, etc. These changes being recognizable and predictable in each of us are probably largely due to maturation.

B. Those changes which are brought about through experience (i.e. observation or activity). Such modifications are based on *learning*. It is important to recognize that this definition must be qualified to exclude changes due to fatigue, illness, drugs, etc. This is sometimes attempted by using the phrase 'a more or less permanent change' in behaviour as a result of experience, but of course some illnesses can have long-term effects and some learning is apparently not permanent as we shall discuss later. From the general definition, however, we can see that changes of this kind are basic to modifications in attitudes, values, knowledge, skills, etc.

Although we shall find it convenient to discuss the development of the individual from these two different points of view (i.e. development as a result of maturation and development as a result of learning), it is important that we realize that these processes are not alternatives to one another. They function together and are simply two facets of the same process of development of a zygote (fertilized egg) into a physically, socially and psychologically mature individual. Obviously there can be no development without the existence of a living organism endowed with the ability to grow and mature. But neither can such a living organism develop unless placed in a suitable environment. Before attempting to describe separately the processes of maturation and learning we must examine their interrelationship more closely.

MATURATION AND LEARNING

Confusion often arises from the use of these two terms because in everyday language both can apply either to a

*There is disagreement among psychologists as to the value of the term 'maturation' in this context. Some prefer the word 'growth', others 'maturing'. Where 'maturation' is used in this book it refers to the concept described in this paragraph.[1]

process of changing or to end-products resulting from this process of changing. 'Maturation' can apply to growth within the individual's body and mind or to the level of performance of which he is capable as a result of this growth. 'Learning' can describe the process of modification within the person so that future responses will be influenced by prior experiences or it can describe the actual changes in behaviour as a result of a period of training which are obvious to an observer. At this introductory level it will be convenient for us to describe the external changes which can be observed and from these to infer what is happening inside the individual.

In very simple terms we can think of maturation as the development of the capacities with which we can learn, and learning as the experiences or activities with which we exercise these capacities.[2] Observation of our fellows shows a basic common pattern of development. We can look at a child and say he is 'about four years old', or his sister is 'a big girl for seven'. Again we think of certain types of response as being typical of an adolescent or an older person. Allowing for slight genetical variation this pattern is fairly constant for all members of the same species. At the same time we are aware of great differences between individuals which are super-imposed on this basic pattern. These variations may be in appearance, levels of attainment, interests, attitudes or a host of other characteristics. Some of these are mainly genetically determined, e.g. colour of eyes, build of body. Others are due in large part to interaction with the environment, e.g. hair-style, values, language. The vast majority of characteristics are influenced by both inheritance and learning. Consequently it is very difficult when observing the behaviour of a whole person to decide exactly which factors are modifying his responses. This matter is of considerable practical importance, e.g. to teachers who need to know the effects of maturation on learning in deciding when and how to teach certain subjects. Again probation officers and other social workers must determine whether deterioration in the behaviour of a previously normal individual is due to a particular stage in his development or is the result of adverse environmental conditions or is a mixture of both.

Psychologists have isolated some of the major problems in distinguishing between maturation and learning and a statement of these may give some perspective in the matter.

A. Many experiences are common to all people from a very early age, e.g. smiles from friendly persons, scowls from displeased persons, the attention of a loving mother or mother-substitute who supplies our essential needs, the existence of a father in a slightly more distant role. Again touch, gravity, temperature change, some pain and insecurity stimulate us all as children. How can these universal experiences be distinguished from the effects of maturation? A good deal of evidence as to the great importance of early experience has been obtained from experimental work on monkeys (e.g. rearing them in the dark or in constant light, confining their limbs to cardboard tubes during their childhood, etc.). It has been discovered that *variations* in stimuli falling on the young animal's sense organs are essential for normal development of the ability to interpret the environment (i.e. they have to learn to use their sense organs once they have developed adequate neuro-muscular links). Evidence from human development is less easily obtained but some information can be gleaned from cases where infants have suffered extreme forms of experience, e.g. great insecurity or pain, limbs in plaster or irons for extended periods. It appears that part of the basic pattern common to the development of all men is the result of common experiences. We all have primary relationships with parents, develop language and imagination, see varieties of colour combinations, suffer from the same basic physical limitations, etc., wherever in the world we live. Perhaps this accounts for some common human activities, e.g. belief in a god, use of rewards and punishment in learning, the telling of folk-tales handed down from previous generations, etc. This whole problem is very complicated, particularly in human beings whose behaviour is so readily modified by experience and social pressures.

B. While maturation may be essential for the development of a behavioural mechanism, we can only recognize the existence of the mechanism when it is used in response to the environment. This at once involves the concept of experience. As we shall describe below some forms of learning (called *imprinting*) can occur very rapidly indeed, e.g. baby ducklings learn to follow a moving object immediately after hatching. Once a behavioural mechanism has developed through maturation, learning improves its efficiency. Chicks can peck from the time they hatch but with experience their aim improves considerably. Young sexually mature birds can build nests but with each successive breeding season their nests become more perfect. In human beings we find that as soon as a child is physically competent to perform a response it tends to do so again and again (e.g. the child who can just walk keeps on walking and soon is rushing about through all his waking hours; the child learning to talk does so incessantly). Learning must be preceded by maturation but then the two processes supplement one another. Consequently periods of rapid growth and maturation are also periods of rapid learning.

C. Another complication arises from the fact that a severely abnormal environment can effect maturation. For example, shortage of food, great pain or anxiety, certain forms of illness or drugs can retard the growth of an individual and alter the ultimate level of development which he achieves. The results of such adverse conditions are obvious in extreme cases. In less severe forms they may also be important but not so easily recognized. How can we distinguish such environmental effects on maturation from those due to inheritance?

D. Even greater problems than the ones already quoted here arise for those psychologists who believe that learning is itself a process of growth of connections between neurons in the brain.

In general we can say that a person gains experience as he matures and he matures during prolonged experiences. If you consider the ability to perform a certain activity, e.g. precision in using a microscope, obviously older children are more efficient than younger ones. You cannot determine whether the more fully grown neuro-muscular mechanisms of the older children determine their superiority or whether their greater experience in general hand-eye co-ordination gives them an advantage. Almost certainly both factors are involved.

This particular example is related to physical maturation. How much more complicated the picture becomes when we consider social and emotional maturity which demand as prerequisites certain types of experience. Take as an example the fear which a six-month old child has of strangers. He must have had prior experiences of parents and siblings to be able to recognize strangers. As he grows up his fear of strangers may remain or diminish depending upon his experience of what effect they have on him. We consider that normal mature behaviour of an adult should not include fear of strangers. To reach this state however the individual must have had suitable prior experiences. Generally speaking, for teachers learning can be considered to be the process of becoming socially and intellectually mature. In order that learning can occur, however, a suitable level of physical maturation is essential.

It is useful at this point to mention the concept of *readiness* as a convenient term for describing the level of maturation and nature of suitable prior experiences essential for mastery of a given new task. To be ready to undertake a course of training to become a shorthand typist you must have the neuro-muscular control to write quickly and legibly and suitable experience and competence in the language which you are writing. A three-month old child is not ready in physical terms to begin to walk. A two-year old child is not ready in terms of experience to learn about summer and winter, or the concepts of miles or centuries. In more subtle forms the problem of readiness determines which subjects are taught to children at different ages. An introduction to the social sciences may have little meaning to the ten-year-old, is of more interest to the fifteen-year-old and is readily intelligible and important to most adults. Let us emphasize the point, however, that chronological age is not, in itself, a very useful guide in predicting performance. What a child is ready to learn depends upon his mental age, relevant past experiences, motivation, teacher-pupil relationship, etc. We shall return to this topic in Chapter 9. Let us now turn to a more detailed study of the processes of maturation and learning.

MATURATION AND DEVELOPMENT

In this section we shall attempt to isolate some of the changes in an individual's behaviour which appear to result from a gradual unfolding of his inherited endowment and to be relatively independent of the environment. Careful observation of large numbers of individuals demonstrate that at certain stages in development particular changes in appearance and behaviour occur in all human beings wherever they may live. Physical examples of such changes are ability to sit, stand, crawl or walk, while psychological examples are emotional differentiation, increase in ability to concentrate and to defer goal attainment, increase in sociability and decrease in selfishness, etc.

As a specific example of a maturation process let us consider communication through speech.[3] A new-born infant can make a noise but his vocal apparatus is not sufficiently differentiated for him to make a variety of sounds. He simply cries when he is experiencing a need. Quite soon, however, it is possible for his mother to distinguish between crying from discomfort (e.g. wind or a wet nappy), hunger and anger due to being put in his pram or left alone. The child at this stage can apparently differentiate between the needs he is experiencing and to a limited extent can communicate the particular type of need to others. By three months of age he will probably also be able to indicate that all his needs are satisfied by making 'cooing' noises.

Gradually the child's ability to make different sounds increases and besides making his own 'baby-noises' he may attempt to imitate his parents especially when they encourage him to do so. 'Da-da' and 'ma-ma' and later other words not only bring approval from adults, but also enable the child to obtain the end he desires. General babbling, on the other hand, is of less use to the child. Observations on the behaviour of children indicate clearly that they can understand a great deal more of what is said to them than they are able to repeat. Presumably this may be due in part to the fact that their vocal apparatus and the nerves supplying it are not yet fully mature. During a child's first year his range of sounds increases and soon he can say simple words and then string them together. Some sounds are more difficult to produce than others because of the fine control of the vocal apparatus which they demand. 'Sw' is often a problem and a child may ask for 'a meetie'. However the child can distinguish between the sounds 'meat' and 'sweet' when said by his parents.

This example of the development of language again indicates the close interrelationship between maturation and learning. All children develop the ability to speak and go through these same stages (i.e. the basic pattern is the result of maturation). The actual language which they come to speak, however, depends entirely on the environment in which they mature (i.e. is due to learning). In general, all new-born babies lack certain characteristics which are found in all adults, e.g. sociability, speech, locomotion. This change from simple infantile behaviour to sophisticated adult behaviour occurs in all people and the general pattern and timing of the phases of this change are universal. The actual form of the adult responses (his language, attitudes, beliefs, knowledge, etc.), however are determined by experience. The adult then is not just a large version of a child. During maturation he has moulded his responses according to environmental pressures. A person brought up in a home environment where controls and pressures appropriate to childhood are enforced in adolescence and adulthood will mature physically but will show behaviour more appropriate to an earlier stage of development. On the other hand a person encouraged to take initiative and decisions appropriate to his age will mature both in body and behaviour.

This concept is of the utmost importance to those teachers who think of themselves simply as imparters of information. If this is their sole function they are probably inefficient and very expensive alternatives to text-books. The prime function of a teacher must be able to encourage his pupils to develop attitudes and behaviour appropriate to their stage of maturation. This more positive approach to the effects of maturation on efficient teaching is much more constructive than regarding it as a limitation on how and when to present subject matter to pupils. To consider maturation as an inborn pattern which unfortunately we can do nothing about and with which we must compromise the logical academic arrangement of our subject matter is deplorable.

Earlier we described how nerve pathways transmit information from receptors to the C.N.S., through the C.N.S. and then out from it to effectors (muscles and glands). Obviously before such pathways are complete this passage of information is impossible. Until sensory pathways are complex enough to carry all the necessary information to the brain it cannot be properly perceived. Even if it reaches the brain, if this is as yet not fully developed, the interpretation and responses of which the brain is capable may be inadequate.

The Processes through which Behaviour Changes

Finally, if motor control of effectors is incomplete or not sufficiently delicate, suitable responses cannot be made by the individual. A basic concept of physical maturation then is the growth of receptors, effectors and neurons connecting them. Further, the more connections there are between neurons, presumably the more pathways are available for nerve impulses to travel through the nervous system and perhaps the greater the variety of behaviour which is possible.

Let us consider the growth of nerve connections more closely.[4] Nerve fibres (axons and dendrites) grow from embryonic nerve cell bodies. Examinations of sections of the cerebral cortex of children dying at different stages of development show that the number of cells present in the brain appears to remain constant. However, the number of connections between neurons increases very rapidly in early childhood and more slowly subsequently. It is obviously of great psychological interest to discover whether more connections develop as a result of brain activity. If this is the case it might in part explain why practice in a particular mental task improves efficiency in it and related tasks. Possible supporting evidence comes from observations on persons who are blinded at birth or soon afterwards by damage to their eyes. The visual areas of their brains, although not damaged, are relatively underdeveloped.[5]

Obviously, then a child cannot perform a given activity until an appropriate level of structural complexity has been achieved. The new-born infant has many muscles, which, as he develops, he becomes able to contract. However, he is not able to use them to cope efficiently with the environment for some time. His co-ordination gradually improves, his movements become less random and more directly orientated towards persons and objects. This may well be correlated with an increase in efficiency of connection between nerve cells in sensory, central and motor pathways. There are many specific examples of this which are obvious to those dealing with small children, e.g. improvement of hand-eye co-ordination, ability to sit, stand, crawl, walk, to hold a pencil and draw at first gross patterns and later finer ones. In general, a child can only perform those acts for which he has the appropriate neuromuscular equipment.

The extent to which behavioural changes are in fact the

result of neuromuscular development and not due to experience is difficult to assess. Some experimental work has been conducted on animals which throw some light on the problem. Creatures are taken at the beginning of a period during which fairly rapid behavioural changes normally occur and their experiences relevant to the responses under investigation are kept to a minimum. In cases where maturation is the major factor underlying these behavioural changes, the fact that the experimental individuals have been unable to practise (i.e. learn through experience) makes little difference to the sequence in which these changes occur and the ultimate end-point reached. A classic example here is the work on the development of swimming in salamander tadpoles.[6] An experimental group was anaesthetized so that the creatures could not move while a control group of normal individuals were practising swimming movements, ultimately becoming competent at movement through water. The anaesthetized group were released from sedation once the control group could swim and it was found that the experimental animals could straightaway swim efficiently without practice. Similar results have been found by preventing baby birds from practising flying until after the normal stage of competency, when they can then take to the air with little difficulty. Observations on human identical twins where one is allowed to practise walking or climbing stairs while the other is prevented from so doing until the first is fairly proficient also support the view that these processes depend to a very large extent on maturation.[7]

As far as the effects of maturation on more complex processes are concerned we have very little information.[8] It is extremely difficult to separate maturational effects from experience and practice. While, to some extent we can observe the gradual unfolding of physical maturation, it is much more difficult to identify maturation in emotional, intellectual and social terms. While we all improve in our ability to generalize and solve problems, our emotional stability and our social acceptability, so much of our improvement depends upon suitable experiences. It is artificial and pointless to attempt to segregate these two aspects of development in such cases and we shall return to a discussion of the interrelationship after looking more closely at learning.

LEARNING AND DEVELOPMENT[9]

We have previously considered 'learning' to be any more or less permanent change in behaviour which results from experience. Such changes may be of many kinds, e.g. the development of skills, the acquisition of knowledge, the modification of attitudes. The field which can be considered under the general concept of 'learning' is therefore extremely wide and, like 'maturation' or 'motivation' can be a possible approach to the whole subject of psychology.

In our first chapter we described how a simple animal like a jelly-fish responds in a stereotyped way to stimuli falling on its receptors. Although to a very limited extent such animals can modify through experience the way in which they react to a given stimulus, inborn patterns of response are generally quite adequate for their simple needs in their fairly constant environment. With more complex animals leading more varied lives it is impossible to conceive of stereotyped responses which will be adequate to cope with all the problems that they are likely to encounter. Consequently they need flexible patterns of behaviour which can be adapted to the circumstances in which the animal finds itself and which can be modified in the light of its previous experiences in that and similar situations.

An individual becomes more efficient in coping with a particular environment as he has more experience of it. At the same time the more specialized and adapted his behaviour becomes the less flexible it is for coping with new situations quite different from the first. For example, a small child with little experience of music will come to enjoy any kind of music frequently presented to him, be it native drums, Scottish bag-pipes, classical music or 'pop'. However, a child brought up very strictly on one particular kind of music only will usually have difficulty in accepting other forms later on. Similarly, older people have much more difficulty in accepting new standards and values than younger ones. We shall return to a fuller discussion of this in those chapters relating to group psychology.

By defining learning as a more or less permanent change in behaviour as a result of experience we avoid problems of including sensory adaptation (e.g. 'getting used to' the feel of your clothes, the ticking of a clock), fatigue, illness, changes in motivation, etc. However, there are still several, apparently different types of response which could come into this field of study. These range from the development of simple habits or the control of reflexes (e.g. not wetting the bed), through remembering (and forgetting) names and faces, to very complex reasoning and problem-solving behaviour. Although it is at present convenient to consider these as separate types of learning, as our knowledge of the processes involved is extended we may well have to modify our views. Certainly in most human learned behaviour it is possible that a combination of several of these so-called 'types' of learning are involved.

Throughout our brief introduction to learning we must keep in mind the fact that learning is the process by which an individual attempts to satisfy his needs by progressive adaptation to the environment. Therefore what an individual learns, or whether in fact he learns at all will depend upon such factors as his present needs (which determine the direction of attention and the level of activity), the present situation (with which his behaviour is designed to cope), his present level of maturation, his relevant previous experience, etc. Also once a change in behaviour is produced, whether or not it is repeated will depend very much on the consequences which the modification brings about in terms of need satisfaction.

In previous chapters some of these themes have already been elaborated. In this section we shall simply indicate some of the main areas in which psychologists studying learning are working. We shall begin with some aspects of remembering and forgetting, not because they are necessarily simple but because they appear to be more easily investigated and described than some other aspects of learning. We shall then very briefly survey some of the most important interpretations of learning suggested by the associationist and field theorist schools. Our theme will be completed by drawing together maturation and learning showing their interdependence in human development under normal circumstances in Chapter 9.

1. *REMEMBERING AND FORGETTING*. All learning is based on the picking up of experiences from the environment, the retention of them within the organism and the subsequent utilization of them in modifying future responses. So we

have progressive adaptation during life without returning to 'square one' for coping with each new situation that we encounter. It is obviously very important to investigate the nature of the process of retention. If a person can revive a prior experience without the assistance of the original stimulus we say that he has *remembered* the experience. If he cannot revive a past experience which previously he could remember, we say that he has *forgotten* it. In our later discussions we shall suggest that perhaps we remember modifications which improve our chances of coping with the environment and we forget those which detract from our success (although we may not be aware of much of this remembering and forgetting).

We generally think of remembering and forgetting in terms of human verbal responses. This is often the case. For example, two children come out of school together on the first day of the new term. Peter's mother asks him what his friend's name is. He says he does not know. At school next day the teacher calls Peter's friend 'Johnny Smith'. Later when Peter's mother presents the same stimulus to him, i.e. 'What is your friend's name?' he responds 'Johnny Smith'. His response to the stimulus from his mother has changed as a result of experience. Peter has learned which in this case involved remembering a name.

Take another common example of remembering, this time of a non-verbal sort. A young kitten urinates in the middle of the carpet. With several experiences of being disapproved of when starting to crouch on the floor, of being lifted on to a soil-filled tray in the corner and of being praised for urinating there, the kitten 'learns to be clean'. It remembers to go to the tray when it needs to. If the tray is moved to a slightly different situation the kitten will hunt for it, remembering some distinctive perceptual feature of it and also its use.

If Peter does not see Johnny Smith for some weeks or if the kitten goes to a cattery while its master is away on a fortnight's holiday, when they subsequently are given a suitable stimulus they will remember the correct response. However, if Peter moved to another part of the country and was not asked to recall Johnny's name until both were adult, or if the kitten was sold and did not return to the kitchen in which it was trained until several years later, then both Peter and the cat are likely to have forgotten the responses which they previously made to these stimuli. It is interesting to note, however, that both can relearn the association much more quickly once they are reminded of it than they could initially.

The kinds of question which psychologists ask about these processes of remembering and forgetting are much easier to pose than to answer.[10] What happens within the individual during retention? Does what is retained (i.e. the memory) remain constant or does it change during retention? What factors influence remembering and forgetting and are there optimum conditions for these processes? How does time influence retention? Is there a difference between long and short term memory? Although much interesting work has been carried out in this field there are still major gaps in our knowledge.

It is useful in theory but often difficult in practice to distinguish between two forms of remembering, namely recognition and recall. We say we *recognize* a person or object when on subsequent perception of it we find it is familiar, e.g. 'I know I have met you before', 'that view is very familiar', 'advance and be recognized'. On the other hand we may be required to *recall* (i.e. to call up again) a piece of information which we have retained from a prior experience and which is an extension of the information available in the present situation, e.g. 'I recall that your name is Peter Brown', 'This photograph was taken at Herne Bay last year'.

On careful analysis it is clear that the main difference between these two activities lies in the extent to which the individual who is remembering is required to indicate the characteristics of the correct response. In recall he must supply all the characteristics, e.g. 'What is the capital of France?' No hint is given as to the nature of the correct answer and all information must come from the memory of the individual. In recognition the individual may only have to isolate those qualities which distinguish the right answer from the wrong ones. For example, is the capital of France, Prague, Paris or Pisa? This is very much simpler. Another example may be taken from criminal identification. To attempt to recall and describe every detail of an individual is much more difficult than picking him out of an identification parade.

In most everyday remembering situations both recognition and recall are involved. Generally some information is supplied which can be recognized while some further details have to be recalled. For example, I see a person in the street. I recognize him and recall that he is one of my students. Again, I go into a classroom and recognize the faces I see as belonging to a group I have previously met. I may, however, be unable to recall which group they are or the names of the individuals. The list of common examples could be extended indefinitely. We can recognize words in a foreign language and recall their English meanings much more easily than the reverse process. We can often recognize a joke or story when we hear it for the second time much more easily than we can recall it when we might want to.

The nature of 'remembering' is not, as yet, understood. An interesting anomalous problem which has caused some speculation is the well-known phenomenon of false-recognition or *déjà vu*.[11] A person in a completely new situation may experience a very strong feeling that he has 'been there before'. Alternatively you can hold a conversation and feel that you have been through it on a previous occasion. 'I knew you were going to say that.' Various explanations have been suggested. It may be that the present situation has some characteristics in common with a previous one and you are generalizing from that. It may be that your 'recognition activities' have got 'out of hand' and you appear to recognize all your experiences for a moment or two. Perhaps this is supported by the finding that there is sometimes evidence of brain dysfunction in individuals to whom *déjà vu* occurs frequently and severely.

We must mention another aspect of remembering which is of great importance to students. Information once learned but then forgotten can usually be relearned much more quickly and easily at a later date than if it were being learned for the first time. This presumably represents a form of remembering of which the individual is not aware.

Before examining more closely some of the factors influencing remembering and forgetting let us remind ourselves of a general point which arose in Chapters 4 and 5. Remembering is rarely a process of exact duplication. We become personally involved in the percepts we form. We are selective of what we perceive and remember and we 'fill in gaps' to make our interpretations more meaningful. In many instances

179

these inaccuracies may not be important or obvious. However clear examples are often seen in the progressive distortions that may occur in accounts of their early days by elderly people.

A detailed account of the practical problems of remembering and forgetting is impossible here. We can only indicate some of the findings of researchers in these fields.[12] From our discussions on perception it will be obvious that the clarity and interpretation of incoming information will have very important repercussions on how well we can retain a memory of it. That which attracts attention, is clearly perceived, properly understood and obviously important to the individual is likely to be well remembered. That which is hardly noticed or seen very briefly, or is learnt 'parrot fashion' or seems unimportant is not likely to be remembered for long.

Once an item has been 'committed to memory' how can subsequent activity effect it? If we learned an item of information previously and now we revise[13] it this will obviously improve our memory of it. If we learn other relevant material which improves our knowledge and understanding of that previous item we shall remember it better. Conversely we may find this new related information easier to learn because of our previous experience. This is the basis of 'transfer of training'.[14] Previously it was believed that subjects like Latin and Greek 'trained the mind' and suited children for any subsequent career. Experimental evidence suggests, however, that this is probably not so and that transfer only occurs either through specific items of information, or through broad principles such as methods, attitudes and ideals. Evidence also suggests that such transfer is not automatic and the learner needs to be shown how these 'transferred' principles apply.

Subsequent activities can also have an adverse effect on previously learned material. A new lesson may make an earlier one less easily remembered especially if they are closely related to one another. Some interesting experiments on this 'retro-active interference' have been performed. If learners commit material to memory, sleep for say 6 hours and then waken and are tested for retention, they are found to be more efficient than comparable groups which learned the same material but were awake and active during the 6 hours before testing. Moreover, the more similar the activity

180

The Processes through which Behaviour Changes

between learning and testing is to the learning experience itself, the greater the loss in retention. This is probably the most common cause of forgetting. The reverse process also occurs where previous learning makes new related learning more difficult. For example, children that have been made to read and write in a slow meticulous manner in school, may well have great difficulty in scanning text-books or taking lecture notes as mature students.

We must take care not to make these processes appear too simple. Many studies have shown other facets of remembering and forgetting.[15] We have already mentioned 'repression' as an example of selective forgetting. Physiological studies on the effects of shock and their causation of forgetting under certain conditions may be very important here also. Again the relationship between remembering and more complex learning has been taken up by some psychologists. Memory is basically associative. We learn our multiplication tables or the alphabet in a given order and often to arrive at a certain piece of information we have to run through a preceding sequence of items. The basis of 'keep-sakes' or knots in handkerchiefs to act as reminders are again examples of the associative nature of remembering. Often in day-to-day experience one thing reminds you of another in some way associated with it. In the next section we must examine the stand-point that perhaps all learning is based on such associations.

Whether or not educationalists consider it desirable, a great deal of memorization is involved in learning tasks both in and out of school. The following suggestions for improving memorization have emerged from experimental findings.[16] As far as the learner is concerned, our earlier discussions indicate the basic importance of motivation. Interest must be stimulated and then maintained. This is usually best achieved through the learner being as active as possible in the learning situation. He should recite, revise, and where appropriate apply and extend the information he is dealing with. If possible he should overlearn by continuing to practise even after he feels he has mastered the material.

Turning to the organization of subject matter it is much more difficult to generalize. The task must first be clearly delimited and defined in terms of what has to be learned from it (e.g. meaning or order). If meaning is important, points giving general perspective should be tackled first. Perhaps a 'whole' approach to the subject followed by more detail on the most difficult areas is best (but evidence is not clear on this point). Where order is important, points to be learned together should be presented together. General consideration of distribution of practice periods, of mock-test situations, of sub-goals and the value of knowledge of results must be taken. The great influence of practical variables here is well summarized in Hunter's book listed in the chapter references.[17]

2. *WIDER INTERPRETATIONS OF LEARNING*. Let us briefly consider some apparently simple forms of behaviour changing through experience. *Imprinting*[18] is perhaps such a case. Chicks and ducklings have an inborn tendency to follow the first moving object which they see after hatching. Under natural circumstances this is likely to be their mother and the survival value of staying close to her is obvious. However, there is no way in which the baby bird can discriminate between its mother and other moving objects. In man-made experiments chicks can be hatched in an incubator and placed in a cage with a match box on a string. As the box moves the chick will follow it. Similar results are found in orphan lambs that form very close attachments to the human being who fosters them.

We have already mentioned *sensory adaptation* by which you 'get used to' a particular repetitive stimulus through adaptation of the sense organs to it. There is also a general tendency to decrease responses to frequent stimuli which prove to be of no importance to the individual. For example, town dwellers accept the roar of traffic and in fact find the countryside too quiet for them. Again horses learn to be docile in traffic and gun-dogs cease to take fright at explosions. As the sensory and motor pathways involved do not appear to be changed through this learning, it is presumed that the behavioural changes are controlled through the C.N.S. The dropping out of responses which are of no value to the individual is called *habituation*. It is apparently the reverse of most forms of learning which we shall describe in that habituation involves not responding to irrelevant stimuli, while most learning involves strengthening responses which are significant and valuable.

The Processes through which Behaviour Changes

These simple examples are apparently unimportant in most complex human learning. However, they do help to emphasize a most important point to which we shall return later, namely that at this very simple level learning can be considered as a kind of bonding process between a stimulus and a response. Physiologically this is of great interest for it makes possible a theory of some form of chemical change in the nervous system being correlated with behavioural change. We indicated such a theory in Chapter 2. At present, however, we have virtually no evidence to support such an interpretation.

When we come to more complex behavioural changes we must remember that the different descriptions and explanations put forward are to a large extent a reflection of the different approaches and procedures of different workers. The problems arising from the profusion of parallel or antagonistic interpretations have had repercussions in many quarters.

Probably the best known work in the field of learning is that due to the Russian physiologist Pavlov[19] and his followers early in this century. Basically, he trained an animal (usually a dog) to respond to a stimulus in a way which, prior to training, it had not done. For example when meat powder is blown into the mouth of a dog a reflex arc is activated which causes saliva to be secreted. This is an inborn response (i.e. it occurs without prior learning). Because salivation is produced without training it is called an unconditioned response (U.R.) to the natural or unconditioned stimulus (U.S.) of meat in the mouth. Suppose now that a buzzer is sounded just before meat powder is blown into the dog's mouth. Although previously the buzzer had no influence on salivary secretion, after a number of joint presentations of meat powder and buzzer, the buzzer will now cause some salivary secretion on its own. The buzzer is called a conditioned stimulus (C.S.). Learning has occurred as response to a stimulus (here the buzzer) has changed from 'no salivation' to 'salivation'.

This whole subject of *Pavlovian* or *classical conditioning* is very much more complex than is generally thought.[20] Some psychologists have attempted to explain all learning in such terms as these and we have several influential theories based on them. Such mechanical concepts, however, may well be too narrow and restrictive for interpretation of more complex learning. Nevertheless, Pavlov's meticulous, systematic, objective studies are of importance from the point of view of method. His findings relate to the grafting on of new stimuli to existing responses. Most human learning, however, can probably be more easily appreciated from the viewpoint of making new responses to a given stimulus.

Another very important interpretation of the learning process based on the concept of associations between two events is that of *operant conditioning*[21] or *trial and error learning*. A major pioneer in this field was E. S. Thorndike.[22] His classical work on cats in puzzle-boxes is fundamental here. A hungry cat was placed in a box from which it could escape only by pressing a 'release lever'. Food was placed just outside the cage and the cat's hunger drive caused him to attempt to escape. He bit, scratched, jumped and climbed around until finally, by accident, he pushed the release level and opened the door. After a small reward (a morsel of food) the cat was replaced in the box and left to escape again. Although the cat was apparently quite unaware of how to release himself, it was found that the time taken for the cat to escape decreased with each trial, i.e. there was a gradual reduction in incorrect responses.

This behaviour was, of course, not reflex. The cat 'decided' how to respond and made a number of quite different responses many of which did not achieve the 'desired' result. *Any one* however which involved the pressing of the release bar was rewarded, whether this involved pushing with nose, paws or hindquarters. This, of course, does not mean that the most efficient mode of response was tried first (or at all). The cat may have pressed the bar when racing madly round the cage. It may have associated this diffuse movement with escape and always performed this activity even though touching the bar with his foot would have been much more efficient. It is entirely possible that superstitious customs associated with certain human activities have a similar origin in that they were first performed in a 'trial and error' fashion in a complex situation where the correct response was not clear. Through subsequent reinforcement they have become integrated into the normal response.

Probably the most important modern exponent of this kind of theory is B. F. Skinner.[23] He suggests that human and animal learning is based on the principle that spontaneous random responses are made to a stimulus and that that which is reinforced will become associated with the original stimulus and be subsequently evoked by it. For example, a young baby will use his vocal apparatus to make a variety of sounds most of which have no meaning to its parents and which are ignored. However a few noises will bring parental reinforcement as when mother comes to the cot and praises the infant who has just uttered 'da'. In future the child is more likely to say 'da' than previously because of the reinforcement he has received from his parent.

Notice the similarities and differences between classical and operant conditioning. Both involve associations between responses and stimuli other than those to which these responses are normally or naturally given. For example, in classical conditioning the dog learns to salivate to the buzzer. In operant conditioning the cat pushes the lever to obtain food. However, there are some very important differences. In classical conditioning the stimulus for initiating the response comes from outside the animal, is under the control of the experimenter and is presented at the same time as the automatic response occurs. In operant conditioning the stimulus (or decision) as to which response shall be made comes from within the learner and is controlled by the learner. Of the variety of possible responses made the correct one is rewarded after its execution and its success is fed back into the organism.

There can be little doubt as to the associative nature of the forms of learning just described. The problem arising is whether or not all human learning can be explained in terms of this stimulus-response bonding. Exponents of operant conditioning hold that the components involved can be made sufficiently complex to meet all known examples of human or animal learning. For a full description of these techniques the interested reader should consult the specialist literature. Here we can only mention two examples. A learner performs again those activities which are reinforced and tends to drop others. By carefully selective reinforcement the teacher can direct behaviour more and more to the end which he desires. This is called *shaping*. In a comparatively simple case this is what happens when a nurse coaxes a patient from his ward by praising and encouraging steps taken towards the door. In

185

more complex instances it is the basis of programmed instruction[24] on teaching machines where the material to be covered is converted into a series of very small overlapping steps and the individual is 'encouraged' to work through them (see below).

Another important point is that of *second order conditioning*. If a buzzer sounds every time a hungry animal obtains a morsel of food then the buzzer sound will take on a pleasant association. A well-fed animal having been previously conditioned in this way will press a buzzer because it finds the sound pleasant. There may well be a parallel with this and the great value which some men put on money.

The mechanical nature of associationist bonding is rejected by many psychologists. They agree that under certain circumstances animals or people can be forced to resort to trial and error approaches to problem solving, e.g. in very complex or novel situations such as escaping from a complicated maze or trying to start a broken clock or television set. But these they say are artificial examples. According to their view we normally attempt to understand and see meaning and perspective in the problem with which we are coping rather than producing random responses and learning through selective reinforcement.

A very large and important group of psychologists called the Gestalt school suggest that mental processes cannot be analysed since wholeness and organization are features of such processes.[25] A well-known worker in the application of Gestalt principles to learning is W. Köhler who stresses that problems are solved and learning occurs, through the perception of essential relationships. Much of his most famous work has been performed with apes.[26] He developed the kind of problem solving situation in which the direct path to a goal was not available but where another indirect but visible path was open. For example he might suspend some food (bananas) from the top of the cage out of reach of the apes but present them with sticks, boxes, etc., with which they could build a 'pathway' to the food. He found that in general the animals would sit for a while viewing the situation and apparently 'puzzling' over the problem. Often a solution would 'suddenly occur' to them (the so-called aha-experience) and they would follow the indirect pathway to a successful

186

completion of the task. This ability to see relationships between parts of a problem and coming suddenly to a solution without previous trial and error approaches is called *'insight'*.[27] Köhler suggests that whenever possible apes and men use insight in problem solving and only use trial and error in the last resort, e.g. when no amount of examining a car's engine will cause it to start we may start a random form of kicking and hammering. In criticism of the work of Thorndike, Köhler suggests that if it had been possible for the cat to 'understand' the puzzle-box situation it would have used insight rather than trial and error in its problem solving.

We have emphasized the work of Köhler in this context. This is only for convenience of illustration. There are many other very important Gestalt psychologists working in related fields, besides important modern extensions of the original school. E. C. Tolman[28] and K. Lewin[29] are two important exponents of the theory that all behaviour is essentially 'goal-directed' and so should not be 'atomized'.

Let us conclude this discussion by repeating that there is still much controversy as to the nature of human and animal learning and whether or not all learning is basically of the same nature. The evidence gleaned from available sources is often conflicting. No one theory as yet explains all the facts. Approaches in general fall into two main groups.[30] First, we mentioned the associationists' interpretation who consider learning to be the establishment of mechanical bonds between stimuli and responses, produced to reduce needs within the organism and strengthened by use. Secondly, we discussed the field theorist approach which rejected the random, trial and error, mechanical analysis of learning and instead considered it to be much more a purposeful attempt to interpret (build up a mental picture of) the problem situation. Obviously this difference in concept is of fundamental importance to teachers who must decide whether to prefer habit-forming drills or meaningful explanations in their teaching.[31]

3. *PROGRAMMED LEARNING.* Much instruction today given to a large number of students by one teacher is clearly unlikely to provide for efficient learning by all class members. In such situations all individuals must work at the same rate,

usually determined by the teacher. Much of the lesson is spent passively by most class members, only a few asking or being asked questions and perhaps having some of their misconceptions corrected.

It is impossible with our present day numbers of learners to remedy the situation through decreasing student-teacher ratios to proportions where these difficulties will not arise. An alternative approach has been made through analysis of the roles of the teacher and the learner, extracting those activities which might be performed by means other than a personal teacher-student contact and devising alternative methods for performing them.

For example, many lessons may best be described as lectures modified by questions and answers. Such lessons are often basically a regurgitation by the teacher of factual information which the students endeavour to write down at the speed at which they hear it. If duplicated copies of the lecturer's notes were distributed to class members prior to the lesson, a much more accurate record would be available to them. Clearly it would be of little use simply to hand out such notes. They must be read, followed, understood and if appropriate, discussed or applied to examples. For a teacher to follow this procedure with a class is extremely desirable. In a large group however, the same limitations of personal involvement and activity apply as in traditional lecturing. A further stage in this sequence is provided by what can be described as a teaching programme. All the relevant information that the teacher wants to present to his class on a given topic is carefully prepared in simple steps, each step being a question or problem that is based on the points previously made. The learner following the material must work through each step (frame) in sequence, mastering each point before being able to proceed to the next.

Moreover, each student works at his own pace, is active in every step and has a check on his understanding of the material as he progresses. In many ways we have a teaching situation closely parallel to individual tuition. The student is rewarded (reinforced) after each response he makes by knowledge of the fact that he is progressing satisfactorily.

A further important point is that each frame has been

produced by the teacher (or some other expert) in conditions less stressful than those existing in front of a class. The fact that each step can be checked and discussed with other experts before presenting it to the students means that any idiosyncrasies or misunderstandings on the part of the teacher can be minimized before the material reaches the students. Also any ambiguities, omissions, etc. discovered in the use of the programme by a class, can be corrected before presenting it to further students.

Programmed instruction can take many forms. It may consist of printed programmes presented to the student through teaching machines of various kinds, or through programmed text books. The frames may be presented in a linear sequence with each step being simple enough to ensure its mastery on first encounter. Alternatively, a branched scheme may be used in which larger steps are taken and learners making incorrect responses are provided with remedial frames to clarify their thinking before being allowed to proceed. Some very sophisticated audio-visual devices for presenting programmes and receiving responses have been designed and computer assisted forms are being developed which greatly increase the potential flexibility of this form of instruction.

Programmed learning has had a very mixed reception among educators, for a variety of expressed reasons. Some of the more negative are legitimate criticisms based on the initial proliferation of poorly constructed programmes by enthusiastic pioneers in this field. Others are the result of apparent prejudice and misunderstanding. Teaching is considered to be an essentially 'human activity', and when B. F. Skinner first proposed techniques by which principles derived from his experiments on pigeons and rats in the laboratory could be translated into human classroom situations much indignation was aroused.

Another criticism commonly levelled is the inflexible presentation which such pre-arranged teaching material must have. A teacher (ideally) modifies his approach according to the performance of his students. A branching programme can only achieve this to a limited extent, a linear programme not at all. However, even though a teacher can detect a wider range of student behaviour than can a preset programme, he is often not able to do much about it in a large class, so perhaps the argument is more academic than is often realized.

A much greater problem relates to the fact that most learners (and teachers) have been trained to expect and accept conventional teaching situations, and they therefore tend to be dissatisfied with a programmed environment. If programmed learning is to become a fundamental technique of teaching, perhaps as part of a self-teaching environment, it would clearly have very great influences on, for example, timetables, streaming, examinations and most important of all on student-teacher attitudes both to each other and to the subject matter.

Many of these changes are likely to be improvements as they will be based on better understanding of the subject by the students and of the students by their teachers. Before this can occur on a really wide scale however, methods for overcoming the problems of setting up machinery for producing and evaluating programmes must be devised. The interested reader can follow many of these topics further in the bibliography.[32] However, here perhaps is a way of at least partially overcoming the gross inadequacies of educational systems all over the world where so much knowledge which is at present available only to the few, could be disseminated to enormous numbers of people to whom it would be of interest and value.

SUMMARY

1. The processes through which behaviour changes may be considered under two headings:

   a. *maturation* dependent on growth of the individual and relatively independent of the environment;
   b. *learning* brought about by experience.

2. These two processes are not alternatives to one another. They are two facets of the all-embracing concept of *development*. Maturation is the process of development of the capacities with which we learn. Learning involves the activities with which we exercise these capacities. They are inextricably entwined.

3. Many problems arise in an attempt to distinguish between maturation and learning, e.g.

190

The Processes through which Behaviour Changes

   a. many experiences are common to all people;
   b. to discover that a behavioural mechanism has matured it must be used (i.e. experience is obtained);
   c. severely abnormal experiences influence maturation;
   d. some explanations of learning are based on the concept of neural growth.

4. The concept of *readiness* is introduced as a useful psychological and educational principle. It describes both level of maturation and nature of suitable prior experiences necessary for the mastery of a new task.

5. There appears to be a basic pattern of human development at the physical, cognitive, emotional and social levels which is presumably due in part at least to maturation. We discuss the development of language as an example but this again emphasizes the close inter-relationship between maturation and learning.

6. The concept of maturation is of prime importance to educators who must realize that they are not just imparters of information. They must also encourage pupils to develop attitudes and behaviour appropriate to their stage of maturation.

7. Physical growth of nerve pathways is necessary before information can be transmitted and interpreted. (Evidence suggests that perhaps connections between neurons develop as a result of brain activity.) A child can only perform those acts for which he has the appropriate neuro-muscular equipment.

8. The interpretation of maturational effects on more complex processes is still in its infancy.

9. Considering 'learning' to be a more or less permanent change in behaviour through experience throws our definition very widely. While it is essential for efficiently leading a varied life in a complex environment the progressive adaptation of behaviour to external pressures is bound to lead to increasing rigidity.

10. There appear to be several forms of learning ranging from control of reflexes to complex problem solving. Do these differ in fundamental nature or only in degree? Important areas in which much psychological investigation is currently proceeding are remembering and forgetting, interpretations of more complex learning and the inter-relationship between maturation and learning in normal human development.

11. There are two major forms of remembering which are to some extent separable:

   a. *recognition* in which the individual is required to distinguish the characteristic features of an item, and
   b. *recall* where he must provide a complete description of it.

191

C.   *Relearning* can be used to demonstrate another example of remembering.

12. Remembering is rarely exact duplication as always the individual is personally involved and his memory of an experience may become progressively distorted. How accurate a particular memory is will be influenced by many factors, e.g. the clarity of the original percept, the nature of the retained material.

13. Once an item of information has been learned subsequent activity may influence the memory of it. This may lead to improvement (revision, transfer of training) or have an adverse effect (interference with or perhaps destruction of the memory). Other factors such as repression, shock, may also influence memory.

14. Memorization is probably much more important in everyday human learning than is generally realized and a few practical suggestions are given for its improvement.

15. Some forms of learning are apparently simpler than others (e.g. imprinting and habituation seem simpler than reasoning and problem solving). These simple forms are of great physiological interest for they suggest that at least some learning may have a chemical bonding basis.

16. More complex learning is open to many interpretations. Two main kinds of explanation are proposed, the stimulus-response associationist, and the field-cognition approaches. Pavlovian and operant conditioning are important examples of the former and the work of Köhler is illustrative of the latter interpretations. No one theory as yet explains all the available facts.

REFERENCES

1. For a useful discussion of the problems and views on this point see Fleming, C. M. *Teaching: A Psychological Analysis* (Methuen, London 1958) pp. 95–118.
2. For a further discussion of concepts of maturation and learning and their interrelationships see Hebb, D. O.: *A Text-book of Psychology* (Saunders, London 2nd ed. 1966; 1st ed. 1958) especially pp. 139–64.
3. See Watts, A. F. *The Language and Mental Development of Children* (Harrap, London 1944).
4. For a physiological discussion of neural growth see Young, J. Z. *The Life of Mammals* (O.U.P., London 1957) pp. 766–90.
5. For a discussion of this in context see Young, J. Z. *The Life of Mammals* (O.U.P., London 1957) pp. 788ff.
6. Carmichael, L. *Psychol. Rev.* Vol. 34, (1927) pp. 34–47.
7. See Gesell, A. and Thompson, H. *Learning and Growth in*

Identical Infant Twins, Genet. Psychol. Monog., 5 (1929) pp. 1–124.

8. For a general summarizing introduction see Mussen, P. H. *The Psychological Development of the Child* (Prentice Hall, Englewood Cliffs, N.J. 1963).

9. For an excellent comprehensive up-to-date discussion of learning see Bugelski, B. R. *The Psychology of Learning* (Methuen, London 1956).

10. For a comprehensive survey of experimental research on memory see Woodworth, R. S. and Schlosberg, H. *Experimental Psychology* (Holt, N.Y. 1954) Ch. 23.

11. See Hunter, *Memory* (Pelican, Harmondsworth 1964) pp. 39–41.

12. See relevant chapters in Collins, M. & Drever, J.: *Experimental Psychology* (Methuen, London 1952; 1st ed. 1926).

13. For some practical suggestions on improving efficiency of revision see James, D. E. *A Student's Guide to Efficient Study* (Pergamon, Oxford 1967).

14. For a brief discussion of 'transfer of training' see Lovell, K. *Educational Psychology and Children* (University of London Press, London 1960) pp. 128–32.

15. An excellent account of 'forgetting' is given in Hunter, I. M. L. *Memory* (Pelican, Harmondsworth 1964) pp. 218–80.

16. For further suggestions in improvement of memory, *ibid.*, pp. 140–3. See also Garry, R. *The Psychology of Learning* (Center for Applied Research in Education Inc., Washington 1963) pp. 55–78.

17. Hunter, I. M. L. *Memory*.

18. See Sluckin, W. *Imprinting and Early Learning* (Methuen, London 1964).

19. Pavlov, I. P. *Conditioned Reflexes* (O.U.P., London 1927).

20. For a discussion of some of the common oversimplifications of Pavlov's work see Barnett, S. A. *A Study in Behaviour* (Methuen London 1963) pp. 157–9.

21. For a brief introduction to operant conditioning see Stretch, R., 'Operant Conditioning in the Study of Animal Behaviour' in Foss, B. M. *New Horizons in Psychology* (Pelican, Harmondsworth 1966) pp. 287–304.

22. Thorndike, E. L. *The Fundamentals of Learning* (Teachers College, Columbia University, N.Y. 1932).

23. See Skinner, B. F. *Cumulative Record* (Methuen, London 1961; 1st edition 1959).

24. For a good introduction see Annett, J. 'Programmed Learning', in Foss, B. M. *New Horizons in Psychology* (Pelican, Harmondsworth 1966) pp. 305–26.

25. See Katz, D. *Gestalt Psychology* (Methuen, London 1951).
26. Köhler, W. *The Mentality of Apes* (Pelican, Harmondsworth 1957; 1st edition 1925).
27. For further discussion of 'insight' see Lovell, K. *Educational Psychology and Children* (University of London Press, London 1960).
28. Tolman, E. C. *Collected Papers in Psychology* (University of California Press, Berkeley 1951).
29. For an introduction to his general theory see Lewin, K. *Dynamic Theory of Personality* (McGraw-Hill, N.Y. 1935).
30. For an excellent treatment of theories of learning see Hilgard, E. R. *Theories of Learning* (Methuen, London 1958).
31. A very readable comparison of associationist and field theorist approaches is given in Russell, R. W. 'How Children Learn – Contemporary Psychological Theories of Learning' in *Studies in Education*, No. 7 (Evans Bros, London 1955).
32. For an excellent introduction to programmed learning and also for further valuable references see 'Programmed Learning' by John Annet in *New Horizons in Psychology*, ed. B. M. Foss (Penguin, Harmondsworth 1966) pp. 305–26.

Chapter Eight

The Integrated Control of Human Behaviour

INTRODUCTION

In the last four chapters we have discussed a number of mental processes (perception, motivation, emotion, maturation, learning, etc.) taking each in turn and examining it separately. While this made our task of description easier and enabled us to see perspective within each topic, the artificiality of such separation was constantly brought home to us. In each chapter we needed to refer to preceding and subsequent chapters to appreciate more fully the points we were discussing. The relationships between perception and motivation, motivation and emotion, motivation and learning and learning and maturation are clear examples here. Further, the observer of human behaviour will realize that apart from it being artificial to describe these processes separately, it is also inadequate to consider them as the sum-total of human mental activity.

We must now take a much wider view of human mental activity within which the processes previously described are basic components but where they are organized, integrated and extended into a complex system much more representative of the mental activities of human beings. The general term applied to these complex 'higher level' activities is *thinking*.[1] Obviously there will be tremendous variety among the activities which are classed as 'thinking'. Some will be primarily

195

concerned with perception and attention, e.g. *think* what you are doing, I was not *thinking* when I stepped off the pavement. Others put the emphasis on remembering, e.g. I cannot *think* where I met him before, I am trying to *think* of the quickest route. While motivation is involved to some extent in the previous examples, in some forms of thinking it is more obvious, e.g. when we express our needs and motives as 'wishful *thinking*' or (as we described in Chapter 5) when we daydream and our flights of fancy are directed by frustrated needs. Again the word 'thinking' can be used as a synonym for 'opinion' or 'belief', e.g. I always say what I *think*, or what do you *think* of the present government? Another general use of the word thinking involves all or most of the previously described processes where they are combined to achieve a given end, i.e. in problem solving.

The problems of formulating a widely acceptable working definitions of 'thinking' are very considerable.[2] Some psychologists follow the interpretation of John Dewey and conceive of thinking in terms of struggling with the environment and solving practical problems. This is quite different from contemplative detached representation of a thinker which is widely used in everyday language. Again, the layman will frequently consider thinking to be confined to reasoning and problem solving, distinguishing it quite clearly from daydreaming and idle fancy. On closer examination it proves impossible to draw a distinct line between these two forms of mental activity.

In general, any definition which narrows down a wide and ill-defined area of study is likely to exclude important information which may help to clarify the particular problems in which we are interested. Let us hold to the very wide concept that thinking is adaptive mental activity where adaptation is both to the external environment and the internal needs of the individual.[3] Thinking, then enables us to respond to the situation in which we find ourselves in the manner most likely to satisfy our existing needs.

Having thrown the net as wide as this we must now select certain focal points around which we can organize our discussion. As in other parts of this book, in order to facilitate the understanding of a complex end-product it is useful to follow a developmental approach. The best known and most comprehensive work in the field of development of thinking is that carried out by the Swiss psychologist, Jean Piaget. Although there are many other eminent workers in the same area a brief consideration of Piaget's work must suffice for an introduction to this vast topic of cognitive development.

Before turning to the theory of Piaget we must clarify our ideas on some of the basic tools of thinking to which we shall constantly refer. Firstly we must consider 'images', percepts revived after the sensory experience has ceased. Such 'past-percepts' are the basic units of much if not all of our thinking. Secondly we must examine the classification of the vast arrays of images which we accumulate during our lifetimes.* This is the process of concept formation. Thirdly we must consider 'language' not only as a means of communication between individuals but also a coding system for quick and efficient thinking. Although for convenience sake we shall look at these topics separately it is clear that they all develop concurrently and are interdependent.

IMAGES[4]

In our discussions of perception we described how we form a succession of 'mental pictures' or percepts representing the situation existing both in the outside world and inside our own bodies. These percepts we interpret according to our present needs, past experiences, etc., and are able to respond to them in a manner most likely to promote our survival or happiness.

Percepts are not lost when we cease to look at, listen to, touch or smell the object which we had previously perceived. They are retained in the mind as 'past-percepts' or *images*. Our percepts were received in a succession determined by the environment we were perceiving, our images also can be strung together in chains but now their order and combination is determined by the needs of the individual in whose mind they are stored. Rather as with a Meccano set we start with a collection of items determined for us (i.e. here percepts of the environment) but we can combine them or organize them

*Many psychologists consider that clear distinctions between images, percepts, concepts, etc., are undesirable. They are separated here for convenience of introduction.

to suit our particular needs and present purposes. This activity is fundamental to the process of thinking. Notice that we can only utilize images derived from previous percepts. We can combine parts of two different percepts and so imagine a mermaid or angel or fairy or we can draw an imaginary scene which we construct from many items each drawn from a different percept. We cannot, however, create an image without utilizing our previous experiences. For example men on Earth when trying to imagine what a creature from outer space might look like must conceive of it as having the qualities of objects or animals found on Earth (which may be quite inappropriate).

In general, how well you can cope with your environmental problems depends on how suitable your past experiences are for enabling you to be successful. If you live in a fairly stereotyped environment, e.g. a tribesman in the jungle, you may simply need to recall complete situations and how you dealt successfully with them before. Such a tribesman can become extremely efficient in his limited environment. Most of us, however, live in such complex variable environments that this kind of reproductive imagery is quite inadequate. We have to utilize creative imagery synthesizing parts of many percepts to deal with the new situation. The necessity for providing children with a wide variety of experiences in order that they may develop into successful, well-balanced, healthy individuals cannot be over emphasized.

There can be no doubt that most of us use imagery in much of our thinking. Whether all thinking in fact involves imagery is a matter of dispute among psychologists and philosophers and there is no point in us following the argument here. Let us concentrate on that area of thinking which is based on imagery.

Just as individuals differ in terms of the efficiency of their memories or the speed and clarity of their perception or the strength of their motivation so they show different degrees of competence in their ability to organize and reorganize their images. These variations are reflected in the creativeness of the person, e.g. in constructing new solutions to problems, in invention, or the production of artistic and literary originals, even in the dreams which he has. Not only do individuals differ in the strength, clarity and flexibility of the images

198

they form, but also they may utilize different sensory modalities from one another, i.e. some form predominantly visual images, others mainly auditory or tactile images, or in appropriate instances images of smell, taste or the sensation of movement. In most people it appears that images are mainly visual with other types of sensation being present but to a more limited extent. Certainly most of us learn more efficiently material which we can see as well as hear and (particularly in young children of limited experience) being able to handle the material also is of great value in this direction. Here then is another reason why teachers should use a variety of forms of presentation of subject matter to their pupils. (We have previously mentioned that such variety helps in clarity of perception, reduction of boredom, and also reinforcement of learning.)

There is another aspect of individual differences in imagery which is of considerable social importance. Different people with different past experiences will view a given situation differently and, if it is a problem situation, will see different solutions to it. How often an outsider can help us to overcome an apparently insuperable difficulty by bringing a fresh mind to bear on it. Many professional bodies call in persons from quite different spheres to advise them on tackling general problems. On a personal level an individual in trouble is more likely to be understood by a fellow of similar background and experiences than by someone of very different background, a student from overseas coming new to this country is likely to be helped most by advice from his fellow countrymen who had similar upbringing to him and have now adapted to the British way of life.

We have introduced the concept of 'understanding' one another in this last paragraph. In this context two people can be considered to understand each other when they view the same situation in similar ways (i.e. they have the same past experiences, present needs, etc., in relation to it.) Consider a common example of a teenager coming in late at night and being challenged by his father for doing so. The lad may complain that his parents do not understand him. (The converse is equally probable.) The situation of the boy coming in late is perceived quite differently by the two parties concerned. The boy sees this as a successful activity indicating his ability to be independent, to act like an adult. The parents view it as an unacceptable situation causing them concern, perhaps making them lose sleep or feel that the control which they have exercised for so long is being taken from them. The two generations *think* differently about the given situation and can be said to misunderstand each other.

In general, when we are talking about everyday events or objects to persons from the same background as ourselves the likelihood of gross misunderstandings is probably small. However, when persons from very different backgrounds discuss even the most basic everyday activities, the case is quite different. Take the new health visitor or social worker meeting a problem family for the first time. How differently they might view, for example, parental responsibilities, disciplining of children, priorities on which money should be spent, etc. As the worker meets more and more problem families her background widens to include suitable past experiences and subsequently she is much more competent to understand and cope with the problems of her future clients.

Two other points in relation to imagery might be mentioned here for they will arise again in later chapters. If one sits quietly in an unobtrusive environment or lies awake in bed, or even performs a humdrum task which does not involve much 'thinking', one finds that 'one's mind runs on' from one thing to another following lines which are of particular interest. Each thought one has can arouse many other related thoughts and the individual must select which one to follow. The line each of us selects will be determined by our present needs or interests or past experiences. If we are concerned about something (e.g. your husband forgetting your birthday, your favourite girl-friend leaving you for someone else, a feeling of fear or guilt) your line of thought will repeatedly return to it ('I can't get it out of my mind'). If a person is suffering from a nagging fear or persistent irrelevant line of thinking a therapist may use 'free association' to attempt to elucidate the problem. The individual is asked to describe his chain of thoughts and any predominant themes become apparent. (The technique is much more complex than we have suggested here.)

Some people have such vivid images that they mistake them for percepts. These vivid images are called *hallucinations*.

200

(There is evidence to suggest that the line of demarcation between images and percepts is by no means clear). In extreme cases these hallucinations can form an imaginary world in which the individual lives, cut off from reality. He may see visions, hear voices, etc., which exist only in his mind. We shall refer to this topic again in Chapter 14.

CONCEPT FORMATION[5]

So far we have discussed images as separate unique items of information stored in the mind. If you consider the vast array of such images which you could collect in a lifetime, it is obvious that it would prove to be very unwieldy unless it was organized in some systematic way. In our modern complex world this problem of organization is a common one. The biologist faced with an enormous diversity of living things, the librarian with extensive collections of books or a department store selling a great variety of articles all have evolved systems of classification which in essence consist of placing more similar items together in a category separate from other less similar items. Those classes which have some common quality can be placed together in a 'higher-order' category and so on until a systematic hierarchy has been constructed using 'similarity' as the criterion for sorting and placing. For example, in a shop, a host of types of sock are all put together on a sock-counter, while slippers are put on another counter, shoes on another, laces on another, etc. Each of these different classes contains many separate items. These classes could all be put into a single category (the footwear department) for greater simplification. This department together with those of dresses, coats, underwear, etc., could all be placed together in a very large category (the clothes shop).

The human mind copes with the information it receives in a similar way. For example we have in our minds the category of 'tree'. Into this go enormous numbers of different items each unique but all sufficiently similar to be classed together and separated from herbs or bushes or seaweed. These latter each have their own separate category yet for simplification all these categories could be put into the higher order class of 'plants'. These mental categories into which we file information

are called *concepts*. It is to a very brief discussion of the
development and utilization of concepts that we must now
turn.

Among the questions which psychologists ask about
concepts, three seem to act as focal points for investigation.
a. How do we first form mental categories out of a variety of
unique experiences? *b*. How do we place a new experience
into an already existing category? *c*. To what extent and in
what ways do categories change with increasing number and
range of experiences? While a great deal of investigation
has been carried out in these fields we are only now beginning
to scratch the surface of the problems involved.

Each item we perceive has many qualities, e.g. of form
(shape, size, texture, etc.), of possible function, of emotion or
memory-arousing ability, and so on. It is the combination of
such qualities that an item presents that makes it unique. We
develop the ability to recognize these individual qualities of
an item, and abstract those of interest to us while ignoring
the rest. All items showing a particular quality can be put
together into a group (or concept) labelled according to the
quality which they share. For example, oranges, balls, the
moon or balloons all have the same shape. We give this a
name (sphere) and put all these objects and any others of
the same shape into a concept to which this name is given.
Again we can extract the function of 'being a centre for the
treatment of patients' from a variety of buildings. Buildings
performing this function we place in the category of 'hospital'.
Hospitals may be big or small, old or new, mental or general,
brick, stone or wood. The only feature which they must share
is the general quality taken as the characteristic of the concept.
If subsequently we come across a mud hut which is used as a
centre for treating patients, then this comes into the concept
of 'hospital'. Another type of concept is related to affective
similarity, e.g. gunfire overhead, being told off, stepping in
front of a car, etc., are all classed as dangerous experiences
because they all arouse the emotion of fear in the individual.

The value of this mental categorization is obvious. We
perceive a variety of experiences. For convenience of coding
we select certain qualities common to several or many
experiences and we learn these qualities. We can recognize
them again in other experiences and so place any new item

in relation to our earlier experiences. Notice however that these categories (or concepts) are invented by us for our own convenience in dealing with the environment. Consequently the categories we form will depend upon our present needs and past experiences. While in concrete qualities such as shape, colour and number there will be very little disagreement between individuals, with more intangible qualities such as beauty, honesty and morality, the effects of learning, motivation, etc., will produce much more varied results.

Concept formation, then, involves making recognizably different items equivalent to one another for ease of interpreting the very complex and variable environment. Efficient thinking is based on the ability to abstract the most important qualities of items while ignoring those of less importance. Skill in concept formation is closely linked with level of development of language and it is to this point that we must next turn.

LANGUAGE

While we generally think of language as a means of communication between individuals, this is only one of its functions; just as language enables us to control and guide other people, so it enables us to control and guide our own thought processes.[6] We have discussed some aspects of language in the form of intercommunication between individuals in various other parts of this book.[7] Here let us concentrate on its use in our own thinking, much of which is performed in words.

A moment's reflection will make clear the fact that many of the images we use in our thinking are word images. Not only would it be very slow but also very difficult to convert into a visual image of an object or event every thought which we perform. Further if we were to think of a single visual image of a single example of our thought content this would be very limiting and usually quite inaccurate for general thoughts. Take as an example the use of the word 'development'. When we use this word in our thinking we do not normally imagine a single actual example of the process. Rather we use the word 'development' having learned by a variety of previous experiences those qualities which this concept represents.

Small children, limited both in experience and vocabulary

form only broad and ill-defined concepts. As they gain more experiences and develop an increasingly precise vocabulary to act as a vehicle with which to describe and classify the qualities of these experiences, so the concepts which they construct become more accurate, detailed and valuable. Notice that the content of an individual's vocabulary is largely determined by the experiences which he has and wishes to describe. In this country our contact with snow is limited and we have but a few words for describing those various states of it which are important to us, e.g. slush, sleet, ice and snow. Any more precise description involves the addition of adjectives, e.g. firm, deep, drifting, powdery. To an Eskimo snow is of the utmost importance, slight variations in its form influencing the whole of his activities. In the Eskimo language we find a very large number of words which describe specific conditions of snow. In a native language from a tropical area there may well be no word for snow at all, or simply one related to white caps of very high mountains. Similarly Zulus who depend very much on cattle for their livelihood have upwards of a hundred terms specifically used in descriptions of them. In English we have very few (although more in the vocabulary of a dairy farmer than of the man in the street). For a person with no contact with a particular type of experience there is no need for a concept or terms to describe it. In human beings, to be deprived of sight or hearing is very serious and affects the whole of the individual's life. We have terms (blind and deaf) to describe these conditions. To be deprived of smell or taste is much less serious and so we have no common term for such deficiencies. As the Soviet psychologist A. R. Luria[8] has said, language is 'the essential means whereby the child finds his bearings in the external world.'

It follows from what we have said above that language development and concept formation are closely interrelated. Language is used for concept description, analysis and synthesis. We use a word to represent a concept and we combine words to make new concepts. You can only form true concepts when you cease to attach the concept label only to a given example of the concept and attach it instead to the general qualities for which the label stands (e.g. big or green, or animal). When we can do this we can combine and compare qualities and refine and improve our concepts. Most complex thinking and learning are performed in words which carry these abstracted and generalized meanings.

THE DEVELOPMENT OF THINKING

Earlier in this chapter we considered the nature of thinking and discussed it in terms of the organization, integration and extension of basic psychological activities such as perception, motivation, learning, etc. A comprehensive survey and interpretation of the development of this process is a colossal task and several different approaches have arisen. The interested reader should consult 'Child Development' by C. M. Fleming in *N.Z.T.C.A. Journal*, No. 5, 1966. Here we shall take the approach of Professor Jean Piaget of Geneva as an example of an investigation of intellectual development and then briefly consider some of his critics.

1. *PIAGET'S THEORY OF THE DEVELOPMENT OF THINKING* Piaget examines the whole sweep of development of thinking from birth to adolescence. His work is based on detailed observations of children both in his own family and in schools to which he has regular access. He has produced a wealth of records and has constructed a theoretical interpretation for many of his findings. Here we can do no more than indicate one or two general points arising from his work.[9]

From his investigations Piaget suggests that during development each of us goes through a series of stages of complexity in our ability to think. We progress from a simple 'reflex' type of organization at birth to formal logical reasoning in the adult.

The individual builds up in his mind a 'working model' of the environment in relation to himself. This model becomes more complicated and detailed both as the nature of the thought processes of the person becomes more complex and as experiences of the environment increase. The model must be constructed in every dimension and detail and is constantly being modified and refined. This mental construct is used in all his thinking (Piaget considers thinking to be 'inward activity') and his level of thinking will be limited by the level of development of his mental construct. At the primitive level this will place great emphasis on the perceptual features of an item, while at more advanced levels fuller understanding through concepts and language will become possible.

By the time we are adults much of our thinking is 'second nature' to us, the mental skills involved having become habits, and we are not usually aware of the mental activities involved. As in so many mental and physical situations it is only when 'things start to go wrong' that we realize what is going on during these activities. When we come up against an intellectual obstacle which we must surmount we ask ourselves how we got to our present position, what the present deficiency in our thinking is and what else is necessary for us to solve our problem.

Piaget, then, sees adult thinking as the end-product of a process of development involving both maturation and learning. Initially it involves 'action in terms of images'. Later as language develops these images are replaced more and more by verbal symbols. Eventually thinking is emancipated from the concrete facts of the environment and can operate freely in the mind of the individual. Such 'abstract thinking' is the basis of the logical, mathematical and scientific thinking characteristic of the adult human mind.

Piaget sees the development of thinking as following into five main stages based on the kind of operation (mental activity) of which the child is capable. The ages ascribed to each stage are representative of the children whom he tested and found competent at these levels of operation.

Stage I from birth to 2 years is called the sensori-motor stage. This name emphasizes the very close link between sensation and reflex response found in very young infants. As they develop, however, their motor responses become more controlled. Co-ordination between, e.g. hand and eye, or eye and ear improves. At the same time the initial lack of comprehension of space, time and the constancy and persistence of the environment is replaced by a crude mental 'working model' with which some understanding and anticipation of their reactions and their surroundings is possible. They expect objects to have a constant shape or size from whatever angle or distance they are perceived. They expect objects to persist even if they cannot be seen. They being to experiment and explore their bodies and their environments. By the time they are 18 months old they will be able to control their environment to some extent. Their 'mental models' will enable them to imagine, plan, remember and pretend. Piaget says their actions are becoming internalized.

Stage II from 2 years to 4 years is the preconceptual stage. In this phase a start is made in the development of concepts but the child is easily confused. However as this stage progresses there is considerable improvement in the ability to classify which is closely linked with the rapid development of language during this period. Words at first represent physical objects, needs and actions. They are also convenient symbols to represent absent objects. They can be manipulated and are used in imaginary games (e.g. sugar and water is dolly's cup of tea, soil is bird's food, mummy is a nurse or a lady on television). This period is one of great expansion and practice at using the ever-improving mental model of the environment. The child spends much of its time asking questions, exploring, experimenting and imagining.

Stage III from 4 years to 7 years is the intuitive stage. The lines of development initiated in early stages continue to progress. More elaborate images are formed and fitted into more precise and systematic schemata. As language develops there is an increase in efficiency and flexibility of thinking. Piaget describes a considerable 'increase in internalization of action' but thinking is still tied much more closely to perception than is the case in the adult. Major limitations in efficient dealing with the environment are obvious in children of this group. For example, they can only consider one dimension of a problem at a time. If you show them a ball of clay and then roll it out into a sausage shape most children will report that the sausage, being longer, contains more clay than the ball did. They cannot, at this stage, look at the whole problem, relate dimensions and appreciate conservation (i.e. here constancy of mass of clay). Similar confusion is found between other dimensions, e.g. distance, length and movement. Another limitation lies in their inability to retrace the steps in their thinking to remedy a mistake or determine how they arrived at a given conclusion. However, in all processes of thinking there is a gradual movement in the direction of more efficient, less perceptually-tied mental activity.

Stage IV from 7 to 11 years is the stage of concrete operations. Piaget uses the term 'operation' for an action which can be carried out in thought and which is reversible. Such thinking operations gradually develop in children during this stage but they can only be applied to concrete objects and cannot be used in relation to verbal concepts until the final stage of development. To quote a classic example, a child at the concrete operational stage can arrange a collection of sticks in order from the shortest to the longest. However, he will not be able to solve the problem: 'If Bill is taller than Fred but shorter than Jim, who is the tallest boy?' until he has passed into the final stage of development. This stage then shows a definite advance towards adult logical reasoning, a dawning of appreciation of conservation, of relationships between dimensions and an ability to reverse thought processes. However, these activities are limited to the level of application to concrete concepts.

Stage V the stage of formal operations which normally extends from 11 years to 14 years but is sometimes never fully attained. This really represents the attainment of fully developed adult thinking. Piaget says that the ability to apply logical rules to abstract problems is the basis of intellectual growth and ability. The individual is no longer tied to actual happenings but can extend his thinking through hypotheses to what might be possible. He can use symbols, manipulate a number of variables at once, combining and reversing them. He can generalize from a few instances and having done so can criticize his own thinking. In general terms, he is concerned with the 'form' of his thinking rather than with the concrete content. Hence the name 'formal operations' for this level of thinking.

The interested reader should consult the original work of Piaget[10] and his colleagues but be warned that these writings are both voluminous and in general difficult and technical.

2. *A CRITICISM OF PIAGET'S APPROACH*[*][11] Obviously the problems of child development are as old as the human race itself. Some early interpretations of child-rearing while generally considered to be inadequate are still not dead in some quarters. As an example some psychologists cite the tendency to put emphasis on classification into types and stages and to ignore variability and range of differences

[*]I am indebted to Dr C. M. Fleming for much of the material in this section.

between individuals. These views can only be justified (say the critics) by collecting illustrative examples to substantiate a previously formulated theory.

Early in this century objective mental testing became established. Large samples of children were observed or interviewed and conclusions were drawn based only on the evidence so collected. These cross-sectional studies when applied to different age-groups gave indications of the ways in which *populations* of children were developing. A major limitation here was that averages and percentages were used to describe results and these failed to indicate variations observable within a group. Great irregularity is found in the mental development of individuals and the value of comparing the average score of 50 six-year-olds is limited.

Since about 1930 great importance has been attached to the case-studies of individuals over long periods. Fleming suggests that 'these render obsolete the previous approaches' and that they 'are now the only methods which offer findings worthy of serious consideration'.

Following this line of argument Piaget's theory of genetically determined stages of growth can be attacked. For example, Fleming vigorously refutes his conclusions based on the vocabulary of children. Piaget records the vocabulary used by certain children in response to certain questions at certain ages and offers this in support of his theory of clearly defined 'stages'. He is presumably assuming that children at a given 'stage' are all alike. Fleming criticizes him for giving no information 'as to the antecedents or the present circumstances of the pupils', or 'of their general mental ability or the kind of teaching which they had received. There was no means of identifying any one pupil at a later age or with respect to a question in another field. It was taken for granted that if a child did not answer a question in a certain fashion he was "biologically" unready for functioning at a certain level of thinking with regard to all other such questions. In the nature of things this was not proved by the type of evidence supplied.'

Summarizing her criticism, Fleming suggests that we should ask three questions of Piaget's enquiries:

i. How were his investigations planned?
ii. What statistical techniques were used in the analysis of their results?

Introduction to Psychology

iii. From these methods and procedures in the author justified in drawing the conclusions which he offers?

Many developmental psychologists stress that the differences between thinking and learning processes of adults and children are quantitative, not qualitative as Piaget suggests. Children develop gradually, at different rates in different circumstances and their maturing at any one time is not of exactly the same pattern as that of others among their contemporaries. The implications for teachers, parents and in fact everyone involved with young people are very great indeed. Nevertheless this area of psychology is still one of the most controversial.

PROBLEM SOLVING

Having discussed some of the basic tools of thinking and the main stages in development of ability to manipulate these tools, let us complete this chapter with a brief examination of one of the major ways in which an adult thinks namely 'problem solving'.[12]

By problem solving we generally mean finding a response which will bring satisfaction of a need in a situation where the way to such an end is not immediately clear. For example, discovering how to cut a piece of linoleum so that it fits neatly round the leg of a gas-stove or defining 'psychology' in a way which is generally acceptable.

Obviously there will be more than one way in which such problems may be tackled. If the individual had absolutely no relevant prior experience he would behave like the cat in the puzzle-box described in the last chapter and would use trial and error. He might snip away at the lino and keep comparing the resulting hole with the stove leg. He might suggest some definitions of psychology and observe whether others agreed with him or not. However, the responses he makes will probably not be entirely random. He is likely to snip in an area which previous experience suggests is about right. He will probably use scissors or a blade for cutting rather than banging a hole with a hammer. Even in a problem where you have no direct knowledge of the situation you will normally have some relevant past experience. If your car has refused to start you may open the bonnet and be unable to decide what is wrong. You are more likely to tap with a hammer or tighten nuts (which *might* prove helpful) than to pour cold water over the engine or give it a coat of paint (which prior experiences of life in general suggest are likely to be harmful). The gradual movement from random to more selective responses in an attempt to solve the problem of communication is seen in the development of language in small children.[13]

In adults there is usually some relevant prior experience available. Providing the problem can be defined and the desired end is known trains of images or their representations can be aroused and directed towards possible solutions. The systematic organization of such trains of mental activity from a problem towards possible solutions we call *reasoning*. Basically this involves seeing relationships between parts of the problem and calling up other relevant information to help in its solution. (We shall return to a discussion of this in Chapter 10 under 'intelligence'.)

In much thinking the individual is apparently aware of the steps through which his reasoning is proceeding. For example, in working out the floor area of an irregular room or deciding how to spend the week's housekeeping money a person may divide the problem up into small portions, solve each in turn and then combine the results. However, at other times, many steps may apparently be worked through without the individual being aware of them as when, for example, the answer to a problem which previously one could not solve suddenly becomes obvious. In our discussions of attention in Chapter 4 we described how we selected and became clearly aware of some aspects of the environment while apparently not noticing others. For example, a person can drive along a road concentrating on coping with traffic and not being aware of his perception of the features of the surrounding countryside. Later if he goes back along this road again without realizing it, he may feel that it is familiar to him. Some perception has gone on without his being aware of it at the time.

There is some evidence to suggest that perhaps thinking may also go on without our being aware of it.[14] When for example we 'sleep on a problem' or in an examination our initial reading of the question paper makes us think that we cannot answer certain compulsory questions, yet when we return to them later we can see the answers much more clearly, presumably some relevant mental activity has been performed in the intervening period. How this comes about is not known. Perhaps trial and error or reasoning processes go on without knowing it, or perhaps redirection of attention away from the problem enables our minds to become more flexible or refreshed in relation to the difficult situation. On returning to it we are better equipped to cope with it.

Often 'problems' met in everyday life are really collections of interrelated problems. These must be separated and analysed before solution is possible. The clear defining of a problem is the first essential step in its solution and is often one of the most difficult.[15] Students frequently have trouble in coping with examination questions until they have mastered this art. Once a problem has been defined its solution can be obtained if recollection of necessary relevant prior experiences is possible and combinations of them to meet the present problem are achieved. These can be made into mechanical processes, machines so programmed being called 'electronic brains'.[16]

Most human problem solving is achieved by breaking down the problem into a series of questions, the answer to each in turn being suggested and tested. For example, a baby cries in the night. His parents ask themselves what might be the cause for his disturbance. The suggestions they put forward will depend on their prior experiences. Is he cold? They could check this by feeling him but this might disturb him more. They might reason that he is in a warm sleeping bag in a centrally heated house and it is not a very cold night anyway. Perhaps he is hungry. They recall his recent apparently adequate feed. Is he frightened or not tired or teething? They put forward as many suggestions as they can 'think of' and attempt to test each one either by direct investigation or by reasoning. If their relevant past experiences are inadequate for them to find an answer to their problem, they may turn to someone with more relevant experience, e.g. a doctor or psychologist.

The basis of problem solving and perhaps all adult thinking involves possessing suitable past experiences which can be efficiently manipulated to meet problems when they arise. Consequently teachers and parents must educate their charges both in factual material and in ability to utilize it'.

SUMMARY

1. The basic mental processes are perception, motivation, emotion, maturation and learning. These are integrated and expanded in the human mind to form a complex system of 'higher level activities' or 'thinking'. This term covers a very wide spectrum of activities and there is much disagreement as to when and how it should be used.

2. The basic units of much, if not all, thinking are 'images' which are 'past percepts' revived after sensory stimulation has ceased. Their revival can be in any combination which suits the particular needs and interests of the individual.

3. Since images are derived from previous percepts how well you cope with present problems depends upon the suitability of your past experiences. Imagery may be pure reproduction of a prior experience, but often it involves the creative synthesizing of several previous percepts.

4. We use imagery in most if not all of our thinking. Just as individuals differ in the efficiency of their memory or perception or in their strength of motivation so they show variations in their ability to imagine. Moreover they differ in the sensory modalities which they utilize.

5. Images are unique to the individual. Therefore different people see the same situation differently and suggest different solutions to it. This in part explains the value of a fresh mind on a problem. In general, people from the same type of background are unlikely to have gross differences of interpretation but great discrepancies can occur, e.g. between a social worker and a problem family over such matters as parental responsibilities, financial priorities, etc.

6. Free association occurs when you are in an unobtrusive environment and you let your thoughts run on. You select those trains of thought which interest you. If you have a persistent fear or need this will tend to recur in your thinking. Some forms of psychotherapy utilize this technique in discovering possible causes of mental disturbance.

7. Sometimes images are so vivid that they are mistaken for percepts. In extreme cases, these hallucinations can form an imaginary world cutting an individual off from reality. He sees visions and hears voices or other sounds which exist only in his mind.

8. The vast number of images accumulated during an individual's lifetime are classified. Their categorization is based on similari-

213

ties, e.g. of form, function, emotional association. Each category is called a concept.

9. This mental categorization is a very convenient method of coding, storing and recognizing experiences. Which categories we form will depend on present needs and past experiences. In concrete qualities such as shape, colour, number, etc. there is probably little difference between individuals. In intangible qualities, e.g. beauty, honesty and morality their effects on learning, motivation, etc. can have much more varied results.

10. Language is not only a means of communication between individuals, it is also a coding system which permits quick, efficient thinking. An individual's vocabulary is determined by the experiences he has had. Therefore language development and concept formation are very closely linked. Most complex thinking and learning are performed in words.

11. Piaget's work on the development of thinking is based on voluminous detailed records of individual children. He has constructed theoretical interpretations of many of his findings, suggesting that each of us goes through a series of stages of cognitive development from simple reflex activity to formal logical reasoning and thinking.

12. Some psychologists (e.g. C. M. Fleming) severely criticize Piaget for his use of small numbers of individuals and his subsequent generalizations. They also accuse him of selectively using his findings to support a preconceived theory.

13. Problem solving is an example of a process using all those areas of thinking previously described. If an individual has no relevant prior experience it is likely that a trial-and-error approach will be used. Generally some past experience is available and the systematic organization of this into possible solutions to the problem is called reasoning.

14. There are strong indications that problem solving behaviour can go on without the individual being aware of it, but the processes involved are not clear. In general, problem solving appears to involve manipulating suitable experiences in original ways to meet new problems as they arise. This surely indicates the areas of responsibility of teachers and parents.

REFERENCES

1. For comprehensive discussions of this field see, e.g., Humphrey, G. *Thinking* (Methuen, London 1951) or Bartlett *Thinking: An Experimental and Social Study* (Allen & Unwin, London 1958).
2. For a useful convenient summary see Thomson, R. *The Psychology of Thinking* (Pelican, Harmondsworth 1958).

The Integrated Control of Human Behaviour

3. The development of the theme of 'thinking as adaptation' is well covered in Krech and Crutchfield *Elements of Psychology* (Knopf, N.Y. 1965; 1st edition 1958) pp. 359–506.

4. For a discussion of the study of imagery see Woodworth, R. S. and Schlosberg, H. *Experimental Psychology* (Methuen, London 1954).

5. An extended treatment of concept formation is given in Bruner, J. S., Goodnow, J. J. and Austin, G. A. *A Study of Thinking* (Wiley, N.Y. 1961; 1st ed. 1956).

6. See Whorf, B. L. *Language, Thought and Reality* (Wiley, N.Y. 1956).

7. Miller, G. A. *Language and Communication* (McGraw-Hill, N.Y. 1953) discusses this area.

8. Luria, A. R. 'The Role of Language in the Formation of Temporary Connections' in Simon, B. (ed.). *Psychology in the Soviet Union* (Stanford U.P., Stanford 1957).

9. For example see Flavel, J. H. *The Developmental Psychology of Jean Piaget* (Van Nostrand, Princeton 1963).

10. For example, see the following books by J. Piaget: *The Psychology of Intelligence* (1950); *The Origin of Intelligence in the Child* (1953); *The Child's Construction of Reality* (1954); *Plays, Dreams and Imitation in Childhood* (1951); *The Childs' Conception of Number* (1952); *The Childs' Conception of the World* (1929). All are published by Routledge & Kegan Paul, London.

11. This section follows the argument of Fleming, C. M. 'Child Development' in *The New Zealand Teachers' Colleges' Association Journal*, No. 5 (1966). For further criticism and alternative interpretations of Piaget's work see: Oakes, M. E. 'Explanations of Natural Phenomena by Adults', *Science Education* 29 (1945) pp. 137–42 and 190–201; Oakes, M. E. *Children's Explanations of Natural Phenomena* (New York Teachers College 1947); Bunt, L. N. H. *The Development of the Ideas of Number and Quantity according to Piaget* (J. B. Wolters, Groningen 1959); Van Hiele, P. M. *Development and Learning Process* (J. B. Wolters, Groningen 1959); Russell, D. H. *Children's Thinking* (Ginn & Co., Boston 1956); Wallace, J. G. *Concept Growth and the Education of the Child: A Survey of Research on Conceptualization* (N.F.E.E.W., London 1965); Lovell, K. 'A Follow-up Study of Inhelder and Piaget's "The Growth of Logical Thinking"', *British Journal of Psychology* 52 (1961) pp. 143–53; King, W. H. 'Symposium: Studies of Children's Scientific Concepts and Interests. 1. The Development of Scientific Concepts in Children', *British Journal of Educational Psychology* XXXI (1961) pp. 1–20; Fleming,

215

C. M. 'Research Evidence and Christian Education', *Learning for Living*, Vol. 6, No. 1 (1966) pp. 10–13.

12. See Wertheimer, M. *Productive Thinking* (Harper, N.Y. 1945).
13. A detailed discussion of this field is given in Watts, A. F. *The Language and Mental Development of Children* (Harrap, London 1944).
14. For a brief but useful discussion of the problems of using the terms 'conscious' and 'unconscious' as applied to thinking processes, see Hebb, D. O. *A Text-book of Psychology* (Saunders, London, 2nd ed. 1966) pp. 286–91.
15. See Wason, P. C. 'Reasoning' in *New Horizons in Psychology*, ed. by Foss, B. M. (Pelican, Harmondsworth, 1966; 1st ed. 1958).
16. An excellent introduction to the workings and possible influence of these machines on human life is given in Sluckin, W. *Minds and Machines* (Pelican, Harmondsworth 1960).

Chapter Nine

An Outline of Normal Human Development

INTRODUCTION

In earlier chapters of this book we have briefly referred to development within specific areas of mental activity. Nevertheless, we have been concerned throughout with the concept of human beings as whole social organisms whose efficiency at coping with life's problems depends to a very large extent on their being able to understand, anticipate and adapt to the behaviour of others. It is beyond the scope of this book to describe in detail the various physical, psychological and social stages through which we pass as we grow up and grow old. However, as subsequent chapters are mainly concerned with interrelationships between individuals further study will be made easier by attempting at this point to integrate these developmental themes and extend them into the social context.

For convenience, we can divide our discussion into two main parts. We will consider first the early development of the individual from conception to starting school,[1] this impressionable period being spent, for the most part, at home and predominantly under parental influence. Subsequently we will examine how the individual develops in the more variable and stressful environment beyond the protection of the home.[2]

EARLY DEVELOPMENT

The behaviour which an individual shows in any given situation to a large extent reflects his historical development. This development has two components. First, there is the evolutionary history of mankind in general and of that individual in particular as reflected in his genetical make-up. Secondly, there are the personal experiences which the particular person has gained during his lifetime.

The life of an individual begins at conception. From then until birth the individual lives in a fairly constant environment to a large extent uniform throughout the whole human race. Although much less variation occurs between individuals before birth than after it, it would be a mistake to suppose that the 270 days or so spent in the womb are *necessarily* unimportant in terms of learning. As we suggested in Chapter 7, many of the behavioural elements shown by all people may be due to the fact that they are all exposed to common environmental stimuli. Perhaps, therefore, the basis of some 'universally human' behavioural characteristics are established in the womb. Evidence here is slight and inconclusive and experimentation is difficult.[3] Nevertheless there is substantial sensory development during this period. The nervous system is capable of activity as can be demonstrated by the production of muscular movements in the foetus not only spontaneously* but also by external sensory stimulation from the third month of pregnancy.[4]

During the intra-uterine period the nervous system develops to an extent which allows the new-born infant to perform activities involving the co-ordination of groups of muscles, e.g. crying, sneezing, yawning and sucking. The fact that you can make a new-born baby cry by slapping it is surely evidence of a sensory-motor link having been already established. With further development in the stimulating external environment the baby's behaviour rapidly increases in variety, skill, strength and endurance. His reaction times improve as do his powers of co-ordination.

While the baby has all the basic human needs which we

*There is increasing evidence to suggest that these spontaneous intra-uterine muscular activities may well be essential for the functional development of muscular tissue itself.

discussed in Chapter 6, he is almost entirely dependent on others (usually his parents) for their satisfaction. There is much controversy as to the degree of importance of early parent-child relationships in the ultimate personality of the individual. It is sometimes said that the first few months of life are crucial in terms of personality development. The arguments behind this belief generally rest on the obvious impressionability of toddlers and the decrease in this flexibility and moulding as individuals grow older. Extrapolating in the other direction, it is suggested that the new-born infant is profoundly influenced by its sensory experiences.

This is an area where experimentation is difficult and much evidence is indirect. For example, Sluckin[5] points out that under the age of about six months it appears unlikely that an infant can distinguish between its mother and other people. Consequently it is improbable that such an infant will have formed an attachment to one particular person. Once the child has reached the stage of being able to form a close tie with one person then the effects of separation are likely to be much more profound than before. Turning to the work of Harlow[6] on infant monkeys, there is some very interesting evidence of the effects of mother-offspring relationships on subsequent behaviour. Apparently baby monkeys need contact with their mothers and to be able to touch and examine them, not only to satisfy their immediate need for security in infancy but also to enable them to produce normal positive sexual and parental responses when they become adult. If these general concepts apply to human beings in a similar way we must surely make parents more alive to the possible importance of their influence on the subsequent mental health of their children (see Chapter 13.)

Initially, mother represents need-satisfaction in terms of food, warmth, cleanliness, etc. If the child experiences further needs, e.g. fear or pain, it will turn at once to its mother for satisfaction and help. Evidence of the importance of suitable mother-child relationships can be gleaned from observations of deprived infants. Children brought up in large impersonal groups, in orphanages, not only appear unhappy, inactive and emotionally disturbed as infants but may also show enduring maladjustments. Apparently, the most sensitive time for such

219

deprivation is between six and twelve months of age. If at this stage or later the young child is isolated from its mother-figure for long periods (several months) it is likely to become irreversibly disturbed. Children spending the first three years of their lives in orphanages are unlikely to overcome such limitations as social and verbal retardation even if they are placed in first rate foster homes. As space is so limited here, let us return to the normal individual and leave the interested reader to consult the abundant literature on the problems of maternal deprivation.

The psychoanalytic school of thought (developed initially by Sigmund Freud) which puts special emphasis on the unconscious mind, attaches great importance to the early relationship between child and mother.[7] Although this relationship is initially tied to feeding and tending behaviour, the security and need-satisfying feelings obtained in these specific circumstances are subsequently generalized to all inter-personal relationships. According to this view the basis of later social adjustment, anxiety, giving and receiving of affection, etc., lies in these early social experiences. Much of the frustration of childhood and later life may therefore be linked with difficult relationships in infancy, e.g. where the child has to accept that sometimes mother is pleasure-giving when she satisfies her child's needs and at other times she is not when she fails to meet his demands. We shall mention this concept again in our discussion of theories of personality.[8]

Bowlby[9] and others also stress the importance of early mother-child relationships in subsequent personality development. In cases of extreme neglect or rejection or over-protection easily discernible marks may be left in the person's make-up. It is surely possible then that in more moderate instances effects of a similar kind but less severe and obvious may also influence the social and emotional adjustment of the individual.

We are not yet in a position where we can be clear about the relationship between early upbringing and later personality development. So many uncontrollable variables operate that assessment becomes very difficult. The earliest social learning normally occurs in the home in relation to a mother-figure. Homes are, of course, infinitely variable. Within any one street in any one kind of neighbourhood the differences between households in terms of attitudes, values, priorities, interrelationships between sexes and generations and many other variables are extremely diverse. Many developmental psychologists suggest that the relationship an infant strikes up with its mother will to a great extent determine its later attitudes towards, and expectations of, other people.

Early social development, apart from relationships with a mother-figure, progresses gradually from a state of comparatively little interest in others at about six months of age to an apparent desire to co-operate with others by about two years. However, environmental circumstances greatly influence the relationships formed and children isolated from their fellows are likely to withdraw into themselves in company to a much greater extent than more socially experienced individuals. Observations of children of nursery school age show clearly how much social development is accelerated by frequent satisfying relationships with other children.[10]

The attitudes of society in general to social relationships are probably very important directives in this development.[11] Society's views impinge on the child mainly through controls first of parents and later of teachers. Early in the child's life friendly acts are rewarded and encouraged while selfish acts are frowned upon. Consequently, social behaviour is reinforced and likely to be repeated. Children who are successful and 'shine above' their fellows are praised, while those lagging behind are encouraged to catch up. Competitiveness is thus rewarded in children and it soon becomes a principle by which their behaviour is controlled. Later in life such concrete forms of comparisons as examinations, social class distinctions, financial differentials, etc., reinforce this principle and can be the cause of much frustration and conflict both within the individual and within society.

We began this chapter by suggesting that it should be considered as a collection of themes. The difficulties of producing a coherent logical description on so many fronts at once are insuperable. This is why the fragments were artificially separated in earlier chapters. Notice however that the concept of 'readiness' applies throughout whether considering ability to produce specific forms of behaviour or to interpret particular types of information. Readiness involves both an adequate level of physical development and suitable prior experiences before mastery of a given situation is possible. This is surely the concept behind our discussion of the effects of early experience on a child. Let us leave the point by looking at a specific example of readiness in infancy, namely toilet-training. This is a subject on which much has been written and here we are only looking at it from the viewpoint of readiness. The age at which toilet-training for a particular individual should occur must surely be related to the stage of readiness when the child is able and wants to co-operate with its mother. Initially the infant cannot distinguish between, for example, its love of food and its love of the giver of food. With experience and maturation the child comes to distinguish between the two and also learns that his mother can provide other need-satisfying services besides giving food. When the child can recognize mother as a person that he wants to please then surely he is ready to be toilet-trained by her. (Basic to much of our education is the need to see our teachers as persons that we want to please.)

Let us mention at this point the use of physical and psychological norms of development. In discussing, for example, individual differences, mental health, mental illness, etc., we shall examine the value of having an estimate of what is average or usual or acceptable in a given society. In terms of maturation and learning psychologists are interested in such norms as, for example, at what age children normally sit, stand, walk, recognize mother or their own name, increase in height, weight, vocabulary, etc., and a host of other items which are conveniently assessed. But we are all individuals and 'the four year old' or 'the adolescent' are umbrella terms covering very wide spectra of variation. The parent who slavishly compares her offspring with such standards, who is overjoyed by any precocity and concerned about any slight falling-short is all-too-common and very unwise. Teachers, nurses and other social workers must be quite clear in their own minds, and make quite clear to their clients, that these norms are simply convenient, limited tools of assessment and variations are not only to be expected but are surely desirable. We all may follow a common maturational sequence of development but anyone with contact with children is aware that this is far from smooth. All have sudden spurts in

222

growth in height, increase in vocabulary or ability to make good relationships with others. Norms are of much less value than the over-anxious parent or over-zealous teacher realizes.

The social development of young children has been closely studied and much has been written on it. There are apparently several closely interrelated stages involved in the development from selfish to socially co-operative behaviour. Initially the infant learns that there are other people in his environment besides himself, e.g. by about the end of the second month he responds to a human voice and by perhaps late in the fourth month can roughly distinguish between positive (smiling) behaviour of another and negative (more threatening) activity. Throughout this early period he learns to differentiate between his now 'self' and the environment. He learns that he is able to control those stimuli which are the result of his own actions but that those stimuli coming from the world outside himself are beyond his control. The progressive realization of differences between people and objects in the environment is another extended and complex developmental process.

As the child becomes more aware of and competent in dealing with his environment, more demands are made upon him to compromise his selfish desires and co-operate with other people. Hand in hand with this comes the need to become not only integrated into the family group but also the desire for independence within it. The whole story of human development is one of integrated change in which specialization and individualization of the person is simultaneously modified by the pressures of social integration. How clearly then we can see that maturation and learning are basic to development. How difficult it is, however, to ascribe relative importance of these processes to any particular item of development.

Normally most of the first five years of a child's life is spent at home, usually in close contact with his parents. As he develops he follows a pattern and achieves a level of attainment which is contained within the limits set by what he inherits from his parents. If he is brought up in a restricted environment devised and regulated by his parents this will doubly impress their qualities and interpretations on his young malleable personality. For example, if a child's parents are nervous or boisterous, intelligent or musical, not only

223

will the child possibly inherit a similar disposition but will be brought up in an optimum environment for developing it. It is hardly surprising that many children do reflect many qualities and behavioural responses of their parents.

Obviously, if the child is to fit easily into the wider, more varied, social environments of school and later of adult life, he needs as much practice in coping with different people and situations as possible. That parents should not be over-protective but that they should do all they can to encourage independence and initiative by presenting the child with a variety of opportunities for extending himself, cannot be overstressed. The point must be emphasized, however, that the understanding of a child is quite different in many respects from that of an adult. We have already mentioned the problems of differentiation between self and surroundings. In the last chapter we examined the problems inherent in coping with several ideas (e.g. shape, size, number and move-ment) at the same time, particularly in the absence of the items being thought about. Another area of difficulty which some adults do not appreciate is that children often are unable to distinguish between fantasy and reality ('You're not really a lion are you, mummy?'). The production of a stimulating but not over-frustrating environment should be the parental aim.

DEVELOPMENT BEYOND THE HOME

Once the child starts school the home ceases to be the only major influence in his life. His language, values and attitudes may be reinforced or modified according to the comparative standards of home and school. His school contacts will be less personal than those of his home and he will have to become more independent (a fact resented by some over-protective parents). He will probably spend time and energy participating in activities of little interest to his parents and so may well have 'less time for' and 'less in common with' them. While children at this stage are increasingly aware of the need for social approval and acceptance, they are still basically very egocentric (e.g. it would be unwise to let a child at the primary school have sole, unsupervised charge of a pet).

An Outline of Normal Human Development

Social development continues rapidly in the period of five to eleven. Friendships early in this stage are usually transient, but as the child becomes more emotionally mature they become much more permanent. By the time the child is eleven he has usually entered the 'gang' stage, liking the company, security, approval and common interest of individuals of the same age and the same sex as himself.[12] He will usually enjoy team games, Scouts or Guides, joining clubs, etc. Often hostility to authority from outside his group is resented and parents and teachers are regarded as a nuisance. As the individual moves into adolescence his ability to cope with the problematic period ahead of him depends very much upon his state of social and emotional readiness which, as we have already pointed out, in turn depends upon his level of maturity and the nature of his childhood experiences.

Adolescence is considered by many psychologists to be initiated by the onset of puberty and to end when the individual achieves social recognition as an adult.[13] (Other definitions, for example, in terms of glandular development or physical maturation, are perhaps more appropriate to the needs of the biologist than to the social scientist). In many ways adolescence is similar to other stages of development in that it involves a complicated integrated movement towards greater physical, psychological and social competence and independence. Therefore the individual is still struggling to adjust his own changing capabilities and social relationships to the new situations in which he finds himself. However, in adolescence, mature heterosexual motivation becomes active for the first time bringing with it new problems and experiences that must be dealt with in a highly restricted and socially acceptable manner.[14] Sexual arousal basically takes the form of positive interests in the opposite sex with very strong desires which cannot be satisfied. It also brings complications relating to other basic needs, for example, insecurity related to new environmental demands, new internal affective experiences, increased sensitivity through changes in bodily proportions, breaking voice, spotty complexion, perhaps the expectation by parents and teachers that their offspring should be more competent and responsible in some areas, while remaining submissive and obedient in others. We could extend this list indefinitely.

Introduction to Psychology

Here, perhaps more than at any stage of development we can see the great importance and interplay of the processes of maturation and learning. There exists the need for independence and freedom given to the adolescent through physiological maturation, but there also exists a lack of necessary experience to be able to tackle the problems of the adult world. How does one learn to cope with freedom without making too many mistakes in the process? This is a general problem by no means restricted to adolescents. Adults, living at home with their parents and suddenly freed by the death of the latter may have great problems of adjustment. Newly 'emergent' nations or previously suppressed social classes obtaining their freedom for the first time also demonstrate the same difficulties. How often the first manipulation of freedom is abuse of it. In the case of adolescents this frequently takes the form of throwing off completely many parental standards and customs. The existence of adolescent fashions in clothes, music and dancing, the mores of gangs and groups and many other 'teenage characteristics' may well be basically a rejection of the authority of the older generation.

Let us leave this phase in development by looking more closely at the problem of insecurity. In some cultures initiation ceremonies are performed at certain well defined points in adolescence which take the individual at once clearly and decisively from the dependence of childhood to the responsibility of adulthood. Here many of the problems of 'growing up' are minimized as the role of the individual and the expectations of society are clear to all concerned. In our culture, however, the individual goes through a prolonged transitional period gradually moving towards adult recognition. Obviously parental attitudes are of paramount importance during this time. The need for understanding and help cannot be overstressed. However, this is often more difficult to achieve than parents (and adolescents) realize. Life is dynamic and changes occur all the time not only within each individual but also in the standards and values of society. The twenty plus years between generations may produce an enormous difference in interpretation of adolescent problems. Parental attitudes not only to sexual matters but also to friends, clothes, occupation, hours of coming home at night, etc., can often be unreasonably antagonistic through failure

226

to appreciate the general social climate in which young people are developing. We cannot attempt to discuss these extremely important, complex problems further here. Let us simply remember that adolescence is a period of very rapid and important development in the lives of each of us, the problems of which are only now being really understood.

The bulk of this book is concerned with the behaviour of adults. We have already indicated some of the continual fluctuations which occur through, for example, motivation and emotion, perception and social pressures. Above these individual variations, however, each of us goes through a series of developmental stages from the vitality of early adulthood to the decline of mental and physical capacities of old age. Let us complete this section by briefly considering some of the general stages through which most of us pass.

The young adult, to a large extent free from adolescent limitations (both inherent in his own personality and imposed by his environment) normally starts work, often gets married and may begin to raise a family. None of these tasks is easy in this modern world. So often jobs available (or accepted) are unsatisfactory in terms of inherent interest, money, prospects, etc. Frequently some form of irksome further education must be taken concurrently with initial employment. This time in his life is likely to be a period of great expense yet minimal earning power. Financial problems are increased with marriage and setting up home. Bringing up a family, while perhaps the ultimate desire of most young people, poses great problems of adjustment. Both partners must lose much of their earlier freedom. The initial excitement of a new baby may wane quite rapidly as the parents begin to feel over-tired, unduly restricted, and have to 'watch every penny'. Often at times of particular strain, for example, the arrival of another new baby, teething, parental illness or financial worry, the tensions in the family may considerably upset mother-child or husband-wife relationships. These are widespread, perhaps normal stages in young adulthood. The importance of varied and suitable prior experiences in enabling individuals to adjust to them cannot be overstressed.

As adulthood progresses and middle age is attained, development proceeds in two directions.[15] On the credit side the person may improve his financial and social standing and his increasing experience of life in the adult world will enhance his efficiency at coping with many human problems. On the debit side, however, there will be a gradual deterioration in physical stamina, in ability to learn and accept new ideas, etc. The family, growing up, will now be leaving home and often parents left behind may feel 'no longer needed'. If this coincides with physiological change, e.g. the menopause in women or more gradual sexual decline in men, or with social change, e.g. loss of one's partner or premature retirement, the effects of the dispersal of the family can be quite dramatic. It is again the mature and mentally healthy individual who comes best out of such stressful situations.

With the approach of old age, major adjustments must normally be made at a time when modification of life-long standards of progressively accumulated status is increasingly difficult.[16] The gradual decline in physical and intellectual capacities which began almost imperceptibly earlier in adulthood often now reach quite obvious levels, perhaps causing anxiety and making clear the need for 'slowing down' or 'handing over the reins to younger people'. While the experience which an individual gleans during his lifetime enables him to interpret problems in which he is well-practised, the rapid advances in modern living often make his interpretations erroneous and inappropriate. He may have great difficulty in accepting new ideas and considers 'the younger generation' to be generally inferior and incompetent.

Examples are all too common of elderly people who have been happy and able to cope well in their life-long haunts but who have deteriorated rapidly on removal to a new locality far away from their friends. However, this must not be misconstrued. Old people need *new* experiences to keep them active and give them an interest in life. Deterioration is far more rapid in the incapacitated or those confined to a restricted environment. This is, in part, why retirement can be such a major problem. Not only does it involve loss of status but also of many major interests and generally the individual lives in a more limited environment than previously.

Here we can see that maturation has progressed very nearly to the end of its run. Experience has been accumulated in the past but the facility for further learning is diminished. Old friends have died, life has changed, youngsters once very

228

much his junior now wield authority which they interpret in terms and values quite different from his own. From the standpoint of this chapter old age can perhaps best be considered as the stage in an individual's life when the processes of behavioural modification that have previously proved so essential for a full happy life now have ceased to be adequate for present needs and adjustments.

SUMMARY

1. The themes of human development introduced in earlier chapters must be integrated and extended into the social context if a clear representation is to be given of the way in which a child grows up. It is impossible to be comprehensive. The areas of study are divided into (a) the early years spent in the home and (b) subsequent experiences beyond the home.
2. Initial development in the womb is apparently mainly the unfolding of genetically endowed patterns. The importance of learning during this period is very difficult to determine. By the time the infant is born its nervous system is well developed.
3. The infant's needs are satisfied by parents. The importance of mother-child relationships is not clear but what evidence is available suggests it may be critical for normal healthy development. The psychoanalytic school put very great emphasis on these relationships.
4. Bowlby and others have examined the effects of maternal deprivation and neglect on subsequent personality development. Together with many other psychologists they suggest that the relationship which an infant strikes up with its mother may determine to a very large extent the nature of other subsequent social relationships.[17]
5. The social development of the child involves a number of extremely complex yet basic processes of interpretation, e.g. differentiating the self from the not-self and then separating various parts of the not-self. As he progresses he must fit into the environment compromising his own selfish desires with those of others. Attitudes of society impinge on the child through his parents. Friendly acts and later success in competition are encouraged. Such emphasis on differentiation between individuals places importance and later anxiety in comparative situations, e.g. examinations.
6. The first five years of a child's life are normally spent at home under parental influence. For this period to be maximally

beneficial for later life, he should be given a wide range of interesting but not over-taxing experiences.

7. Once at school the child tends to move away from his parents in both interests and activities. His social awareness increases and he is likely to make friends of his peers. Parents and teachers play a much less prominent part than previously.

8. In adolescence his development continues often at an increased rate. It is, moreover, complicated by the emergence of mature heterosexual motivation. The physical, psychological and social adjustments necessary at this time are likely to upset previous balances. Insecurity is everywhere and the importance of parental understanding cannot be overstressed.

9. Problems of the young adult are tied mainly to leaving home, starting work, getting married and raising a family. This is a period then of great turmoil and little security, great expense and minimal earning power.

10. While middle age may bring an improvement in social standing and experience it also represents a deterioration in physical and psychological performance levels. These may lead to some difficulties of adjustment which increase with approaching old age.

REFERENCES

1. See Gesell, A. *The First Five Years of Life* (Methuen, London 1954) or Isaacs, S. *The Nursery Years* (Routledge & Kegan Paul, London 1929).

2. For a detailed survey of child development see Carmichael, L. (ed.). *Manual of Child Psychology* (Wiley, N.Y. 1954).

3. See Hocker, D. *Evidence of Prenatal Function of the Central Nervous System in Man* (American Museum of Natural History, N.Y. 1958).

4. For example, see Spelt, D. K. 'The Conditioning of the Human Foetus in Utero', *Journ. Exp. Psychol.* (1948) 38, pp. 338–46.

5. See Sluckin, W. 'Early Experience' in Foss, B. M. (ed.). *New Horizons in Psychology* (Pelican, Harmondsworth 1966).

6. See Harlow, H. F. and Zimmerman, R. R. 'Affectional Responses in the Infant Monkey', *Science*, Vol. 130 (1959): pp. 421–32.

7. Burlingham, D. and Freud, A. *Infants without Families* (Allan & Unwin, London 1943).

8. See Freud, A. *Introduction to the Techniques of Child Analysis* (Nerv. Ment. Dis. Monogr., 1928) No. 48. Also Klein, M. *The Psychoanalysis of Children* (Hogarth Press, London 1932).

9. See for example Bowlby, J. 'The Effects of Mother-Child

Separation: A Follow-up Study', *Brit. Journ. Med. Psych.* (1956) 29, pp. 211–47.

10. Hattwick, L. A. and Saunders, M. K. 'Age Differences in Behaviour at the Nursery School Level', *Child Develp.* (1938) 9, pp. 27–47.

11. Elkin, F. *The Child and Society* (Random House, N.Y. 1960).

12. Thrasher, F. M. *The Gang* (University of Chicago Press 1927).

13. For a discussion of the psychology of adolescence see Hurlock, E. B. *Adolescent Development* (McGraw-Hill, N.Y., 1955).

14. Sex problems as they appear to adolescents are discussed in Jordon, G. W. and Fisher, E. M. *Self Portrait of Youth* (Heinemann, London 1955). Physiological and behavioural disturbances are covered in Tanner, J. M. *Physical Maturing and Behaviour at Adolescence* (Nat. Children's Home, London 1959).

15. See Wallis, J. H. *The Challenge of Middle Age* (Routledge & Kegan Paul, London, 1962).

16. Cumming and Henry, *Growing Old* (Basic Books, N.Y. 1961).

17. For a fuller discussion of this problem see Fleming, C. M. *Adolescence: Its Social Psychology* (Routledge & Kegan Paul, London 1963).

Chapter Ten

The Differences Between Individuals

INTRODUCTION

In previous chapters of this book we have discussed some of
the more important aspects of psychology which apply to
each of us. However, it is obvious from observation of
persons around us that although we all can think and learn,
that we all have emotions and interests, attitudes and abilities,
we each differ from our fellows in the degree and way in
which we display these characteristics. Some people think
more clearly than others, some learn quickly and efficiently
while others are poor in this respect. Again, the interests of
individuals are very diverse as are their emotional responses
to a given situation. These variations between persons are
very important to us in our everyday life.[1] We are social
creatures, living and working together. There are different
jobs to be tackled in our society for which we must select the
most suitable individuals, for example, a person who would
make a good nurse may not necessarily be satisfactory as a civic
leader or machine operative. People who must work together
need to be compatible in terms of ability and interest if they
are to form an efficient team. Some members of society are so
different from their fellows that they may have difficulty in
fitting into their environment, for example, the genius, the
mentally deficient or the habitual criminal. In this chapter we
shall be examining these individual differences from two
points of view. Firstly, we shall consider why we are all
different from one another and discuss the factors which

make us as we are. Secondly, we shall examine the importance and problems of being able to assess the degree to which we differ in these various characteristics.

THE FACTORS WHICH MAKE EACH INDIVIDUAL UNIQUE

It is convenient to divide these into two groups: a. those we inherit, i.e. which are present from the very start of our lives, and b. those we acquire, i.e. which affect us during the course of our lives.

A. INHERITED CHARACTERISTICS.[2] Each person starts life as a fertilized egg (zygote) which is formed by the union of a sperm from his father with an egg from his mother. Present within this zygote are chemical units (genes) which are the 'blueprints' according to which the zygote will develop. These genes lie together in long strings (chromosomes). The inherited characteristics of an individual are determined by the chromosome content of his zygote (and consequently all other cells in his body because they are derived from this zygote). All animals of one species have the same number and arrangement of chromosomes and therefore are all similar to one another. Animals of different species have different chromosome numbers and arrangements and therefore develop differently from one another.

Major chromosome differences indicate major differences in genes. However, slight changes in number, type, strength, position or combination of genes in a chromosome, while not greatly affecting the appearance and general structure of the whole chromosome, will in fact give a slightly different blueprint. Consequently, individuals of the same species developing from zygotes with slightly different gene-contents will be different from each other in small ways, for example, hair colour, body build, etc.

Chromosomes are present in pairs in all the cells of an animal's body except in the sperm and eggs where they are single. There are twenty-three pairs of chromosomes in human cells and twenty-three single chromosomes in human sperm and eggs. In the zygote, therefore, we find twenty-three chromosomes from the father pairing with twenty-three from the mother. This means that for every characteristic of the future body the zygote carried a pair of genes, one from the mother and one from the father. The number of genes in a chromosome is very great. In the process of division and separation of chromosomes in the production of gametes there occurs a shuffling of genes. Therefore each gamete has its own particular gene complex. When fertilization occurs two gametes unite each with its own unique gene content. The new zygote has inherited part of its genetic material from one parent and part from the other but its own particular arrangement is unique. The only exception to this rule occurs when a zygote splits in half and develops into two separate offspring with the same genetic constitution. The resulting individuals are called 'identical twins'.

The importance of actual gene distribution is probably very great for many human characteristics. It is likely that any one characteristic is determined by several pairs of genes acting together, and so their relative positions may greatly influence their activity.

The study of inheritance (genetics) is a science in its own right. We cannot go into it in detail here, but the reader unfamiliar with the subject would be well advised to consult an elementary biology text on this fascinating and vitally important topic.[3] Let us simply note the following points in relation to inheritance of characteristics:

   i. The genes which govern a person's development come partly from his father and partly from his mother.
  ii. The gene-content of a person is determined at fertilization and cannot be changed subsequently.
 iii. The action of genes affects every cell in the person's body.

B. ACQUIRED CHARACTERISTICS. From conception onwards the new individual is dependent on exchange between itself and the environment if it is to grow, develop and survive. At first this exchange is basically related to obtaining food and oxygen from the mother's body and passing back waste material to it. After birth these biological functions are still performed but now in relation to the outside world. Once the child begins to lead an independent life, however, it has to cope with a much more complex, demanding environment. It picks up experiences relating to its surroundings through its sense organs. It must respond to these experiences in such a

234

way that it copes with the external situations which produced them (see Chapters 1 and 2). We have previously discussed the way in which experiences can be stored within a person's mind for use in solving problems encountered later. What is stored within a person's mind will depend upon the particular experiences he has had. Obviously two persons having different stores of past experiences both coming into contact with a common new experience will respond to it differently. For example, a biologist and an artist will both have stores of past experiences orientated to their particular way of thinking and attitudes towards life. If both were presented with a newly discovered, very unusual tropical flower their interests and responses to it would be quite different. Similarly, attitudes towards an outbreak of industrial unrest and strikes will be different for workers, management and uninvolved men-in-the-street. We have discussed in earlier chapters the importance of past experiences in dealing with and understanding present problems. Let us leave the point here by simply stating that many of our present characteristics are dependent upon our previous experiences.

Our genes determine our potential level of development (that is, the level which we could attain under ideal circumstances). However, whether this level is reached or not depends upon the environment presenting all necessary conditions and opportunities. For example, the potential strength which a person can develop in his biceps muscle depends upon the genetic inheritance he receives from his parents. Under no circumstances can he exceed the limit set by these genes. In order to obtain maximum possible efficiency in this muscle, however, adequate supplies of food and oxygen must always be available, all waste products must be quickly removed, regular and correct exercise must be practised, etc. It is virtually impossible to achieve ideal conditions for maximally efficient development of any physical or psychological characteristic of an individual. Therefore persons always tend to reach a level of attainment which is lower than their 'potential level'. The attained level we call the 'actual level' of performance of the characteristic under consideration. Many obvious examples of the difference between levels of attainment as a result of differing environmental conditions can be found in the literature relating to experimental work on plants and animals.[4] Take pea plants or snap-dragons, mice or insects, and carefully select large numbers of individuals of as nearly identical genetic constitution as possible. Divide them into two groups. Satisfy all the needs of one group (that is, make it a *control*) while keeping the other group short of food or at a low temperature. The development rate and success of the second experimental group will be much lower and the ultimate level attained by this group much inferior to that of the control. Similar environmental effects can be seen on the psychological development of human beings.[5] In a home where there is no interesting, worthwhile literature, no instructive discussions with parents but simply a dull, uneducative atmosphere where questions rarely arise and are never answered, one finds children growing up apathetic to knowledge and prepared to accept an unimaginative, humdrum life. Such children placed in homes where there is an active, interesting quest for knowledge, however, are likely to develop an appetite for new information and to demand a stimulating environment to satisfy it. Today, with universal education and the increase of mass media of communication, for example, television, radio, instructive literature, fewer children are growing up in extremely uninspiring environments and consequently there are fewer 'automatons' prepared to do humdrum jobs.[6] Another example of the effects of the environment on the psychological development of children can be seen in homes where the parents take all decisions and allow their offspring no responsibility. Such children are likely to grow up lacking in self-confidence and become weak adults unable to assert themselves, take decisions or carry responsibility. Similar children allowed to take initiative are much more likely to be able to hold their own with their fellows.

Although we have been discussing environmental effects mainly in terms of restrictions placed on the individual by external factors, this is in fact only one of the ways in which we are moulded by our surroundings. We learn a great deal by imitation and we tend to copy our parents, teachers and friends. We copy not only actual behaviour and speech patterns but also attitudes, interests and values. Consequently, in a household where the parents are Roman Catholic the children will be also. Had they been born of Methodist parents they would have grown up Methodists. Similarly, with politics, racial prejudices, attitudes towards other persons, animals, the law, etc., we copy our parents and adopt their standards. When we leave home and meet other persons of different points of view it may well cause us to be disturbed and feel insecure as our basic, life-long beliefs and values are questioned for the first time. As our experiences of other points of view increase in number, we may well modify our previous ideas. In general we can say that the limits of our possible development are set by genetical considerations. How nearly we reach these potential limits and what form our actual level of attainment takes depends to a large degree upon the environment in which we develop.

THE MEASUREMENT OF DIFFERENCES BETWEEN INDIVIDUALS

Techniques for measuring qualities of concrete objects involve comparisons between the specific item under consideration and predetermined standards. For example, the length of a piece of string is ascertained by comparing it with a ruler which is marked out in feet and inches. These units of length are determined before measuring the piece of string. Moreover, they are acceptable to and used by many other people. The units are arbitrary and fixed by common agreement. Other objects whose lengths are to be measured are compared with this standard. Similarly, volumes of liquids may be measured by pouring them into measuring cylinders or jugs which are graduated in units, for example, pints or litres. According to the number of units filled by our liquid we record the volume as so many pints or litres. Again, thermometers measure temperature or clocks measure the passing of time by comparing the specific item being assessed with previously determined standards or scales that have wide acceptance and which can be reproduced.

When measuring human characteristics, comparison again is the technique used. In principle, a given stimulus is presented to many individuals and their responses are observed. For example, a question is asked and the answers received are recorded and marked, or a problem is set and the times and techniques used to obtain the correct solution are noted. From this variety of responses the tester can obtain information regarding the performances of the most successful and least successful candidates and the average candidates in the group tested. For example, student nurses may be asked to complete a vocabulary test. Perhaps the best candidate can obtain 90 per cent of the right answers while the weakest only gets 31 per cent correct. Suppose the average (or norm) for the group is 63 per cent. Now give the test to any new student nurse you wish to assess on this characteristic and compare the result she obtains with the standard you have constructed from the performance of other student nurses. It is important to notice that the standards obtained for one group of persons can only be applied to individuals of approximately the same age group, background, training, etc., as the original group tested. For example, a standard obtained for eleven-year-old school children might show that in a mathematical test the scores ranged from 65 per cent for the top child to 12 per cent for the weakest group member, while the average mark was 41 per cent. If this standard was now applied to an eight-year-old taking the same test it is unlikely that even if he was top of his class of eight-year-olds in arithmetic he would get more than perhaps 40–50 per cent. However, a modern languages student in his early twenties, although perhaps not at all good at arithmetic, would probably do better than 65 per cent. This is an obvious example but it is very important to recognize this underlying principle that a standard obtained for a particular group of people is a comparative standard within that group and it should only be applied to other individuals similar to members of that group. For example, the child from the small country school who has always been top of his class is considered to be bright by his parents and teachers. When he moves to a grammar school at the age of eleven he is now in quite a different group from his previous classmates. Different standards must be applied to assess his performance. Failure to realize this can cause much distress to the child and his parents who may feel that 'he has gone downhill since he went to the big new town school'. Again, standards which are established by persons living in one country cannot be applied to individuals brought up in a different way of life. British people frequently refer to persons of other nationalities as being over-amorous or temperamental, backward or un-reliable. These other persons, in return, consider Britons to be staid, cold or unsociable. Similarly, British adults often think that American children are precocious because they are applying British standards to children brought up in a different society. These examples illustrate the danger of applying standards formulated for one group to the behaviour of quite a different group. In our discussion of assessment of individuals we must consider the construction of standards and scales against which we can evaluate the behaviour of these individuals. For our conclusions and assessments to be accurate it is essential that we constantly bear in mind the need for our scale to be suitable for the individuals under investigation.

The needs of modern society make the assessment of the psychological characteristics of individuals a very important issue.[7] The enormous number and variety of mental tests now available are evidence of this fact. We shall concern ourselves with three major groups of test which are of particular interest to the layman. In this chapter we shall consider tests of achievement (for example, examinations) and intelligence tests, while in the next chapter we shall discuss personality tests.

EXAMINATIONS

As our first example of techniques for comparing individuals let us consider school examinations. These disruptive and emotionally charged events have affected the lives of most of us at some time or other. Their prestige in our examination-conscious society tends to cause students and teachers and often also parents and employers to develop illogical attitudes towards them. Let us start then by trying to view them in perspective.

In everyday contact with other people, we constantly exchange information through speech and gesture, writing and facial expression. By carefully formulating questions or remarks and observing the responses of others to them we can learn a great deal about our fellows. Let us analyse more closely the stages in a two-way conversation between, for example, a ward sister and a visitor to her ward.

The visitor may formulate in her brain a question relating to the student nurses whom she observes making beds in the ward. She asks this question of the ward sister who interprets it in the light of her own past experiences, attitudes, motives and interests which may well be quite different from those of the visitor. Again, according to information in her brain, the sister will produce a reply to the visitor's question and transmit it back to her via effectors and receptors.

By careful formulation of questions and observation of responses the visitor can discover the sister's attitudes towards the younger generation, to discipline and change, what sort of training she had herself, whether she is more concerned with happy personal relationships than with immaculate tidiness and regimentation, etc. The sister's behaviour (that is, her answers) reflect towards the subject of the visitor's question.

The visitor, in her turn, will interpret the sister's replies in the light of her (the visitor's) attitudes and motives. If the visitor is a ward sister from a similar hospital and with similar experiences, she will consider our sister's responses to her questions to be very wise and quite correct. However, should the visitor be a student nurse who has suffered under an unsatisfactory régime which is apparently being duplicated in this ward, then her interpretation of the sister's views will be far less generous: 'old stick-in-the-mud, won't change with the times', etc. This personal, or *subjective*, element of interpretation comes into all forms of communication and will very considerably affect the way in which we sum up the person to whom we are speaking.

Examinations are techniques designed to minimize subjective effects.[8] They attempt to assess the abilities and past experiences of a person in a more scientific and accurate way than by casual observation as described above. Nevertheless, the same communicating techniques are utilized. Assessment is made more efficient by controlling the presentation of stimuli and the recording and marking of responses. Ideally all candidates for an examination should have followed identical courses. The examination itself should present all students with identical questions in identical circumstances and the answers produced should be assessed in identical terms. Then any variations between assessments will reflect differences in the mental processes of the students.

From our knowledge of psychology and our own personal experiences, however, we can be sure that there are many factors affecting student performance in an examination other than the mental capacity of the individual. Let us consider the nature of some of these factors:

A. All the information needed to answer a question comes initially from the environment. If the subject was not taught to the student his response will be nil. Even if the teacher did present the topic to the class, the student may not have perceived it correctly, for example, may not have been paying attention, may have grasped an example rather than an underlying principle. Again, if a student has a language problem or a sensory deficiency (poor eyesight or hearing), faulty percepts may be formed which prevent full understanding of the techniques involved. The teacher may have presented the material in a form which cannot easily be adapted to the questions on the examination paper or she may have only touched superficially on the aspect of the topic which is required by the particular question set. There is no doubt that teachers and teaching situations can very much affect students' examination results.

B. Once the information relating to the topic has entered the student's brain, all the various complex interrelated processes and capacities of the mind come into play. How efficiently the material taught can be held in his mind will depend not only on how well it was perceived but also on how good his memory is and whether he has refreshed his memory (that is, revised) just before the examination. Again, the ability of the student to think, that is, to manipulate and reorganize information in his mind to suit his present needs, must be considered. The type of examination question influences results in this context, for a question which simply requires recitation of lecture notes (that is, tests memory) is measuring an ability quite different from one which asks the student to 'work things out for himself' (that is, tests capacity to think). The student's interest in the subject and need for success in the examination (that is, his motivation) will affect the effort that he puts into perceiving and retaining the material to be learnt and also the way in which he tackles the examination paper. All these and a host of other factors active in the candidate's central nervous system will influence his examination performance.

C. In the actual examination situation, many factors will be reflected in the student's answers. Luck in being presented with a question which he can answer or which sparks off the correct train of thought. Familiarity with this type of situation. How well he is feeling both mentally (for example, tired, nervous) and physically (for example, in pain from ulcers, hungry, needing to urinate) will exert important effects; so also will environmental factors like temperature, ventilation, noise, comfortable desks, etc. Opportunity for copying is another effect which can be placed in this category of factors in the examination situation which may affect student performance.

Consequently, one cannot tell from a single examination result just what factors were responsible for producing the mark obtained. The implications of this problem are considerable throughout our educational and social system. Are we justified in adopting the point of view that we are assessing candidates as whole persons able to deal with complete situations and so it is no disadvantage to be measuring a complex of so many factors? Should we promote a person to a position of responsibility because he was successful in an examination which he could have passed through possessing a photographic memory or being well taught or by being extremely lucky? Should we expect that because a man has passed 'professional examinations' based on factual knowledge, skill and logical argument in order to become a lawyer, teacher or doctor that he should have qualities which will make him a paragon of virtue, a leader of men, or a model for the rest of society? Our society is riddled with such problems as these. The fact that many of them are implicit in our attitudes rather than openly expressed makes them all the more dangerous. A great deal of psychological investigation has gone into the whole problem of what examinations really do measure and their findings have been of great importance to educators.

A fuller discussion of the more applied aspects of examinations is outside the scope of this text. Studying and revising for examinations,[9] setting and marking papers, evaluation of different forms of examinations, criticisms of their shortcomings as assessment techniques and of their effects on our educational system and a host of other problems could fill many volumes. Let us restrict ourselves to asking why we use examinations and whether or not they are successful tools for these purposes.

We have suggested that an examination is basically a controlled form of communication where a common stimulus is presented to a number of individuals and their responses are carefully recorded. Any variations between responses to this common stimulus will reflect differences in the mental processes and stored information within the brains of the individuals. There are many variations on this basic plan. [10] For example: *a.* oral, written and practical examinations each employ their own sensory and motor pathways; *b.* Essay examinations present complex stimuli, the responses to which give measures of many qualities simultaneously, for example, knowledge, style of thinking, range of past experiences, vocabulary, etc. Objective or short-answer questions attempt to measure one quality at a time, for example, factual knowledge or reasoning ability or specific skill. (The psychological tests we shall discuss below can be considered advanced forms of objective test.) *c.* Another major variation on examination techniques depends upon whether the stimuli are presented and responses are obtained all 'at one sitting' and under fairly easily controllable conditions (as in a final examination) or whether the process is continued over an extended period where much less control is possible (as in continuous assessment).

In selecting an examination technique we must first ask ourselves exactly what it is that we wish to assess and then consider which of the tools available will perform the task most efficiently. [11] Among the more important uses to which examinations are put are the following:

A. To test students' competence in knowledge or skills. This is usually the function of an end-of-term examination or a weekly test or some other technique for ensuring that each member of the class is coping with the work being presented to him. It is also a function of final examinations where students are required to reach a certain standard of proficiency before being considered qualified in a given subject.

B. To assess the adequacy of a teaching method. This function may be considered as another aspect of *A.* above but there the emphasis is put on 'feed-back' to the teacher as to the suitability of his approach for the particular class being taught. It is obviously important that a student-teacher, or even an experienced teacher tackling a new subject, should utilize examinations for this purpose.

Introduction to Psychology

C. To place members of a group in order of merit. This is necessary where the number of candidates exceeds the number of places available. In our competitive and heterogeneous society persons of different levels of attainment are needed to perform different tasks and fill different positions. To select the most suitable person for a particular job its requirements must be defined in examinable forms, for example, possession of certain knowledge, skills, attitudes and interests; capacity to manipulate apparatus and materials; problem solving ability; accuracy in observation, interpretation and measurement, etc. The candidates can then be ranked according to their success in such tests and can be allocated to appropriate levels of responsibility within the field covered by the examination.

D. To provide a goal towards which both students and tutors can work. We have discussed in Chapter 6 the importance of 'motivation' as the dynamic driving force behind activity. Reference to that chapter and to our own experience will illustrate the importance of this function of examinations. The extent to which this is a desirable function is a matter of great educational and philosophical dispute.

So far we have been discussing examinations which attempt to assess what has been learned during a special course of training, for example, an O-level French course, an introductory nursing course, or a term's work in mathematics. The results of these examinations reflect performance accurately only within the context of the subject being examined, and the interests and attitudes engendered by it. Frequently, however, we need an estimate of a student's general level of thinking, problem solving ability, etc., not tied to any one specific subject. We might, for example, wish to predict the likely future achievement of a student. Suppose that we want to know whether a particular candidate will make a good member of a profession whose work will take him into fields not encountered in his school curriculum. Can we tell from examination results in mathematics, history and Latin whether a student will make a good nurse or administrator or officer in the forces? How do we select candidates for further courses of training? In our educational system, movement from primary to secondary and secondary to tertiary educational courses is based on assessment of the individual not only in terms of his past attainment but also on what it is hoped he will achieve in the future in a new environment and frequently working in new fields of study.

A central educational problem revolves around the question 'Can examinations fulfil satisfactorily these various functions for which they are at present utilized?'[12] Let us consider briefly what we can and cannot expect to learn from traditional, short-answer and practical examinations.

Traditional examinations consist of questions which require logically constructed answers using written or spoken sentences and normally involving description, explanation, discussion or problem solving. They have several advantages over other types of test. They evaluate style (that is, the way in which a candidate thinks without being prompted); they assess a student's range of experiences; they provide opportunity for expression of original ideas; they are easy and cheap to produce and so can be designed expressly to suit the needs of a particular group of students.

However, they have great disadvantages. How desirable is it to require a candidate under stressful conditions to attempt to express, for example, her scientific or nursing ability in writing (a slow, laborious process introducing many extra variables between students)? Inaccuracies are increased by then asking the examiner to attempt to assess the original qualities from this written script. Again, such examinations sample only a small section of the syllabus (for example, ten questions set on a year's work). Marking is likely to be very subjective (as we described earlier in this section). Oral forms of traditional examination are open to all these criticisms, especially subjectivity on the part of the examiner who may be influenced by the candidate's voice, appearance, etc. The candidate again may be upset by the sight of the examiner. The stressful effect of the examination on the student's performance is likely to be even more marked in an interview. Again, unless the examination is recorded, answers are only temporarily available and later checking is impossible. Examinations of several students by the same examiner must be spread out in time or else different questions must be given to each candidate. Both of these situations introduce extra variables. Usually oral examinations are very brief when compared with three-hour written papers. The British preference for the traditional type of examination seems to be due mainly to the fact that we are used to them. Students feel that they can do themselves justice in them, and examiners believe that they can learn much about candidates from them. Nevertheless, close scrutiny suggests that many of the functions which they are supposed to perform can be much more efficiently carried out by other forms of test.

Short-answer or objective tests are particularly favoured in the U.S.A. and are slowly gaining acceptance in Britain. In this form of assessment the examiner analyses the information which he is going to require from the students and organizes it into a large number of short questions. The answers to these questions are either right or wrong (as opposed to the various degrees of success found in essay and interview evaluation). Subjective effects in the marking of answers are obviously kept to a minimum (although the extent to which they enter into the framing of questions is a matter of considerable dispute). The advantages of such examinations are obvious. Marking is quick, easy and objective and can be carried out by unskilled assistants using a marking scheme. The answers required normally involve a tick or underlining or one or two words and so the candidate spends most of his time thinking rather than writing. Also a large number of questions can easily and fairly sample the whole syllabus in a one-hour examination.

The limitations of objective tests have probably been over-emphasized by diehard educationalists in this country. Among the more valid criticisms may be mentioned particularly the problems of setting the examination paper. Subjective effects influence question form and content, the whole process is very time consuming and in order to obtain the answers required the questions sometimes become rather artificial. The candidate's ability to express himself is not tested and guessing effects make desirable the use of statistical corrections of results.

Practical examinations give the examiner the advantage of observing the examinee actually performing under conditions similar to those in which he will subsequently work. This must surely outweigh any adverse criticism that may be levelled against them. Nevertheless, the examiner should be aware of the limitations of this form of test and must attempt to minimize them. The major problems fall into three categories:

246

The Differences Between Individuals

a. the stressful nature of the examination situation;
b. the very limited sampling of the syllabus which is unavoidable in a single examination;
c. difficulties of control, subjectivity and unpredictability which are constantly present.

How then should we examine candidates to get as complete and accurate an assessment of them as possible? The major difficulty appears to be that different types of examination are each measuring different qualities. A combination of these various techniques will give a more comprehensive assessment of the complete person than can any one form alone. Perhaps the crux of the matter lies in the fact that we cannot hope to evaluate a person efficiently in all these various characteristics at once. If we try to do so inaccuracies are likely to occur. For a more rigorous assessment of individual differences we must turn to 'psychological tests'.

PSYCHOLOGICAL TESTS

These can be considered as forms of assessment where greater care is taken in establishing just which qualities are being evaluated than is the case in most examinations. Psychologists have produced what are called 'standardized educational tests' which specifically evaluate such activities as oral arithmetic, vocabulary and language development, reading, etc.[13] They have also constructed tests which attempt to assess interests,[14] special abilities and aptitudes,[15] personality characteristics. This last form of assessment will be considered in the next chapter. Here we will discuss some aspects of psychological testing of 'intelligence'.[16]

In our discussions of examinations we emphasized the importance of careful definition of the qualities to be assessed before devising tests to evaluate them. This we must also attempt to do in the case of 'intelligence'. When the layman uses the word it is frequently in an imprecise sense, as a 'rag-bag term' for, for example, ability to solve problems, think abstractly, even to learn. It is very often surrounded by an aura of disrepute and mistrust, partly because of lack of understanding of what it involves but also partly because of the fear and loathing which most of us have of being summed up

247

accurately by our fellows. We discussed this at length in Chapter 5.

If we turn to more informed interpretations of the meaning of 'intelligence' we again find great discrepancies among psychologists as to exactly how the term should be defined.[17] Let us put the concept of intelligence into perspective before attempting to formulate a precise definition of it. When we discussed school examinations we attributed performance in an examination at the end of a course to two factors:

a. The information available in the environment to be learned during the course of study, that is, what the teacher has taught, what the students have read, etc. This should be more or less common to all class members following the course.

b. The individual abilities of the students to learn from this available information. These will be different for each student and will depend on inherited mental characteristics and the extent to which they have been developed in relation to the subject matter of the course.

In intelligence tests we are also concerned with performance in an examination-type situation, but here we are not assessing how much a person has learned from a particular course of study in a given subject. Rather we are attempting to evaluate the general level of thinking, understanding of relationships, solving of problems, etc., that the person has attained during his development and upbringing in life in general. Therefore, an individual's performance in an intelligence test will depend on:

a. The information from the environment which has been available to be learned during the person's lifetime. This will vary between individuals according to the surroundings in which they have lived. For example, a person brought up in a competitive, inspiring environment will have encountered many more complex and varied experiences of all kinds than if he were confined to much less stimulating surroundings. The number and type of experiences he has had will also depend upon how long he has been in contact with such information, that is, upon his age.

b. The individual's abilities to cope with the situations which the environment presents. If you take persons from the same culture and of the same age group and compare their performances in a test based on experiences found in everyday life,

The Differences Between Individuals

differences in result will reflect differences in inherited mental characteristics and the extent to which they have been developed in the individuals in relation to life in general.

If we wish to assess individuals in terms of their general ability to cope with the environment, perceive what is important, solve problems, utilize past experiences in interpreting new situations, etc., intelligence is obviously a basic factor to be taken into account.

However, as our discussions in previous chapters have suggested, while intelligence may underlie all these complex processes, they are nevertheless quite different from each other and involve a good deal besides intelligence. To define intelligence, therefore, we must attempt to extract this common factor from these intelligent processes. The first person to attack this problem successfully was Charles Spearman.[18] By statistical techniques which are outside the scope of this discussion he analysed intellectual activities and produced evidence that suggested the existence of one fundamental ability underlying all intelligent processes. This he called the general factor of intelligence (g). For each individual activity there was also a specific factor (s) which was shared with no other activity. For example, the intellectual factors underlying John's ability to play the violin consist of 'g', John's general ability which is involved in all his intelligent activities, and 's', John's specific ability to play the violin.

This 'two factor' theory has since been modified in the light of subsequent evidence. Spearman originally thought that 's' factors were each entirely specific to individual tasks. For example, if a person plays the piano and the violin, although 'g' is common to both these activities, he will have 's' $_{(piano)}$ and 's' $_{(violin)}$ which are quite different and separate from each other. Nowadays, however, it is widely accepted that this is not the case. Spearman's concept of a specific factor for one activity may include some elements which also occur in the so-called specific factors for other related activities. These elements which are shared between related functions are normally called group factors. Let us take an example to illustrate this modern conception of a 'three factor' theory. Which factors determine the intellectual performance of a schoolboy in mathematics, physics and French? All will involve 'g', his general factor of intelligence. Maths and physics will both

249

involve, to varying extents, the group factor of numerical ability. Physics and French will both share his verbal ability group factor. Finally, each subject will have its own specific factor confined to itself.

The extraction and definition of group factors is a difficult task. While there appears to be little doubt as to their existence, the exact nature and limitations of each is a great problem. The most firmly established appear to be verbal ability, spatial ability, numerical ability, mechanical ability, musical ability and perceptual speed, although several others are suspected. In many cases of new suggested group factors, however, the evidence is as yet unconvincing.

Limiting the concept of intelligence in this way has given us orientation and perspective within the topic. However, before we can reliably assess a person's intelligence, we must translate these factors into measurable terms. From this point of view we can look upon an intelligent person as one who, when tackling a problem, can discover what aspects of the situation are important to its solution, and can also call to mind other relevant ideas which will help him. Specifically then, intelligence is a measure of two abilities:

    i. to see the relevant relationships between objects or ideas in a problem situation;
    ii. to call up other relevant ideas.

We can illustrate these concepts by the following diagrams, where squares represent ideas or objects and a circle indicates the relationship between them:

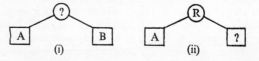

Let us use this form of representation to illustrate some simple examples of questions which will be familiar to anyone who has ever taken an intelligence test.

Example 1. Underline the word which does not belong in the same category as the rest:

cat; dog; cabbage; rabbit; hamster

The Differences Between Individuals

Here the student is required to determine relationships between pairs of items in the list and select the odd-man-out:

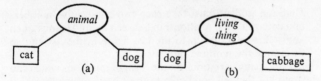

All these comparisons reveal the relationship of 'animals' except those involving 'cabbage' which give the relationship of 'living things'. Therefore, underline 'cabbage'.

Example 2. Underline the word which does not belong in the same category as the rest:

cat; radish; cabbage; mountain; rabbit

Here all comparisons involve the concept of 'living things' except those including 'mountain'. Therefore 'mountain' is the word which should be underlined.

Example 3. 'Tall' means the opposite of (high, big, short, thin).

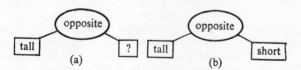

In this case the student is given one idea and a relationship and is asked to select a second idea which completes the picture.

Example 4. What is the opposite of 'tall?'
This question is based on the same principle as Example 3, but here the student has to recall the correct word rather than recognize it from a list.

Example 5. Wet is to dry as big is to – – –?
This type of question involves both the abilities involved in intelligence. The student must ask himself:

a. What is the relationship between wet and dry?

b. What is the opposite of big?

Example 6. Supply the next number in the following series:

$$1, 3, 5, 7, - - -$$

Here the student must take each two consecutive numbers and determine the relationship between them. He must then apply this relationship to the last figure in the list and so determine the required number.

There are many variations on the form of questions which can be used but they all boil down to these basic principles which we have been discussing. The criticism is often levelled that such questions are so artificial and unrelated to the problems of everyday life as to be useless. However, if any process of constructive thinking is carefully analysed, be it passing an examination, bringing up a family, doing research or anything else, it will be found that it can be resolved into a large number of these very simple, straightforward questions.[19]

We can only briefly mention a few of the practical aspects of intelligence testing here, and persons likely to be involved in administering such tests should consult some of the specialist books listed in the bibliography.[20] In constructing a test it is of course essential to select questions which measure 'g' rather than group or specific factors. (If you wish to assess musical or mechanical ability, special tests have been devised using questions involving these factors.) It is impossible to formulate a single question which involves nothing but 'g'. Consequently, a variety of questions must be set which measure many different group and specific factors. The summing or averaging of performance in these questions will tend to cancel out these unwanted factors.

Tests can be given to isolated individuals in the form of standardized interviews and this is the technique used by psychiatrists and clinical psychologists in diagnosis of mental disorders. It is also used in the assessment of very young children. However, individual testing is very time consuming and it requires the services of a skilled tester. Under normal circumstances where intelligence tests are to be used on large numbers of persons, a group test is preferable. These involve presenting a large number of questions of different types to a group of candidates simultaneously. These questions may be given orally, although it is more usual to have them duplicated

The Differences Between Individuals

in a question book. Under controlled conditions and in a given time, the students are required to answer as many questions as they can. The answer sheets are collected by the invigilator, marked by comparison with a marking scheme supplied by the constructor of the test and the marks obtained converted into some acceptable measure of intelligence by comparison with a simple table. Such a system enables this type of test to be used by a wide variety of teachers, selectors, etc., with little or no psychological training.

Earlier in this chapter we emphasized that marking or assessing is basically comparative. Suppose that your three-year-old child can say 100 words. Is she forward or backward for her age? Obviously you must determine how many words each of a very large number of three-year-old children can say, extract an average or arrange them in order of merit and compare your infant's performance with this scale.

A similar technique is used for comparing intelligence. A series of tests have been devised and given to persons of different ages. Each test is designated according to the age at which the average child passes it; for example, a Year Seven test can be passed by 50 per cent of the children in their seventh year, that is, between six and seven years old. If we test an average seven-year-old child he will pass a seven year test but will fail an eight year test. If we take a bright seven-year-old he might well pass both seven and eight year tests. The first (average) child has a chronological age and a mental age, both of seven years. The second (bright) child also has a chronological age (C.A.) of seven years but has a mental age (M.A.) of eight years.

We could express differences between C.A. and M.A. in terms of an individual being, for example, 'one year forward' or 'two years backward' from average, but this is too imprecise. For a child of C.A. nine years to behave like a child of ten years (that is, to have an M.A. of ten years) is far less unusual than for a child of C.A. one year to behave like a child of M.A. two years. It is normal practice to express advancement or retardation in terms of their ratio to C.A. This is achieved by dividing M.A. by C.A., the result being called the mental ratio (M.R.). For example, a child of C.A. seven years with M.A. nine years has a Mental Ratio of $\frac{M.A.}{C.A.} = \frac{9}{7} = 1\frac{2}{7}$. Such fractions are very inconvenient to handle and write and consequently it is usual to multiply M.R. by 100 to remove the fractions. This final figure, that is, M.R. $\times$ 100 is called the individual's intelligence quotient or I.Q. For example, the child with M.R. $\frac{9}{7}$ mentioned above will have an I.Q. $=$ $\frac{9}{7} \times 100 = 128$. Average persons obviously have I.Q. $= 100$ (that is, M.A. $=$ C.A. and so M.R. $= 1$). I.Q.s above 100 indicate persons of higher than average intelligence, and of under 100, persons of lower than average intelligence.

This technique works quite well when assessing the level of intelligence of children. However, a person's intelligence ceases to increase after the age of 15–16 years. Consequently, although his M.A. stays at about 16 his C.A. goes on increasing. To overcome this difficulty we can use a constant denominator of about 16 years. It is more usual, however, to employ a different technique for comparing the performances of adults. This is called the percentile rank (P.R.) method. In this case, all the persons taking a particular test are arranged in order of merit. The list is then divided into 100 equal groups, each group being called a percentile. The members of the top group have a percentile rank of 100, of the bottom group a P.R. of 1 and an average individual a P.R. of 50.

If you are told that an individual has P.R. $= 75$ in an intelligence test, this means that he is more intelligent than 74 per cent of the population and less intelligent than 25 per cent. This P.R. technique can be used in any sort of test. It can be particularly valuable in describing examination results. To say that a student got 90 per cent of the marks in an examination tells us very little unless we know how difficult the paper was. But to say that he had a P.R. of 67 tells us that he did better than 66 per cent of the other candidates taking the paper.

There are many other aspects of intelligence that space does not permit us to discuss here. Let us simply leave the topic by reminding ourselves that although there are many gaps in our knowledge of its nature and many reservations in public opinion as to its usefulness, it has been the basis of much successful diagnosis and selection between individuals. In particular it has been widely used in clinical studies of problem and subnormal children and in selection of children at $11 +$. A field of growing importance is the application of intelligence and other forms of testing to vocational guidance, so important in our modern way of life with its specialization and division of labour.

SUMMARY —

1. All human beings are similar yet each is unique. It is important that we should understand how and why we differ from one another and also how we may attempt to assess the degrees of variation between individuals.

2. Factors responsible for our similarities and differences may be placed in two categories:

   a. inherited characteristics present from conception onwards;
   b. acquired characteristics which come to influence us during the course of our lives.

3. In the development of the individual genes and chromosomes determine the potential level of attainment of the individual in both physical and psychological terms.

4. The actual level which is attained within these genetically determined limits depends upon the environment within which the individual develops.

5. The concept of measurement involves comparisons with standards. This is as true for psychological characteristics as it is for length, weight, time or any other variable. In a psychological test a standardized set of stimuli (questions) are presented to the group of persons being tested. Their responses (answers) are recorded and compared with a standard (marking scheme) or with each other.

6. It is obviously essential that the standard you use is suitable for the individual with whom you are using it. Different age-groups, cultures, nationalities, etc., demand different standards.

7. Examinations can be considered as carefully controlled forms of communication where stimuli are standardized and responses accurately observed and compared either with a standard or with each other.

8. Many factors affect a candidate's performance in an examination, for example, his teacher and the way in which he was taught, the examination paper, and luck as well as psychological factors active in his own C.N.S., for example, memory, intelligence, relevant past experiences, motivation. Consequently, a single examination result does not tell one very much about

which factors were responsible for the mark obtained. This is of great practical importance in a society where personal advancement is often based on examination results.

9. The types of examination so far discussed have attempted to assess what has been learned during a special course of training, for example, an O-level French course or a study-block in a nurse training school. The question arises 'to what extent can such examination results be used to predict future achievement either in these subjects or in life in general?'

10. Traditional essay-type examinations, short-answer objective-type tests and practical examinations each assess different qualities. To obtain the best overall evaluation of an individual a combination of these techniques should be used. However, such human assessment leaves much to be desired. Psychological tests attempt to provide a more rigorous assessment than normal examinations achieve. As our example we considered intelligence tests.

11. The major problem of identifying intelligence really boils down to extracting the common factor from a variety of intelligent processes, for example, the ability to cope with the environment, to solve problems, to see what is relevant and important.

12. The first person to attempt this successfully was Spearman. By statistical techniques he analysed a variety of intelligent activities and extracted one fundamental factor underlying them all. This he called 'g' (the general factor of intelligence). He also determined for each act a specific factor, 's', which he believed was shared with no other act. This concept of intelligence is embodied in Spearman's Two Factor Theory.

13. Nowadays the concept of group factors as factors shared between related tasks has been added to Spearman's theory. The major group factors which are generally accepted are verbal, spatial, numerical, mechanical and musical abilities and perceptual speed.

14. Intelligence can be looked upon as a measure of two qualities:

   a. the ability to see relevant relationships between objects or ideas in a problem;
   b. the ability to call up other ideas relevant to the problem.

15. Assessment of these two qualities determines the form and content of questions used in intelligence tests. Although the questions themselves may appear artificial and unrelated to the problems of everyday life, analysis of any problem-solving behaviour can be achieved through these two processes.

16. Intelligence tests may be oral or written and given to individuals or groups according to the needs of the tester. Whatever form

is used the instructions issued with the test must be strictly adhered to. The marks obtained are converted into an acceptable measure of intelligence by a standard procedure laid down in the instructions accompanying the test.

REFERENCES

1. Lindgren, H. C. *Psychology of Personal and Social Adjustment* (American Book Co., N.Y. 1953) discusses social implications of individual differences.
2. For a useful discussion of the principles of genetics see Mottram, V. H. *The Physical Basis of Personality* (Pelican, Harmondsworth, revised ed. 1952), pp. 11–51.
3. For further detail on inheritance of human characteristics see Carter, C. O. *Human Heredity* (Pelican, Harmondsworth 1962).
4. Reid, L. *The Sociology of Nature* (Pelican, Harmondsworth 1962) and Leach, W. *Plant Ecology* (Methuen, London, 3rd ed. 1949); both consider environmental effects on plants and animals.
5. Bowlby, J., abridged and edited by Fry, M. *Child Care and The Growth of Love* (Pelican, Harmondsworth 1953) discusses some effects of parents on the development of children.
6. Riessman, F. *The Culturally Deprived Child* (Harper, N.Y. 1962).
7. See Vernon, P. E. *Intelligence and Attainment Tests* (U.L.P., London 1960) and Vernon, P. E. *The Measurement of Abilities* (U.L.P., London 1956).
8. For a discussion of many psychological aspects of examinations see Vernon, P. E. *Intelligence and Attainment Tests* (U.L.P., London 1960).
9. See Adams, J. *The Student's Guide* (English Universities Press, London 1964), pp. 227–48, or James, D. E. *A Student's Guide to Efficient Study* (Pergamon, Oxford 1966).
10. See Vernon, P. E. *Intelligence and Attainment Tests*.
11. *Ibid.*
12. *Ibid.*
13. For an examination of some standardized educational tests see Burt, C. *Mental and Scholastic Tests* (Staples Press, London, 1949).
14. As examples of interest tests see Kuder, G. F. *Kuder Preference Record* (Science Research Associates, Chicago 1942) or Strong, E. K. *Vocational Interest Blank* (Stanford University Press, Stanford, Cal. 1927).
15. Vernon, P. E. *The Measurement of Abilities* (U.L.P., London, 2nd ed. 1956).
16. For a very useful introduction to the subject of intelligence see

Knight, R. *Intelligence and Intelligence Tests* (Methuen, London 1933).

17. *Ibid.*, pp. 16–40.
18. *Ibid.*, pp. 7–15.
19. Burt, C. *The Distribution and Relations of Educational Abilities* (King, London 1917).
20. The following will give many references to further reading while at the same time providing a comprehensive background to intelligence testing. Vernon, P. E. *Intelligence and Attainment Tests* (U.L.P., London 1960); Vernon, P. E. *The Measurement of Abilities* (U.L.P., 1956); Burt, C. 'The Meaning and Assessment of Intelligence' in *Readings in General Psychology*, Halmos, P. and Iliffe, A. (eds.) (Routledge & Kegan Paul, London 1959).

Chapter Eleven

The Uniqueness of Each Individual

INTRODUCTION

This chapter continues our discussion of individual differences and the problems and importance of their assessment. We have considered methods of comparing people in terms of their past achievements in a given course of study and also techniques for predicting performance in terms of general intelligence or special aptitudes. While, for particular purposes, these are extremely valuable measures to obtain, in everyday life most of us tend to assess individuals as whole persons rather than in terms of isolated characteristics.

In this chapter we are concerned with this problem of 'how to assess a person as an integrated whole'. We all do this (with varying degrees of success) whenever we attempt to understand the behaviour of another person. But on what criteria do we base our assessments? Are these the best criteria for the purpose, and, if they are, can we be sure that we apply them correctly and fairly? We spent the whole of Chapter 5 discussing how we frequently misinterpret ourselves and what is going on around us.

You can demonstrate for yourself that in contacts with other persons you select certain features to which you pay attention. The first time you meet a new individual you will notice some specific characteristics of him, perhaps his height, colour of his eyes, his clothes, some feature which reminds you of a previous acquaintance, and so forth. (Two persons meeting a stranger for the first time and subsequently comparing views will discover that they probably noticed quite different features, and so got different impressions of him.) On subsequent meetings with this new acquaintance you will find that the obvious features which struck you at first no longer catch your attention (you have become used to them), and now you notice other details in their place. For example, a class of young children were introduced to their new teacher who had a very pronounced French accent. For the first few minutes of the lesson the children were obviously fascinated by her voice and paid little attention to anything else. After quite a short time, however, they stopped noticing her speech and carried on with their work as if she had no such accent, i.e. they now paid attention to the subject matter which she was discussing.

Obviously you form an impression of a person according to the features which you observe. You will have clearer percepts of the characteristics which attract your attention, than of those which go unnoticed. Ask a group of your friends what they notice most about persons to whom they are introduced and you will find points of view varying from where and how they met the individual, what he was wearing and how he talked, to apparent intellectual ability and common interests with themselves. When you ask them why these features are important and how they interpret them, frequently they cannot tell you. Such an unsystematic and unreliable method of assessing individuals is obviously quite useless for efficient selection of persons within our society. (Nevertheless the majority of amateur interviewing panels have much prestige even though their work is covered by this statement.)

Psychologists have been concerned for a long time with seeing persons as integrated wholes. The sum-total of all our physical and psychological characteristics is called our *personality*.[1] If you consider the previous chapters of this book as pieces of a jig-saw puzzle, then this chapter on personality can be considered as the overall picture. Analogies are often misleading and many psychologists would say that the jig-saw concept may be inadequate. Perhaps it is better to consider the individual aspects of a person's make-up as bricks and personality as the whole house, built of bricks but held together with cement. At our present state of knowledge it is better to assume that personality ought to be studied 'as a whole', any analysis giving an incomplete picture (just as analysis of protoplasmic constituents gives an incomplete picture of the living cell). Of course, such an approach makes the process of accurate, efficient assessment and comparision of individuals very difficult indeed.

In this chapter we shall concentrate on three major aspects of personality study. We shall begin with a discussion of basic concepts of the relative effects of inherited and acquired factors in personality development. We shall then very briefly consider some of the main theories relating to the nature of personality. Finally we shall outline some of the more important techniques for personality assessment.

INHERITED AND ACQUIRED FACTORS IN PERSONALITY DEVELOPMENT

In the last chapter we outlined briefly the importance of both our genetical make-up and the environment in which we develop, as controlling forces in making us the individuals we are. Both of these factors obviously affect the complete personality, both physically and psychologically. The genes (blue-prints), according to which our characteristics are determined, are duplicated from the original fertilized egg and are identical in each cell of our bodies (including our brains). The environment in which we grow up affects all our physical and mental processes. Some children are overfed or undernourished, others lack exercise or get insufficient sleep and the results are reflected in the personalities of the individuals concerned. Similarly parents and teachers, while bringing children up in the way which they think best, may, consciously or otherwise, encourage careful accurate observation or engender slapdash habits, may give practice in learning by understanding and thinking or insist on rote-learning or immediate blind obedience without giving reasons. Some of these environmental effects are reflections of peculiarities of the parent or teacher and consequently will vary between families or classes in the same society. Others however represent the standards of the society itself which are reaching the child by way of its particular family or school and will be common to all members of that society. Later these standards will impinge upon the child directly and continue their modifying and controlling function.

261

It is useful to extract two basic concepts in the description of personality. *Temperament* is the physical and physiological basis of our personality which is to a large extent inherited. *Character* is the acquired aspect of personality which manifests itself in standards, attitudes, values, etc., which the individual picks up from the environment. As our discussion will show, however, it is very difficult to separate completely these two concepts.

A. TEMPERAMENT. It is impossible to give a short definition of this term which will be acceptable to all schools of psychology. It refers basically to the inborn aspects of personality, and most people agree that this restricts it to the 'feeling' or emotional functions (but see Chapter 6). The 'knowing' and 'willing' functions of personality are acquired through experience and therefore are not normally included in discussions of temperament.

As both physical characteristics and temperament are based largely on inheritance there is good reason for supposing that they might be closely linked, but here there is a difficulty. While a person's height, strength, athletic abilities or physical deficiencies may be largely based on genetic endowment, their development and final form and their value or otherwise to the individual will be determined by the environment. The same applies to internal anatomical and physiological considerations, for example, the strengths of needs and drives, hormone balance, the structure of the nervous system and so forth.

The question then arises: 'Can we be sure that any variations in personality are due to inheritance?' May they not all be the result of environmental effects? This is a difficult standpoint to refute and evidence must be indirect. It is certainly true that infants show considerable temperamental variations which are hard to explain in terms of environmental influence. Some are very active, others constantly sleepy, some are content to be nursed by any stranger, others are embarrassingly fearful. Again observable changes in the functioning of the brain, e.g. damage from accident, or deterioration with age, will bring about quite striking personality changes. Persons with peculiar electrical brain patterns may have abnormal personalities, e.g. some problem children and aggressive psychopaths. Certain brain operations and the use of electro-convulsive therapy also have observable physical effects on the brain which can be related to changes in personality. Further evidence comes from the endocrine system. For example, if the thyroid gland of a previously normal person suddenly becomes overactive, the individual will become much less stable and more anxious than before. Conversely a decrease of thyroid secretion will change the individual's personality in the direction of mental and physical lethargy.

Apart from these very obvious psycho-physical connections our knowledge of the actual importance of inheritance in personality determination is meagre. Whether a child is aggressive or fearful, inquisitive or shy, cheerful or sad, etc., depends upon both what he inherits from his parents and the environment which his parents create for him to develop in. How his parents treat him, whether he is an only child or a member of a large family, the economic and educational standard of the home, and a host of other factors determine the direction and extent to which his inherited characteristics are developed. Environmental conditions so effect the manifestations of inborn characteristics that we cannot disentangle them. Let us simply state that we shall use the word 'temperament' to mean that part of our personality which is based on physical and physiological foundations and which therefore forms a fairly stable framework within which acquired characteristics develop.

B. CHARACTER. This can be considered as the sum-total of those aspects of our personalities which, although developing within the framework created by our inherited characteristics, are basically the result of environmental effects. For example a person's values, attitudes, morals and interests represent the results of experiences which that individual has perceived. Consequently character is much more easily controlled than is temperament. By subjecting an individual to certain types of experience we can 'train' his character.

In our discussion of maturation and learning in Chapter 7 we mentioned the permanent effects on a person's behaviour of early experiences.[2] The forms of behaviour resulting from the influences of such early experiences will be constantly practised throughout the formative years of a child's life and by the time he is mature will be almost as ingrained in his personality as are his temperament characteristics. (We often talk of such acquired effects as being 'second-nature' to the person.) On top of these more or less permanent features of character we find superficial short-term features which are related to the immediate circumstances in which the individual finds himself. This kind of 'external mask' which can be put on, for example, at an interview for a job, going home to meet your girl-friend's parents, etc., is as much part of your character as are your political or religious views. A combination of these two aspects of our characters enables us to be relatively stable within ourselves and able to recognize and expect certain behaviour forms in others ('that is typical of him', 'cannot believe that of her', 'quite out of character'). At the same time, however, each of us can be flexible and produce suitable responses in a variety of situations, for example, a school teacher behaves differently when talking to a good child, a naughty child, another teacher, the headmaster, a visiting parent or an inspector.

We have discussed various aspects of these environmental influences in other parts of this book. Let us simply remind ourselves that all living animals (human or otherwise) are in a constant state of exchange with the environment. Biological need satisfaction (see Chapter 6) is the most primitive manifestation of this exchange and an upset in terms, for example, of shortage of food, or sexual opportunity or excessive pain or heat, will influence the immediate behaviour and perhaps also the subsequent development of the individual. At the human level we find that other psychological needs (e.g. security, acceptance by others, respect, interest) are also essential for a full and successful life.

In the infant, helpless and dependent, these needs are very largely satisfied by its parents. Not only do its parents keep it alive and well by supplying requirements essential for life, but as it grows older they control and direct its behaviour through manipulation of these need-satisfying requirements. If it responds as they wish it to, it will be rewarded perhaps with food or some other material gift, but often with love, praise and acceptance. If it behaves in an unacceptable way its parents may withhold food and acceptance ('go to bed with no supper', 'I don't love you any more', 'if you do that again I shall run away') or they may cause it physical discomfort, etc. All rewards and punishments be they administered by parents

and teachers on children or by society or adults, can be analysed in terms of need satisfaction.[3]

The young child develops values and attitudes towards its
family and friends according to the principles outlined above.
Whether the person grows up optimistic, helpful and polite or
aggressive, selfish and demanding will depend upon both the
mind and body with which he is born, and the environment in
which he develops. A key to understanding much of the
behaviour which a person shows lies in the concept of
'functional value'. Normally, behaviour is produced which
deals with the environment in the most useful way for the
individual performing it. If a child discovers that reacting in a
certain way gives good results he will practise this technique.
For example, if a small child finds that in order to obtain his
fair share of life's good things he has to fight and compete
with his brothers and sisters he will do so. If on the other hand
his parents require that all their children shall sit back and
wait until they are given their quota then he will be less aggressive as a result. When the child reaches maturity he will be so
used to behaving in certain ways that he will have difficulty in
modifying his responses.

In Chapter 4 we discussed the importance of past experiences
in the interpretation of new percepts. Even when environmental circumstances are quite different we still use partially
relevant past experiences. For example, the man who is a
policeman or sergeant-major at work may regiment his
children at home, or the girl 'kept down' at home often cannot
relax when she is at her boy-friend's house in the presence of
his very much more liberally minded parents. In everyday life
one can see young impressionable children sharing an
environment with adults and adopting the standards (social,
moral, political, religious) of those adults. Subsequently,
when these patterns are firmly established and the child enters
society as an individual in his own right, he will continue to
apply these standards. If his home life has taught him to
respect other persons and their property he will continue to do
so. If taught to be careful with money, to keep himself to
himself, to be a snob, to admire honesty or to disregard the
law, these tendencies will be present in his deep permanent
character.

This concept raises a very complex philosophical, social and educational problem. A person acquires his values and standards from the environment in which he is brought up. When subsequently he has to make value judgements about his own or other societies, about their nature, problems, possible improvements, etc., he uses as his standard for comparison the past experiences which he has gleaned from his own society. While such inside information can give some indication of the origins and development of problems which arise, at the same time, lack of experience of other ways of life makes for narrowness of interpretation and incomplete understanding. A schoolmaster cut off from the outside world can put quite ridiculous emphasis on a detail of presentation of homework while disregarding important aspects of his subject which his pupils will need to appreciate after leaving school. Again the nursing profession may have great difficulty in revising their systems of student recruitment and examination unless they obtain information from outside sources. Communist and capitalist countries may be unable to understand one another because of the differences in standards which they are applying in interpreting circumstances and suggestions.

The importance of the environment and particularly of parent–child relationships in the subsequent production of certain types of behaviour has been brought out by substantial investigations into the origins of problems of delinquent children. While generalizations can over-simplify human situations, it appears that frequently children are malicious, cruel and defy authority when they have been constantly rejected by their parents or their parents quarrel or live apart. Other manifestations of lack of security occur when parents neglect their offspring either intentionally by going out drinking or not bothering to cope, or unintentionally where there is no father, and mother must work, or where parents are not physically or mentally competent to run a home. Children of such families may join gangs or steal in order to make good their need for security in as positive a manner as they can. We are all familiar also with the shy, sensitive, anxious type of child who feels inadequate at home either through fierce and unsuccessful competition with other brothers and sisters or through over-critical, demanding parents.

Although we have emphasized the underlying constancy and stability of an individual's personality, we have also mentioned that a person's behaviour at any time depends very much upon the circumstances in which he finds himself and the other people sharing his environment. This is very obvious in the case of a person who 'puts on a good show' to impress visitors or inspectors, but is normally far less efficient and well-organized. Again the strong-willed aggressive head of an office or school may be quite meek (even 'henpecked') at home. This type of experience is common to us all in perhaps less extreme forms. For example, you would behave quite differently when throwing a party for a group of your teenage chums from when you have a tea-party for several elderly aunts, even though the environment and basic activity (i.e. eating and communicating) may be the same. Again, the sudden appearance of an authoritarian figure in a previously noisy group can modify the behaviour of individuals concerned and 'put a damper on things'.

Because people behave in certain ways under certain circumstances it is quite easy to obtain a wrong impression of a person. A schoolteacher met only in class where he is teaching his specialist subject can easily create the impression that he is 'always right' and the idea that he is fallible and human may not occur especially to his younger pupils. Many people have similar misconceptions of the width of ability of doctors or lawyers or may think clergymen are morally much better than they actually are. Many of our likes and dislikes among people are due to misunderstandings based on inadequate experience of them ('he's all right when you get to know him'). We shall discuss this concept more fully in Chapter 12. We must always bear in mind the fact that although society is built up of interacting individuals, each individual is constantly being moulded by his society. Personality then can be considered to be the result of adaptation of an individual to his physical and social environment.

THEORIES OF PERSONALITY

Throughout the history of civilization attempts have been made to classify individuals in terms of their personality characteristics. The reasons underlying these attempts range from a practical need for selection and prediction to an academic or individual interest in oneself in comparison with others. The major problem in this process is the selection of measurable criteria which correlate with personality characteristics. In the past, physical measurements have formed the basis of such classifications but today, with the development of suitable psychological tests the emphasis has moved towards assessment of behaviour in response to given stimuli. Such studies are still in their infancy and no one theory yet put forward explains all the known facts or is universally acceptable. This does not, of course, mean that most of this apparently conflicting material is wrong. It is quite conceivable that different workers are looking at the same basic concept from different points of view and are consequently arriving at different interpretations of the nature of personality.

One of the earliest classifications of personality-types is attributed to Hippocrates (400 B.C.) who suggested that a person's behaviour was to a great extent determined by the relative quantities of body-fluids (or humours) which he possessed.

Predominant Humour	Type of Behaviour	Personality Type
Blood	unstable, excitable, gay	sanguine
Phlegm	lethargic, slow	phlegmatic
Yellow bile	easily angered	choleric
Black bile	pessimistic	melancholic

Although such a classification is too limited to explain the great variety of personality types which we can observe around us, its emphasis on the basic importance of the chemistry and physics of the body in determining behaviour-forms has by no means been rejected. W. B. Cannon has done a great deal of most interesting work on the role of hormones in personality determination. He analysed the effects of over- and underactivity of each ductless gland in terms of behaviour changes, for example:

Ductless Gland		Behaviour Forms
Thyroid	overactive	domineering, excitable
	underactive	lethargic, lazy, dull
Gonads	overactive	aggressive, self-confident
	underactive	withdrawn, artistic, musical

Although in extreme cases such hormonal influences can have a marked effect on personality, it is probably more realistic to regard them as 'colouring' factors than as basic personality determinants.

Several classifications in terms of external physical appearance have been attempted. At first sight this is a very reasonable line of approach. We constantly assess other people in terms of their faces, voices, clothes, etc. Advertisements stress the importance of make-up, deodorants and a host of other aids to beauty in improving our personalities. Again, a lost limb or some other disfigurement can considerably affect an individual's behaviour, attitudes and relationships with others. Obviously, many of the characteristics in such personalities are the result of learning as described in our discussion of 'functional value' above. Two abortive attempts at classification in such terms can be quickly dismissed. *Phrenology* was based on the concept that certain mental faculties, e.g. intelligence, reasoning, memory, were located in specific parts of the brain, and the better developed the faculties were, the more nervous tissue would lie in these areas. By carefully feeling the skull (which follows the brain contours) the phrenologists believed they could determine which faculties the individual was best endowed with. The faculty theory of psychology has now been rejected and so has phrenology. *Physiognomy* suggests that personality is linked to physical characteristics in a very direct way. Proportions of the face and head, texture of the skin and hair, etc., were considered to be indicative of personality. For example, a receding forehead or a 'weak' chin, small eyes or a flabby mouth were considered to represent undesirable qualities in psychological terms as well as in physical appearance. While such physical features are obviously dependent upon inherited endowment and glandular secretion and may therefore be linked to temperament, their relationship to the individual's total personality is too indirect and obscure to be valuable.

A very interesting concept was put forward early in this century by a psychiatrist, Ernst Kretschmer.[4] He observed that schizophrenic patients (see Chapter 14) tended to be thin, fragile persons while manic depressive patients were usually plumper and rounder. Patients in mental hospitals are likely to show extremes of personality characteristics which may well be present in more moderate form in members of the normal populace. Consequently, Kretschmer devised a classification in terms of physique based on his psychiatric observations but applied to the general public.

Personality Type	Physical Characteristics	Behaviour
Asthenic	slight and tall	stable, idealistic, withdrawn, unemotional
Pyknic	plump and short	unstable, tolerant, social, emotional
Athletic	muscular, broad and tall	intermediate between above
Dysplastic	abnormal or underdeveloped	tendency to feel inferior

Application of this classification to the general public has not borne out Kretschmer's predictions completely although there may well be some correlation between physique and behaviour. It is a common human experience to think of a jolly happy-go-lucky person as being short and fat, e.g. Friar Tuck, or John Bull, while a withdrawn miserable type is portrayed as a lean, tall person, e.g. fairy-tale witches, or Scrooge. However, so many other factors also appear to be involved in personality formation that to base selection or prediction on such criteria is obviously impossible.

The last type of classification of personalities in terms of physique which we shall mention here is that put forward by Sheldon in 1942.[5] He classified individuals in terms of the relative proportions of tissues derived from the different parts of the original fertilized egg (or zygote) from which they developed. The zygote divides many times giving a ball-like mass of cells. As development proceeds the ball becomes hollow with an accumulation of cells at one end. These cells differentiate into three layers:

an inner layer or endoderm giving rise to the digestive tract,
an outer layer or ectoderm giving rise to the skin and nervous tissue,
an intermediate layer or mesoderm giving rise to muscle, skeleton, blood, etc.

In the completely formed body each of these cell types is represented. Sheldon had 4,000 young men photographed naked from the front, back and side. He then rated each of them on a seven-point scale for each of these tissues. He postulated three extreme combinations:

270

The Uniqueness of Each Individual

   a. the endomorphic type who was round and soft bodied (rating 7:1:1);
   b. the mesomorphic type who was muscular and large boned (rating 1:7:1);
   c. the ectomorphic type who was delicate, thin, sensitive (rating 1:1:7).

Most people were, of course, intermediates having ratings (or somatotypes) of e.g., 4:3:5, 5:4:2, 4:4:4 etc. (See Sheldon's own work for more accurate interpretations of photographs and ratings.)

Having systematically categorized physical characteristics Sheldon now selected samples of individuals for personality assessment. In a series of interviews each candidate was rated in terms of a large number of psychological characteristics. Sheldon claimed to have established three personality types each linked to a somatotype.

   a. Viscerotonic (related to endomorphic) who likes comfort, is relaxed and jolly, prefers company, is tolerant and easy going, is emotional and needs affection;
   b. Somatotonic (related to mesomorphic) who likes adventure, is aggressive and energetic, likes to be 'in charge', is insensitive, objective and direct;
   c. Cerebrotonic (related to ectomorphic) who likes privacy, is restrained and apprehensive, hides his feelings and lacks self-confidence.

Although when Sheldon carried out his investigations he claimed to obtain very high correlations between somatotype and personality type, other workers have not confirmed his findings and much research is still required to substantiate this theory.

In general we can say, that while in theory physical characteristics could form a very convenient basis for classifying personality, in practice such schemes prove inadequate. While the form and function of a person's body will exert a powerful influence on his behaviour there are many other psychological aspects which are not taken into account by the physical approach.

This concept of types, so convenient in biological terms, has also been extended to psychological characteristics. We talk of people as good types or bad, sensitive or thick-skinned, sociable or withdrawn. In general such classifications are meant to be superficial and are simply convenient ways of describing individuals in everyday language. C. J. Jung developed a much more comprehensive personality classification along these lines but on a more scientific basis. He allocated persons to two categories, *introverts* who were withdrawn, shy, antisocial and more interested in things than in people and *extraverts* who were sociable, outgoing and interested in other people. While such a scheme is simple and attractive it does not work well for the majority of individuals. Most of us are usually intermediate between these categories, while occasionally we may be either extraverted or introverted. In fact, Jung's theory shows all the characteristics which have caused modern psychologists to reject type classifications. People are distributed over a continuous scale from, for example, extravert to introvert or from good to bad, with the majority falling in the middle of the scale and not near the two extremes as a type theory would suggest. Again, such theories are bound to be artificial as they give quite unnatural prominence to some selected part of an individual's personality instead of assessing the whole person. It is very difficult to take environmental effects into account in most type theories, and as we have said many times before, these are of great importance in determining the response of an individual.

Many psychologists prefer to describe an individual in terms of relatively permanent characteristics of his personality, e.g. his stability, aggressiveness, cheerfulness or degree of sophistication. These characteristics (or *traits*) are part of the personality of each of us being well developed in some individuals, poorly defined in others while most of us are normally distributed between these two extremes. Such traits are obviously a very convenient way of describing an individual and form the basis of everyday descriptions of people in ordinary conversation. In such everyday discussions we tend to notice only those traits which are very well or very poorly developed (e.g. the neurotic or the very placid, the sophisticated or the very crude) and ignore the traits of only average development. This introduces a further complication for what is 'average' or 'normal' depends upon other people in the environment. For example, a scientist may be considered very methodical and logical at home but only average at work, a student's dress and behaviour may be unconventional in the

The Uniqueness of Each Individual

street but normal in his class-room situation. Again a particular trait may be considered in a favourable light when the person follows your own inclinations, e.g. he may be 'reliable' and 'consistent' but should he go against your wishes you may think him 'rigid' and 'inflexible'.

In psychological investigations, it is important that all relevant traits in a personality must be noted even if they are not all investigated. Some form of objective assessment must then be utilized to avoid personal preferences and prejudices. Again the large number of traits which can be described must be organized into a convenient form for investigation. Techniques based on statistical analysis have been devised for extracting general categories of apparently closely related traits and for which specific tests can be constructed. Unfortunately, different workers in this field vary very much in the number and content of the trait categories which they have isolated. Eysenck[7] suggests that there are three major dimensions in which individuals differ:

a. introversion – extraversion
b. emotional stability – neuroticism
c. normality – psychoticism

On the other hand Cattell[8] claims to have established a dozen or more categories:

a. easy going, frank – reserved, obstructive
b. intelligent – mentally defective
c. emotionally stable – neurotic
d. dominant, aggressive – submissive, complaisant
e. cheerful, witty – depressed, pessimistic
f. interested in others – neglectful of others
g. adventurous – withdrawn
h. independent – dependent
i. cultured – crude, awkward
j. understanding – suspicious, jealous
k. conventional – unconventional
l. sophisticated – sentimental

The most important point for our purpose here is that these are attempts to describe personality in an objective manner. Much fuller accounts of these and other theories can be found from the bibliography.

While such trait extraction and description is a very important first step in personality determination and assessment it suffers from the inadequacy of not describing the inter-relationships and relative importance of these different traits. Again behaviour varies so much with different situations that it is impossible to give an accurate and consistent description of an individual through a simple list of traits. We need some form of description which takes into account the general pattern of interaction of traits with one another and at the same time considers the effects of the particular environmental situation in which the individual's personality is being investigated, i.e. we need a *dynamic* theory of personality. We must attempt to assess personality as a whole, but not try to force individuals into rigid, preconceived type-classes in so doing.

In strict psychological terminology dynamic theories of personality are those which put emphasis on the adaptation of an individual to the situation in which he finds himself at the particular moment of observation. Consequently a person's responses are not simply a manifestation of his particular traits, but are the result of his traits reacting with present environmental circumstances. Another very large school of theories put emphasis on the importance of personality development. They consider the genetical endowment of the individual as a framework within which previous experiences, health, need satisfaction and frustration, etc. are able to build up a complex but fairly stable individual.

Within each of these two approaches again different workers have taken different stands. Some consider human personalities as all sharing certain universal properties which can be scientifically assessed while others emphasize the uniqueness of the individual. Many psychoanalytical theories attempt to explain personality in terms of certain patterns of development found in each of us but determined or directed according to experience. Learning theories are more concerned with specific examples of reward and punishment which shape development. Some such theories attach great importance to the role into which the individual is cast through his place in society, his nationality, sex, age, socio-economic status, etc.

We shall not attempt a full description or evaluation of these theories here. Let us simply mention a few of the more important workers in this field. Pride of place must go to the Viennese physician, Sigmund Freud, the founder of psychoanalysis[9] (see Chapter 14) not only because of the very great influence which his work has had on psychology as a whole, but also because of his reputation among the public at large. Freud's theory is based on the concept that the *libido* (the energy of the sexual instinct) of the individual is the driving force behind all his behaviour and consequently underlies his whole personality. He stressed that the way in which libido is developed or frustrated during childhood to a very large extent determines adult behaviour. His great emphasis on the instinctive basis of behaviour caused much of his work to be rejected by his contemporaries, and many subsequent workers in this field, while still acknowledging some of Freud's basic concepts, have attached more importance to environmental and cultural influences than he did. We shall mention the work of some of these Neo-Freudians below.

Freud considered that there were three major aspects of personality. The *Id* is the instinctive (primary) driving force behind our behaviour. It demands immediate satisfaction of biological needs and we are unaware of its activity. The *Ego* is the conscious will or reason that controls behaviour so that the demands of the id are modified in the light of environmental pressures. The *Super-ego* is a kind of conscience or ideal standard built up through experiences during life. Its function is to maintain standards of behaviour at a level demanded by society and its effect is to produce a feeling of guilt when it is not observed. Freud considered that at any one time for each individual the id will be seeking pleasure and need gratification, the environment enforcing limitations and the super-ego imposing its acquired level of standards. The way in which the ego resolves these various components is expressed in the individual's personality. Sometimes the id is dominant, for example in sexual assault or rape. Sometimes the super-ego is dominant, for example, when one fights for a principle to one's biological detriment. Nevertheless his emphasis was on the importance of libido and he went on to construct a theory based on the effects of gratification or frustration of biological needs at different stages in the individual's development.

Many other theories of personality have been put forward. They differ mainly in where they put their main emphasis. A. Adler[10] (1930) for example, instead of stressing libido, ranked the desire for superiority as the prime factor in personality development. He sees each of us striving to perfect himself both as an individual and as a member of society and so our personalities reflect our own shortcomings and the success with which we redress them. K. Horney[11] (1937) changed the emphasis on to the importance of basic anxiety aroused by any form of insecurity which the individual experiences. E. Fromm[12] (1941) again considered the prime motivating factor in personality determination to be based on insecurity but he sees it in the specific context of the growing child gaining in independence and responsibility. The individual's inadequacies in his new role cause him to feel insecure, lonely and afraid and he attempts to 'escape from freedom' by making new relationships which help him to satisfy his new needs. The individual's personality is determined by the way in which society satisfies or frustrates these basic needs. Other theories go on to extend the importance of the motivation of the individual. H. Murray[13] (1938) for example, considers that there are some twenty categories of need which must be considered in personality determination. On the other hand H. S. Sullivan[14] (1953) stresses the importance of interpersonal relationships and considers that the study of personality should not be restricted to the study of the individual.

Let us conclude our discussion of personality theory by very briefly introducing the work of G. W. Allport[15] (1937) as an approach very different from that of Freud. Allport considers that 'personality is the dynamic organization within the individual of those psychophysical systems that determine his unique adjustments to his environment'. He postulates that personality can be described in terms of traits of two different categories: (a) *common traits* which are qualities exhibited by everyone and in terms of which individuals can be compared and (b) *personal traits* (or *personal dispositions* as he calls them) which are personality features unique for each of us and dependent upon our capabilities and experiences. Some traits will be of paramount importance in the person's make-up while others will be less influential. It is the organization of these traits within the individual that characterizes his personality. A very important feature of Allport's theory is his concept of 'Functional Autonomy of Motives' which we introduced in Chapter 6. This states that activities originally performed to satisfy a particular need may later become motivating in their own right. For example, a child may learn to read initially to meet the demands of his parents and teachers but subsequently may enjoy reading for its own sake. Again a teenager may decide to become a teacher through identification with an admired form-master. Later when the 'adolescent crush' has subsided the student may find his intended career an acceptable goal in its own right.

Notice that while Allport accepts that experiences during development will to some extent shape an individual's personality, he also emphasizes the importance of the contemporary situation in a full description of personality. He believes that we should be concerned with present values, attitudes and interests whatever their historical development may be. He puts stress on consciousness of the here and now as opposed to Freud's obsession with the importance of early experiences and parental attitudes. He is less concerned with the permanent fundamental nature of the id and more interested in the 'patterned individuality' of the person in his contemporary situation. Allport's theory represents a more positive forward-looking approach to personality than the compulsive, repetitive concepts of Freud.

We cannot follow this discussion further here. Let us leave the point by saying that while as yet we have no universally acceptable theory of personality, some suitable working hypothesis is essential for the development of methods of personality assessment. Different approaches have suited the needs of workers in different fields. The interested reader must follow these up for himself.[16]

ASSESSMENT OF PERSONALITY

In any form of evaluation, be it of building materials or physical fitness, works of art or human personality, it is obviously important that the evaluator should be in a position to (a) decide exactly what he wants to assess, (b) ensure that this is, in fact, what he is assessing, and (c) take precautions to make his assessment as accurate and reliable as possible. From our discussion above, it is clear that there are no universally acceptable approaches to these problems in personality assessment. Nevertheless, the practical demands of society dictate that some form of assessment of personality for use in selection and guidance must be produced. A great deal of research has gone into investigations in this field and many different 'tools of assessment' have been constructed.

We must consider the nature of some of the more important of these techniques and note some of their values and limitations. We must remember, however, what tremendous problems they are attempting to cope with. For example, each of us is unique and for most of the qualities in which we shall be assessed the concepts of right and wrong do not apply. In general, for selection purposes, comparisons must be made between the individuals under consideration, e.g. the applicants for a job, or the candidates for a place on a course. In terms of clinical assessment and guidance, e.g. of a psychiatric patient, or a youth whose potentialities are being evaluated for possible employment, the individual must be compared with what society considers to be normal or desirable under the circumstances (see Chapter 13). Again, our personalities are dynamic depending to some extent on the environmental conditions in which we find ourselves. Any assessment concerned with adaptation to one set of circumstances (e.g. an unnatural testing situation) may not assess the whole personality as it might show itself under more normal circumstances. As our final example of a complicating factor we can note that the assessor is always subjectively involved in the evaluation either in the way in which he puts the questions or in the manner he assesses the answers.

In attempts to reduce these and other distorting influences a variety of approaches to personality assessment have arisen. An assessor may endeavour to evaluate the whole person in terms of his general appearance and behaviour, or he may prefer to extract certain selected features which he considers to be crucial. He may set fairly objective tests where a mechanical form of assessment is appropriate or he may prefer to obtain information which has to be interpreted subjectively by an assessor (preferably trained to do so).

Which form he chooses must depend upon the purpose he has in mind. A relatively subjective informal approach may be adequate for an internal promotion within a school or hospital where everyone is known as an individual. On the other hand, a highly technical objective tool whose administration and

The Uniqueness of Each Individual

interpretation requires special training may be more efficient for selection of, say, student nurses into the profession from a large unknown population. As we shall discuss later a combination of techniques is generally the most efficient method for indicating the general pattern of psychological activity of the whole individual while at the same time elucidating particular traits, attitudes and interests.

Let us consider first some techniques which attempt to limit the number of qualities being assessed in a given test. Measures of physical and physiological factors come into this category, but in general their results are not very promising. Those functions affected by the autonomic nervous system are sometimes used in clinical interviews. These form part of an individual's responses to the test-situation over which he has no control. Measurement of changes in blood sugar content or electrical conductivity of the skin as a result of an emotive experience (e.g. a word or picture representing an idea taboo to the subject) have been attempted. This skin conduction technique is the principle on which lie detectors are constructed. Again E.E.G.s[17] (see Chapter 3) have also been considered but their value is limited at present to the diagnosis of certain abnormal states such as epilepsy and psychopathic personalities (see Chapter 14). Other studies based on psychosomatic concepts and expressive movements, e.g. walking, speaking, handwriting[18] have not proved very useful in the practical assessment of personality. The same can be said for Sheldon's somatotype classification. It must be noted however that an individual's physical characteristics must and do influence much of his personality through the limitations and potentialities that they place on him. However, at our present level of knowledge we must admit that we cannot assess accurately an individual's personality in terms of physical measurement.

Let us consider next personality assessment through paper and pencil tests where the individual is required to answer a series of questions about himself. We cannot cover the wealth of forms available here but must simply note a few basic principles.[19] In the previous chapter we introduced the concept of objective-type examinations in which the examiner so organized his questions that he severely limited the amount of information required in each answer. In some types a series of possible answers were given and the examinee had to select the right one. A similar technique can be used in personality assessment but here there is no right or wrong answer. Instead the individual's choice of answer from those available supposedly indicates characteristics of his own personality.

In some cases a question and possible answers are embodied in a list of statements from which the individual must indicate his choice by ticking the most appropriate suggestion, for example:

I am extremely social and hate being alone
I usually enjoy company
I am of average sociableness
I am rather shy and retiring
I like my own company and resent the presence of others

In other tests the individual is presented with questions to which he must answer yes, no or don't know, for example:

Are you an unsociable person?

Another variation consists of giving statements to which the candidate must answer true or false or perhaps rate himself on a scale from 5 to 1 according to the extent to which he thinks the statements applies to him, for example:

I am a sociable person

Score of 5 means that he thinks he is very sociable, or 3 that he is of average sociableness and of 1 that he thinks he is unsociable.

Such tests may be designed to assess one trait at a time (e.g. extraversion/introversion) or they may attempt to evaluate the overall level of adjustment. Some types consist of direct questions about the individual's work, leisure activities, interests and attitudes but these are likely to be very unreliable especially when the candidate knows or thinks he knows what the tester wants from him. Other forms attempt to compare the resemblance of patterns of answers of an individual with those of other people already allocated to certain groups. For example Strong's Vocational Interest Blank[20] evaluates interest in and suitability for entrance into a given profession not by asking questions obviously based on knowledge of that profession but by selecting items over a very wide range of topics. The patterns of scores of large numbers of people

The Uniqueness of Each Individual

engaged in a variety of occupations are recorded and used as a standard for comparison. The pattern of responses of the new candidate is recorded and compared with these standards and if he answers in a manner typical of an engineer or an artist or a musician then results indicate that he might well be an appropriate recruit for that profession. The Minnesota Multiphasic Personality Interview[21] performs the same function for psychiatric deviants distinguishing between, for example, schizophrenics, paranoiacs, psychopaths, hysterics, depressives (see Chapter 14). In general although these tests have apparent potential, still much work is needed to improve their validity and reliability.

The techniques we have been describing involved self-ratings by the individual. Other personality questionnaires have been designed for the assessment of an individual by his associates. Again unless great care is taken, personal preferences and prejudices can distort the findings. There is a tendency to be over-generous in estimations ('what would he like me to say?' 'suppose he was assessing me'). Again you can be over-influenced by ratings in one or two qualities. If you like a person you tend to rate him highly on all favourable issues, e.g. intelligence, honesty, maturity, stability, while if you dislike him you may be much less generous in your ratings. These generalized influences are called *halo-effects* and we shall return to them when discussing interviewing below.

In general we can say that despite their widespread use in the U.S.A. personality questionnaires have some way to go before they are readily available as valuable tools for selection and guidance. Nevertheless a great deal of ground-work has been done and all the indications are that refinement and efficiency will continue to increase.

In the personality questionnaires described above the assessor decided which information would be extracted by carefully limiting the questions which he asked. While such an approach has the obvious value of being capable of scoring and evaluation in a fairly objective manner, it imposes great restrictions on the individual being tested. *Projection tests*[22] are designed to avoid many of these restrictions. The principle embodied here is one which we have introduced elsewhere in this volume (e.g. in our discussions of perception and communication). All our activities have some personal element in them. The amount may be small, for example, when taking a pulse rate or reading aloud from a text-book, or it may be very considerable when expressing opinions or writing a fictional story. If a test could be devised which encouraged an individual to project a very great deal of his personality on to the environment through creative or imaginative acts, then this should enable us to assess him without distorting the results by using narrowly directed questions.

Among the most well known of the projection tests is the Rorschach Ink-Blot Test which consists of a number of cards on which ink has been spilled. Each card is then creased down the middle to give a symmetrical blot. The individual is asked to interpret the blot and according to the way in which he does so, e.g. the number of items he sees, the nature of the items as animal, human or inanimate, whether he selects part or all of the blot for interpretation, etc., the skilled tester can come to conclusions about the experience or fantasy of the individual. The validity of these tests is disputed and the interested reader can follow the discussion further in the references.

Another popular projection test is the Thematic Apperception Test which requires the individual to tell stories about ambiguous pictures. These reflect the aims and fears, hopes and disappointments, interests and attitudes of the individual. As in all such tests the results are difficult to interpret as there are no easily obtained, generally acceptable standards of assessment. This test, together with the Rorschach test, is frequently used in the diagnosis of abnormal personality. Painting and drawing are also used in the diagnosis and treatment of the maladjusted. With children, free play evaluation has been developed. The difficulties of interpretation are considerable, however, and assessors need special training.

The chief value of projection techniques is that they elucidate information not readily obtained by other means. However, they seem to be more valuable in isolating abnormalities than in educational selection or vocational guidance. An obvious problem with these tests is that the information obtained reflects so many unique qualities of the individual being assessed that comparisons between persons is very difficult. A technique which to some extent limits this problem is that of sentence completion. Here, the first part of possible emotive sentences are presented to the subject who is asked to complete them, for example:

I want to know . . .
As a child I . . .
What annoys me . . .
I am best when . . .
My father . . .
I failed . . .

Though faking is possible, often much valuable emotionally toned material is obtained. This technique then compromises by being dependent on projection by presenting ambiguous stimuli but at the same time bringing in sufficient restriction to make scoring and comparison feasible.

Let us complete this very brief introduction to techniques of personality assessment by looking at methods which attempt to evaluate the way in which the whole individual copes with general environmental situations. There are two main ways in which this approach has been developed. Either the individual is observed over a long period under natural conditions (which are very difficult to control), i.e. he is continuously assessed, or he is subjected to intensive interrogation for a short period under artificial but more easily controlled conditions, i.e. he is interviewed.

Past behaviour and experiences are often a useful guide to the understanding of an individual's present problems. When social workers or clinical psychologists compile case histories[23] they collect and interpret information relating to their patients from a variety of sources. They delve into family history, experiences in early life and at school, occupational record after leaving school, health and interests, marital problems and many other areas of experience. Such biographies are normally made in retrospect, their value only becoming apparent when the individual's physical, mental or social health breaks down. There are obviously great limitations to their detail and accuracy and much more efficient reports could be obtained if a cumulative record could be built up for each of us during our lifetime. In a school or hospital where an assessment of each individual must be made at some time or other such cumulative records should be kept.

Each of us keeps a cumulative record in our minds of our fellows as we 'get to know them better'. However, such a collection of data is likely to be very unsystematic and is not easily accessible to others. If an accurate, carefully documented written record could be kept at frequent, regular intervals, for example, during a child's education or a patient's stay in hospital, or better still, over extended periods of an individual's life, this would be very valuable.[24]

Obviously, the detailed nature of the record will depend on the use to which it will be put. In Britain today most of us have medical and dental records, many firms keep staff records, bank managers keep customers' records and the State keeps criminal records. Within a hospital for each patient several records each with a different emphasis may be kept by, e.g. the ward sister, the doctor and the almoner. In an educational establishment, depending upon the needs of the students and staff, records of various kinds are necessary. Attendance and medical records, home and socio-economic conditions, examination successes, performance in tests of general or specific abilities, aptitudes, interests, temperament, etc., levels of adjustment and maturity and many other qualities may all find themselves in a cumulative record. (The success with which these are assessed and recorded is another matter.)

For practical details of recording the interested reader should consult the bibliography. Let us simply note here that this whole process is much more difficult than many assessors appear to think. We have already mentioned halo effects above. While we must try to avoid such personal identification as to make our assessments inaccurate, at the same time we must know our charges well enough to be able to understand and assess them at more than a superficial level. Assessments made by different raters under different circumstances and then combined are more likely to be accurate evaluations than the opinions of one individual alone. The problems of combining such ratings are lessened if carefully defined questions are drawn up and 5-point scale marking is used (instead of imprecise terms like 'good', 'adequate', 'could do better', etc.). It is obviously essential that such record cards as are drawn up should be filled in accurately and regularly with dates and other relevant documentation. A carefully designed and executed scheme of this sort can be a most useful guide to a student's progress.

Often when selecting individuals into a profession a synopsis of a cumulative record compiled by other persons is needed. This usually takes the form of a testimonial, reference or confidential report. These reports sometimes go beyond describing past performance and attempt to predict, for example, what a good teacher or nurse the individual will make with suitable training. The rather meagre evidence available so far suggests that if reports are based on a few factual assessments of specific characteristics they may prove to be of some use. If, however, they consist of subjective generalizations about whole persons by head-teachers or matrons who pride themselves on being 'shrewd judges of character' then they are likely to be inefficient.

Persons asking for such confidential reports would do well to stipulate specific characteristics in which they are interested and which they believe a person with extensive contact with a candidate can assess more accurately than they can with a test, for example, such qualities as honesty, sympathy, persistence, punctuality. It is helpful to construct a number of questions on each quality, possible answers being given in a list of statements of which the rater has to tick one. For example:

Is the student capable of working on her own?[25]
  a. needs constant prodding;
  b. needs occasional prodding;
  c. carries out ordinary assignments of her own accord;
  d. completes suggested supplementary work;
  e. seeks and sets herself extra tasks.

Such questions as these involve less comparison with other students than the more traditional approach asking the assessor to comment on 'how well a student works on her own' or even asking 'how good a student' the assessor finds the individual. It also removes imprecise terms like good, average, poor, etc., which mean different things for different assessors. Having directed the assessor's thoughts to such qualities as you are interested in, if she is then invited to write a short testimonial explaining and elaborating on her previous answers this may add useful additional information without detracting from her earlier comparatively objective answers.

As our last example of a technique for personality assessment let us consider the interview. The great popularity and widespread use of this technique has engendered a great deal of research into its advantages and shortcomings. It is impossible here for us to do more than indicate a few of the major areas of interest.[26]

It is useful to consider interviews as carefully controlled conversations focusing around those characteristics of the individual which are to be assessed. These characteristics may relate to suitability for selection into or advancement within a profession or institution, for example, at selection into a teacher-training or nursing course, or for promotion to head of department in a school or principal tutor in a hospital. Alternatively, the interview may attempt to diagnose the particular problem which an individual may be faced with, as in a case of social or psychological maladjustment. In both categories the concept of comparison is used in assessment. We present our interviewees with certain stimuli (i.e. questions or problems) under controlled conditions and we carefully record their responses. If selection or advancement is the intention then candidates are compared with one another. If diagnosis and treatment is required the individual's responses are compared with those of 'normal' members of society.

A major difficulty in interviewing is that the assessors are, to a very large extent, using techniques of communication which are part of normal everyday human contact. They ask questions, note answers, observe gestures and facial expressions, they are sympathetic and suggestible. From these activities in non-interviewing situations they attempt to assess the past experiences, attitudes, values, interests, etc., of their friends, neighbours, colleagues and others with whom they may make daily contact. In Chapter 5 we discussed how very easy it is to misinterpret, to become personally involved in an answer and to read much more into it than was intended by the person to whom we are speaking. We are used to applying techniques involved in interviewing in a much more haphazard way in everyday personal contacts.

To make interviewing as efficient as possible, two questions must be asked and the answers applied rigorously to our procedure. Firstly, what information do we wish to obtain from the candidate? Secondly, which of this required information can be gleaned from an interview? Certain important qualities obviously can be evaluated to some extent in an interview, e.g. fluency and expression in language, physical appearance, demeanour, ability to strike up acceptable relationships with others, behaviour under stress. Again, by questioning one can check information from other sources on the individual's professed experiences and interests. However, our normal everyday 'assessments' of our fellows go far beyond these limits. We attempt to evaluate such qualities as moral fibre, emotional stability, intelligence, etc. These activities are so much part of our life that we may not be aware of their existence when we use them (like the rules of English grammar). Interviewers are often not aware of what they are assessing and so their findings may be of little value.

Many problems which arise during the stress and strain of an interview are very hard to avoid. We have already mentioned subjective interpretations by the interviewer. These can take many forms. So much information about the candidate is available during an interview that the assessor must be selective. He may choose unwisely and concentrate on some comparatively unimportant points while ignoring some other much more valuable information. Again, a single point arising in a discussion can spark off a whole train of thoughts in the interviewer's mind, for example, a common interest or birth-place or an antagonistic view from his own can colour the assessor's whole impression of the candidate. These subjective effects can influence the candidate's responses also. There are reports of mothers actively resenting advice on maternal matters from unmarried nurses and social workers. Again, young interviewers can antagonize more mature candidates simply because of the age difference.

A major shortcoming of interviews is that the behaviour, manner, appearance, etc., of candidates under these stressful, artificial conditions may well not be representative of them. Most interviewers expect some 'impression-creating' by candidates who obviously want to put on 'as good a front as possible'. Some of this impression-creating may go on without either interviewer or candidate being aware of it. In investigations into the accuracy of legal testimony it was found that the actual form of a question could greatly affect the nature of the answer to it.[27] This is particularly common when the most acceptable answer is implied in the question. For example, '*Didn't* you see your attacker?' is more likely to cause a doubting person to answer 'yes', than the question '*Did* you see your attacker?' So in an interview '*Do* you want to specialize?' is less likely to be answered positively than '*Don't* you want to specialize?' '*Did* you like school?' than '*Didn't* you like school?' in instances where the candidate is in doubt on the matter. For an extension of this problem consult the bibliography.[28] In general let us say that the interviewer wants the candidate to do most of the talking with as little influence as possible from what he thinks the interviewer wants him to say.

There is much debate as to how reliable interviews are as tools of assessment. Their critics describe instances in which they add very little to the efficiency of selection by other methods. Their advocates, while accepting that interviews have severe limitations, point out that at our present state of knowledge, the other forms of personality assessment which we have introduced above are not very satisfactory. They indicate other advantages of interviews over paper and pencil personality tests. Interviews can be flexible and are comparatively easily employed (when compared with the preparation, interpretation and validation of written tests). Again they may have a 'psychological advantage' when candidates believe that they have a chance to 'do themselves justice', while assessors often like to meet the candidates and 'sum them up'. Again, if you are selecting or promoting an individual into a post where the kinds of quality assessable in an interview (e.g. speech, appearance, sociability) are important, then obviously this is a valuable technique to employ.

Finally, if we are to use interviews to any extent in personality assessment it is very important that we should train interviewers in their art. Trained experienced interviewers can be efficient selectors. The nature of such training is beyond our scope here and the interested reader should consult specialist texts on the subject.[29]

Let us complete our discussion here by briefly considering how these concepts of personality assessment can be applied in practical situations. Some of the points we have made are usually implicit in assessment procedures even though they may not be expressly stated.

The first step in any selection or promotion assessment must be to state in general terms, the sort of person you are looking for, e.g. a potential nurse or teacher, a child of high academic ability, a person capable of leading others, etc. This general concept must then be translated into specific assessable terms, e.g. intelligence, suitable past experience, ability to work hard, interest in the new role. Thirdly the assessor must consider which of the available tools of assessment are competent to evaluate these characteristics. We find, for example, that students applying for admission to nurse training schools, colleges of education or universities are often assessed by means of:

 a. examination results which reflect intelligence and relevant past experiences;
 b. an interview which gives a picture of fluency, appearance, sociability, demeanour, etc.;
 c. a confidential report which provides extended assessment of behaviour under normal working conditions.

Sometimes an intelligence test or a paper and pencil personality test is added together with a language test for students from overseas.

The scores obtained on these tests cannot be simply averaged or summed up as they are each measuring something different. (To do so would be comparable with adding the temperature to the atmospheric pressure on a particular day to get an overall picture of the meteorological conditions.) Some of these tools can give specific evaluations, e.g. I.Q. or grade of examination result. Others are usually more subjectively assessed, e.g. a satisfactory or unsatisfactory confidential report or interview. In general, for selection the assessor should set a minimum standard for each technique, candidates with scores falling below this being rejected. For promotion the person should be selected who performs best in the technique (or combination of techniques) which the assessor thinks is most important. Any generalizations on such a vast and variable subject as this, however, are likely to be inadequate. The interested reader would be well advised to turn to one of the excellent texts specifically concerned with personality assessment.

SUMMARY

1. Frequently we need to assess individuals as whole persons rather than in terms of specific characteristics as we described in the previous chapter. The sum total of an individual's personal characteristics whether inborn or acquired, constitute his *personality*.

2. It is theoretically convenient to distinguish between two major aspects of personality: *temperament* which is the physical and physiological basis of personality, and *character* which describes those acquired aspects picked up from the environment. In practice, however, it is impossible to separate these aspects because genetical endowment cannot produce an end-product without a suitable environment and the environment can produce nothing without an organism capable of development.

3. Although each of us has a fairly constant, permanent aspect of personality which can be recognized and identified with us, there is also a very adaptable aspect which enables us to cope with the demands of the particular environment in which we find ourselves.

4. Motivation and need satisfaction are basic to the concept of acquired aspects of personality. Each of us develops and uses behaviour which is functionally valuable to us in terms of rewards and punishments.

5. Early experiences are subsequently used in the interpretation of later percepts. Attitudes inculcated into children often persist in later life. We acquire the values and standards of the society in which we are brought up. When, subsequently, we have to assess the standards and values of our own or other societies we tend to do so in a manner biased towards those with which we are familiar.

6. Personality can be considered as the result of adaptation of an individual to his physical and social environment. There have been many attempts to classify personalities for both practical and academic reasons. The need for measurable criteria meant that originally physical characteristics were utilized. With the development of psychological tests more and more emphasis has been placed on behavioural measures.

7. Many physically based systems were propounded but have proved to be inadequate, e.g.:

   a. Hippocrates' classification based on humours;
   b. Cannon's emphasis on endocrine secretions;
   c. Phrenology, the study of proportions of the skull;

The Uniqueness of Each Individual

    d. Physiognomy which considered that there was a direct relationship between psychological characteristics and physique, e.g. dimensions of the head, texture of the skin and hair.

8. Kretschmer suggested that there is a relationship between overall physique and characteristic type of behaviour. While his conclusions may be useful in the assessments of mental patients his results are not confirmed for the general populace.

9. Sheldon classified physique in terms of proportion of endoderm, mesoderm and ectoderm in the adult body. He then interviewed persons classified in this way and collected clusters of behavioural characteristics which he said correlated highly with these physical categories. However, his work needs considerable substantiation before it can be accepted.

10. The concept of type classifications has been extended to purely psychological approaches, e.g. Jung's theory based on extraversion/introversion is well known. A major difficulty in type theories is that people do not fall into well-defined categories but are distributed over a continuous scale with the majority lying towards the centre.

11. Many psychologists now prefer the concept of traits (relatively permanent characteristics of personality) as convenient descriptive techniques. Eysenck and Cattell attempt to describe personality objectively. However they perhaps fail to take adequate account of (*a*) the dynamic interrelationship between traits and (*b*) the effects of the environment on personality.

12. There have been many attempts at producing a comprehensive theory of personality. Some approaches stress interaction with the environment, others emphasize development, some are concerned with elucidating universal human qualities, others with the uniqueness of the individual. Sigmund Freud and G. W. Allport offer widely diverging approaches. As yet no universally acceptable theory exists, different approaches to personality demanding different interpretations.

13. Despite the diversity of theories of personality it is essential that some practical techniques for personality assessment should be available. Many different techniques have been devised, each putting emphasis on particular aspects of personality which are important to the originator of the test. Which form an assessor chooses depends upon the purpose which he has in mind.

14. Some techniques attempt to limit the number of qualities which they assess. We mention some physical tests which have been developed but which as yet are not of very great value in selection or promotion. Paper and pencil personality tests exist in a variety of forms. Although these are very popular in the U.S.A.

they still leave much to be desired as reliable tools of assessment. Nevertheless much groundwork has been completed in this field and perhaps their value will increase in the future.

15. Projection tests may be used by trained psychologists. The individual being assessed is given creative or imaginative tasks in which he can 'project' his personality on to the environment. For example the Rorschach Ink Blot Test and the Thematic Apperception Test. Free play, painting and drawing may be used also. In general these projection tests seem to be more useful in isolating personality abnormalities than in selection and promotion assessments.

16. Among the most widely used assessment techniques are those which try to evaluate responses of the whole person to the general environment. These may be extended evaluations under natural conditions which are often very hard to control (i.e. continuous assessment) or intensive, short interrogations under artificial but more easily controlled conditions (i.e. an interview).

17. For efficient personality assessment for selection or promotion purposes it is generally best to use a combination of techniques.

REFERENCES

1. For a discussion of problems in defining 'personality' see Allport, G. W. *Personality: A Psychological Interpretation* (Constable, London 1937).

2. For a detailed discussion of the importance of early experience see Fiske, D. W. and Maddi, S. R. *Functions of Early Experience* (Dorsey Press, Homewood, Ill. 1961).

3. See Stott, D. H. *Delinquency and Human Nature* (Carnegie United Kingdom Trust, Dunfermline 1950).

4. Kretschmer, E. *Physique and Character* (Routledge & Kegan Paul, London 1925).

5. Sheldon, W. H. and Stevens, S. S. *The Varieties of Temperament* (Harper, N.Y. 1942).

6. Jung, C. G. *Psychological Types* (Harcourt, Brace & World, N.Y. 1923).

7. Eysenck, H. J. *Dimensions of Personality* (Routledge & Kegan Paul, London 1947).

8. Cattell, R. B. *Description and Measurement of Personality* (Harrap, London 1946) and *An Introduction To Personality Study* (Hutchinson, London 1950).

9. See Freud, S. *An Outline of Psychoanalysis* (Hogarth, London 1949).

10. Ansbacher, H. L. and R. R. (eds.). *The Individual Psychology of Alfred Adler* (Basic Books, N.Y. 1956).
11. Horney, K. *The Neurotic Personality of Our Time* (Norton, N.Y. 1937).
12. Fromm, E. *Escape From Freedom* (Rinehart, N.Y. 1941).
13. Murray, H. A. *Explorations in Personality* (O.U.P., London 1938).
14. Sullivan, H. S. *The Interpersonal Theory of Psychiatry* (Norton, N.Y. 1953).
15. Allport, G. W. *Personality* (Holt, N.Y. 1937).
16. For a short description and critique of many important theories of personality see Hall, C. S. and Lindzey, G. *Theories of Personality* (Wiley, N.Y. 1957).
17. Walter, W. G. 'Electro-Encephalography' in *Recent Advances in Psychiatry* (Churchill, London 1944).
18. Allport, G. W. and Vernon, P. E. *Studies in Expressive Movement* (Macmillan, London 1932).
19. See Vernon, P. E. *Personality Tests and Assessments* (Methuen, London 1953).
20. Strong, E. K. *Vocational Interest Blank* (1927) and *Vocational Interests of Men and Women* (1943) both published by Stanford University Press.
21. Hathaway, S. R. and McKinley, J. C. 'A Multiphasic Personality Schedule (Minnesota)', *Journal of Psychology* (1940) 10, pp. 249–54.
22. Bell, J. E. *Projective Techniques* (Longmans Green, London 1948).
23. Skottowe, I. *Clinical Psychiatry for Practitioners and Students* (Eyre & Spottiswoode, London 1953), pp. 78–111, discusses practical details involved.
24. See either Fleming, C. M. *Cumulative Records* (U.L.P., London 1945) or Walker, A. S. *Pupil's School Records* (Newnes, London 1955).
25. From Vernon, P. E. *Personality Tests and Assessments* (Methuen, London 1953), p. 107.
26. *Ibid.*, pp. 20–31.
27. Moore, E. H. 'Elements of Error in Testimony', *Journ. App. Psych.*, 19 (1935), p. 447.
28. Muscio, B. 'The Influence of the Form of a Question', *Brit. Journ. Psych.*, 8 (1916).
29. Oldfield, R. C. *The Psychology of the Interview* (Methuen, London, 1941). Also Maccoby, E. E. and N. 'The Interview: A Tool of Social Science' in Lindzey, G. *Handbook of Social Psychology* (Addison-Wesley, Reading, Mass. 1954), pp. 449–87.

Chapter Twelve

The Behaviour of Groups of Individuals

INTRODUCTION

In previous chapters we have been concerned mainly with the behaviour of individual human beings and have only mentioned interrelationships between such individuals where they helped to clarify points under discussion. In this chapter we shall change our emphasis completely and focus our attention on the ways in which people who live together affect each other's experiences and behaviour. We have frequently referred to the fact that information from the environment (both from the present situation in which we find ourselves and from past experiences stored in our minds) plays a major part in determining how we behave. As we live in close contact with other human beings they will figure largely in the experiences we perceive. Consequently, our lives will be greatly influenced by the persons with whom we live. In fact many psychologists believe that our immediate associates have a more important effect on our lives than any other factor.[1]

Before investigating these effects any further we must consider the nature of relationships between people living together. Obviously different individuals in our environment will impinge upon our lives to greater or less extents. Friends or relatives sharing our home will be much more involved with our daily experiences than similar individuals living fifty miles away. For example, a teenager living at home with his parents will be influenced by them and his behaviour will be modified to be acceptable to them. Suppose he then obtains a place in a college some distance from his parents' home or he marries and he and his wife go to live in a house of their own. Quite soon the influence of his parents' way of life wanes and new factors relating to the different environment come into play. His outlook and behaviour will change. (People say 'he has grown away from his parents'.) He will find it increasingly difficult to return to his parents' home. How often do we hear people in such situations say: 'I like to return home for short periods but . . .'; 'I do not know how I ever lived at home for all those years'; 'I do not think that if my parents came to live with us, we could ever hit it off.' These examples clearly demonstrate that the effect of individuals on the lives of one another is dependent upon the number and types of experience which pass between them.

In psychological terms we describe a number of individuals living together and affecting each other as a 'group'.[2] In a group, therefore, all the individuals share some common experiences. But depending upon the number of persons in the group, so their relative effects on each other will vary. It is common practice to divide groups into categories according to the number of individuals composing them.

A. PRIMARY GROUPS are small intimate collections of individuals who greatly affect each other. The best examples here are the family[3] to which we belong and the small group of close friends which we make outside the family. From such groups we receive help, understanding, companionship and love. With them we share difficulties and joy. We are well known within such a primary group and our activities are interpreted in terms of what other members of the group know about us, not only in the present situation, but also in previous situations. In other words, in a primary group we are known and judged as whole persons, taking into account our attitudes, interests and past experiences, making allowances for shortcomings over which we have no control. It appears to be essential for the satisfactory psychological development of an individual that he should belong to at least one primary group. Children brought up in institutions[4] where no personal relationships can be made are psychologically stunted. Today in such institutions every effort is made to put children into small units with nurses or house parents to act as 'anchors' of primary groups made up of such children. In boarding schools children often live in 'houses' or are divided into 'dormitories' which partially fulfil this need for personal groups. Adults collect around themselves small groups of friends who often have something in common with them. A person who has no family or friends is missing a great deal and his life is very empty. We need close relationships with others to develop fully and live happily. Today, with the emphasis on stream-lining, large organizations, etc., the task of forming a small personal group of friends becomes increasingly difficult. Many psychologists believe that the effects of this situation are responsible for some of the social problems of our times, and as the process continues so our difficulties will grow. The need to feel important and acceptable as a person to a group of other individuals is apparently a basic biological and psycho-logical requirement of us all. Neglect of this need or absence of opportunity for its fulfilment can only have harmful results. We shall return to this topic in the chapters devoted to 'mental health' and 'mental illness'.

B. SECONDARY GROUPS are again collections of individuals all affecting one another, but in these cases the relationships are formal and impersonal. They are based on a superficial knowledge of other group members and are concerned less with the individuals as complete persons and more with their functions in the particular relationships under consideration. For example, the customers bringing their cars to the reception office of a large garage form, with the garage employees, a secondary group whose common aim is to keep the customers' vehicles in working order. The backgrounds and personal peculiarities of the group members are unimportant. The aim of the group is to perform efficiently one specific function and other aspects of the individuals involved are ignored. Such groups are essential in our modern way of life for us to co-operate and attain efficiently goals which would be beyond the reach of smaller, less specialized concerns.

It will be apparent from this description of group types that the criterion for distinguishing between primary and secondary relationships is really how well you know other members of the group. In a very large group, e.g. a school, a hospital, a trades union, you can only know a few people really well. These intimate friends will form a primary group to which you belong. You and your friends will also be part of the large secondary group consisting of all the members of the school or hospital, etc. The dividing line between the members of the primary group of your special friends and the secondary group beyond them is not clear cut. A slight change in your activity within the secondary group may cause you to learn more about certain people previously outside your primary group. You find that as you know them better you treat them as your friends and they may become part of your close primary circle.

If you consider all the persons that ever, in any way, impinge upon your life you can arrange them in order of how much you know about them. Complete strangers have nothing about them with which you are familiar. You have not seen or heard of them before, you do not know what their jobs are, where they live, how old they are. When you meet such individuals for the first time the only information you have about them is what you see and hear at that first meeting. Any percept you form (i.e. any mental picture you construct) of these individuals is based on this one (perhaps quite atypical) experience of them. If you meet them again, however, your relationship on your second encounter will not only be based on what you see and hear at this second meeting but also on the information stored in your mind from your first meeting. When you have collected previous information about a person in this way he is no longer a stranger but an acquaintance. Continue this process and your acquaintance may become your friend, perhaps eventually a close friend or even your best friend.

In order to obtain information regarding another person it is usually necessary to share the same environment with him and to exchange experiences with him. So we know best the people with whom we live and work providing they present us with experiences from which we can learn about them. Some people are difficult to get to know because the information which they allow us to perceive of them is scanty, ambiguous or unpredictable. This process of collecting relevant information enabling us to get to know other individuals better has already been referred to in our discussion of perception. It furnishes much of the mental background that goes into our percepts. Depending on whether previous encounters with a person were pleasant or not we shall look forward to meeting them again or not.

We carry in our minds information collected from previous encounters and use this in our percepts of subsequent meetings with the individual concerned. Suppose, however, that we were going to meet a person that we had not met before. Suppose also that we were furnished with some information about him, e.g. his age, occupation, opinions. We will form in our minds a mental picture of what we expect he will be like, basing our assumptions on our experiences of other people in his age group, occupation, etc. It is quite likely that if we do this we shall be wrong in our preconceived picture of him ('he wasn't a bit as I expected him to be!'). For example, suppose we have heard and seen on television, newspapers, films, that teenage students with long hair and motor bicycles had been taken into custody for certain delinquent activities. If this had been our only experience of such individuals we might well jump to the conclusion that the long-haired student to whom we are introduced is a potential delinquent. There is no rational reason why he, any more than anyone else, should misbehave. However, this tendency to over-generalization or *stereotyping*,[5] as it is called, is very widespread. We often hear 'the younger generation' or 'the older generation' being decried in general terms in this way. Again we may attribute a whole series of characteristics to a person because we have heard that he is a socialist, an ex-officer from the R.A.F., etc. We shall have to return to this problem later in this chapter because of the great difficulties that can often arise in communication between groups or individuals who hold incorrect stereotypic impressions. Let us leave the point for the moment by restating the fact that the basis of a relationship between two or more individuals is the past experiences which they have shared. Two strangers have no common past experiences and therefore have no group-relationship. Two close friends have a great deal of shared past experiences. What form a relationship between two people will take will depend upon the number and nature of the experiences they share.

INDIVIDUALS AND GROUPS[6]

Groups are made up of individuals and so obviously will vary according to the type of person of which they are composed. A club or a housing estate, a school class or a hospital ward, a neighbourhood or a nation, each will have its own character-istics which are determined by the individuals within it. However, as we have explained before, an individual is affected by his environment and when such a person is a member of a group many of the experiences he picks up from his environ-ment are determined by the group to which he belongs. This being the case, it is very difficult in practice to study the psychology of the individual in isolation from group effects, while at the same time the psychology of the group is based on the behaviour of its component individuals. It is worthwhile at this point examining a little more fully the interdependence of the group and the individuals comprising it.

Why do individuals form groups? We discussed in an earlier chapter the concept of social motives which direct our be-haviour in such a way that we co-operate with other people. The group is the result of these driving forces in action. There are many advantages to be obtained from living together. Apart from the obvious biological sex-need for propagation of the species and for the feeling of security against the environ-ment that living with others can bestow, there is the great benefit of specialization (technically called 'division of labour') which team-work allows. Also in this connection, social life with overlapping generations enables knowledge and skills to be passed on. It is interesting to notice that for most people there is also great psychological satisfaction to be obtained from group activity. Praise, criticism, appreciation, company and friendship are only obtained when more than one person is concerned in an activity. To lead a full and satisfying life all our mental energy forces must be utilized. Several of these can only function in group situations, e.g. gregariousness, sub-mission, assertion, love and hate, parental care or sexual activity. These forces are absent from the behaviour of the individual in isolation. It follows, therefore, that the mental activity of a group is not just the sum or average of that of its individual members but in fact includes many forces not demonstrated by isolated persons. This explains to a large extent why people behave differently in company from when they are alone. We shall return to this point in our discussion of 'communication' below.

Obviously, the characteristics of the group in economic, social, physical and psychological terms are determined by these same features as they are present in individuals.[7] For example, a number of working-class, low-paid, very religious individuals will form a working-class, poverty-stricken, religious community. Such a group will decide on values and attitudes which are acceptable to most members of the group. These will give standards, rules and laws which the group will enforce by means of rewards and punishments. Persons being born into the group will grow up moulded by these standards and so will perpetuate the way of life of the group. New persons entering the group from outside may well find difficulty in adjusting to the standards of the community. It is important to realize that the values, standards, attitudes, etc., of the group within which we live are not absolute or universal standards but depend upon the ideas and desires of the members of that group. They are designed to safeguard individuals within the group and to keep the group united. For example, in Wild West films where the law-abiding Christian members of a wagon train are confronted by members of an outlaw gang one sees clearly how the two groups have evolved different standards of behaviour and control according to their different needs. The rule of the gun is out of place for restraining God-fearing men, women and children, but is more effective than preaching when dealing with murderers and villains. The fact that different cultures, nationalities, classes, etc. have different standards of behaviour is of the utmost importance when widely divergent groups try to communicate with each other. Misunderstanding, mistrust and friction is often the result of such encounters.

We have said that the attitudes, abilities, interests and ambitions of members decide the standards which the group will expect of new persons entering it. It may well be, however, that in some cases a person may be born into a group to which he is unacceptable or a member of a group may change his behaviour so that he no longer fits in with the requirements of the group to which he belongs. Such persons are described variously as mentally deficient, mentally ill, law-breakers, anti-social or otherwise abnormal depending upon the way and the degree to which they diverge from that which is acceptable to the majoirity of group members. Consequently, what may be considered against the law in one country may be perfectly legal in another. What is a sexual perversion in one culture may be quite normal in another. A person may be considered of high intelligence in one community, but only average in another.

How much deviation from these standards can be tolerated will depend very much on the nature of the group to which the individual belongs. Normally in primary groups, where individuals are well known and their behaviour can be predicted, much more liberty can be allowed. This will mean that among such primary groups there can be wide variation. For example, consider the families living in any one street. In each house the individuals develop their own interests and attitudes, routines and standards. Outside the house, however, when the individuals become members of the larger secondary group of the town or country in which they live, freedom is much more restricted and laws much more stringently enforced. Here much individuality is lost and persons are concerned to conform with what is socially acceptable. Anyone who does not so conform is considered odd or anti-social. For any group to be stable and co-ordinated, however, some degree of freedom and self-expression is desirable to avoid mental tensions within its members. In our modern life based on large secondary groups, such personal freedom is becoming more and more limited. This may well be part of the reason behind the increase in industrial friction, law-breaking, etc., which are such problems of our times.

THE RELATIONSHIPS OF INDIVIDUALS WITHIN GROUPS

So far we have been discussing groups as if they were collections of interacting individuals haphazardly placed together. A little reflection, however, will show that this is rarely the case. For members of a group to co-operate and work together for the common good, it is essential that they should operate each within certain limits which are agreed by and known to other members of the group. Just what these limits are and how rigidly they are enforced will obviously depend upon the individuals concerned, the task being undertaken and the nature of the group in which the limits are imposed. Normally today in primary groups (e.g. family circles) limitations are comparatively few and flexible to allow individuals

Introduction to Psychology

as much liberty as possible. In the Victorian family, however, the reverse was the case and relationships tended to be formal, rules strict and punishments severe. In present-day secondary groups we find that constant enforcement of regulations is necessary to ensure efficient operation. Consider the havoc caused by a few men working on a conveyor belt in a car factory deciding to 'go slow' for a few days. In schools and hospitals also the widespread trouble that could result from a few persons failing to comply with regulations makes the enforcement of restrictions on liberty essential for the good of the group. As we shall discover in the next few pages, in order that the group shall survive and be maximally efficient, each individual must do what is best for the whole group rather than follow his own specific interests.

In working towards the common aim of the group, different individuals, in the light of their varying skills, backgrounds, limitations, etc., are given certain tasks to perform. For example, one person who is able, experienced and capable of commanding respect and co-operation from others may become leader, while other young, inexperienced, unskilled individuals may be the messengers and general subordinates of the rest of the group. The position in the group which an individual holds is called his *status*.[8] We speak of a person's position being of higher or lower status according to the amount of responsibility that he has within the group. For example, matron has a higher status than a ward sister, while a student nurse has comparatively low status. Similarly, within a school the head teacher has high status but in relationships with the Local Education Authority his position is comparatively minor. According to your status you will be required, within the limits discussed above, to perform certain types of behaviour. For example, a teacher is required to educate his pupils, a doctor to treat his patients. Such activity, as is determined by your status, is called your *role*[9] within the group. How rigidly defined a person's role will be depends upon the type of group and nature of the task in which he is employed. For example, the role of father in a family is much more flexible than that of a machine mechanic in a factory. The limitations on a child or patient at home are likely to be much less rigorously enforced than if that same child was at school or the patient in hospital. Many people, especially children, find the comparatively flexible roles of the primary group much easier to fulfil. The tendency in our modern way of life to move from the small personal community to the large secondary group runs contrary to this preference. We can expect, therefore, that the number of social misfits within our society is likely to increase.

By the nature of the lives we live, each of us belongs to more than one group at a time. For example, a married man belongs to his own small family circle of his wife and children, a larger family circle including all his other relatives, and other groups composed of, for example, his neighbours, his friends, his workmates, his political party, other members of his religion, town, nation. Each of these forms a group to which he belongs. It is very likely that his status will vary between groups. For example, as a father he might be head of his own household, but at work he might be a very lowly member of a large concern. On the other hand, we may find a woman who, at work, is a responsible sister in charge of a hospital ward, at home is the youngest daughter of whom no one takes much notice. If we are to be able to cope with the status changes necessary for us to fit into each of the groups to which we belong we must be versatile in our behaviour. We all know the type of person who is a typical school-ma'am or business executive or sergeant-major all the time and never properly fulfils family or other roles required outside his work. Such people have not properly developed the technique of adjusting themselves according to the situation in which they find themselves. Such adjustment is not always easy for any of us. A child starting school or a patient entering hospital may well not know how to behave. Adjustment to a new situation depends on learning. Once you have been in a situation for some time you know just how to respond to it, what to expect of it and you can cope with it much more easily than before.

Another major difficulty can arise from belonging to several groups at once. Earlier in this chapter we pointed out that one picks up one's values and attitudes from the group in which one lives. It may well be that the values held by different groups to which you belong will differ among themselves, e.g. your political views may clash at some points with your family or national loyalties, or your trades union ties may be incompatible with your religious beliefs. Such conflicts frequently occur in the lives of most of us and can be the cause of frustration, social unrest and the weakening of the groups to which we belong.

Within a group made up of many individuals, all these various relationships, adjustments and frustrations are active at once. The overall condition of the group as a result of them is termed its *morale*. Morale is a measure of the co-ordination and organization of the group and consequently of its efficiency to direct itself and achieve its aims. A group with high morale is composed of individuals making satisfactory relationships between themselves. In order to achieve this situation, the individuals must be prepared to compromise or even ignore their own desires and interests for the good of the group as a whole. This is the basis for insisting in team games that all members of a side should work together to score goals and that individuals should not try to glorify themselves by 'going it alone'. At home or at work we each of us modify our selfish natural desires so that we behave in a way acceptable to others. In other words, we, as individuals, are working not only to our own ends but also for the overall good of the group. In order that high morale may be obtained, it is vital that all members of the group should share common aims and be prepared to go all out to attain them. In such a task the importance of direction and control by a good leader is paramount. Examples abound in every sphere of well-led groups which are successful, while those with poor leaders or no leaders at all are disorganized and inefficient. The class with the uninterested teacher, the firm with the weak employer, the nation with a corrupt head of state are all too common examples of unsuccessful groups. The closely-knit community of the early Christian Church or the British nation during the world wars are indications of how efficient, well-led groups can be.

The leader,[10] however, is not the only person of importance within a group. He is generally the co-ordinator and organizer of other people within the group but it is these subordinates and their relationships with one another that are the material from which the group is composed. To be efficient these group members must have a general overall impression of the aims and organization of the group to which they belong. They must see themselves and their functions in perspective so that they can be maximally efficient. They must make the correct relationships[11] with their fellows, feel accepted and respected by them and be able to understand and communicate with them. To this end the use of a common form of dress or way of speaking and behaving, or shared interests and type of training can all be invaluable in integrating a group and putting members at their ease. We have previously mentioned the desire to conform which our basic nature developed by our mode of education bestows on us all to varying extents. Linked with this point the need for praise and appreciation in uniting a group is very important, especially when continued performance demands a great effort by group members. In order that individuals can work together for the common good of the group, it is important that they should be able to pass information from one person to the next. This passage of information is called *communication*.

COMMUNICATION[12]

We said earlier that the basis of a relationship between two or more individuals is the past experiences which they have shared. In order to share an experience, we must be able to pass information from one person to another. In this way we can discover how our fellow group members are responding to the common experience, what they are doing, thinking and feeling both about the situation in general and about us in particular. We are constantly communicating with other people. We become so used to it that we tend not to realize its vital importance until something goes wrong (in much the same way that we are only aware of our teeth or our stomachs when they ache). When our communication system breaks down, trouble results. Family upsets, separation and divorce, industrial unrest and strikes, delinquency, crime and even war are some of the results of bad communication and lack of understanding between parties involved in a relationship.

The uses to which we put communication in our normal everyday activities are extremely varied. We may be describing an experience or expressing a feeling; we may be trying to instruct or influence our fellows or we may be communicating for entertainment, gossip or abuse. The rules and regulations under which we work and the demands we make on other people all are based on the passing of information between individuals. Obviously then, communication is an aspect of group behaviour which is of the utmost importance. It tells us how we are coping with our environment and our relationships with others and how other people are responding to us.

Let us consider what is involved in a conscious act of communication. We can divide the process into the following main stages:

a. Preparation of the message, i.e. consideration of its content and form.
b. Transmission of the message, i.e. speaking, writing, gesticulating.
c. Reception of the message, i.e. hearing, seeing.
d. Interpretation of the message, i.e. understanding what it means.
e. Reaction to the message, i.e. changing our behaviour or thoughts as a result of the information received.

In two-way communication, e.g. in a conversation between two people, the reaction of one of the persons to information received might well be the process of preparation of an answering message which he is going to transmit back to the other individual.

Communication can be considered as an extension outside the body of the processes of transmission of information previously described within the body. In Chapter 1 we discussed the way in which information from the receptor cells is carried along sensory nerves to the central nervous system. Here the information is interpreted and decisions are taken. Messages are then sent down motor nerves to effectors by the activity of which the person behaves. These processes of transmission within the body are all included in communication. To them is added the passage of information from the effectors of one person, through the environment, to the receptors of another. We shall not consider here the activities of the effectors and receptors in the transmission and reception of information. Any elementary biology or nursing text-book will give adequate coverage of the anatomy and physiology of the major sense organs, the vocal apparatus, facial muscles, etc., which are involved. From our point of view the main topics to examine further are the psychological aspects of preparation and interpretation of messages.

Earlier we mentioned that there are many different functions of communication from reporting a factual happening to abusing or entertaining others, from expressing a feeling or 'letting off steam' to reading to a friend from a text-book. Whatever the reason behind a conscious act of communication we have to prepare the information in our minds before we can transmit it. Consequently, whatever we say or write will be strongly flavoured by our own values, ideas, motives, past experiences, etc. In some instances our personal contribution will be small, e.g. when we are imparting some factual material more or less as we perceive it, as when counting a pulse rate, reading from a book, etc. In other cases the information in the message may be generated or constructed almost almost completely within our minds, e.g. when describing how we feel in certain circumstances or expressing our views on a controversial problem.

Usually, information we are passing on has both these components present to varying degrees, i.e. it consists of actual information picked up from the environment which has been coloured or moulded by our own mental activities and knowledge. It is very difficult when listening to another person reporting an event to know just how accurate are the statements he is making. Although he may not intend to mislead and misrepresent, his memory of the actual happening is likely to be distorted. His report will emphasize those aspects of the event to which he paid most attention and which suited his interests or prejudices. The fact that the amount of information he can remember from any one situation is limited will mean that he will have been selective in what he remembers and his mental picture will be incomplete and disjointed. On relating the instance he is likely to fill in the gaps with what he thinks may have happened. Frequently, also, a person plays a larger and more important part in his memory of an event that he did in the original situation. The great importance to be attached to these personal inaccuracies of reporting has been the subject of much controversy as to the use of legal testimony.

Apart from these personal considerations, another complication which must be taken into account is the fact that communication is often a reaction to the environment. For example, in a conversation I speak to my friend whose reply is a response to my communication. My next response is likely to depend upon what he said to me and so on. Such a process is an example of what is called *feedback*. The degree of feedback varies very much in relationships between different individuals. Some people are easy to talk to (i.e. their responses are easy to reply to). Others give short, curt replies to which it is very difficult to respond. Yet other persons go on talking regardless of the responses of those around them, for example, bores are very insensitive to the reactions of people to whom they are talking.

The type of environment you are in considerably affects the way in which you communicate. People around you determine the limits of what you say and often how you say it. Among friends you can be less formal and reserved, at work you will be more technical and so on. Jokes and smutty stories may be perfectly acceptable among a group of men on a 'pub crawl' but would be most unsuitable at a children's party. Experts at cross-examination know that when reporting an incident you try to show yourself up in the best possible light.[13] You are loath to admit to the gaps in your memory of the incident. As we said on p. 288 when you are unsure, by careful questioning, you can be persuaded to give the answers that the questioner requires. A good deal of investigation into the effects of the form of the question on the answer received has been carried out. It indicates very strongly that testimony varies considerably with the circumstances under which it is given.

The effect of previous recall of an incident on the nature of subsequent reports is also very important. Suppose that you witnessed an accident and later when you got home you told the story of what you had seen to your family. Subsequently, you go to the police station to make a statement. The memory of the report you gave to your family is fresher in your mind than is the accident itself. Any suggestions, explanations or associations added by yourself or your family when you told your story previously now may possibly become part of your testimony at the station. If this process of retelling the story of an incident happens frequently enough, the final report can be quite different from the original occurrence. This is very noticeable in old people who relate tales of their childhood with great regularity. Careful recording of such stories shows that with repetition the facts become more distorted (usually in favour of the narrator).

The final environmental effect on communication that we will mention here is the way in which you see the person to whom you are speaking, i.e. upon the relationship you have with that person. If you are hostile, your information may be given brusquely, if at all, while if you are friendly, you will co-operate and provide all that is necessary. You may be trying to impress your fellows and so distort your information in favour of yourself, or you may have something to hide and so provide little information or even give false information, i.e. you may lie.

We have been concentrating so far on the processes of preparing and transmitting information. Now let us consider how a message, once received, is interpreted by another person. If the receiver has had just the same past experiences, interests, attitudes, values, etc., as the giver of the information, then he will interpret what is being said exactly as the sender means him to. But, of course, no two people ever have exactly the same experiences in their lives and so no two individuals have identical interests, etc. Consequently, we each tend to interpret the information we receive in a way which is different from that which the transmitter meant us to. Such a situation inevitably leads to misunderstandings. Such misunderstandings are frequently and easily seen when young children and adults communicate with one another, but instances often happen between adults (particularly when two people do not know each other very well, false impressions can easily be formed). Generally, when communication occurs between two people gross misunderstandings are avoided by the feedback principle mentioned above. However, in classroom situations, where feedback from the pupils is often not forthcoming, it is difficult for the teacher to know how to modify his information to suit the needs of the group, and class members may fail to understand the material being communicated to them. Consequently, question and answer form an essential part of classroom communication.[14] This whole topic of problems of misinterpretations of information is discussed in Chapter 5. Let us leave the matter at this point by reiterating the fact that while the passing of information between individuals is essential for group relationships, this communication is the end result of a host of preparatory mental processes of which we are unaware. We cannot know what motives, attitudes or prejudices initiated a particular reaction in another person. Generally speaking, we do not know exactly why other people speak and behave as they do. It is our task within our group to try to interpret such information as satisfactorily as possible. Providing we have all been brought up in the same general environment we shall have a good chance of success. Nevertheless, it is often very difficult to understand persons of a different generation or culture from our own.

Our surroundings affect us in many ways from conception onwards throughout life. As far as communication is concerned, we develop physical structures, e.g. vocal cords, lips, tongues, teeth, muscles, sense organs, which are the organs of information transmission and reception, but experience and practice are necessary for our communication to become efficient. This experience and practice can only come from watching and copying others round about us. Initially, these are our parents, brothers and sisters, but later our school teachers and friends play an increasingly important part. From such other persons we learn the meaning of words and gestures, how to speak and write. From them we pick up attitudes and prejudices, values and interests.[15] They give us the standards by which we come to judge ourselves and others. If you take a very large group, e.g. a nation, a hospital community or a school, and examine the relationships within it, you will find that it tends to divide up into smaller groups in which persons with similar interests or backgrounds or jobs tend to congregate together. For example, in our British society we have social classes based on financial or educational criteria; clubs and societies based on interests, such as drama, tennis or mothercraft; political parties, trades unions, religions, etc., within which all members have something in common either in ideals or intentions or attitudes. Within each of these sub-groups of our society, characteristics are reinforced and so the different collections of people grow further apart in terms of these characteristics, e.g. interests, behaviour, aims, education standards, etc. Depending upon the group in which you find yourself, so your standards will change to meet what is acceptable to your fellow group members. Great friends in the primary school may grow apart from one another on entering different secondary schools.

Again, you will often hear a mother complain of the deterioration in her son's behaviour 'since he's got in with a bad lot at school'. This picking up of standards, attitudes, etc., from the environment is a form of communcation.

It is interesting to note that many of our values, interests and prejudices are not necessarily transmitted to us through spoken or written words. There are other very effective methods of communication within a group which we must briefly consider. They mainly boil down to copying the behaviour of those round about us. You can see the value of this process from a biological point of view. In a group all individuals must act and think and feel as a whole or else their effectiveness may be cancelled out. If we all tend to copy the actions, thoughts and feelings of our neighbours we shall 'keep in step' with one another, our co-operation will be greater and as a group we shall be more efficient. It is in these three categories of action, thought and feeling that copying mainly occurs. A small child sees its mother taking clothes-pegs from a basket to fix washing to the clothes-line. It will itself take pegs out and hold them up to mother. Such copying of action we call *imitation*. In adults the same type of situation occurs, for example, when one or two people stop in the street and stare or point at a window on the first floor of a house. Soon others stop and stare and a crowd begins to form. Again, if you are in an audience at the theatre and your neighbours begin to clap, you are likely to follow suit to remain one of the group.

Copying or sharing of thoughts is called *suggestibility*. This is the unwitting process of accepting the ideas and opinions of another person. Intentional asking for instruction from a fellow group member is basic to the learning process.[16] Frequently, however, when we are together in a group we pick up ideas or suggestions from another person without realizing it. A persuasive politician can be talking about the type of problem that we as individuals are struggling to cope with. By listening to his line of argument we can easily come to think that his views and ideas are in fact our own. We now think in the same way that he does. We have been subjected to the process of suggestion by him. Again, an advertiser can describe a situation which we might have experienced ourselves. He explains how he sees the problem and how his product will solve it. When we meet that problem again ourselves our minds at once return to the product which it was suggested would fill our need. We now think of this solution as being our own, i.e. we are sharing the thoughts of the advertiser; we have fallen prey to his suggestion.

Sympathy or 'feeling with others' is another important form of communication. The 'atmosphere' at a football match or in the theatre is much more stimulating when you are a member of a large audience than when you are alone. A touching scene involving other persons can make a bystander feel happy or sad. The joy of a child opening its Christmas presents can make the parents very happy. Sharing the feelings of those around us is familiar to us all. It is however very difficult to explain how and why we are so affected.

In this chapter we have been concerned with the fact that although each individual is capable of experiencing, learning, thinking and behaving in his own individual way, how he performs these functions depends very much on the environment and group to which he belongs. In the next chapter we shall examine the need for compromise between a person's selfish desires and the demands of the environment. In the last chapter we shall discuss some of the problems which arise when a person is unable to come to terms with himself and his surroundings.

SUMMARY

1. Experiences from the environment greatly affect our behaviour. As persons around us figure largely in these experiences they have important influences on our lives. A number of individuals living together and sharing experiences constitute a *group*. Depending upon the size of the group the relative effects of one individual upon another will vary. We can classify groups according to the number of individuals of which they are composed.
2. *Primary groups* consist of a few individuals each knowing one another intimately, for example, a family circle or a group of close friends. Individuals in such groups are regarded by their fellows as complete persons and are not judged on single encounters. Membership of such groups is essential for satisfactory development and subsequent happiness of the individual.
3. *Secondary groups* are larger impersonal collections of indivi-

duals, more concerned with transitory and isolated relationships than with complete understanding of each other. In our modern world this type of group is essential for the effective attainment of complex and postponed goals.

4. The basis of a relationship between two individuals is the past experiences which they have shared and the common goals to which they are working. Strangers have no shared experiences, while friends have many. Previous experiences of another person are utilized in the formation and interpretation of future percepts of that individual.

5. There is a tendency to attribute certain characteristics to an individual because he belongs to a certain group. Within limits this is quite a useful technique providing that the generalizations made are correct. However, over-generalization is called *stereotyping* and can cause gross misunderstanding and difficulties in communication.

6. Groups are made up of individuals and therefore vary according to the type of person of which they are composed. Conversely, individuals are influenced and modified by the groups to which they belong. These two interrelated concepts of group psychology cannot be separately evaluated.

7. The standards of a group are established to unite it and safeguard its members, and are based on concepts which are acceptable to the majority of the persons concerned. These standards are different for different groups. New members born into a group are initiated into the particular values of that society through their parents and teachers. Mature persons transferring from one group to another may have great difficulty in adapting to the new standards now expected of them.

8. The degree of deviation from these standards which the group can permit will depend on the nature and functions of the group. For the common good individuals must co-operate and integrate their activities within the frameworks which society lays down.

9. The position which an individual holds within a group is called his *status*. It is usually assessed in terms of the degree of responsibility which he carries. The type of behaviour which society demands of an individual is called his *role*. Roles are usually much more flexible in primary groups than in secondary groups. As flexible roles are more easy to fulfil the current trend towards more and larger secondary groups makes life more difficult for the individual and may be a factor in the creation of more social misfits than was previously the case.

10. Major problems of adjustment arise when an individual belongs to several groups in each of which he has a different status.

These problems are accentuated when these various groups each have different sets of values and standards.

11. *Morale* is an overall description of the co-ordination and organization within a group. It is assessed in terms of the degree of compromise by individuals between their own selfish interests and the common good of the group.

12. For a group to be maximally efficient, information must pass constantly and accurately between members. This is the function of *communication*.

13. An act of communication involves subjective elements in the preparation and interpretation of messages. The extent of distortions as a result of these influences are difficult to assess. In normal conversation misunderstandings are corrected to some extent by processes of 'feedback'. It is particularly important in teaching to ensure that what is being presented to the students is being correctly interpreted.

14. Communication techniques are obviously the result of learning. What you say, how you say it, the meaning of gestures and actions, are all determined by the group to which you belong.

15. Not all communication takes the form of language. We are influenced by others when we copy their actions (imitation), their thoughts (suggestion) or their feelings (sympathy).

REFERENCES

1. Berg, I. A. and Bass, B. M. *Conformity and Deviation* (Harper, N.Y. 1961), discuss the effects of group pressures on the individual.

2. Homans, G. C. *The Human Group* (Routledge & Kegan Paul, London 1951). See also Lindgren, H. C. *The Art of Human Relations* (Hermitage, N.Y. 1953).

3. Fleming, C. M. *The Social Psychology of Education* (Routledge & Kegan Paul, London 1959), pp. 39–48, discusses family influences in child development. See also Bossard, J. H. S. *The Sociology of Child Development* (Harper, N.Y. 1948).

4. See Fleming, C. M. *The Social Psychology of Education*, p. 89, discusses the effects of institutionalization on children.

5. See Vernon, P. E. *Personality Assessment* (Methuen, London 1964) esp. pp. 25–45, for a discussion of stereotyping in personality assessment.

6. For an excellent introduction to the relationship between individuals and groups see Fleming, C. M. *The Social Psychology of Education*, pp. 39–66.

7. Bovard, E. W. 'Social Norms and the Individual', *Journal of Abnormal and Social Psychology* 43 (1948), pp. 62–9.

The Behaviour of Groups of Individuals

8. Argyle, M. 'The Concepts of Role and Status' in Halmos, P. and Iliffe, A. in *Readings in General Psychology* (Routledge & Kegan Paul, London 1959), pp. 185–97.
9. Argyle, M. 'The Concepts of Role and Status', op. cit.
10. Krech, D. and Crutchfield, R. S. *Theory and Problems of Social Psychology* (McGraw-Hill, N.Y. 1948) deals with morale and leadership in Chapter II.
11. Guetzkow, H. (ed.) *Groups, Leadership and Men* (Rutgers University Press, New Brunswick, N. J. 1951) is a series of papers covering research in human relations.
12. Price-Williams, D. R. *Introductory Psychology: An Approach For Social Workers* (Routledge & Kegan Paul, London 1958), pp. 118–48.
13. *Ibid.*, pp. 125–34 deal with problems of testimony.
14. Hughes, A. G. and Hughes, E. H. *Learning and Teaching* (Longmans, Green, London, 3rd ed. 1959; 1st ed. 1937), pp. 390–408.
15. Miller, N. E. and Dollard, J. *Social Learning and Imitation* (Yale University Press, New Haven, Conn. 1941) discusses the ways in which social pressures arise.
16. See Murphy, G. *Experimental Social Psychology* (Harper, N.Y. 1937) for a discussion of the effects of suggestion on learning.

Chapter Thirteen

Coming To Terms with Ourselves and Our Surroundings

INTRODUCTION

It is surely the aim of each of us to live a full, contented life in congenial surroundings where we can be happy and at the same time make other people happy.[1] However, our own personal experiences together with the discussion in earlier chapters of this book on the make-up of the individual and relationships between individuals indicate that such an end is likely to be very difficult to attain. It is an examination of some of the problems involved in achieving this end to which this chapter is devoted. The popular, convenient yet virtually indefinable term used to describe the concepts involved here is '*mental health*'.

Most persons when asked what they understand by 'mental health' as used in contexts of campaigns, conferences, flag-days, etc., will define it in terms of absence or avoidance of mental illness. While this is a very negative approach to the concept it is one which our discussions on 'attention' in Chapter 4 might well lead us to expect. As long as our lives run smoothly we take the factors involved for granted. It is only when 'things go wrong' that we become really aware of the offending 'things' at all. We notice our teeth when they ache, our digestive tracts when we are constipated or suffering from indigestion. We become aware of Koreans or the British dockers only when their activities begin to interfere with our lives. We may take our wives and families for granted until relationships become strained. We are not fully aware of the dangers of unemployment, famine or war until events bring them into the realms of possibility. There is a tendency to accept normal functioning passively and only to become active when the status quo is disrupted.

Such an approach is not very helpful to us in our discussion here where we are concerned with a positive identification of health. Let us consider the World Health Organization definition of 'health' as our starting point. This describes health as 'a state of complete, physical, mental and social well-being and not merely an absence of disease or infirmity'. This definition has the great merit of putting 'physical health' in perspective and in relationship to other forms of well-being. Physical health (that is, the efficient working of the body with all its various organs and systems co-ordinated and integrated) is certainly a vital aspect of a completely healthy person. However, contrary to popular usage, in itself physical health is not commensurate with complete health. This latter also implies living in an environment which promotes well-being. We talk about a healthy community when discussing concepts of morals, values, standards and amenities. We use expressions like 'the health of the economy', 'unhealthy attitudes in industry or the younger generation', 'healthy signs of competition,' etc. This social concept of health is very important as we shall soon describe. For most of us it boils down to relationships and need satisfaction at home, at work or through the society in which we live. If we are frustrated or unhappy at home, or insecure or repressed at work our health will soon suffer.

The physical health of the individual and the social health of the environment are two vital aspects of the concept of mental health. The third major component relates to the efficient, co-ordinated functioning within the individual of the processes described in this book. We might attempt to define mental health as a state of balance both within the individual and within the environment. The difficulties which are raised in attempting to interpret such a definition in specific terms are very great and an analysis of some of them form the bulk of the rest of this chapter.

THE NATURE OF MENTAL HEALTH

At several points in this book we have discussed the use of comparisons between individuals in our assessment of one another, for example, when considering criteria of intelligence, attainment, personality evaluation. This same technique is utilized in describing 'healthiness'. However, with such a wide and ill-defined field it is very difficult to decide just what you should be comparing. The layman usually bases his assessment on *belief* of what is normal and healthy and this generally boils down to 'like me' or 'like I wish I was'. The social worker takes a criterion of normality based more on what is *statistically representative* of society. In helping an individual to achieve healthiness in these terms he is enabling him to fit in better with his fellows while still achieving personal satisfaction. However, both the lay and specialist concepts of mental health are extremely difficult to define.

The crux of the problem of normality[2] has been discussed in the chapter on personality. We are each of us unique and all have different abilities, potentialities and needs which must be utilized and satisfied if we are to be balanced and fully developed individuals. The concepts of normality in legal, statistical, social or biological language are specialized and geared to those particular disciplines. In the field of mental health, the normal state represents a condition of full and co-ordinated development of potentialities and satisfaction of needs in a manner which is acceptable both to the individual himself and to other persons sharing the environment with him. From this point of view one can see that a career woman or a family woman, a business tycoon or a milkman, an artist or an engineer can all be mentally healthy although they all have quite different personalities and achieve quite different end points. This concept of normality has a multiplicity of educational, social and other implications mainly beyond the scope of this book. We shall however mention some of these in this chapter and the next. For example, vocational guidance and assessment of the potentialities of an individual with a view to selecting a suitable working environment for him is of increasing importance in this modern technological age with its considerable specialized division of labour. Again, in the next chapter we shall introduce some of the problems related to psychiatric treatment which attempts to restore an individual to a state of mental health appropriate to himself, should he stray beyond the limits acceptable to himself or society.

We have said that to avoid tensions and frustrations within the individual all his potentialities must be expressed and satisfied. Moreover, these various potentialities must work together in harmony. This inevitably means setting up a goal or ideal towards which he can direct his physical and mental energies. For balance within the environment we must each live and work in a situation with which we can cope, which stretches yet satisfies us and in which we can make progress both for the benefit of ourselves and our fellows. We can, therefore, consider a mentally healthy person as one who sets himself a socially acceptable goal and successfully works towards it. This at once brings in the vital concept that mental health is dynamic. It involves both adaptation and self-fulfilment. It is constantly changing according to the needs and stage of development of the individual and the environment in which he finds himself.

As in so many areas of psychology, it is comparatively easy to state a problem in theoretical or ideal terms. It is much more difficult to translate theory into practice. We have touched on some obvious problems working against the attainment of a mentally healthy state in previous chapters. An individual's selfish desires may well be incompatible with the needs of the rest of society. Again, the demands of different groups to which an individual belongs may be diametrically opposed to one another. Frequently a person's physical or mental limitations may prevent him from playing the part which society expects of him (for example, he may be unable to adjust to difficult situations or be of an unsuitable level of intelligence). A major problem to which we shall return later is that societies are often controlled and directed by persons who themselves are not as mentally healthy and balanced as they should be, for example, 'empire-builders', 'power-seekers'.

When the environment puts a very great strain on an individual his responses may well prove inadequate to cope with it. Such extremes will be discussed in the next chapter. Here we shall confine ourselves to conditions which remain within socially accepted limits. We have said that 'mental health' is a dynamic concept. The changing features involved may be environmental or integral parts of the individual. It is to a closer examination of these features that we must now turn.

INDIVIDUAL FACTORS INVOLVED IN MENTAL HEALTH

In Chapter 9 we described the way in which each individual goes through a series of changing phases during the process of development. These are of both bodily and behavioural kinds, for example, a gradual increase in physical size and strength, development of language ability, attitudes becoming progressively less self-centred and more socially acceptable, etc. The general features of development are inborn and basically similar for all people. However, the rate of development and the ultimate end point attained depend partly on genetic factors but also to a large extent on the environment. This developmental process is called maturing.

Mental health obviously embodies the concept of maturing.[3] At any particular stage in a person's life, a state of balance within himself and within his environment must depend to a large extent upon how far the individual has developed. For the adult person to be completely healthy it is essential that all his naturally emerging tendencies at each phase of development should have been fully expressed and satisfied. We shall return to the problems of frustration and repression and their relationship to mental illness in the next chapter. Let us note here that in the normal process of growing up it is essential that at each stage of development an individual should enjoy all the experiences which he is ready to cope with so that his education may be as full and rich as possible. Only after each phase of development has been fully worked out can the individual pass on satisfactorily to the next stage. The whole concept of immaturity is bound up with the perpetuation of infantile, childish or adolescent behaviour into adult life.

Let us take a specific example of this concept of maturing and its relationship to mental health. The underlying principles controlling the development of behaviour may be briefly considered first. The small child is helpless and insecure in the new, complex and ever changing world of persons and objects. Most of his activities are selfish, often animal-like and geared to physical survival and comfort. As he grows older he matures and becomes less self-centred. Experience shows him how he should behave in order to achieve the end he wants, while retaining the approval of others. On reaching adolescence he becomes accepted more and more into the world of adults where emphasis is placed on the social environment rather than on the physical. He has to learn to behave in an adult manner, to forget himself, to co-operate with others and generally work for the good of the community.

A small child gets enraged when he is thwarted in something which he wants to do, for example, his pile of bricks or a sandcastle is knocked down, but he is less bothered by factors not immediately concerning him – for example, what the neighbours think of his tantrum. As he gets older, physical thwartings become less important to him while social relationships affect him more and more. He will be more concerned about what the neighbours think about him than about his inability to achieve some desirable physical goal. As an adolescent he will be greatly put out by unfavourable comparisons made between himself and others, he will feel inadequate and insecure in the company of more competent adults, he will be looking out for personal snubs and will often be quite disproportionately angry or aggressive as a result. Many of the problems of adolescence are probably due to the fact that while these young people are going through a period of physiological, physical and psychological upset we expect them to participate in adult social life for which they have little relevant experience. As suitable experiences accumulate, however, the adolescent learns to know what to expect, can see perspective and generally is able to cope with his social environment. He becomes an adult who, if he continues to mature, will become even less concerned with problems of his own personal relationships and will turn his attention to such activities as the amelioration of problems of minority groups, and injustices to his profession or nation rather than to himself.

This example of the process of maturing involves the development of several tendencies, for example; love being turned away from self and towards others; aggression from physical fighting to overcoming social and economic obstacles;

fear from physical dangers to social injustices. While the process of maturation as manifested in the details of behaviour is very variable depending upon the person involved and the environment in which he finds himself, we are all familiar with adults who behave in an immature manner. For example, the mother who puts on a great show of dominating her children in public or who speaks in an 'artificially refined' voice on the telephone, in order to create an impression of her own standing; persons who think only of today and do not care about the future; individuals concerned only with self-glorification and who ignore or abuse possible competitors; teachers and parents who bully and take advantage of their charges. These examples could be multiplied indefinitely.

Because of the complexity of human nature, the limitations and conflicts of the environment and the excessive demands of modern society on the individual, no one is ever completely mentally healthy. The extent to which he falls short of this ideal depends both on genetic and environmental factors. Some inborn tendencies, such as fear, aggression, sex, are biologically essential for the continued existence of the individual and the race. Although they form part of the make-up of each of us their relative strengths vary from person to person according to genetic endowment. These tendencies must be expressed or sublimated (see Chapter 5) if the individual is to remain mentally healthy. Repression or frustration of these desires will result in mental tension and possibly subsequent mental illness. Other tendencies such as curiosity and maternal care seem to be more easily obliterated (perhaps because they are of less primary importance for survival). A person who has had certain basic personality components destroyed will obviously grow up a weaker and less fully rounded person than he otherwise would. He is less likely, however, to be fundamentally disturbed when the lost components are those such as parental care which is not so vital for the continued existence of the individual.[4]

In summarizing this section then we can think of a mentally healthy person as being one who has fully satisfied all his needs, expressed and developed all his potentialities and gleaned as many varied and relevant experiences as possible in so doing. (Failure to develop potentialities and satisfy needs will lead to frustration and tension and deterioration in mental

322

health.) These individual characteristics must be integrated and harmonized so that they are all directed to a common goal. (Lack of such co-ordination will lead to conflict, frustration and deterioration in mental health.) The end to which the individual is working must be acceptable both to himself and to the society in which he lives. (If this is not the case the person may become both dissatisfied and a social misfit, either of which must lead to deterioration in mental health.)

SOCIAL FACTORS INVOLVED IN MENTAL HEALTH

The division of our discussion into 'individual' and 'social' factors involved in mental health is bound to be somewhat artificial and arbitrary because of the considerable interaction occurring between these two aspects of an organism-environment relationship to which we have frequently referred in this book. All living creatures are moulded by their surroundings and Man is no exception to this principle. But in the case of Man his remarkable ability to adapt the environment[5] to suit his own needs makes our isolation of internal and external factors extremely difficult. Ever since Man learned to cultivate crops and domesticate animals, to build shelters and use fire, to communicate and co-operate with his fellows his pattern of existence has become increasingly unnatural. His environment, physical as well as social, is to a large extent man-made. While, theoretically, this should mean that it is ideally suited to human requirements, in fact many pressures and tensions exist within such an environment which tend to disrupt Man's well-being. In this section we shall consider two of the environmental forces which work both for and against mental health, viz. communication and leadership.

1. *COMMUNICATION*[6] We discussed in the last chapter some of the values of living together in groups and stressed particularly the importance of belonging to at least one intimate primary group, for example a family. Frequently, however, family groups composed of grown-up children and elderly parents sharing a home find that as many needs are frustrated as are satisfied by the arrangement. The major disruptive factor suggested by people in these situations is often 'lack of understanding' on the part of all concerned. We

discussed the factors behind such misunderstandings in Chapters 4 and 5. Breakdowns of communication are major social and industrial problems of our times, for example between parents and children, between management and trade unions, between nations. The reasons for this are easy to see. Exchange of information, views, attitudes, etc., between individuals is essential for the co-ordinated activity necessary for social life. However, due to the complex, personal nature of the preparation and interpretation of messages passed between persons it is extremely easy for distortion and misunderstanding to occur. But these same qualities of 'vitalness' and 'personal involvement' mean that such distortions can have far-reaching and often undesirable effects.

As an obvious example let us mention 'advertising'. A lengthy discussion of the moral and social problems involved is out of place here.[7] We are mainly concerned with the psychological principles underlying this form of communication. We have discussed in some detail in earlier parts of this text the concept that our present behaviour is coloured to a great extent by previous experiences. Depending upon the nature of our past experiences of a particular person, object, idea, etc., we shall have a tendency to respond to it in a predetermined manner when we meet it subsequently. Such a 'readiness' of interpretation we call an *attitude*.[8] We may be fully aware of our attitudes (for example, towards politics or religion) or only partly aware (for example, perhaps towards racial discrimination where what we say we feel when put to the test may prove to be only partially correct) or not aware at all (for example, towards our children or workmates; we may be quite surprised when told by observers that we have a certain way of responding of which we were not aware). Closely allied to attitudes are opinions. An *opinion* is an expectation about behaviour or events. For example, 'It is my opinion that if a nuclear war broke out mankind would be annihilated'. An opinion poll asks people what they think will be the result of, for example, a general election, or the effects of a particular new tax which has just been introduced.

Attitudes and opinions then are based on previous experiences. Advertising, propaganda, brainwashing, are all techniques for influencing attitudes and opinions by subjecting individuals to particular types of experience which they will utilize in deciding on subsequent patterns of behaviour. Most advertising consists of one-way communication channels from a poster, a film, an individual, etc., to a number of persons. Depending upon the present needs and past experiences of the population to which it is directed, the effects of the advertising will vary. Obviously, such advertising is biased in favour of the product or idea concerned and the information given is distorted by stressing its good points and its competitors' weaknesses. In order that attention should be paid to the advertisement some interest factor (for example a catchy tune, a pretty girl, a well-known personality, a free gift) may be linked with it, and the basic advertising information is perceived almost incidentally.

In most cases of advertising the individual being persuaded has at least some idea that he is likely to be misled and can, if he wishes, take appropriate action. Nevertheless, many people put great faith in the printed word or the expert 'medical adviser', 'chief research chemist', etc., of many television and newspaper advertisements, probably because of an *attitude* developed early in life towards text-books and school teachers. Breakdowns and distortions of communications in more general terms are often less easily discerned. If individuals are given faulty information about, for example, political, religious, national or class problems during the early years of their lives, they will grow up with unsatisfactory attitudes and opinions (that is, *prejudices*)[9] towards these problems. Such attitudes can be 'caught' by imitation of parents, teachers and fellows as well as being actively 'taught' by them. This problem has been discussed in the last chapter. It is essential that we should all be constantly aware of these dangers and that those concerned with teaching the young should be particularly careful about cultivating socially acceptable attitudes and opinions in themselves and their charges. Attitudes change as one goes through life collecting wider and more varied experiences. Social forces can be very effective in this modification of attitudes, for example, mass media, social clubs, family relationships and responsibilities. We shall return to the importance of attitude development and modifications later in this chapter when discussing methods for general improvement of mental health.

2. *LEADERSHIP*[10] Within any social group one finds

members with varying degrees of responsibility and importance. Some individuals are of low status, following instructions and taking little responsibility while others are of higher
status, issuing instructions, co-ordinating and organizing the
activities of the rest of the group. The extent to which an
individual guides and directs others and exercises authority
over them is a measure of his *leadership*. Leaders are very
important group members not only because of their effects
on the persons in their group but also because they often
act as the point of contact between their own group and other
groups and therefore can greatly influence the relationships
so created. As teachers, nurses and social workers of all
kinds are required to act as leaders in their own particular
fields, it is important that we should discuss this topic fairly
carefully.

As with so many psychological concepts, leadership is a
comparative term. It occurs to varying extents at all levels of
society. Within a family, father is likely to be leader, but within
a community composed of many such families and fathers,
there will emerge leaders of these leaders. Such is the system
in any hierarchy. In school, a teacher leads her class, teachers
are led by the head who in turn is controlled by his Local
Education Authority, while all L.E.A.s are responsible to the
Department of Education and Science. In hospital the pattern
of student nurses responsible to staff nurses and sisters who
in turn are controlled by matrons and the administrative hierarchy also demonstrate varying levels of leadership. In an
ideal society made up of perfect individuals such a scheme
would seem to be most efficient. However, close examinations
of existing situations often indicate that much is left to be
desired.

We must ask ourselves 'what makes a good leader?'
because if some individuals are likely to be better leaders than
others it is important that we should be able to identify and
select these candidates for posts of responsibility. In animal
societies the leader is generally the individual who has superior
qualities over his fellows (for example, in terms of strength,
size of horns, colour of plumage). Some psychologists suggest
that a similar type of selection occurs in human societies,
that is, the leader epitomizes (as far as possible) what the rest
of society regards as ideal. Other workers believe that leader-

ship qualities are more subtle than this would suggest. Certainly the types of leader emerging in different groups of similar constitution can vary very much. For example, if the elected group representatives from different but comparable classes in a college are compared some may be found to be studious, stable and knowledgeable, others fun-loving, extraverted and frivolous. Also one group may select different leaders in different situations, for example, a single class may choose one person as their representative on academic matters, another as their social organizer, while if the group on a day trip was involved in an accident yet another member might prove the most efficient leader in the crisis.

When attempting to establish basic principles as to what constitutes a good leader, one must attempt to put aside the superficial variations created by the nature of the particular group under examination. This is not easy when generalizing about, for example, a family group, a platoon of service men, a nation, the Roman Catholic Church, a class of school children and a psychiatric rehabilitation unit. However, in all these instances the leader must show at least the following characterestics:

A. He must be a good group member, aware of the aims and ideals of the group and prepared to help them to reach these ends even at the expense of his own desires and ambitions. In a competitive environment, where the leader is in a favourable position for self-glorification, it is extremly difficult for him not to abuse his opportunities, as many groups know to their cost.

B. In comparison with other members of his group he must show up favourably, for example in intelligence and experience, otherwise he will be unable to guide and assist his fellows successfully. He must be able to take decisions quickly, correctly and with confidence. He must be objective, fair and reliable.

C. He must be acceptable to the group as a whole. This is a dynamic process, leaders falling from or gaining favour during their period of office. Basically, it boils down to being able to communicate with other group members, being sensitive to their needs and reactions and being competent to deal with the problems which arise.

D. He must want to lead because one only succeeds com-

327

pletely in the tasks in which one wants to (see Chapter 6 on the importance of motivation). Equally, in order that the group shall be successful the leader must motivate his fellows to follow his direction. He must be competent not only to decide on the line which the group should follow but to set the pace and, through administration and communication, ensure that all his charges are participating in a manner which stretches and satisfies them as individuals while at the same time they are being used to the maximum benefit of the group as a whole.

While it is comparatively easy to state the characteristics which you consider to be desirable or essential in a competent leader, it is quite a different matter when you come to select a suitable individual for the task. The most reliable way of ensuring that a person will make an efficient leader is to promote him to that position of responsibility and observe how the group behaves under his control. Such a technique, however, is normally out of the question, although it represents to some extent the situation found when student teachers on teaching practice are given charge of a class for a short while. Another method of identifying possible leaders was first developed in officer-selection procedures[11] for the services and now has been extended to many industrial and even educational fields. Here a group of possible candidates for promotion are put together in a problem situation or set off in a discussion. Their behaviour is observed particularly with reference to their influence on other group members. In such a situation some individuals, by virtue of qualities inherent in their personalities, will make useful contributions to the situation, will be listened to and acknowledged as potential leaders by their fellows. Other persons may well prove to be most unsuitable for posts of responsibility and be insignificant or even disruptive in their effects on the rest of the group. It is on this personal differentiation that individuals are elected as leaders by other members of the group. 'Who would we like to lead us? So-and-so appears to be responsible, to know where he is going, I like him, he seems fair, he is very able.' And so by a vote among group members this individual will be elected as their leader.

Frequently, however, a leader is appointed from outside the group by a selection committee sometimes far removed from the individuals for whom the new leader will be responsible.* They select a candidate whom they consider suitable in terms of background, experience, interview-technique, etc. (We discussed this matter in the chapter on Personality.) A major difficulty arising in selection for promotion is that while an individual may make an excellent nurse or teacher, shining above her fellows and therefore being the apparently obvious choice for advancement, she may in fact be most unsuitable for the administration and responsibility that promotion demands of her. The group to which she is appointed now has a weak leader, while the group which she has left has lost a valuable member.

Each of us has his own ideas and standards as to what the aims and functions should be of the group to which we belong. The higher an individual's status within the group the more chance he will have of ventilating his views and of having them put into practice. This does not mean, however, that the contributions of more lowly group members are necessarily of less value. Generally, in a group of individuals of wide and varied experience, everyone benefits from communication in all directions, both to and from the leader and between other group members. Not only does this ensure that full use is made of the knowledge and skills of all group members, but also that the individuals concerned can feel important and involved in the functioning of the group and so morale will be strengthened. Where this multi-directional communication is linked with wise delegation of responsibility, we have what is termed a *democratically organized group*.

On the other hand, if the leader issues orders by virtue of his position and accepts no discussion or consultation, delegates no responsibility and shows disapproval of demonstrations of initiative among members of his group, then we talk of such leadership as being *dictatorial* or *autocratic*.

One frequently hears discussions, particularly among intending teachers, as to the relative merits of these two forms of leadership, and generally very little agreement can be reached.[12] The crux of the problem is that leadership is based on a relationship and so, like all other relationships, depends upon the individuals involved in the relationship and the end

*Such an individual is often called a 'head man' or 'boss' as opposed to a leader.

which it is desired to achieve. There has been a general trend from autocratic to democratic relationships from Victorian times to today. This is true in personal relationships in home, school and work as well as in more general attitudes in government, law and the Church. In general, it is true to say that where members can usefully contribute to the efficient functioning of their group, it is of considerable benefit both to themselves and their fellows that they should do so. However, there are situations where authority and direction is better situated in the hands of one individual, for example in the case of an emergency on a hospital ward or in an accident in the street. The autocratic approach also has a place in the classroom when a teacher is introducing a topic to a class with no previous relevant experience of it.

In most practical situations, a mixture of both approaches is usually appropriate. Because of his status and role the leader must have a considerable influence on decisions taken for or by the group. However, where competent experienced individuals constitute at least part of the group they are usually required to make some contribution to its running. Studies in many fields indicate the importance of some form of leadership. Under laissez-faire discipline, group members show lack of integration and understanding of the objectives for which they are aiming. They behave in an irresponsible manner and morale is low. Inadequate control and leadership in the home will lead to the development of poor, selfish attitudes and possibly delinquency and criminal activities; in the school it will result in inefficient learning and in society in general it will lead to moral, social and economic decline.

We have been discussing communication and leadership as two major environmental factors influencing mental health.[13] We could take a host of other problems relating to the selfishness of individuals within society, the adverse effects of competition and fear of others, resistance of the individual to change, the difficulties and prejudices of inter-group tensions, etc. Space, however, is limited, and to give a more complete picture of 'mental health' let us now turn to a brief discussion of some of the ways in which individuals manage to retain some balance within themselves while at the same time adjusting to the ever changing, often hostile environment. We must also consider how social workers, be they in schools, hospitals or the community at large, can help to ameliorate the problems which do arise.

THE MAINTENANCE AND IMPROVEMENT OF MENTAL HEALTH

We have constantly referred to the basic concept of motivation as the driving force behind our activities. In all living organisms there is a tendency to behave in a manner which will enable the individual to survive, maintain and, if possible, increase his efficiency in coping with the situations in which he finds himself. In human beings we refer to the importance of this tendency when we say 'we can only help people who will help themselves' or we talk of 'the need for a will to live or recover', etc. While, in common parlance, these phrases usually refer to physical illness, they are equally applicable to social and economic situations and also are basic to the improvement of mental health. We have discussed the need for setting ourselves socially acceptable, personally satisfying goals towards which we can work in order that we shall attain some high degree of mental health. Often we need help in discovering and attaining these end points and it is the prime function of social workers of all kinds to assist persons needing such help. In its widest sense this applies as much to nursing a patient back to physical health, or educating a pupil to attain full development of his intellectual abilities as it does to social guidance in promoting adjustment and security within the community.

It is obvious that the better the health of an individual, the more easily will he redress any deterioration in his well-being and the more efficiently will he maintain and improve his present state. For example a physically healthy person is resistant to disease and recovers quickly from minor illnesses, while a physically unhealthy individual is prone to all kinds of illness, and can be very badly affected by quite a mild infection or can be extremely upset by a slight shock. Equally, a socially and economically healthy person can maintain and advance his position in society with little guidance from others, while the poverty-stricken or socially maladjusted individual needs constant help and direction. The balanced, happy, healthy

331

individual can normally preserve and improve his general mental well-being without external assistance. We shall discuss the situation of persons not capable of such self-help in the next chapter.

The fundamental prerequisite for being able to help oneself and others in attaining well-being in physical, social or mental contexts is that each of us should understand not only his own problems but also those of other people. This is indeed a tall order. It is impossible to put down on paper the specific practical steps which every person should use in attempting to cope with the problems of himself and others because each of us is unique and the number of environmental situations which each of us may encounter is legion.

The intention behind this book is to outline some of the underlying principles and processes basic to an understanding of the mental activities of human beings in general terms. How these manifest themselves in particular situations depends on many factors, environmental and genetic, past and present. We have followed a widely used procedure for attempting to apply a pure science to practical problems. Take an analogy with meteorology. The weather forecaster on television or radio starts his explanation and prediction by discussing such wide concepts as high and low pressure areas, temperature and pressure gradients, fronts and air currents, etc. From this he moves to an outline of 'the general situations' which is a discussion of the likely weather forms for the whole country based on prior experiences of similar meteorological conditions. Finally, specific predictions are made for each region of the country taking into account geographical structure, distance from the sea, time of year, etc. Quite often these specific suggestions are different from the actual conditions which develop. The more one knows about the underlying principles of meteorology the more one can appreciate why the promised sunny periods or scattered showers have not replaced the persistent heavy rain that was expected to move rapidly eastwards clearing the country before dawn. Perhaps the wind dropped or changed direction as a result of an unusual combination of circumstances, which meteorology, still in its infancy, has not yet learned to anticipate. While this type of wrong forecasting can upset our plans considerably, we cannot do much about it, and a knowledge of why a particular chain of events occurred may not be of any great practical value to us.

In psychology we follow a similar approach to this in our application of experimental findings to everyday problems. This book has outlined some basic principles and has attempted to state 'the general human situation'. Exactly how people behave in specific circumstances may be quite different from what you might expect as an observer versed in general principles. Unlike the situation in weather forecasting, however, this does not mean that the general principles are of little value to you. On the contrary, they suggest the possible reasons for discrepancies between a person's actual response and what you (or, perhaps more important, what society) expects of him. In this way the social worker may be able to see solutions to the problems of others whom he is trying to help. When any of us can see another person's problems in perspective and can understand their causes, even though we may not be able to ameliorate them directly we shall be more tolerant of the persons concerned and may well respect their views in the light of their particular backgrounds and difficulties. This does not mean that we will agree with them or accept their attitudes and ideas. It does mean, however, that we will be in a better position to appreciate their problems and live with them as people.

The problems relating to poor mental health can be traced to causes either in the individual, or in the environment or (more usually) to a mixture of both. Persons may have great difficulty in coping with situations in which they find themselves for a variety of shortcomings in their own personalities. For example, they may be emotionally immature, yet be required to take posts of some considerable responsibility, as when a young student nurse has to act as 'mother' to a group of juvenile patients, or a student-teacher on school practice has to be responsible for a rowdy class of teenagers only two or three years her junior. Again unsuitable past experiences can make a person quite incapable of coping with a specific situation. For example, a young child who has always had his mother as a major part of all his previous percepts, will find that situations in which she is absent (perhaps when starting school or going into hospital) can be quite intolerable. Again the head of a large firm, or a high ranking officer in the services may find it extremely difficult on entering hospital to submit to the controls of a young student nurse. The last personality factor we shall mention here relates to the necessity for correct motivation in order to achieve complete well-being. A boy may 'feel too tired' to mow his father's lawn but can play a strenuous game with his friends and show no sign of fatigue. On a sunny afternoon you can read a novel or complete a crossword puzzle much more easily than you can tackle homework or revision for an examination. The difference between those activities which you can tackle successfully and those which you find difficulty in completing relates to the degree of 'need satisfaction' which each possesses. In order to achieve complete mental health an individual must be aware of what is involved in this concept and then want to achieve it.

No matter how well balanced an individual may be he will at times find himself in frustrating or unacceptable situations. In such instances he must respond to the problem in one of three ways. First, he may attempt to reform the situation, e.g. the teacher joining the staff of a school with lax discipline may control his class so strictly and punish so severely that he achieves order where previously chaos was rife. Secondly, he may 'put up with' the situation and change his own views to fit in with the environment. This tendency to compromise is so drilled into us as children that we tend to conform often without realizing that we are doing so. For example, we smile and talk politely to our neighbours whom we may actually dislike but with whom we do not wish to quarrel. Thirdly, we may withdraw from the frustrating situation and look for an easier environment, for example, we may ignore our neighbours by staying indoors when they are in their garden. We may avoid topics of conversation on which we have strong, unorthodox views. Again a teenager may be very quiet and shy in the presence of adults for fear of appearing inadequate or being made to look a fool. The mentally healthy person copes with such problems in a realistic way. Some persons always run away from conflicts, others always acquiesce and accept, a few always challenge and fight. It is a sign of emotional maturity and mental health when a person attempts to evaluate each situation and takes the action most appropriate to deal with it.

Coming to Terms with Ourselves

Let us take as an example of the interplay of these two factors, the treatment of juvenile delinquency.[14] Research indicates that children who break the law may be unbalanced within themselves, or may live in environments which fail to satisfy their needs for security, acceptance, respect and interest, or (as in the majority of cases) may suffer from a combination of these two factors. If a child is found guilty of breaking the law there is a variety of methods of attempting to deal with the situation. If the misdemeanour was obviously the result of a temporary lapse in discipline which the offender and his parents can remedy then he will return home on condition that he makes every effort to avoid a repetition. If, at the opposite extreme, the home from which the child comes is so bad that not only is it impossible for him to cope with it at present, but also it is unlikely to give him the necessary opportunities and experiences essential for him to be competent to deal with life's problems as an adult, then he is likely to be removed and put into a new, more satisfactory environment, e.g. an approved school. The majority of cases are intermediate between these two extremes. The home environment may not be so degraded as to justify complete removal of the child from it, yet, on the other hand, it may appear unlikely that the child will be able to reform in that environment without help extra to that which his parents are able to give. In such instances a probation officer may be introduced into the situation both to control and direct the existing situation along socially acceptable lines and at the same time to act as a source of advice and experience for the child to learn how to cope both with his present and future problems.

Situations such as the ones we have just described are, of course, undesirable. Their amelioration is a major social task and needless to say an extremely difficult one. We have repeatedly stressed the need to educate persons to understand the principles underlying human problems in order that they can help themselves and others. This education must be very carefully planned with an emphasis always on perspective. To become obsessed with the shortcomings of yourself and others is extremely undesirable.

Radical changes are apparent in some areas of educational thinking. For example, a much more realistic approach is

335

being adopted in some quarters to the education of parents for their future tasks. For years we have given a full and careful training to student-teachers for their role *in loco parentis*. Nurses and other social workers are prepared for their future careers by specialists in their particular fields. Yet we have relied almost exclusively on the development of natural tendencies in young people who are about to produce and bring up a family of their own. It is hardly surprising that in so complex and unnatural an environment as obtains in our society such inborn tendencies often prove inadequate. While specific, immediate problems especially with young children can be taken to a doctor, health visitor or other social worker, the general organization of day to day life within the family is based on uninformed and often faulty attitudes and opinions incorporating personal past experiences which may leave much to be desired. While compulsory instruction of parents may well be unacceptable to most people and is not suggested here, the extreme popularity of parent-craft classes already being run successfully in some areas indicates that much wider provisions of such facilities is a vitally important step in the improvement of mental health.

Closely allied to this problem is the question of whether sex-education should be taught in educational institutions. Is it desirable that children be taught 'the facts of life' by a person specially trained for the task? Should such instruction be given outside the emotional and personal atmosphere of the home? Is it important to include the subject as part of the normal school curriculum, so that it is not thought of as something 'different' or 'special'? If different children mature (both physically and psychologically) at different rates, at what point should the topic be introduced? In the light of modern social and economic problems should topics such as birth control, abortion, homosexuality, etc., be introduced? It is not the object of this book to attempt to answer such questions. Nevertheless the attainment of a state of complete mental, physical and social health is dependent upon satisfactory solutions being found to such problems.

The educational field is full of problems of this kind. Should social science be taught in schools? Are teenage children sufficiently mature to be introduced to the concepts of psychology and sociology? Should a course in economics and general world problems be introduced at some time into the curricula of all senior pupils? Would this help international co-operation? Do our school days fit us for future lives in the modern world? Unless they do, can we hope to become fully mature, mentally healthy adults? The modern world with its tremendous scientific and technological knowledge is a very complex place to live in. Man has much control over his environment and so needs to be constantly re-educated in terms of attitudes, understanding and judgment in many fields from the practical and economic to the moral and aesthetic. With the continual increase in industrial efficiency and automation a man in his twenties today may well have to adapt himself to several different jobs during his lifetime. A narrow training in a specialist skill may be of less value to him than a wide liberal education.

Increase in industrial efficiency is bound to bring with it increase in leisure time.[15] Leisure is a very difficult concept to define. It can be thought of as time when you are not engaged in your vocational work, but rather in activities which you select from your own choice. In order that you should know what is available for selection and also that you should choose activities which are likely to be most valuable to you, education for leisure is essential. The introduction of such courses in schools and colleges will encounter opposition from public opinion. We still suffer in this country from the after-effects of the Victorian era, which considered that any pleasant activity was probably evil and so was not to be encouraged. Nevertheless efficient use of leisure is so important to the mental and physical health of the person, that public re-education in this matter is vital and urgent.

In many ways health-promotion attitudes and schemes are being incorporated into education. Instances range from the provision of liberal education through part-time schemes for young industrial workers, to training and rehabilitation schemes for prisoners and long-term hospital patients. Two major areas of direct application of psychological principles to everyday life are in vocational guidance (where persons are tested to discover the type of work for which they are best suited) and in various fields of industrial psychology (where careful analysis of practical problems has enabled greater efficiency to be achieved).

337

It is extremely difficult to attempt to summarize a chapter of this nature whose scope is really commensurate with psychology itself. The main conclusion that can be drawn relates to the fact that we are all bound to encounter conflicts in our lives. When we do so we must adjust to each situation as it arises, attempting to see perspective, recognizing and accepting our own limitations and those of other people. We must use our own abilities for the good of the group concerned, be it family, class, profession, nation or the human race. If we are responsible for other people through our roles as parents, teachers, nurses or whatever, we must encourage them to become valuable productive members of society, capable of creating good and useful relationships with others. It can only be through a combined effort of all members of society that we can hope to bring about an overall improvement in mental health, leading to a reduction of tension between individuals and between groups. This should result in a decrease in many fields of conflict, including mental illness, criminality, family and industrial strife and eventually even war.

SUMMARY

1. We all want to be happy and at the same time make other people happy. The attainment of this state is basic to the concept of mental health. Mental health is very difficult to define without introducing comparisons with mental illness. It may be described as 'a state of balance within oneself and within the environment', but this at once brings in the ideas of physical and social health which are, in fact, inseparable from mental health.

2. Healthiness is comparative. We are all unique. Consequently any criterion used in recognition of a mentally healthy person must be of a wide and general nature. In ideal terms a person is mentally healthy when his abilities have been developed in a full and integrated manner and his needs have been satisfied in a way which is acceptable both to himself as an individual and to others sharing his environment.

3. To be mentally healthy a person must adjust both to his own changing needs and capabilities and to his ever-changing environment. Consequently mental health is a dynamic concept.

4. As an individual matures he goes through a series of bodily and behavioural changes. At any particular state of his life, what can be considered to be mentally healthy depends upon his level of

maturation. In order to maintain a tension-free state both within himself and within the environment, each individual should attempt to achieve the following conditions:

   a. to satisfy his needs, develop his potentialities and widen his experience as fully as possible appropriate to his level of maturation;
   b. to integrate the various aspects of his mental, physical and social characteristics and direct them towards a given end;
   c. to select as such a goal one which is acceptable not only to himself but also to the social group to which he belongs.

5. The modern human physical and social environment is to a large extent man-made. Theoretically, therefore, it should be ideally suited to his requirements. However, pressures and tensions exist within such environments, which tend to disrupt Man's well-being. Two major social forces often responsible for such breakdowns are discussed in this chapter, namely communication and leadership.

6. Communication is the essential process of passing information between group members. However, due to the complex, personal nature of the preparation and interpretation of such information it is very easy to distort and misunderstand. Breakdowns in communication are major political, social and industrial problems of our times. Advertising is an obvious example of distortion of communication and because of its obviousness can be anticipated and to some extent coped with. Many more insidious forms of distortion may occur in the transmission of, e.g. political, religious or racial attitudes and opinions, many of which are often caught by imitation.

7. A leader is an individual whose responsibility it is to direct and integrate the activities of other members of the group to which he belongs. For maximum efficiency it is desirable to select for this role a person who:

   a. is prepared to put the needs of the group before his own selfish ends;
   b. compares favourably with other group members;
   c. can be relied upon and is fair and objective;
   d. is acceptable as a leader to the rest of the group;
   e. wants to lead.

While selection procedures for potential leaders should take these factors into account, in many cases, this is not done with consequent adverse effects on the mental health of the other group members.

8. Every individual has his own views regarding the aims and

functions of the group to which he belongs. The higher his status within the group the more chance he will have of them being put into practice. If any group member has special ability or experience, full use should be made of this whenever possible. This not only improves the efficiency of the group, but also satisfies the need for self-involvement of the individual concerned. In such cases multi-directional communication and certain delegation of responsibility is advantageous to all concerned. This type of group organization is called *democratic*. Sometimes, however, consultation and delegation may detract from efficiency, e.g. in an emergency where swift, bold action is essential. Here the leader must usually take responsibility and act at once on his own initiative. Such organization is termed *autocratic* or *dictatorial*. In many social situations a mixture of these two approaches is most efficient.

9. Each individual must strive towards a personally satisfying socially acceptable goal if he is to be mentally healthy. The better your present state of health (be it physical, mental or social) the more efficiently can you prevent its deterioration and the more easily can you improve upon it. The role of the social worker is to assist persons in a poor state of health to help themselves to achieve a suitable goal.

10. Causal factors of poor mental health may be personal inadequacies of the individual or undue environmental stresses or a combination of the two. In order that an individual may improve his state of mental health he must be able to isolate and understand the problems involved and must want to correct them. For efficient reduction of his problems he must be prepared to be flexible in the selection of suitable responses. In some cases this may involve altering his own attitudes and responses, in others it may mean a modification of the environment to reduce stresses, even to the extent of completely withdrawing from the difficult situations. The hall-mark of mental health, however, is the selection of the most appropriate response to each situation that arises.

11. In the increasingly complex and unnatural modern world people need more and more help to cope with life's problems. The training of nurses, teachers and other social workers must be constantly modified to suit these changing requirements. The introduction of parent-craft classes on a nationwide scale is indicated as a method for improving mental health. A new look is also needed at how well our present school curriculum educates children for later life. In general we need a very much greater effort than is made at present to attempt to understand the human problems of both individuals and society.

Coming to Terms with Ourselves

REFERENCES

1. For an attempt to promote better understanding of the problems of mental health see G. Thorman *Toward Mental Health*, National Mental Health Foundation Public Affairs Pamphlet No. 120 (1946).
2. Jones, E. 'The Concept of a Normal Mind' in Halmos and Iliffe (eds.) *Readings in General Psychology* (Routledge & Kegan Paul, London 1959) pp. 167–84.
3. See Fleming, C. M. *The Social Psychology of Education* (Routledge & Kegan Paul, 1959) especially pp. 67–78.
4. See Hadfield, J. A. *Psychology and Mental Health* (Allen & Unwin, London 1952) which develops this concept.
5. Thomas, W. L. (ed.) *Man's Role in Changing The Face of The Earth* (University of Chicago Press, 1956) discusses man's relation with the natural world.
6. For a fuller discussion see Price-Williams, D. R. *Introductory Psychology: An Approach for Social Workers* (Routledge & Kegan Paul, London 1958) pp. 118–48.
7. See Brown, J. A. C. *Techniques of Persuasion* (Pelican, Harmondsworth 1963).
8. Rosenberg, Houland, McGuire, Abelson and Brehm *Attitude Organization and Change* (Yale University Press, New Haven Conn., 1960) discusses attitudes and their modification.
9. Allport, G. W. *The Nature of Prejudice* (Addison-Wesley, Reading, Mass. 1954).
10. Jennings, H. H. *Leadership and Isolation* (Longmans, Green, N.Y., 2nd ed. 1950; 1st ed. 1943) gives an introduction to interpersonal choices studied in a correctional institution. See also Brown, J. A. C. *The Social Psychology of Industry* (Pelican, Harmondsworth 1958) pp. 219–44.
11. Vernon, P. E. and Parry, J. B. *Personnel Selection in the British Forces* (U.L.P., London 1949).
12. Hollander, E. P. *Leaders, Groups and Influence* (O.U.P., London 1964).
13. For a useful survey see Taylor and Chave *Mental Health and Environment* (Longmans, London 1964).
14. See Andry, R. *Delinquency and Parental Pathology* (Methuen, London 1960) and Burt, C. 'Recent Discussions of Juvenile Delinquency' *Brit. Journ. Ed. Psych.*, 19 (1949).
15. Pieper, J. *Leisure: the Basis of Culture* (Pantheon, N.Y. revised ed. 1964).

Chapter Fourteen

Failure to Come to Terms with Ourselves and Our Surroundings

INTRODUCTION

In the previous chapter we described a mentally healthy person as an individual who is balanced and free from tension both within himself and in relation to his environment. Theoretically then a person who is imbalanced and not completely adjusted within himself or his surroundings can be considered to be mentally ill. The major short-coming of such a definition as this is that all of us could be considered mentally ill, often for most of our lives. For example, a person may wish to achieve a goal which society prevents him from reaching and so he is frustrated. Can we say then that all children in school counting the minutes until the end of the arithmetic lesson are mentally ill? Are motorists driving up and down looking for parking spaces which are not available mentally ill? Again a person's own limitations may prevent him from reaching a particular goal. But are people taking driving tests before they are competent to pass or are children entering for the eleven plus examination even though they are of below average I.Q. necessarily mentally ill? Each of us may wish to follow two different (perhaps antagonistic) lines at the same time. A father might feel sick and wish to go to bed, yet his desire to take his child to the zoo as a birthday treat prevents him from retiring. He is imbalanced within himself from his two conflicting desires, and also perhaps may be unable to cope efficiently with his environment if he is unwell. Yet surely only a purist would describe this man as mentally ill.

Because of the complexity of human nature and the stressful, unnatural situations in which we often find ourselves, we all frequently experience conflicts, frustrations and tensions, we all make inappropriate responses from time to time and we can then be described as temporarily imbalanced. But to include 'flying off the handle', being bored or anxious, making a stupid remark or laughing when someone trips on the kerb, as being necessarily symptomatic of mental illness would be akin to including a broken finger-nail, a scratch on the hand, or a hole in a tooth as being examples of physical illness. While in the purist sense this may be true, in common usage these characteristics on their own would be considered normal. They *may be* symptomatic of a much more serious condition, e.g. holes in teeth might indicate a calcium deficiency throughout the body, while mistakes in responses to the environment might be symptomatic of a person losing touch with reality. If the condition of the person worsens in respect of these symptoms then tests or observations become necessary to determine the nature and extent of the illness. If, however, the individual is able to carry on a normal life which is acceptable both to himself and others sharing the environment with him then these individual peculiarities are not considered symptomatic of mental illness. It is only when a person is sufficiently maladjusted as to be unable to conduct his life in a normal way that he is considered to be mentally ill.

At once, of course, all the problems of 'comparing individuals' are raised again. What is a normal life? How can you tell whether your responses are acceptable to other people when the conventions of our society make normal people 'say the right thing', 'cover up their real feelings', 'be loyal to a friend or colleague of long standing', etc.? At what point does a person's maladjustment sufficiently interfere with his conduct to make him socially unacceptable? The virtual impossibility of answering these questions satisfactorily is obvious. We have all come across individuals who are not having psychiatric help and yet without doubt have extremely adverse effects not only on the conduct of their own lives, but also the lives of their families and perhaps also their colleagues at work. Take the fairly common case of a person who attains a post of

343

responsibility when young and competent. As he gets older and becomes progressively senile he finds difficulty in adjusting and so cannot cope with his environment, yet by virtue of his status he has a tremendous influence on the activities of the groups of which he is leader. In the competitive world of business the effects of such people will often be minimal and short-lived, but in teaching, nursing, and other less competitive fields the problem can be extreme.

While we shall return to specific examples of mental illnesses later in this chapter, let us briefly consider here the extent of the problem. In Great Britain, one in nine women and one in fourteen men can expect to have treatment in a mental hospital at some time in their lives. In fact nearly half our hospital beds are taken up by psychiatric patients. But this is by no means the whole story. Nearly twice as many patients are being treated in the community as are being cared for in hospital. The situation which exists here is basically similar to that described in the last chapter for the treatment of delinquency. If you are trying to help a person to move from an abnormal socially unacceptable state to a more normal, socially acceptable state, be it the reforming of an offender or the treatment of a mental patient, you will have more chance of success in a normal social environment than in an institution cut off from society. Provided that the person concerned can cope with the environment, initially with the help of his family and a social worker but later perhaps, more or less on his own, his rate of recovery is likely to be speeded and the end result more satisfactory if he is treated in the community. In attitudes towards mental illness there has been a considerable modification over the last two centuries. No longer do we think of demons possessing the minds of the mentally sick. Treatment is far from punitive and medical knowledge continues to make great strides. Nevertheless, in this field more than in most, there is a great need for re-education of the population to remove the stigma that psychiatric illness frequently carries.[1]

THE NATURE OF MENTAL ILLNESS

In our discussion so far we have frequently referred to the inability of the psychiatric patient to cope with his environment. This is the main characteristic which distinguishes a mentally abnormal person from a normal one. There are no general activities which in themselves universally indicate mental illness. Crawling on your belly in the gutter, while extraordinary in a London shopping-centre, may be quite acceptable and sensible in a front-line village in wartime when snipers lurk in the houses lining the street. Again to pump water through your neighbour's sitting-room window may or may not be socially acceptable, depending upon whether or not his house is on fire. These examples are extreme, but they represent the point of the general argument that a person is mentally ill when his responses to the environment are sufficiently inappropriate as to interfere with the normal running of his own or his fellows' lives.

Such unsatisfactory responses may take many forms. They can conveniently be classified as follows (a) Abnormalities of doing including the examples we described above as well as more general distortions ranging from virtually complete immobility to incessant, apparently meaningless (often rhythmic) movements no matter what the environmental situation. (b) Abnormalities of speech which may range from voice peculiarities such as stammering, to the creation of new words which are meaningful only to the patient himself, or refusal to respond to a question even though he is quite aware of the answer. (c) Abnormalities of feeling which may either be of increased intensity (e.g. a person may be very elated or depressed to an extent quite out of keeping with the situation in which he finds himself) or of decreased intensity (e.g. he may show indifference, apathy and coldness in situations where a normal person would be emotionally involved) or distorted (e.g. his mood may be quite out of keeping with what he thinks about a situation or he may experience rapid changes of mood for no apparent reason). (d) Abnormalities of thinking involving both distortion of content, e.g. hallucinations, and of form, e.g. flight of ideas, or great difficulty in developing a train of thought. Often both content and form are abnormal, e.g. in phantasy or obsessions with some obscene, repetitive idea. (e) Abnormalities of orientation both in space and time where the patient is unable to determine where he is, what day it is, etc. (f) Abnormalities relating to the ability to form judgments or to reason out simple problems. We shall return to examples of these disturbances later in our discussions of specific types of mental illness.

We have said that one of the main characteristics of a mentally ill person is that his responses are inappropriate to his environmental situation, e.g. his movements or answers may be meaningless, his thoughts or feelings may be unsuitable, his orientation, judgment or reasoning may be faulty. This concept of mental illness as maladjustment suggests that there are two main factors which contribute to a person's mental state, namely the personality of the individual and the environment in which he finds himself.[2] When we say that Mr X is a normal individual we mean that he copes with his problems at home in a manner satisfactory to himself and his family, that he is successful in his business commitments and that he fulfils the role which society expects of him. Suppose, however, that this previously normal man is now subjected to a greatly increased environmental load, e.g. his wife dies and leaves him with a young family, or his business commitments become very heavy and dealing with them completely exhausts him mentally. Now he may well be unable to cope, he may have a 'nervous breakdown', i.e. he may become mentally ill. An excessively demanding environment then can cause a previously normal person to become mentally ill (as the results of prisoner-of-war interrogations in the last war indicate). Of course some people 'break down' more easily under stress than do others. How prone you are to mental illness depends upon your personality. Some persons cannot cope even with a normal environmental load, for example the mentally defective, or persons with special disabilities of sight or hearing, or individuals who are over-anxious or senile or have inferiority complexes. We shall mention many more examples later in this chapter. An environmental load which is acceptable to normal people can prove too much for an individual of weak personality and cause him to show signs of mental illness. Such persons may appear to cope perfectly well in a sheltered environment, e.g. in a home where they are protected by other members of their family. Should their relatives no longer care for them, then the weak individuals may have to be taken from society and put into a quiet problem-free environment such as a psychiatric hospital where they will be able to cope. The name 'asylum' originally given to such institutions, means 'a refuge'.

In the investigation and treatment of a mental patient the psychiatrist needs a great deal of information. While a detailed discussion of case-taking would be out of place here,[3] it will be obvious from our previous discussions that this information might conveniently be grouped under three major headings.

A. THE GENETIC ENDOWMENT OF THE PATIENT.[4] While it seems likely that some inherited factor is present in most of the major groups of mental illness, it is very difficult to assess its specific importance in relation to other factors acting on the individual after conception. Apart from the difficulties of determining the nature of the inherited weakness in a potentially mentally ill person, the whole study of human genetics is difficult and slow. Long intervals between generations coupled with the small numbers of reproducing individuals involved and the inadequate and subjective records of family histories all complicate the issue. Nevertheless so vital is an understanding of the principles involved here not only for the care of potential or actual mental patients but also in advising certain persons not to marry or have children that every effort must be made to elucidate these problems as quickly as possible.[5]

B. PREVIOUS EXPERIENCES OF THE PATIENT. Obviously by having the right type of previous experience to deal with the common problems of our environment, we become increasingly successful at coping with them. Equally obviously, if we have unsuitable past experiences we may be temporarily or permanently prevented from coping with future problems. Those which the psychiatrist may encounter are infinitely variable. They range from malnutrition or infection in the womb, to disease, injury or the effects of drugs in adult life. They may be physical (as suggested above), psychological (e.g. traumatic or otherwise harmful experiences at home, in school or at work), or social (e.g. due to wartime conditions, unemployment, industrial depression). They may be limited to certain times in the individual's life* (e.g. puberty, leaving

*Many psychologists suggest that there is a tendency to make too much of the influence of physical changes on psychological processes.

home, child-bearing, menopause), or they may be more or less constant throughout life (e.g. as a result of an unsympathetic parent, husband or boss). It is often extremely difficult to isolate any particular factors as being primarily responsible for a person's mental illness. Generally a combination of many different circumstances is involved.

C. PRESENT SITUATION OF THE PATIENT. Some environments are obviously unsuitable for the promotion of mental health, e.g. the home dominated by an unbalanced parent, or the society which cannot satisfy the needs of its members. Many situations, however, cannot be considered universally unsatisfactory and yet may be causing mental illness in some individuals in those situations. How well a person can cope with the demands of a particular environment will depend both on his inherited capacities and the previous experience which he has had. In other words, the stress likely to be created in an individual by a given situation is dependent not only on the situation itself but also on the nature of the person concerned and his familiarity with such situations. Another aspect of this problem relates to the speed at which the difficult circumstances arise. We said in the previous chapter that mental health is 'dynamic' and that as individuals we must constantly adapt ourselves to both internal and environmental changes. Mental illness can be considered as a lack of such adjustment. Under normal circumstances a person adapts himself slowly and almost imperceptibly as he matures and ages and as his environment evolves. Suppose, however, that a sudden change occurs either within the person (e.g. at puberty or menopause) or in the environment (e.g. sudden death of your husband or an enormous success on the football pools). Such circumstances can considerably and immediately change the person's whole internal-external balance. Very great adjustments are necessary to restore a state of balance. Often it takes some time to get over the change and during this period of adjustment the person may become mentally ill.

Although it has been convenient to divide causative factors in mental illness into these three categories, in any case which you take the behaviour of an individual whether normal or abnormal is the resultant of the interplay of all three factors. [6] Looking from my window at children playing in a park I can see great variety in their roles and responses to one another.

The behaviour they are showing at this moment depends (*a*) on the specific situation and relationship in which they find themselves (*b*) on the capacities which they inherit from their parents (*c*) on their previous experiences of similar situations. Again consider a student who as a child was physically strong but who suffered an illness at adolescence which has left him partially paralysed. Subsequently the disability he developed affected his physical and psychological experiences and has to a large extent determined the situation in which he finds himself today both through physical limitations, and psychological and social attitudes and pressures. In any case of mental illness these three groups of factors will be involved, although their relative importance will vary from case to case.

It will be apparent from what we have said so far that just as we could not easily separate mental health from other forms of well-being, so also mental illness cannot be isolated from physical and social illness. For example, unemployment indicates lack of social well-being. Its effects on the individual may also be physical (malnutrition, inadequate clothing and shelter, etc.) or psychological (insecurity, lack of self-respect, no interest in life, etc.). However, the person may have become unemployed through physical or psychological shortcomings. It is often impossible to disentangle the causative factors in such cases. Consequently we must consider people as units with physical, psychological and social characteristics. While the symptoms of an illness may appear in one sphere (e.g. as an ulcer, or as depression) the causes might be in quite a different sphere (in the first example through psychological worry, in the second through a long painful physical illness). Although doctors may specialize in psychiatric, internal or social medicine they must all have training in each of the three branches of the subject.

The main concept which we must bear in mind for the rest of our discussion in this chapter is that we are less concerned with being able to *describe* a mental illness as with being able to *understand* it. In this way it should be possible to treat the causes of the illness rather than simply trying to dispose of the symptoms. The chief difficulty in such understanding lies in the lack of specific links between causes and symptoms in many psychiatric illnesses. The same symptoms may be shown by different people for a variety of causes. For example, depression may be caused by factors ranging from the after-effects of a simple common infection to an intra-cranial tumour, or from a neurotic state in an overworked housewife to a psychotic condition in a manic-depressive patient (see next section). Again the same causative factor in different individuals can produce quite different clinical pictures. Take, for example, the responses of a group of children found to be in need of special schooling and so removed from the security of the environments of their homes. Some will be unable to concentrate on their work, others will become very naughty (i.e. begin to perform antisocial acts). Some will become aggressive, others very shy. Some may develop physical clumsiness or begin to wet the bed, while still others may demonstrate infantile habits (thumb sucking or nail biting) or even psychosomatic illnesses. For our purposes here it will be convenient to discuss inappropriate forms of behaviour under two main headings:

a. *Mental illness* where we shall consider individuals whose nervous systems have developed sufficiently fully and who have encountered adequate experiences for them to have been able to lead a normal life but who have subsequently deteriorated into an abnormal condition.

b. *Disorders of mental development* where we shall discuss cases of incomplete mental development or inadequate utilization of mental equipment, e.g. backwardness and retardation.

FORMS OF MENTAL ILLNESS

Under this heading we are considering all persons who have at some time led a normal life but who are now behaving abnormally. We will not reiterate our previous discussion of the difficulties of defining 'normality'. Let us simply remind ourselves that the distinction between normal and abnormal is not clear cut and it is often impossible to pinpoint the precise onset of a mental illness. Part of the reason for this is that many psychiatric symptoms differ only in intensity from those in normal behaviour (e.g. anxiety, depression, concern with detail). Another factor hindering recognition is that initially the signs and symptoms often appear in a very minor form. They may gradually become more pronounced but persons sharing the environment with the patient adapt themselves to his 'funny ways'. Outsiders entering the environment, however, may well wonder how his friends and relatives 'manage to put up' with such an abnormal person. While the stranger can often tell that something is wrong and the psychiatrist normally can diagnose the problem and suggest treatment, the patient and his immediate fellows may have great difficulty in recognizing the existence of abnormality. Consequently, many patients do not receive psychiatric help as early as they should, thus making their treatment and cure more difficult.

It is convenient to distinguish between two major categories of mental illness, the psychoneuroses and the psychoses. The psychoneuroses (sometimes shortened to neuroses) are mental illnesses which, although affecting the happiness of the individual, making him perhaps over-anxious, fearful for no cause or in some other way abnormal, are not so severe as to profoundly disturb his whole personality and cause him to lose contact with reality. The psychoses involve severe disorganization of personality with changes of thought, feeling or intellect which may be so extensive as to prevent the patient from seeing the world as his normal fellows see it. There is much discussion as to whether or not psychoneuroses and psychoses are quite different types of condition or whether they are only differences in degree of maladjustment. This problem need not trouble us further here except to notice that while patients to whom the term 'neurotic' is applied can be generally accepted back into society following their readjustment, psychotics are permanently barred from some posts, for example, in the services and professions, and may be prevented from free entrance to certain countries. Consequently, it is common practice to limit the use of the term 'psychotic' to extreme mental upsets and to class milder disturbances as 'neurotic illnesses'.

1. *PSYCHONEUROSES*[7] (*NEUROSES, 'NERVOUS BREAKDOWNS'*) Everyone at some time makes inappropriate responses to the environment, or feels tense and anxious in his own mind and providing there appears to be adequate reason for these maladjustments they are considered to be normal. Many people, particularly under stress, may deviate in their feelings, thought and judgments to a degree which would not be considered normal, but realizing their own imbalance, can so talk and behave that no one else is aware of

351

their stressful situation. In many instances such imbalances correct themselves when the problems causing them are resolved. In slightly more severe cases behaviour may be affected to an extent only noticed by close friends and relatives, for example, an individual may be more irritable or anxious than previously. Here we have a gradation from normal to slightly neurotic behaviour. Should the individual's behaviour become even more inappropriate to his environment, his responses be ineffective (e.g. through lack of self-confidence or courage) or exaggerated (e.g. anxious and fearful in situations which normal persons accept as non-threatening) and the patient be aware of his predicament, then he is suffering from psychoneurosis (we say he is having a 'nervous breakdown').

Among the most common psychoneuroses are *anxiety states*. They are particularly prevalent in persons who worry a great deal and are fearful even when there is no danger to disturb them. Although they will tend to rationalize and say that they worry as a form of 'insurance policy' in fact they are generally converting a psychological fear of personal inadequacy into terms more acceptable to themselves. Because they set themselves high standards, and through their anxiety reduce their efficiency they frequently break down under the self-imposed strain. The results of this breakdown may be mental or psychosomatic (e.g. gastric and duodenal ulcers are common in such individuals).

Obsessional neuroses are very similar in some ways to anxiety states. Here the patient experiences unwanted thoughts which are not related to the situation in which he finds himself and yet he cannot prevent them. This results in his feeling conflict and anxiety but in this case related to a particular anxiety. We all have such experiences: 'I cannot get that tune out of my mind' or 'I keep going through that unfortunate meeting I had this morning', and we may say that the repetition 'is driving me mad' or 'getting on our nerves'. What is irritating to us as occasional experiences to normal persons can create great anxiety in obsessional personalities. The thoughts upon which such persons dwell may relate to a variety of concepts, from the meaningless to the obscene, from physical health (hypochondria) to religion. In some cases obsessional responses may show themselves in behaviour. Within the realms of normality, the meticulously tidy or the scrupulously clean person may be classed as an obsessional. More abnormal forms such as avoiding walking on the cracks between paving stones, performing meaningless ritualistic acts, counting stairs, etc., are all well known.

Phobias are uncontrollable fears which can often lead to extreme maladjustment. While it is considered normal to be afraid of an actual terrifying experience, even though it may now be passed but is likely to return again, for such fears to unnecessarily pervade and interfere with all aspects of an individual's life is obviously abnormal. An infant has an inborn fear of falling. It is natural for him to be concerned about danger from falling when as an older child he climbs trees or as an adult, he scales rocks and mountains. However, intense fear of going upstairs, or climbing on to a stool to reach a book from a shelf is quite inappropriate to the situation and is considered abnormal. Other fears, such as dread of closed spaces (claustrophobia) or of open spaces (agoraphobia) are found in some people. Fear of the dark is very common in children and also in a surprisingly large number of adults. Evidence suggests that this fear of the dark is learned, probably through frightening childhood experiences such as nightmares or being woken by a frightening noise, or feeling alone and unwanted by parents happily having supper downstairs. The crux of the nature of a phobia is that it represents an excessive fear of certain objects or situations even though the person knows that there is no danger present. He normally wishes to be rid of the unreasonable fear but is unable to do anything about it himself.

Hysteria (the name is derived from the Greek word hysteron, meaning the womb, because it was once thought to be an illness of women, due to the wandering of the womb within the body). While hysteria is found particularly in young women it also occurs in older women and men of all ages. The early psychiatrists limited the concept of hysteria too much by confining it to certain forms of behaviour of adult women. There is a tendency today, however, for laymen to use the word too widely by applying it to any form of dramatic or exaggerated behaviour. Psychologists restrict the use of the word to reactions which are produced or prolonged to protect the patient from something he wants to avoid, or to help him fulfil a wish or satisfy a desire. For example, the neurotic soldier may become paralysed or lose his voice, he may suffer from nausea or cry or laugh in an uncontrollable manner when he is told that he must return to the front-line in the face of great danger. Such patients differ from persons suffering from anxiety states in that once the stressful situation has been resolved, they return to a more cheerful condition. It is very important to distinguish hysterical reactions from malingering. While the latter constitutes a conscious attempt to deceive in order to avoid an unpleasant situation, in hysteria the patient is never clearly and fully aware of his motivation.

Psychoneuroses, then, are failures of adjustment of which the individual himself is usually aware, although the causes of his illness are often not clear to him. The normal person behaves, thinks, and feels in a way which deals appropriately with the situation in which he finds himself. He is happy or sad, aggressive or anxious in any situation to a degree which is considered normal by other people sharing his environment. (What is considered normal varies from group to group, e.g. Spaniards tolerate emotional levels which might be considered extreme or unacceptable to Swedes.) This production of normal behaviour, feeling or thought is controlled by the nervous system of the individual concerned. Take a simple example of response to an environmental danger. When the danger is perceived the autonomic nervous system takes appropriate action by raising the rate of heart beat and respiration, digestion ceases and certain hormones are secreted. The central nervous system controls mental responses, making the individual alert, causing him to pay attention to important stimuli and in general making him ready to respond. A combination of the control of the A.N.S. and C.N.S. produces the right sort of responses of a suitable magnitude to deal with the danger.

Suppose, however, that these controls go wrong, e.g. the effect of the A.N.S. on the heart may be to produce palpitations, on the gut to cause indigestion, or more generally throughout the body to bring on sweating or trembling. Again the C.N.S. may make the person over-anxious or elated, cause him to pay attention to the wrong aspects of his environment, or make unsuitable responses. In these malfunctions in relation to a physical danger, the person could be seen to be responding inappropriately and he might fall victim to the danger.

Failure to Come to Terms with Ourselves

The stressful situations to which psychoneurotics make wrong responses are rarely physical. They are commonly due to mental conflicts often between the individual's own desires and limitations and the controls and demands of society. However, the same type of malfunctioning of response can be seen here as we described above. Psychosomatic disorders, e.g. digestive, respiratory or circulatory upsets may arise. Over-anxiety, depression or elation can occur or paying gross attention to unimportant items (as in phobias) or performing unsuitable reaction (as in obsessional activities, or paralysis). These are manifestations of inappropriate activities of the A.N.S. or C.N.S. or both.

The causes of such breakdowns in efficiency of response are hard to identify. They are not diseases as much as reactions to stressful circumstances which may be due to an increase in environmental load or to a decrease in capacity of the individual to cope with them. The principle of treatment in such cases is to discover and remove the conflict which is causing the individual to make inappropriate responses. We shall briefly consider some techniques for such treatment, after we have discussed some rather more serious mental disorders, namely the psychoses.

2. *PSYCHOSES*[8] As we have previously discussed, the exact distinction between psychoneuroses and psychoses is a matter of debate. For our purposes it is enough to take as our criterion that psychoses involve severe disorganizations of personality which may eventually lead to such changes of thought, feeling or intellect as to prevent the patient from seeing reality in the same terms as his fellows. His attitudes to all his experiences may be coloured by one overriding emotion, e.g. depression, elation, aggression or suspicion, or he may show no emotional response at all. He may have hallucinations (false perceptions) and delusions (false beliefs) which prevent him from participating in social activities and in extreme cases be not only a nuisance but a danger both to himself and to others. Unlike the psychoneurotic patient, the psychotic is not usually aware that he is abnormal. He therefore resents suggestions that he is not coping adequately with life's problems and so rarely co-operates with attempts to help him.

It is very difficult to classify psychoses in a form acceptable to all psychiatrists. It is convenient to separate those forms which are the result of observable physical or physiological changes in the individual (i.e. the *organic disorders*) from those which have no obvious physical or physiological counterpart (i.e. the *functional or psychogenic disorders*). It must be noted, however, that many psychologists and psychiatrists maintain that just because there is no observable physiological change involved in the psychogenic disorders this does not mean that such a change does not occur at a level at which our experimental techniques are at present insensitive.

Organic psychoses are changes in behaviour resulting from physical or physiological changes in the brain (normally the cerebrum). Such alterations in brain structure may be due to deterioration of brain cells, such as is found in senile dementia (loss of mental powers with advancing age) or in hardening of the arteries of the brain. Again it may be due to damage through physical injury or the growth of a tumour. In a small proportion of cases of epilepsy also, behavioural deterioration may occur (but with modern treatment this is becoming less common). Poisons of different sorts may affect the functioning of the brain. These poisons may be the toxic products of illnesses such as rabies, tetanus or diphtheria, they may be the results of over-activity of ductless glands, e.g. the thyroid, or they may be drugs taken by the individual, e.g. alcohol, morphine, cocaine. All organic psychoses show some behavioural disturbance. Certain psychoses tend to show certain characteristic symptoms, for example, senile dementia often involves impairment of recent memories, loss of logical thinking, inability to take decisions, while toxin reactions often involve mental confusion and loss of emotional control. However, due to the complexity of the functioning of the brain it is often very difficult to see a constant direct relationship between brain disease of a certain area, or the action of a specific toxin and a well-defined characteristic set of symptoms. Due to such factors as local compensatory mechanisms and integration by, for example, circulation through large areas of the brain, the appearance of symptoms of mental illness is often slow and of a general nature, behaviour gradually deteriorating until a level is reached where professional assistance is essential.

Now we must turn to the *psychogenic or functional psychoses* in which the changes involved in behaviour cannot be directly related to observable changes in the central nervous system. Evidence from several sources indicates that perhaps these illnesses have physiological counterparts, for example, the use of drugs such as tranquillizers whose effects are physiological, help to remedy some functional disorders. Again, the percentage of persons suffering from functional psychoses remains fairly constant even in times of war and economic hardship when the stressful nature of the environment may be expected to increase the incidence of disorders resulting from environmental stress. Other evidence based on genetic studies indicates that there is probably an inherited susceptibility to many of the particular types of psychosis. The relative importance of constitutional weakness of the individual and environmental pressure upon him is difficult to assess and probably very variable in these 'functional psychoses'. It is common practice to classify these disorders into three groups, according to the aspect of mental functioning which is most disturbed:

- *a*. the affective disorders involve emotional imbalance;
- *b*. the schizophrenic disorders involve peculiarities in how the patient thinks;
- *c*. the paranoid disorders involve peculiarities in thought content, i.e. what the patient thinks.

Each of the categories is so complex that we can only indicate generalizations here. The interested reader is referred to the bibliography at the end of this book.

AFFECTIVE DISORDERS. Most of us are sometimes high-spirited and sometimes sad, but to be normal the circumstances in which we find ourselves should indicate that such emotions are appropriate. Affective psychotics experience prolonged and profound changes of mood, e.g. elation, depression, anger or fear, quite out of keeping with their circumstances. *Depression* is very common (affecting nearly 1 per cent of the population). The sufferers may be aware of their inappropriate feeling and so obtain professional help. In advanced cases, however, such insight rarely exists. Often patients show physical deterioration as well as psychological maladjustment. They may not wish to go on living and in extreme cases may attempt suicide. *Mania* is an exaggeration of mood in the opposite direction from depression. Patients are overcome with tremendous feelings of joy and exhilaration. They may be excessively active, eating and sleeping very little and consequently becoming exhausted (in extreme cases death may result). This activity may take various forms, for example, the patient may undertake greater responsibilities and enterprises, run greater risks, become more aggressive or sexually active than before. In most cases of mania there is little insight by the patient into his condition and he may be extremely difficult to deal with both during and after his illness.

SCHIZOPHRENIC DISORDERS. These are the most common types of psychosis. The characteristic deviation from normal of schizophrenic patients is that their mental activities (particularly their thought processes) are not integrated into a coherent whole designed to cope realistically with the environment. The lack of harmony between mental activities of a schizophrenic and what would be considered appropriate responses of a normal individual vary very much in degree and kind. In a mild form the patient may lose interest in his work and family and become withdrawn and emotionally unresponsive. In more advanced cases hostile or dangerously impulsive outbursts of activity may occur, or the patient suffering from delusions and hallucinations may enact a kind of day-dream fantasy to himself. In other extreme forms some patients cease to walk or talk or make any response to the environment, even neglecting their own personal cleanliness and toilet habits. Despite their high incidence in our society, very little is known about the causes and treatment of this extremely grave group of mental disorders.

PARANOID DISORDERS. In mild forms this type of disorder may be confused with schizophrenia for the behavioural peculiarities shown by paranoid patients are also based on systematic persistent false beliefs (i.e. delusions) about the environment. The main difference between the two forms of illness becomes more apparent in extreme cases. While the grotesque hallucinations and delusions of the schizophrenic make his responses, thoughts and emotions illogical and incomprehensible to normal people, the delusions of paranoid patients are often quite feasible, although they are wrong. For example, such a patient may believe that he is very rich, or that all his friends and relations are plotting against him. He behaves in a way compatible with these false beliefs and so he becomes increasingly maladjusted to his environment. It is as though he were using advanced forms of projection and rationalization (see Chapter 5) to interpret his environment according to his own values and attitudes. The paranoid patient often behaves in quite a normal, socially acceptable manner until that part of his sphere of activity which is affected by his delusion is touched upon.

3. *PSYCHOPATHIC PERSONALITIES*[9] In everyday language the term 'psychopath' is often used to describe any mentally ill person who is violent. In the strict psychological sense this expression has a much more specific meaning. It refers to a group of mentally abnormal persons who are not mentally deficient and who are not included in the previous categories of psychoneurotic or psychotic types. They are usually unreliable, selfish, unsympathetic and antisocial. They have not developed the moral standards and values of the society to which they belong and consequently form a high proportion of offenders against the law. Comparatively little is known about the causes and possible treatment of psychopaths and the interested reader is referred to the book of D. K. Henderson (1939) listed in the bibliography.

TREATMENT OF MENTAL ILLNESS

For treatment to be effective it must obviously be directed at the causes of an illness. We have already described how these causes might be psychological in nature (e.g. stresses and strains within the mind of the patient, or between the patient and his environment) or of a physical or physiological kind (e.g. toxins in the blood or degeneration of nervous tissue). Consequently treatments fall into two main groups, those which are basically related to psychological analysis and re-education, and those which are physical or chemical in nature.

1. *PSYCHOTHERAPY*[10] (the treatment of disorders by psychological methods).

If a normal person has a conflict in his mind, or is having difficulty in coping with his environment, parents, work, etc., it often helps a great deal if he can talk to some other sympathetic but uninvolved individual. While in some cases this listener may be able to make helpful suggestions, the main value of the interview usually comes from the troubled person talking and thinking about his own problem. By so doing he is making a conscious attempt to resolve the conflict and will feel much better for having done so because he will have reduced his own mental tension.

A similar technique is used by psychotherapists who are specialists at listening to and helping mentally ill people in order that they can solve their own problems as far as possible. The first stage in psychotherapy involves elucidation as far as possible of the causes of conflict. This requires self-expression by the patient in a form which can be analysed by the therapist. While talking is the most common type of such self-expression, other forms may be used, for example, play analysis and therapy are sometimes used with children, or drawing or painting analysis may be useful in other situations. It is of prime importance in this type of treatment that the patient should co-operate with the doctor. Consequently such psychotherapy is much more widely used with psychoneurotics who are aware of their problems and want to solve them than with psychotics who are generally not aware of their peculiarities and resent attempts to assist them. When the patient has told the therapist all he can about his problem he may have given some important indications of the cause of his conflict. He will also have given the doctor some information as to the type of patient he is dealing with. It is often necessary now for the therapist to delve deeply into the roots of the patient's problem to attempt to discover whether there exist further disturbances of which the patient is not aware.

Various techniques have been developed for this purpose. One of the best known is *psychoanalysis*[11] which is based on the work of Sigmund Freud. Freud said that many of the mental events of which a patient is conscious in fact represent other unacceptable past experiences which the individual has managed to repress. The psychoanalyst attempts to help the patient to remove the disguises of those intolerable past experiences so that the true situation may be seen in perspective and the tension which it created may be released. This is a lengthy process often involving several visits per week for two or three years.* For details of techniques involved the

*Some psychologists are very critical of psychoanalysis for they feel that excessive verbiage encourages invalidism.

reader should consult suitable works mentioned in the bibliography. In general terms the procedure is to put the patient in a relaxed frame of mind and ask him to give an account of every thought entering his mind (free association). This is very difficult for the patient at first, not only because he may not wish to divulge his personal thoughts, but also because our culture demands that we think before we speak and we are used to carefully selecting what we say. The interpretation of dreams is also an important aspect of psychoanalysis. We have described Freud's approach to analysis here. There are other forms such as that based on the work of Jung,[12] which takes into account not only the past experiences of the individual but also the history and culture of the race to which he belongs.

The major differences between simple psychotherapy and psychoanalysis are that (a) psychoanalysis is much deeper and more far-reaching than the quicker, more superficial simple interview and (b) in the simple interview the psychiatrist discusses, persuades and suggests ideas to the patient instead of leaving him to work out his problems alone. In both types of approach the patient builds up confidence in the doctor which may help him to recover, although the degree of independence attained is sometimes greater in simple psychotherapy. For this and other reasons (e.g. time and money involved) simple psychotherapy may be preferable in many cases of early psychoneurosis. So much depends, however, on the personality of the patient concerned. If he is basically adequate but has an overriding specific problem which is interfering with his mental balance, then simple psychotherapy may well be satisfactory. If his problem is more deep-seated and general, however, some more far-reaching analysis is probably indicated.

There are many variations in such techniques.* We shall leave them by mentioning what appears to the layman to be the most spectacular of them, namely *hypnosis*.[13] This term is applied to the artificial inducement of a dream-like state of heightened suggestibility in which the patient, although in many ways appearing to be asleep, is able to maintain contact with the psychiatrist. Such trances can also be induced by the

*The interested reader should consult the bibliography for accounts, e.g. of Rogerian techniques and social psychiatry.

use of hypnotic drugs. The suggestibility of the patient enables the doctor to influence him to remember and disclose emotions and experiences which he had previously repressed. While in some cases the results of this treatment can be excellent there are several drawbacks. Only about one in four of the general population can be hypnotized at all. Of those who can, some are unable to accept on waking what has been brought to light during the trance. Again many psychotherapists are dubious regarding the value of recall under conditions so much controlled by the hypnotist. The ultimate place of this technique in psychotherapy is still in doubt.

Throughout this book we have stressed the importance of satisfaction of needs both physical (e.g. food, warmth, freedom from pain) and psychological (e.g. security, acceptance, self-respect, a variety of interests) for a full and happy existence. For the mentally ill such satisfaction is essential to prevent further frustration and deterioration. It is very easy for normal busy nurses and relatives just to give the patient 'something to keep him quiet' to free them for their other duties. The field of occupational therapy[14] has developed rapidly in recent years, being concerned not simply with occupying the patient but with carefully prescribing suitable occupations for each individual, appropriate to his physical and mental conditions. By discovering his interests and capabilities his energies can be so directed as to enable him to perform a constructive activity for the benefit of himself and sometimes also of the community. The development of libraries, handicraft centres, painting and music groups as well as more vocational rehabilitation centres are common examples of such therapeutic techniques.

The ultimate aim of psychiatric treatment is to fit the patient for returning as an acceptable member to society. Although individual therapy is usually necessary to determine the exact nature of the patient's problems and to give him personal contact and confidence in the therapist, some form of group therapy is often desirable also to make rehabilitation complete. Group techniques[15] while being economical from the hospital's point of view also help the patients in several ways. For example, they can see that they are not unique in their illness, and improvement in mental health is infectious in many cases. Again several psychological needs can be satisfied within the group, which enable patients first to become useful members of the hospital community and subsequently perhaps useful members of society outside the hospital. Such group therapies may take the form of drama which the patients produce and act, clubs to which they belong, recreation and games sessions, as well as vocation-orientated classes and groups. The integration of suitable patients into society again is gradual, by an introduction and extension of parole, eventually in appropriate cases leading to complete discharge.

2. *PHYSICAL TREATMENT* A detailed description of these techniques is out of place here.[16] Among the more important types that we may mention are the use of drugs, electro-convulsive therapy and brain surgery.

When a mental illness is the result of some infection or poison in the body (e.g. as a result of some fevers or diabetes or the effects of alcohol) then *chemotherapy* may be necessary to correct the imbalance while general medical procedures must be used to remove the causative factor. Other drugs have specifically psychological action, e.g. antidepressants, sedatives and energizers. The use of tranquillizers has been of great importance in the modification of management of over-excited, aggressive patients who now can be sedated, and so the need for restrictive practices for the protection of the patients themselves and for others has been reduced. Insulin treatment is a special case which we will mention because it is known to many lay persons although it is obsolescent in this country. Sugar is essential for normal brain functioning and an adequate level of concentration in the blood is maintained by a fine balancing mechanism. When the level of sugar in the blood rises, e.g. after a meal, a hormone called insulin is secreted by the pancreas, the effect of which is to cause sugar to be removed from the blood and stored for future use. If such removal of excess sugar from the blood did not occur, it would be excreted through the kidneys and lost from the body. If insulin is injected into the body, the sugar supply to the brain is depleted and coma or semicoma results. This comatose condition is found to be very helpful in alleviating certain schizophrenic conditions, especially those occurring in adolescents as a result of an emotional disturbance. The mode of action of this technique is not understood.

We have already referred to the electrical activity of the

brain in Chapter 3. The passage of a small electric current through the front part of the cranium for a fraction of a second has been found to have very beneficial results for some mental patients, especially persons suffering from depression. This treatment is called electro-convulsive therapy (E.C.T.), for when administered without anaesthetic and muscle relaxant drugs, the patient after becoming unconscious gives a bodily convulsion. Normally such drugs are used, both to reduce the anxiety of the patient regarding the treatment and also to prevent the occurrence of physical accidents, e.g. fractured bones, which might result from bodily convulsion. The patient normally recovers consciousness after about ten minutes and following a short period of confusion, becomes fully conscious and can usually return to his daily occupation in a matter of a few hours. The risks to the patient from this kind of treatment are very small and are far outweighed by the great benefit afforded through the alleviation of his abnormal state.

Cerebral surgery has a place in psychiatric treatment in certain cases. Obviously where mental illness is the result of say an accessible brain tumour which can be removed safely, an operation is indicated. The operation of leucotomy which involves severing certain nerve tracts between the thalamus and the frontal lobes of the cerebral cortex (see Chapter 3) is another well-known surgical procedure. Its mode of functioning is not understood and it is only resorted to when other techniques have failed. While it usually reduces tension, worry and restlessness, it may also bring undesirable changes in personality, e.g. indifference and weakening of judgment and foresight.

DISORDERS OF MENTAL DEVELOPMENT

In the previous sections of this chapter we have been concerned with persons who had previously attained normal mental health but had subsequently deteriorated. Now we must turn to those individuals whose mental development has been imperfect and who have never achieved normality.[17] It is convenient to divide them into two major groups:

> *a.* Those who lack the capacity to attain a level of mental development normal for the race and culture to which they belong.

Failure to Come to Terms with Ourselves

Such short-comings may be of a general nature throughout all mental functions (such a condition being called *oligophrenia*) or they may be specific as, for example, in tone-deafness, partial blindness (the so-called *special disabilities*);

b. Those who through adverse environmental conditions have not attained a level of mental development which fully extends their capacities (such persons are said to be *retarded*).

The level of attainment of an individual can be assessed in general terms by observing the success with which he copes with his environment. Special tests may be used to obtain more valid and reliable estimates. The problem of deciding the limits of normality again arise as they did in our discussions of mental illness. It is particularly difficult to decide whether a child is mentally deficient or not as all individuals develop at different rates and the fact that at a certain age an individual appears to be less able than fellows of the same chronological age may simply indicate that he is a late developer.

It is always easier to spot the extremely abnormal individual than it is the person who only slightly deviates from levels of general acceptability. All workers concerned with dealing with people are aware of the difficulties of coping with patients, clients, pupils or relatives who, while not deviant enough to merit specialist professional care, are sufficiently at variance with their fellows to constitute a nuisance. We have mentioned such cases at various points in earlier chapters. Here we are mainly concerned with a brief introduction to more extreme forms of abnormality.

1. *INDIVIDUALS INCAPABLE OF ATTAINING A NORMAL LEVEL OF MENTAL DEVELOPMENT* We are all aware of persons in our society who exhibit some pronounced degree of mental deficiency caused either by genetical or environmental factors. The law recognizes several categories of such individuals, the terms for which are widely (and often imprecisely) used in everyday language.

Idiocy is a state of mental deficiency so severe that the individual cannot protect himself from everyday physical hazards. He becomes lost when momentarily parted from his guardian; he burns or otherwise hurts himself in situations in which the normal person would find no hazard. In severe cases he has little facility for recognizing and communicating with others. In intelligence tests his I.Q. would be below 20.

Imbecility is a state less severe than idiocy, but in which the individual cannot manage his own affairs nor be taught to do so. Some of the higher grade imbeciles can acquire useful simple motor skills such as scrubbing floors or polishing brass under supervision. I.Q. range is between 20 and about 50.

Feeblemindedness is a state not as incapacitating as imbecility but in which individuals need care and supervision and must be constantly controlled for the sake both of themselves and the rest of the community. Their I.Q. range is between 50 and 70. In U.S.A. the term *moron* is used for persons of this level of intelligence.

Above the level of the feebleminded it is convenient to have a category of persons who, while not being as mentally deficient as those previously described, are still unable to cope with the normal demands of society. Their I.Q.s fall in the range 70 to 85 and they are variously described, for example, as *dull* or of *inadequate constitution*, and so forth. It is difficult to generalize about characteristics of this group. While an individual may be quite unable to deal with the pressures of a stressful environment such as may be found in the competitive world of a family man living in an urban area, he might adjust and cope quite adequately if as, say, a country dweller he was living at home with his protective parents, and going off into the fields to perform simple straightforward tasks. It is interesting that many vagrants, criminals and prostitutes fall into this category of mental inadequacy.

It is quite beyond the scope of this book to discuss the tremendous range of types of mental deficiency with which psychiatry is familiar.[18] In outline it is convenient but perhaps limiting to consider three categories of causative factors any or all of which may occur together in a particular individual.

A. Inherited factors of general mental weakness. Genetical studies indicate that mentally deficient parents tend to produce mentally deficient offspring.

B. Inheritance of a particular pathogenic condition. Evidence of inheritance is not conclusive in all cases of the conditions mentioned here, but in many instances genetic constitution is believed to be a prime cause:

> *Gargoylism* in which the individual is physically stunted, adopts a crouching posture, and the eyes are set wide apart, often looking outwards.

366

Microcephaly in which the skull is small and cone shaped, the frontal regions being underdeveloped.

Hydrocephaly where there is an excessive amount of fluid in the skull resulting in an enlargement of the head. This condition may be present at birth but also can develop subsequently due to intra-cranial infections.

Mongolism in which the individual has certain Oriental features, e.g. slanting eyes and broad nose; the tongue is enlarged, fingers are short, joints are lax and there are many other distinguishing features. The cause of this condition is unknown, but may be genetically determined, as Mongols have an extra chromosome in the cells of their bodies. It appears to be related to advancing age of the mother, at the time of the Mongol conception.

C. Factors external to the brain which may affect its development. These can take many forms, e.g. injury at birth or before (perhaps through the mother falling heavily); through poisons entering the foetus through the placenta and circulating to the brain as when the mother has syphilis, or suffers from German measles in the first three months of her pregnancy; or through irradiation of the mother's pelvic region during pregnancy by certain types of radio-active ray. Again if the individual's thyroid gland is underactive, *cretinism* results which affects both physical and mental development. While individuals suffering from such afflictions as we have outlined here are found in our society, they will not normally be encountered by teachers, and nurses and other social workers required to deal with such cases will receive special professional instruction.

2. *INDIVIDUALS NOT MAKING FULL USE OF THEIR POTENTIAL CAPACITIES* In the last section we were discussing individuals whose level of mental attainment was subnormal due to inevitable factors implicit in their nervous systems. Here we are concerned with people who have been held back (retarded) by defective upbringing and who have not had a chance to extend their capabilities *to anything like* their full extent.

We must couch our definition in these rather unspecific terms because as we stated earlier in our discussion of individual differences, none of us ever reaches his full potential level of attainment. How far below this potential his actual level of attainment falls depends to a very large extent on environmental factors. In our modern society with its great variety of opportunity, most of us develop many of our capabilities to a considerable extent. We may still, however, be held back in our pursuit of and accomplishment in e.g. games or music if facilities for experience in these fields are not available. We shall be concerned here with individuals who have been subjected to such abnormal circumstances that their *actual* general level falls very far short of their *potential* general level of attainment.

In a wide sense the term 'retardation' can be applied to anyone whose mental development has been impeded. Consider the very talented individual who, under suitable circumstances would have excelled, for example, the schoolmaster whose musical genius only manifests itself in playing the church organ on Sundays, the farm worker who writes wonderful poetry or paints outstandingly well. We are all familiar with examples of persons who, because of the practical needs of a bread-and-butter job, have neglected or been unable to make full use of their talents. Such people can 'get by' but only as average members of the community and not as the leading lights in their special field that they could have been. Of course this is frustrating for the individual, a great loss to the subjects concerned and to the community at large and is to be greatly deprecated. Today, with universal education in this country, coupled with vocational guidance, financial assistance, etc., problems such as these are happily decreasing in number.

In the more specific sense in which we shall be using the concept of retardation for the rest of the chapter we are considering individuals (especially children) whose actual level of performance is definitely below normal. We can think of two major but overlapping categories:

a. Those who would be normal if brought up under normal circumstances but who through adverse conditions, such as poor health, socio-economic problems, undesirable parental pressures, etc., fall far short of normality. For example, young men called up for national service who initially cannot read and write but who subsequently learn quite quickly. Again, the gardener or cleaner in a school for maladjusted children who describes some of the long-staying pupils as being 'perfectly normal' might well be observing persons such as we are con-

368

sidering here. (There could, of course, be complications not apparent to a layman.)

b. Those who, while being of below average intelligence could in an appropriate environment with proper care and treatment be accepted into society among its weaker members. When such persons are brought up in a competitive critical environment where little understanding of their problems is attempted then they are likely to achieve a very low level of attainment.

In considering manifestations of retardation we must remember that while it is common practice to confine the term to impeded psychological development, as we have said earlier in this chapter such disturbances can show themselves in various spheres of activity. For example, *physical upsets* such as clumsiness, awkwardness at games, poor co-ordination, illegible handwriting, stammering, accident proneness; *emotional upsets* such as instability, poor attitudes to work or other people; *intellectual upsets* which may be specific short-fallings in subjects like maths or grammar or general poor performance in all subjects involving intellectual facility; *social upsets* which can be generally described as naughtiness or, in extreme cases, delinquency. It is obviously quite artificial to attempt to separate these categories, and abnormal activity in any one sphere may be indicative of much more widespread disturbance.

We must, of course, be careful not to attribute every peculiarity which a child shows to mental retardation. Some problems are genetically determined, e.g. certain types of physical awkwardness, nervousness, aggression. Others are brought on by the physical conditions in which the child is operating, e.g. chairs which are too high or too low, apparatus which is too stiff, heavy or complicated. These are problems which science and handicraft teachers often experience when teaching children from eleven to eighteen years of age in the same laboratory or workshop. Again problems arise through actual physical limitations of the children, e.g. partial deafness, rheumatic joints. At times of very rapid physical growth (e.g. in the early teens) bones sometimes grow much more quickly than muscles and consequently clumsiness and lack of co-ordination result to the consternation of the child as well as his family and teachers. Here, due to the limitations of space we shall confine ourselves in the main to mental retardation as a result of adverse psychological experience. Even this, however, may manifest itself in all the various forms suggested above.

Why do these unsatisfactory forms of behaviour develop? In earlier chapters we have emphasized the ways in which marks of parental, school and other influences are left on our personalities.[19] In the most obvious case, unsatisfactory teaching will affect attainment in the subject which is being poorly taught. But attitudes of teachers can have many other more widespread effects. A boy in a primary school was able and well at the top of his class throughout his first four years. In the fifth form his mother was the class teacher. She, probably to avoid jibes of favouritism, was very hard and critical towards her son and often appeared quite unfair to him. His behaviour deteriorated both in and out of school which aggravated his mother's attitude towards him. The vicious circle was not broken until the end of that year by which time the child was near the bottom of his class, nervous, unhappy and a much less valuable member of the school.

Problems can be even greater when home and school demands are in conflict. For example, the children of servicemen who must change school when their parents move, whose attendance is often irregular and who generally feel insecure. Again discipline at home may be too strict or too lax to enable the child to fit happily into the school environment. Inadequate sleep or food or too much homework can also cause tensions between school and home. While parent-teacher associations are, in many instances, doing a grand job in ameliorating some of these problems of conflict, one can still find parents who interfere unduly with the education of their offspring, and teachers determined to exclude rigorously all forms of parental influence.

Although school either alone or in conflict with the home can exert some considerable influence on a child, it must be accepted that the home and family are usually responsible for most of the retardation which may occur in a child's development.[20] There are many reasons for this. Bonds with parents are stronger and their influence greater than can be the case with outsiders. Children do not go to school until they are four or five years old and even then spend only a few hours of weekdays during term-time away from home. Each child is part of a group at school, while at home it is an individual. There are many other reasons also why parental influence is very great. We all know examples of children crushed and suffocated by over-protective, dominating parents. We see infants who are forced by parents to behave like little adults. They become precocious or disturbed, feeling guilty about matters which should not yet concern them. We find nervous children who suck their thumbs, bite their finger-nails, wet the bed or show many of the mental defence mechanisms discussed in Chapter 5. Such disturbed behaviour may be permanently characteristic of children from very bad homes or may be quite transitory as when a child from a normal home goes through a difficult period, e.g. at puberty, or moving house, or when one of its parents is ill.

How can we deal with such problems? The answer must lie in understanding the cause and removing it. While this may appear to be stating the obvious, how often it is too much trouble for a parent or teacher to go to these lengths. They may become angry with a child who has an irritating twitch or who is very shy or who cries easily. 'Pull yourself together', 'snap out of it', 'be your age', 'cry baby'. Far too many people in positions of responsibility abuse their authority, criticize unfairly and use standards based on adult behaviour to judge the responses of children. While to prolong a negative list of undesirable practices is pointless, it is important that we should be clear that such approaches are often quite useless. If the child is disturbed through fear or insecurity, as is often the case at adolescence, the obvious remedy is to be found in a friendly atmosphere free from criticism.

Let us say a word on the concept of 'naughtiness'. Some parents and teachers adopt the attitude that life is a struggle between themselves and their charges, and that the latter have a store of behaviour patterns 'specifically designed' to irritate 'their betters'. Such an approach suggests that the whole process of bringing up and educating children will be an unpleasant chore but teachers and parents (if worthy of the name) will assure you otherwise. It is much more constructive to think of naughtiness as behaviour which is unacceptable in our modern society but which probably has survival value in other circumstances, e.g. fighting, asserting oneself, climbing trees and throwing stones. The undesirable effects of crushing these impulses were discussed in Chapter 5. The only satisfactory answer is to find a socially acceptable outlet for these activities. Teachers find that discussions and class participation helps a great deal in cutting down irrelevant talking. Woodwork, handicraft, gardening and art encourage constructive rather than destructive use of a child's curiosity and talents. Competitive activities, e.g. sports and quizzes or project and problem solving, are methods for reducing physical aggression.

Trying to remove the cause of the naughtiness or redirecting the energy available for it is far more effective than punishment. An interested, busy child is not naughty. A child shut up alone in its bedroom is more likely to err. If a child is reacting against the present régime, making the environment even more unpleasant is unlikely to relieve the situation. Let us take an obvious example here of a child of five years who cried aloud for several nights running because it was afraid of the dark. The parent slapped the child and it no longer disturbed his sleep. He was satisfied that he had 'cured' the socially unacceptable behaviour. Surely he could see that all he had done was to introduce into the situation an even greater need (here pain avoidance) than that existing previously (i.e. fear). He certainly had not cured the trouble as the child's later greatly increased fear of the dark indicated. Although this is a very obvious example it demonstrates an all-too-widespread attitude towards naughtiness. As parents and teachers we must always attempt to understand causes and remove them, rather than take the easy way out and introduce yet another conflicting need into the situation. This is not to say that one should never punish. It is rather saying that punishment is a very poor second to understanding coupled with positive redirection of the child's behaviour. Some psychologists believe that the reaction of teenagers against their parents, in particular, and adult society in general is basically a revolt against the suppression to which they have been subjected.

Closely related to our discussion here is the subject of juvenile delinquency. We can think of this as extreme naughtiness that extends to law breaking. The interested reader should consult the bibliography.[21] The crux of the matter seems to be that while the delinquent has the same needs and motives as the normal child, these have been so frustrated as to produce quite antisocial forms of behaviour. The delinquent needs to be accepted but his family has rejected him. He has found comrades in a similar plight, and formed a group (or gang) in which he is accepted and feels secure. If the norms of this group demand violence against other groups in society then he will join in this type of behaviour. He will steal and lie to remain a member of the group and perhaps improve his standing within it.

We must be careful not to over-simplify the problems involved. Some individuals are more prone to throw away acceptance by society than are others. The child who has had a good home might become a social misfit, especially if he 'gets in with the wrong sort'. But evidence suggests that the vast majority of delinquents suffer from unsatisfactory need fulfilment. Many come from broken homes and have had little security and affection. Others have had no suitable outlet for aggression, exploration, curiosity, competition, etc., and so 'let off steam' by means which damage the rights and property of others. To climb trees and throw stones into a lake is something which most children do. The proportion of country dwelling delinquents is small. In a town where there are no suitable recreational facilities provided children climb drainpipes and fences and throw stones through windows. Their behaviour is illegal but is not really different from the activities of their country fellows or children from towns in which playgrounds are provided for release of their energies.

Much time and thought is being expended by social workers of all kinds in attempting to alleviate the problems of troublesome and delinquent children. A major obstacle can often be the blind, ignorant prejudice of members of 'the good old days brigade'. 'Too much psychology and not enough stick', 'these problems have only arisen since psychology was invented', and other negative comments are still far too common. While in earlier times problem children existed but were ignored or flogged into quiescence, today society is conscious of its responsibility to help them to lead full, normal, socially acceptable lives.

Frequently the cause of maladjustment lies in the environment in which the child lives. If this is so, the environment must be modified, for example, the parents may need re-educating in their responsibilities, or the teaching method at school must be changed. If these changes cannot be brought about by the parents or teachers alone, then help must come from outside, e.g. from a probation officer or some other suitable social worker advising in the home, or educational psychologists at school. Often retarded children can be put in a class of educationally sub-normal individuals and receive special teaching in an environment in which they are comparable with their fellows. There are obvious disadvantages against such segregation.[22] These are perhaps accentuated when children are sent to special schools for difficult pupils. The pros and cons of this arrangement are beyond the scope of our discussion here. It is, however, worth noting that the results which can be obtained with many very disturbed children when taught in special classes geared to their specific needs and cared for by interested specially trained staff are very heartening indeed.

SUMMARY

1. We described a mentally healthy person as one who is balanced within himself and within the environment. Most of us are imbalanced to some extent and consequently do not enjoy full mental health. Slight imbalance is considered quite normal in our society and it is only when an individual becomes so maladjusted that he cannot conduct his life in a way acceptable to himself and others that we describe him as 'mentally ill'. The problem arises as to how one distinguishes cases of 'slight imbalance' from cases of mental illness.
2. The main characteristic which differentiates the mentally ill person from the mentally healthy one is his inability to cope with the environment in a socially acceptable manner. Inappropriate responses may take an infinite variety of forms usually classified under abnormalities of (a) doing (b) speaking (c) feeling (d) thinking (e) orientation in space and time (f) judgment and reasoning.
3. The concept of mental illness as a form of maladjustment suggests that there are two main factors which contribute to a person's state of mental well-being:

    a. the personality of the individual;
    b. the nature of his environment.

    When an individual is mentally healthy his personality is competent to cope with his present environment. Suppose, however, that the environment becomes very stressful, then his personality may not be able to deal with the now more difficult circumstances and his responses may become inappropriate. Alternatively, a weak individual may be able to cope adequately with a protective environment such as might be created for him by his parents. Suppose he is removed from his home or his parents die and he finds himself in more stressful surroundings but still within limits which could be dealt with by normal persons. He may well not be able to cope and his responses may be unsuitable.

4. To investigate and treat a psychiatric patient a doctor needs much information. It can be classified theoretically into:

   a. genetic endowment of the patient;
   b. previous experiences of the patient;
   c. present circumstances of the patient.

However in most cases each of these three factors is involved to an extent not easily determined. Another problem lies in the inter-relationships between mental illness and physical and social upset. From all points of view it is essential to consider a person as a unit with physical, mental and social characteristics. Consequently psychiatrists are less concerned with trying to describe mental illness and more with attempting to understand it.

5. In our discussion of inappropriate responses to the environment we shall distinguish between:

   a. mental illness where individuals have previously been able to lead a normal life but have subsequently deteriorated;
   b. disorders of mental development where either there has been incomplete development, or inadequate utilization of the mental equipment.

6. Mental illnesses are usually classified under the headings of:

   a. psychoneuroses (or *neuroses*) in which the individual, although mentally disturbed, is not so ill as to lose contact with reality;
   b. psychoses in which personality disorganization is so severe as to prevent the patient from judging the world by the same set of standards that his normal fellows use, i.e. he does lose contact with reality.

There is much discussion as to whether or not psychoneuroses and psychoses are different types of condition or whether they are only differences in degree of maladjustment.

7. Some of the more important forms of mental illness are:

a. psychoneuroses:
    anxiety states
    obsessional neuroses
    phobias
    hysteria
b. psychoses:
    organic psychoses
    affective disorders
    schizophrenic disorders
    paranoid disorders
c. psychopathic personalities.

8. Treatment of an illness must always be directed at its cause. Causes of mental illnesses may be psychological or physiological and consequently treatments fall into categories designed to attack these forms of upset.

    a. Psychotherapy is treatment of mental disorder by psychological methods: e.g. simple psychotherapy, psychoanalysis, hypnosis, occupational therapy, group psychotherapy.
    b. Physical treatment may be by drugs (chemotherapy) electro-convulsive therapy or brain surgery.

9. Disorders of mental development can be divided into:

    a. those in which an individual is incapable of attaining a normal level of mental development either in general terms (*oligophrenia*) or through some specific disability;
    b. those in which an individual is prevented from making full use of his potential capabilities through adverse environmental circumstances (*retardation*).

REFERENCES

1. Yellowlees, H. *To Define True Madness* (Pelican, Harmondsworth 1953) pp. 1–26, discusses some of the problems in this field.
2. Hunt, J. McV. (ed.) *Personality and the Behaviour Disorders* (Ronald Press, N.Y. 1944) gives a useful survey.
3. Skottowe, I. *Clinical Psychiatry for Practitioners and Students* (Eyre & Spottiswoode, London 1953) pp. 78–111, gives a concise account of suitable techniques for case-taking.
4. Slater, E. 'Mental Disease Heredity' in *British Encyclopedia of Medical Practice* (2nd ed. 1950) gives an excellent summary of available knowledge in this field.
5. Carter, C. O. *Human Heredity* (Pelican, Harmondsworth 1962)

is a very readable comprehensive account of some major problems and applications of the study of human inheritance.

6. Skottowe, I. *Clinical Psychiatry for Practitioners and Students*, (Eyre and Spottiswoode, London 1953) pp. 35–78, gives a detailed discussion of important factors concerned in mental illness.

7. Any psychiatric text-book will extend our discussion of types of mental illness. For a specific treatment of neuroses see Ross, T. A. *The Common Neuroses* (Arnold, London, 2nd ed. 1937).

8. For a useful discussion introducing problems of describing psychoses see Skottowe, I. *Clinical Psychiatry for Practitioners and Students.*

9. Kahn, E. *Psychopathic Personalities* (O.U.P., London 1931) gives a lengthy description of psychopathic types and attempts to systematize this complex subject.

10. Diethelm, O. *Treatment in Psychiatry* (Thomas, Springfield Ill., 2nd ed. 1950) gives an excellent discussion of treatment by psychotherapy.

11. Jones, E. *What is Psychoanalysis?* (Allen & Unwin, London 1949) is a good introduction. Also Hall, C. S. *A Primer of Freudian Psychology* (World Publishing Co., Cleveland, 1954) is very useful. The beginner reading Freud's own work should start with *An Outline of Psychoanalysis* (Hogarth, London 1949).

12. Cox, D. *How the Mind Works* (English Universities Press, London, 1964) gives a simple introduction to Jung's psychology. Another useful account is Fordham, F. *Introduction to Jung's Psychology* (Pelican, Harmondsworth 1959).

13. Marcuse, F. L. *Hypnosis, Fact and Fiction* (Pelican, Harmondsworth 1959) is an easy to read, comprehensive introduction to the theory and techniques of hypnosis.

14. Haworth, A. and McDonald, E. M. *The Theory of Occupational Therapy* (Williams & Wilkins, London 1940).

15. Foulkes, S. H. and Anthony, E. J. *Group Psychotherapy* (Pelican, Harmondsworth 1957) is a good general introduction to the subject and includes many references for further detailed study.

16. Sargent, W. and Slater, E. *An Introduction to Physical Methods in Psychiatry* (Livingstone, Edinburgh 1948) gives a detailed description of physical techniques.

17. Clarke, A. M. and Clarke, A. D. B. *Mental Deficiency: the Changing Outlook* (Methuen, London 1958) is an excellent introduction to further study.

18. Carter, C. O. *Human Heredity* (Pelican, Harmondsworth 1962) gives an introductory account of mental disturbances in which there is a probable genetic predisposition.

19. Wall, W. D. *Education and Mental Health* (Harrap, London

1955) deals thoroughly with the relationship between school and mental health.

20. Bowlby, J. abridged and edited by Fry, M. *Child Care and the Growth of Love* (Pelican, Harmondsworth 1953) gives a very useful summary of findings in the field of mother-child relationships.

21. For full discussions of delinquency and many further references see Bovet, L. *Psychiatric Aspects of Juvenile Delinquency* (World Health Organization, Columbia 1951); Stott, D. H. *Delinquency and Human Nature* (Carnegie U.K. Trust, Dunfermline 1950); Burt, C. *The Young Delinquent* (U.L.P., London 1925).

22. Cleugh, M. F. *The Slow Learner* (Methuen, London 1957), examines the problems of remedial teaching of school children.

Chapter Fifteen

Conclusion

This volume has attempted to indicate some of the major areas which psychologists cover in their descriptions and investigations of human behaviour. A wealth of information has been gathered on all fronts in the behavioural sciences. There is a tremendous amount which has still to be elucidated but it is surely the responsibility of all persons concerned with human problems, be they nurses or teachers, parents or employers, to make themselves familiar with the principles of these sciences.

It is easy to overstate apathy and antagonism to a subject in which there is much personal involvement. Appearances can be deceptive and often people who express hostility to psychology may in fact be more interested in it than they are prepared to admit. Nevertheless when talking to many members of the general population about such problems as bringing up a family, coping with the elderly or the mentally sick, tackling the rise in juvenile crime or the decline of moral standards, it is often obvious that they base their reactions on prejudice and hearsay, failing to look for evidence to back their conclusions, or separating fact from opinion.

It is interesting, albeit most unsatisfactory, to find that while many people will consult and follow the advice of a practitioner of a physical science, for example a heart specialist, an agricultural chemist or a construction engineer, they believe that they can be their own experts in psychological and social matters. One meets persons who state that behavioural problems in general can be ameliorated by some sweeping measure

379

such as increase in unemployment, the extended use of physical violence in school, or even an enforced religious revival. Others admit that the subject is very complex but believe that they are more competent to interpret their own specific problems than the 'remote academic specialist'. Others again frankly admit that they do not know what the answers to these problems are but remain apathetic to the issues involved. While one may have sympathy with some of these basic attitudes, it is quite inexcusable that an effort should not be made to attempt to understand the relevant findings of the social sciences when these are readily available.

Turning from the general public to the specific professions concerned with human problems the situation is, in general, more enlightened. Nevertheless all too many potential teachers are concerned primarily with their academic subject and consider the education aspects of their course (including psychology and sociology) as adjuncts tacked on to their main field of interest. Again, many student nurses may become well versed in the causes and treatment of mental illness, but are woefully unaware of the concepts underlying the behaviour of the normal person. Such situations are no less reprehensible than the parent who decides upon a career for his son without considering his offspring's interests or abilities, or the general public view that secondary modern school children are second-rate individuals. All these examples indicate the failure of people to recognize the importance of an under-standing of the principles underlying the behaviour of the individual and of society.

Changes in educational techniques, child guidance, voca-tional selection, attitudes towards mental illness, etc., indicate that society as a whole is desirous of humanitarian change. It is much easier to make constructive modifications when you have some insight into how and why people behave as they do. This book has been written in the hope that it may whet the appetites of some individuals concerned to better understand themselves and others, so that they may go on to read further and learn more about the social sciences.

BIBLIOGRAPHY

CHAPTER 1

Suitable texts for more intensive general study once the general principles outlined in this text are mastered.

1. Hilgard, E. S. *Introduction fo Psychology* (Methuen, London 1957).
2. Munn, N. L. *Psychology: The Fundamentals of Human Adjustment* (Harrap, London, 4th ed. 1961).
3. Morgan, L. T. *Introduction to Psychology* (McGraw-Hill, N.Y., 2nd ed. 1961).
4. Cohen, J. (ed.) *Readings in Psychology* (Allen & Unwin, London 1964).
5. Halmos, P. and Iliffe, A. *Readings in General Psychology* (Routledge & Kegan Paul, London 1964).

CHAPTER 2

1. Eccles, J. C. *The Neurophysiological Basis of Mind* (O.U.P., London 1953).
2. Geldard, F. A. *The Human Senses* (Chapman & Hall, London 1953).
3. Hebb, D. O. *Text-book of Psychology* (Saunders, London, 2nd ed. 1966; 1st ed. 1958).
4. Hebb, D. O. *Organization of Behaviour* (Science Editions Inc, N.Y. 1961; 1st ed. 1949).
5. Morgan and Stellar. *Physiological Psychology* (McGraw-Hill, N.Y. 1950).

CHAPTER 3

1. Ashby, W. R. *Design for a Brain* (Chapman & Hall, London 1952).
2. Grey Walter, W. *The Living Brain* (Pelican, Hardmondsworth 1961).
3. Sluckin, W. *Minds and Machines* (Pelican, Harmondsworth 1960).
4. Wooldridge, D. E. *The Machinery of the Brain* (McGraw Hill, N.Y. 1963).

CHAPTER 4

1. Blake, R. R. and Ramsey, G. V. *Perception: an Approach to Personality* (Ronald Press, N.Y. 1951).
2. Dember, W. N. *The Psychology of Perception* (Holt, Rinehart & Winston, N.Y. 1961).
3. Gibson, J. J. *The Perception of the Visual World* (Houghton Mifflin, Boston 1950).
4. Vernon, M. D. *The Psychology of Perception* (Penguin, Harmondsworth 1962).
5. Vernon, P. E. *Personality Assessment* (Methuen, London 1964).
6. Von Bekesy, G. *Experiments in Hearing* (McGraw-Hill, N.Y. 1960).

CHAPTER 5

1. Anderson, J. E. *The Psychology of Development and Personal Adjustment* (Holt, N.Y. 1956).
2. Gordon, Harris and Rees *An Introduction to Psychological Medicine* (O.U.P., London 1936).
3. Hart, B. *The Psychology of Insanity* (C.U.P., London 1941).
4. Hepner, H. W. *Psychology Applied to Life and Work* (Prentice Hall, Englewood Cliffs, N.J. 1950).
5. Lindgren, H. C. *Psychology of Personal and Social Adjustment* (American Book, N.Y. 1953).
6. Saul, L. J. *Emotional Maturity* (Lippincott, Philadelphia 1947).
7. Symonds, P. M. *Dynamic Psychology* (Appleton-Century Crofts, N.Y. 1949).

CHAPTER 6

1. Bindra, D. *Motivation: A Systematic Reinterpretation* (Ronald Press, N.Y. 1959).
2. Brown, J. S. *The Motivation of Behaviour* (McGraw-Hill, N.Y. 1961).
3. Duffy, E. *Activation and Behavior* (Wiley, N.Y. 1962).
4. *Studies in Education No. 7* (University of London Institute of Education, Evans 1955).
5. Young, P. T. *Motivation and Emotion* (Wiley, N.Y. 1961).

CHAPTER 7

1. Fleming, C. M. *Adolescence: Its Social Psychology* (Routledge & Kegan Paul, London 1963; 1st ed. 1948).
2. Hadfield, J. A. *Childhood and Adolescence* (Penguin, Harmondsworth 1962).

3. Hilgard, E. R. *Theories of Learning* (Appleton Century Crofts, N.Y. 1955).
4. Hunter, I. M. L. *Memory* (Penguin, Harmondsworth 1963).
5. Kohler, W. *The Mentality of Apes* (Pelican, Harmondsworth 1957; 1st ed. 1925).
6. McGeoch, J. A. and Irion, A. L. *The Psychology of Human Learning* (Longmans, London 1952).
7. Osgood, C. E. *Method and Theory in Experimental Psychology* (O.U.P., London 1953).
8. Russell, W. R. *Brain, Memory, Learning* (O.U.P., London 1959).
9. Skinner, B. F. *Cumulative Record* (Appleton-Century Crofts, N.Y. 1961).
10. *Studies in Education No. 7* (University of London Institute of Education, Evans 1955).
11. Valentine, C. W. *The Normal Child* (Penguin, Harmondsworth 1956).

CHAPTER 8

1. Bartlett, F. C. *Thinking: An Experimental and Social Study* (Allen & Unwin, London 1958).
2. Humphrey, G. *Thinking: An Introduction to Its Experimental Psychology* (Methuen, London 1951).
3. Johnson, D. M. *The Psychology of Thought and Judgement* (Harper, New York 1955).
4. McKellar, P. *Imagination and Thinking* (Cohen & West, London 1957).
5. Thomson, R. *The Psychology of Thinking* (Penguin, Harmondsworth 1959).
6. Watts, A. F. *Language and the Mental Development of Children* (Harrap, London 1944).

CHAPTER 9

1. Carmichael. *Manual of Child Psychology* (Wiley, N.Y. 1954).
2. Flavell, J. *The Developmental Psychology of Jean Piaget* (Van Nostrand, N.Y. 1963).
3. Gesell, A. *The First Five Years of Life* (Harper, N.Y. 1940).
   — *The Child From Five to Ten* (Hamish Hamilton, London 1946).
   — *Youth: The Years from Ten to Sixteen* (Hamish Hamilton, London 1956).
4. Hurlock, *Child Development* (McGraw-Hill, N.Y. 1964).

5. Klein, J. *Child Rearing Practices* (Routledge & Kegan Paul, 1965).
6. Mussen, P. *The Psychological Development of the Child* (Prentice Hall, Englewood Cliffs, N.J. 1965).
7. Stone and Church. *Childhood and Adolescence* (Random House, N.Y. 1957).
8. Winnicott, D. W. *The Family and Individual Development* (Tavistock, London 1965).

CHAPTER 10

1. Anastasi, A. *Psychological Testing* (Macmillan, N.Y. 1955).
2. Cronbach, L. J. *Essentials in Psychological Testing* (Harper, N.Y. 1964).
3. Freeman, F. S. *Theory and Practice of Psychological Testing* (Henry Holt, N.Y. 1956).
4. Guilford, J. P. *Fundamental Statistics in Psychology and Education* (McGraw-Hill, N.Y. 1950).
5. Knight, R. *Intelligence and Intelligence Tests* (Methuen, London 1933).
6. Thomas, T. *The Science of Marking* (Murray, London 1930).
7. Thorndike, R. L. and Hagen, E. *Measurement and Evaluation in Psychology and Education* (Wiley, N.Y. 2nd ed. 1961).
8. Vernon, P. E. *The Measurement of Abilities* (U.L.P., London 1956).
9. Vernon, P. E. *Intelligence and Attainment Tests* (U.L.P., London 1960).

CHAPTER 11

1. Cattell, R. B. *An Introduction to Personality Study* (Hutchinson's University Library, London 1950).
2. Eysenck, H. J. *The Structure of Human Personality* (Methuen, London 1953).
3. Hall, C. S. and Lindzey, G. *Theories of Personality* (Wiley, N.Y. 1957).
4. Hunt, J. McV. *Personality and Behaviour Disorders* (Ronald Press, N.Y. 1944).
5. Mottram, *The Physical Basis of Personality* (Pelican, Harmondsworth 1952).
6. Oldfield, R. C. *The Psychology of the Interview* (Methuen, London 1941).
7. Stagner, R. *The Psychology of Personality* (McGraw-Hill, N.Y. 3rd ed. 1961).
8. Vernon, P. E. *Personality Tests and Assessments* (Methuen, London 1953).

9. Vernon, P. E. *Personality Assessment: A Critical Survey* (Methuen, London 1964).

CHAPTER 12

1. Argyle, M. *The Scientific Study of Human Behaviour* (Methuen, London 1957).
2. Brown, J. A. C. *The Social Psychology of Industry* (Penguin, Harmondsworth 1954).
3. Fleming, C. M. *The Social Psychology of Education* (Routledge & Kegan Paul, London 1959).
4. Homans, G. *The Human Group* (Routledge & Kegan Paul, London 1951).
5. Isaacs, S. *Social Development in Young Children* (Routledge & Kegan Paul, London 1933).
6. Klein, J. *The Study of Groups* (Routledge & Kegan Paul, London 1956).
7. Maier, N. R. F. *Principles of Human Relationships: Applications to Management* (Wiley, N.Y. 1952).
8. Newcomb, T. M. *Social Psychology* (Holt, Rinehart & Winston, N.Y. 1965).
9. Sprott, W. J. H. *Social Psychology* (Methuen, London 1952).

CHAPTER 13

1. Bernard, H. W. *Towards Better Personal Adjustment* (McGraw-Hill, N.Y. 1957).
2. Bowlby, J. abridged and edited by Fry, M. *Child Care and the Growth of Love* (Penguin, Harmondsworth 1953).
3. Brown, J. A. C. *Techniques of Persuasion* (Penguin, Harmondsworth 1963).
4. Fenton, N. *Mental Hygiene in School Practice* (O.U.P., London 1949).
5. Flugel, J. C. *Man, Morals and Society* (Pelican, Harmondsworth 1955).
6. Hadfield, J. A. *Psychology and Mental Health* (Allen & Unwin, London 1950).
7. Lindgren, H. C. *Psychology of Personal and Social Adjustment* (American Book Co., N.Y. 1953).
8. Sears, R. R., Maccoby, E. E. and Levin, H. *Patterns of Child Rearing* (Harper, N.Y. 1957).
9. Soddy, K. (ed.). *Mental Health and Infant Development* (Routledge & Kegan Paul, London, 1955).
10. Wall, W. D. *Education and Mental Health* (Harper for Unesco, London 1955).

CHAPTER 14

1. Burt, C. *The Causes and Treatment of Backwardness* (U.L.P., London 1953; 1st ed. 1937).
2. Clarke, A. M. and Clarke, A. D. B. *Mental Deficiency* (Methuen, London 1959).
3. Freud, S. *On Dreams* (Hogarth Press, London 1952).
4. Fyval, T. R. *The Insecure Offenders* (Pelican, Harmondsworth 1963).
5. Hadfield, J. A. *Dreams and Nightmares* (Pelican, Harmondsworth 1954).
6. Henderson, D. K. *Psychopathic States* (Chapman & Hall, London 1939).
7. Jones, E. *What is Psycho-analysis?* (Allen & Unwin, London 1949).
8. Morgan and Lovell. *The Psychology of Abnormal People* (Longmans, London 1928).
9. Rogers, C. R. *Counseling and Psychotherapy* (Houghton Mifflin, Boston 1942).
10. Skottowe, I. *Clinical Psychiatry for Practitioners and Students* (Eyre & Spottiswoode, London 1953).
11. Stafford Clark, D. *Psychiatry Today* (Pelican, London 1952).
12. Stott, D. H. *Saving Children From Delinquency* (U.L.P., London 1952).
13. Valentine, C. W. *The Normal Child and Some of His Abnormalities* (Pelican, Harmondsworth 1956).

USEFUL FOLLOW-UP BOOKS FOR TEACHERS

1. Cleugh, M. F. *Psychology in the Service of the School* (Methuen, London 1951).
2. Cronbach, L. J. *Educational Psychology* (Staples Press, London 1958).
3. Fleming, C. M. *Teaching: A Psychological Analysis* (Methuen, London 1958).
4. Hughes, A. G. and Hughes, E. G. *Learning and Teaching* (Longmans, London, 3rd ed. 1959; 1st ed. 1937).
5. Isaacs, S. *Intellectual Growth in Young Children* (Routledge & Kegan Paul, London 1930).
6. Jersild, A. T. *Child Psychology* (Staples Press, London 1955).
7. Lovell, K. *Educational Psychology and Children* (U.L.P., London, 8th ed. 1965).
8. Peel, E. A. *The Psychological Basis of Education* (Oliver & Boyd, London 1956).
9. *Studies in Education No. 7* (University of London Institute of Education, Evans 1955).

10. Valentine, C. W. *Psychology and Its Bearing on Education* (Methuen, London 1950).

USEFUL FOLLOW-UP BOOKS FOR NURSES

1. Altschul, A. *Aids to Psychology For Nurses* (Baillière, Tindall & Cox, London 1962).
2. McGhie, A. *Psychology as Applied to Nursing* (Livingstone, Edinburgh 1966).
3. Odlum, D. *Psychology, the Nurse and the Patient* (Nursing Mirror, London 1959; 1st ed. 1952).
4. Williams, J. *Psychology for Student Nurses* (Methuen, London 1954).

USEFUL FOLLOW-UP BOOKS FOR SOCIAL WORKERS

1. Argyle, M. *The Scientific Study of Social Behaviour* (Methuen, London 1957).
2. Price-Williams, D. R. *Introductory Psychology – An Approach for Social Workers* (Routledge & Kegan Paul, London 1958).
3. Guntrip, H. *Personality Structure and Human Interaction* (International Universities Press, N.Y. 1961).
4. Homans, G. C. *The Human Group* (Routledge & Kegan Paul, London 1951).
5. Krech and Crutchfield. *Theory and Problems of Social Psychology* (McGraw-Hill, N.Y. 1948).
6. Stott, D. H. *The Social Adjustment of Children* (U.L.P., London 1958).
7. Carstairs, G. M. *Studies in Social Pathology* (*series*) (Pelican, Harmondsworth 1965).

Index

Index

Brain, 44, 46, 47–9, 53–77, 79ff, 89ff, 262–3; development of, 54–9; evolution of, 54–6; fore-, 58, 75, 157; hind-, 55, 60–1, 75; mid-, 55, 61; dorsal part, 58; new-, 55–7, 75; human, 58–64; stem, 60–2, 75; tumours of, 72

Bridges, K. M. B., 158, 164

Brown, J. A. C., 341

Bruner, J. S., 215

Buddenbrock, W. von, 43

Bugelski, B. R., 193

Bunt, L. N. H., 215

Burlingham, D., 230

Burt, C., 258, 378

Cameron, N., 164

Camouflage, 91

Cannon, W. B., 163, 164; on hormones and personality, 268, on personality, 290

Carmichael, L., 192, 230

Carr, H. A., 104

Carter, C. O., 257, 377

Case histories, 283

Cattell, R. B., 292; personality categories of, 273, 291

Central nervous system, 21–4, 65, 67, 72–6, 148, 162, 172; psychology and, 21–3, 72–4; evolution of, 44–6; main functions of, 45; development of, 50–4; and biological needs, 137ff; and behaviour, 182; development of in prenatal period, 218ff, and examinations, 255–6; and psychoneuroses, 354–5; and psychoses, 357

Cerebellum, 60–1

Cerebral cortex, 62, 65–72, 76–7, 157, 364; cells of, 70–2

Cerebral Cortex of Man, The, 77

Cerebral hemispheres, 71, 76

Cerebral surgery, 364

Challenge of Middle Age, The, 231

Character, 262, 263–4, 290

Chemotherapy, 363

Child and Society, The, 231

Child Behavior and Development, 163

Child Care and the Growth of Love, 164, 257, 378

Child Development, 164

Child's Conception of Number, The, 215

Child's Concept of the World, The, 215

Child's Construction of Reality, The, 215

Children, development of, 158, 218–24

Children's Explanation of Natural Phenomena, 215

Children's Thinking, 215

Chromosomes, 233

Chronological age, 253–4

Clarke, A. D. B., 377

Clarke, A. M., 377

Claustrophobia, 353

Cleckley, H. M., 130

Cleugh, M. F., 378

Clinical Psychiatry for Practitioners and Students, 293, 376, 377

Collected Papers in Psychology, 194

Collins, M., 193

Coming to terms with ourselves, 316–40; failure of, 342–76

Common Neuroses, The, 377

Communication, 305–12, 314, 323–5; breakdowns in, 323–5, 339

Compensation, 115–16

Compliance, 118–19

Compulsions, 118–19

Conception, 233

Concepts, 196, 201–3; formation of, 213–14

Conditioned Reflexes, 193

Conditioning, 183–6; classical, 183–5; operant 184–5; Pavlovian, 183–6; second order, 186

Conflicts, 120–4, 129; ignoring existence of, 120–2; retreating from, 123–4

Conformity and Deviation, 314

Controls, 236

Conversion hysteria, 119

Convulsion hysteria, 119

Co-ordination with environment, 44–78; organs of, 45–9

390

Index

Index

Index

Index

Index

Index

Index

397

Index

398

Index

Index